PATERNOSTER BIBLICAL AND THEOLOGICAL MONOGRAPHS

The Power of the Cross

Theology and the Death of Christ in Paul, Luther and Pascal

PATERNOSTER BIBLICAL AND THEOLOGICAL MONOGRAPHS

A full listing of titles in this series appears at the end of this book.

SERIES PREFACE

At the present time we are experiencing a veritable explosion in the field of biblical and theological research with more and more academic theses of high quality being produced by younger scholars from all over the world. One of the considerations taken into account by the examiners of doctoral theses is that, if they are to be worthy of the award of a degree, then they should contain material that needs to be read by other scholars; if so, it follows that the facilities must exist for them to be made accessible. In some cases (perhaps more often than is always realised) it will be most appropriate for the distinctive contribution of the thesis to be harvested in journal articles; in others there may be the possibility of a revision that will produce a book of wider appeal than simply to professional scholars. But many theses of outstanding quality can and should be published more or less as they stand for the benefit of other scholars and interested persons.

Hitherto it has not been easy for authors to find publishers willing to publish works that, while highly significant as works of scholarship, cannot be expected to become 'best-sellers' with a large circulation. Fortunately the development of printing technology now makes it relatively easy for publishers to produce specialist works without the commercial risks that would have prevented them doing so in the past.

The Paternoster Press is one of the first publishers to make use of this new technology. Its aim is quite simply to assist biblical and theological scholarship by the publication of theses and other monographs of high quality at affordable prices.

Different publishers serve different constituencies. The Paternoster Press stands in the tradition of evangelical Christianity and exists to serve that constituency, though not in any narrow way. What is offered, therefore, in this series, is the best of scholarship by evangelical Christians.

PATERNOSTER BIBLICAL AND THEOLOGICAL MONOGRAPHS

The Power of the Cross

Theology and the Death of Christ in Paul, Luther and Pascal

Graham Tomlin

Foreword by Alister McGrath

PATERNOSTER PRESS

First published 1999 by Paternoster Press

Paternoster Press is an imprint of Authentic Media,
P.O. Box 300, Carlisle, Cumbria, CA3 0QS, U.K.
and
P.O. Box 1047, Waynesboro, GA 30830-2047, U.S.A.

British Library Cataloguing in Publication Data

ISBN: 0-85364-984-7

Typeset by the author
Printed and bound in Great Britain by Nottingham Alpha Graphics

To Janet

CONTENTS

PART I: Paul and the Cross in the Church at Corinth

PART III: Blaise Pascal's Theology of the Cross

CONCLUSION

FOREWORD

The cross has always been of central importance to the Christian faith. It is perhaps understandable that attention has generally been paid primarily to the relation between the cross and salvation, particularly the manner in which the death of Christ can be seen as the basis of human redemption. Yet the cross has an even deeper significance, in that it acts as a window into the nature and purposes of God. The phrase 'a theology of the cross' has been widely used to refer to a way of doing theology which takes the cross as its starting point for our knowledge of God.

In this important and learned study, Graham Tomlin explores the contours of the theology of the cross, by engaging with three of its major representatives: Paul, Luther and Pascal. Throughout the work, Tomlin combines first-class scholarship with a real concern to establish the contemporary relevance of this theology, grounded in a firm understanding of postmodern thought. The result is a model of the engagement of past and present, showing how the church of today can learn from the hard-won theological insights of the past. As Tomlin makes clear, the theology of the cross is no academic exercise, but a passionate engagement which recalls the church to the foot of the cross. Tomlin demonstrates beyond doubt that the theology of the cross is not simply a matter of historical interest; it is of major importance to the church, as she seeks to remain faithful to her true identity and mission. In an era which is intensely suspicious of power, the theology of the cross offers us a way of maintaining Christian integrity, and responding to the criticisms directed against any form of truth-claim by writers such as Jacques Derrida and Michel Foucault. Tomlin's masterly analysis of his subject shows how the rich heritage of the Christian tradition can continue to be of service to the church today, as it prepares to enter into the third millennium.

This learned and lucid book will challenge and encourage any who are concerned about Christian truth and integrity. I enthusiastically recommend it.

Alister E. McGrath
March 1999

ACKNOWLEDGEMENTS

I am profoundly grateful to many people who have helped in the writing of this book. The supervisors of the doctoral thesis on which it is based, Professor David Catchpole and Dr. Alastair Logan of the University of Exeter were always encouraging, attentive and wise. In Oxford, Alister McGrath first kindled my interest in the theology of the cross, and has kindly contributed a foreword. David Wenham acted as a valuable sounding-board for my ideas on 1 Corinthians, and Richard Parish generously gave time and interest to the section on Pascal. Others who kindly offered help and advice include Don and Peta Fowler, Professor Richard Bauckham, Richard Burridge, Simon Chesters, Neil Mancor and many others. I am particularly indebted to Jeremy Mudditt and the staff of Paternoster Press for their work in helping prepare the book for publication. I am therefore conscious of how much I have relied upon the support and help of many over the past years; needless to say, any mistakes which remain are mine, not theirs.

I am also indebted to those who have enabled me to find both time and finance to conduct the research. John Skinner, my vicar in Exeter, encouraged the project at an early stage, the Principal and Fellows of Jesus College, Oxford kindly allowed me a sabbatical term from my work as Chaplain to the College in 1993, and Dick France and the staff of Wycliffe Hall willingly covered for a term's leave in 1995. The Philpotts Education of the Clergy Trust, St Luke's College Foundation in Exeter, and the All Saints Educational Trust all made generous grants towards the costs of the research.

Wycliffe Hall and Jesus College have both proved stimulating and enjoyable places to learn and teach. I am deeply grateful to staff and students in both places who have helped me understand the theology of the cross more fully, both by their questions, ideas and examples. Lastly I must mention my wife Janet, without whose constant encouragement, practical Christian wisdom and considerable sacrifice I could not have worked on this at all, and Sam and Sian, without whom the book might have been completed much sooner, but then life would have been far less fun.

Graham Tomlin
Wycliffe Hall, Oxford
Easter 1999

Preface

In 1988, Jürgen Moltmann concluded a brief study of the tasks facing theology towards the end of the twentieth century with these words:

> The modern critique of religion no longer makes any critique of the content of faith, but is a purely functional critique of the psychological, political and social effects of this faith. It no longer asks whether it is true or false, but only whether it has the function of oppression or liberation, alienation or humanization.[1]

His words raise a number of interesting issues, one of which concerns the relationship between theology and the forms of church and social life which it engenders. The suspicion Moltmann identifies is that through the Christian era, the church has frequently exercised the functions of oppression and alienation, and that all too often, the church's official theology has backed up its claim to power. In fact, the issue of *power* is one of the most sensitive facing theology in the current context, in the light of sustained analysis of the operation of power within societies, and of its relationship to knowledge and truth by a number of significant thinkers.

Taking their cue from Nietzsche, several 'postmodern' theorists have asserted that all claims to truth are in reality disguised claims to power. Jean-Francois Lyotard famously defined postmodernism as "incredulity towards metanarratives".[2] After the fall of the great 'stories' (including Christianity), there can be no legitimisation by appeal to truth or reason, but rather, only by functional or technological criteria: precisely Moltmann's point.[3] The result is Lyotard's call to "wage a war on totality",[4] in that such absolute truth is now impossible, and that any such claim to ultimate truth actually operates as a bid for power over others. Jacques Derrida likewise calls for an 'armed neutrality' towards all claims to truth: his celebrated and complex notion of *différance* is antagonistic to all claims to unitary ultimate truth, for example for or against the existence of God, or any systems built upon such foundations.[5] As language cannot refer to anything outside itself, and "meaning is neither before nor after the act",[6] any discourse, including theological discourse, cannot claim to tell the Truth, and must be seen instead in terms of how it functions, whether in repression or liberation.

The work of Michel Foucault, to whom we shall return, has helped to educate a whole generation to be suspicious of the hidden operations of power within society. Truth, he argues, is not discovered, but is created as a social construct to legitimise power relations within that society.[7] Foucault teaches us to be aware, even wary, of the ways in which power produces a truth to legitimise it, and truth produces power to make it seem unquestionable.

All of this poses serious questions for theology; as Anthony Thiselton puts it: "These perspectives constitute the most serious and urgent challenge to theology, in comparison with which the old-style attacks from 'common-sense' positivism appear relatively naïve."[8] In particular, it raises the question of how power works in relation to theological discourse, and within the community where theology often operates, the church.[9] If 'truth' is purely a social construct, simply a means of legitimising claims to power, what status can theological claims to truth possess? In the face of such a challenge, how can theology avoid becoming just another claim to power, and the church avoid being implicated in the same power-games which operate elsewhere in society? To return to Moltmann's point, how can the church avoid becoming another agent of oppression and alienation, and instead, become a focus of liberation and humanisation? To put the question in another form, does the Christian theological tradition hold the resources to meet such a challenge?

In 1927 Emil Brunner wrote about Luther's insistence on the cross as the centre of Christian theology:

> The feeling of the Church has been quite sound on this point; but where she went wrong was in her frequent forgetfulness of the meaning of the phrase: *in hoc signo vinces*; in that over and over again she herself lost the key to the meaning of this sign... The whole history of Christianity, and the history of the world, would have followed a different course if it had not been that again and again the *theologia crucis* became a *theologia gloriae*, and that the *ecclesia crucis* became an *ecclesia gloriae*.[10]

The theology of the cross has received a good deal of attention since Brunner's words, in the aftermath of the Second World War, both among the victors and the losers. Both German and Japanese theologians explored this theme in some depth in coming to terms with their post-war experience,[11] but it surfaced also in the heady optimism of post-war North America, in the works of Douglas J. Hall.[12] While Kazoh Kitamori in Japan and Jürgen Moltmann in Germany wrote their theologies of the cross out of the experience of darkness and destruction of the losers in war, Hall turned to the *theologia crucis* not in a context of despair, but of optimism. Hall found that Moltmann's original 'Theology of Hope' was not what the over-confident "officially optimistic" U.S.A. of the 1960s and early 70s needed to hear.[13] In the era of American expansionism and the Vietnam war, Hall felt that only the theology of the cross "takes its stand within the experience of negation. It neither minimises the

evil and apparent absurdity of life, nor does it absorb the negative,
finally, into a triumphant positive."[14] The theology of the cross has
therefore been used both to offer comfort and to challenge
complacency in the post-war West. This is a truly versatile theology,
which can speak in different historical settings, both to those who
exercise power, and those who are on the receiving end of its
operation.

This book sets out to show how the theology of the cross has
offered a critique of theologies which undergird claims to power by
the church, or certain groups within the church, theologies which
have done so by importing ideas into Christian theology which are
essentially foreign to it. It aims to demonstrate both the *subversive*
nature of this type of theology, undermining and deconstructing
claims to power, but also its essentially *communal* nature, seeking
to build community and relationship. It will also seek to demonstrate
how this 'thin tradition'[15] can claim a long history within Christian
tradition, but has more often been kept alive[16] through traditions of
popular piety than in the official theology of the church. It argues
that the theology of the cross speaks of a God who can be known
only through the experience of a profound powerlessness before
him. This experience then becomes the key to a new understanding
of power, as the ability to surrender rights, privilege and power for
the sake of others. The cross needs to be understood not only as
atonement, but also as the defining moment for the revelation of
God, and of his people.

Three theologians have been chosen as examples of this type of
theology, each offering a distinctive angle on these questions. Paul
serves as the starting-point, an initial biblical reference point,[17]
necessary to root the study in the origins of the Christian tradition,
an important factor if this is to be represented as authentically
Christian theology. Furthermore, his teaching in 1 Corinthians 1-2
played a vital role in the reappearance of this theology at various
crisis points of church history, so it will be important to examine
how Paul's theology of the cross works. Luther has also commonly
been regarded as a major historical reference-point for the theology

of the cross.[18] In the subsequent history of the Reformation, this aspect of his theology did not achieve as much prominence as his teaching on justification, or the primacy of Scripture for example, and it was not until the renaissance in Luther studies which followed the appearance of the Weimar Edition from 1883 and the work of Karl Holl, that the role of the cross in his theology was duly recognised.[19] As one of Paul's most influential interpreters, Luther provides us with a valuable case study of the way in which this type of theology was transmitted, its location within the Christian tradition in the intervening years, and therefore its relation to the dominant lines of theology through the medieval period.

Blaise Pascal has not generally been regarded as a theologian of the cross, and one initial task will be to establish this as a major structural element of his theology. In fact Pascal has not always been taken with great seriousness as a theologian, a factor which may account for the lack of analysis of the role the cross plays in his thought. Works on his theology tend to focus on other areas of his thinking, for example his teaching on grace, notably in his *Ecrits sur la Grâce*.[20] This book will argue that the cross plays a major structural role at significant points in his thought. Pascal also provides a useful counterbalance to Luther. They stand on different sides of the European confessional divide, Luther as the originator of the Reformation, Pascal standing within the time and traditions of the Catholic Reformation. Pascal's inclusion as a foil to Luther shows that this type of theology is not tied to one side or the other of post-Reformation European theology, has the ability to transcend otherwise opposed positions, and to continue to offer its critique of the abuse of power under a wide range of historical settings.

On the other hand it is clear that both are working in highly charged polemical contexts, Luther against forms of late medieval theology and the papal church, Pascal in (among others) the Jansenist struggle with the Jesuits. Both are theologians of protest, ranging their voices against much larger forces at work within the church of their day, and despite differences in their situations, both provide examples of the theology of the cross in operation, subverting those larger forces and the ideologies which legitimise them.

One further point can be made about the inclusion of Pascal. Luther was not a major influence upon Pascal's thought, and as we shall see, there is little evidence that Pascal had read him at all. If one of the themes of this study is the influence of 1 Corinthians 1-2 in sustaining this type of theology in history, then these two can be seen as interpreting the themes of this passage independently from each other. This is important in elucidating the effect of Paul's theology of the cross on both of these theologians, rather than risking the possibility that his teaching has in one case been filtered through the other. Modern Protestant theologians who have explored the theology of the cross, such as Kierkegaard, Barth or Bonhoeffer were all profoundly influenced by Luther, making the choice of such figures less useful for an analysis of the influence of 1 Corinthians on subsequent *theologiae crucis*. The recent revolution in Pauline studies has emphasised how much he has been interpreted in post-Reformation Protestant theology through Lutheran eyes. This 'new perspective on Paul' has sought to free him from this Lutheran straitjacket. The choice of Pascal enables an exploration of the influence of Paul's *theologia crucis* and the contours of the theology itself, in a region uninfluenced by Luther.

Although the theme of the *theologia crucis* as polemical theology directed against theologies of power provides the focus of the work, in each part the balance will of necessity be different. For Paul, the key question is the elucidation of the polemical context. The state of the Corinthian church and the provenance of the ideas and behaviour Paul encounters there are by no means agreed upon by scholars. The major part of the first section will therefore suggest a new interpretation of the evidence, which shows how his theology of the cross, developed explicitly in 1:17-2:5 yet permeating the letter, functions as a response. For Luther, while the polemical context has been well described in recent scholarship,[21] the origins of his theology of the cross are much less clear. While showing how Luther's thought was influenced by 1 Corinthians 1:17-2:5, a major focus will be to offer new insights into the way in which this type of theology was mediated to Luther. Therefore, this study examines the origins of Luther's theology of the cross within patterns of late medieval piety and devotion, and the way in which this theology provided Luther with an answer both to his own early spiritual problems, and also to the wider ecclesiastical and theological context. With Pascal, in the absence of previous study in this area, the first task will be to try to describe and explain the place occupied by the cross within Pascal's thought, and the way in which it operates as a vital structural principle for him. We will then proceed to demonstrate how this theological framework enabled him to conduct a polemical campaign on three fronts, against the scepticism of Montaigne and contemporary Pyrrhonism, against Cartesian rationalism, and against the power of the seventeenth century Society of Jesus. Throughout, the theology of the cross will be portrayed as a theology of protest against the illegitimate use of power within the Christian church.

Notes:

[1] J. Moltmann, *Theology Today* (London: SCM, 1988), 93.
[2] J-F. Lyotard, *La Condition Postmoderne: Rapport sur le Savoir* (Paris: Editions de Minuit, 1979), 7.
[3] "Où peut résider la légitimité, après les métarécits? Le critère d'operativité est technologique, il n'est pas pertinent pour juger du vrai et du juste." ibid., 8.
[4] J-F. Lyotard, "Answering the Question: What is Postmodernism?," reprinted in *Modernism/Postmodernism* (ed. P. Brooker; London: Longman, 1992), 139-50 (here, 150).
[5] Cf. J.D. Caputo, "Mysticism and Transgression: Derrida and Meister Eckhart," (ed. H.J. Silverman; *Derrida and Deconstruction*, New York: Routledge, 1989), 24-39, esp. 28-9.
[6] J. Derrida, *Writing and Difference* (London: Routledge, 1978), 11.
[7] "Each society has its régime of truth, its 'general politics' of truth: that is, the types of discourse which it accepts and makes function as true; the mechanisms and instances which enable one to distinguish true and false statements, the means by which each is sanctioned." M. Foucault, *Power/Knowledge:Selected Interviews and Other Writings 1972-77*, ed. C. Gordon (New York: Harvester Wheatsheaf, 1980), 131.

[8]A.C. Thiselton, *Interpreting God and the Postmodern Self* (SJT: Current Issues in Theology; Edinburgh: T. & T. Clark, 1995), 16.

[9]In the range of institutions surveyed by Foucault, the church does not escape attention: it is implicated particularly in his interest in the role of the confessional as a symbol of intrusive power in the history of sexuality: M. Foucault, *The History of Sexuality* (3 vols.; London: Allen Lane, 1979-88). French original 1976-84.

[10]E. Brunner, *The Mediator* (London: Lutterworth, 1934), 435. German original, Tübingen, Mohr/Siebeck, 1927.

[11]In Japan, K. Kitamori, *A Theology of the Pain of God* (London: SCM, 1966) Japanese original, Shinko Shuppansha, 1946. In Germany, e.g. J. Moltmann, *The Crucified God* (London: SCM, 1974) German original, Munich: Kaiser, 1973; E. Jüngel, *God as the Mystery of the World* (Edinburgh: T. & T. Clark, 1983) German original, Tübingen: Mohr/Siebeck, 1977.

[12]Starting with D.J. Hall, *Hope Against Hope: Towards an Indigenous Theology of the Cross* (WSCF Books 1.3.3; WSCF: Geneva, 1971).

[13]Ibid. 15.

[14]Ibid. 37.

[15]The phrase comes from, Douglas Hall, who described the *theologia crucis* as "…that 'thin tradition' which has functioned like an antiphon beneath the high triumph song of Christendom." Ibid., 34.

[16]D.J. Hall, *God and Human Suffering: An Exercise in the Theology of the Cross* (Minneapolis: Augsburg, 1986), 114.

[17]E.g. Hall, *God and Human Suffering*, 105-6.

[18]Kitamori, Moltmann, Jüngel and Hall all use Luther extensively in their works.

[19]B. Lohse, Martin Luther: *An Introduction to his Life and Work* (Edinburgh: T. & T. Clark, 1986), 223-4.

[20]E.g. J. Miel, *Pascal and Theology* (Baltimore: John Hopkins, 1969).

[21]A.E. McGrath, *Luther's Theology of the Cross* (Oxford: Blackwell, 1985).

Part I

Paul and the Cross in the Church at Corinth

One: **Introduction**

THE CROSS AND THE CONTEXT

Why did Paul begin his first letter to the young church at Corinth by drawing their attention to the cross of Christ? What was happening in the church which made Paul feel that at this point in their development, they particularly needed to hear again this 'word of the cross'? These are the fundamental questions which lurk behind this section of our explorations. Moreover, these questions are asked because in the past, the study of Paul's theology of the cross has not always taken such contextual considerations very seriously.

German theologians have tended to identify the cross as the centre of Pauline theology more readily than English-speaking ones.[1] This may well be due in part to the lingering memory of Luther, and in part to Germany's post-war experience.[2] This tendency gathered pace and depth in the 1960s and 70s with a series of works[3] addressing issues which had become crucial pastoral and dogmatic questions within the post-war German Church.[4] The most influential of these was Ernst Käsemann's 1969 essay "Die Heilsbedeutung des Todes Jesu nach Paulus",[5] which has rightly been called a "landmark in modern interpretation".[6] Käsemann's essay distinguished Paul's own interpretation of the cross from the tradition which he had received. The tradition saw the death of Jesus as an act of God's love and grace, the turning point of the ages, where human sin was defeated. Käsemann argued that Paul, while not dissenting from this interpretation, took it a stage further, seeing in the cross "the divinity of God revealed", in that the cross reveals human bankruptcy before God, and human inability to transcend this either by achievement or by religion.[7] Thus, Käsemann's understanding of Paul's theology of the cross is marked out by his stress on the theological significance of the cross, as opposed to its purely Christological or soteriological significance. Because it resounds with *theo*logical implications, the cross can never be seen as purely a preparatory stage on the road to the resurrection, a "chapter in the theology of the Resurrection", but rather, in Käsemann's memorable phrase, remains always "the signature of the one who is risen".[8]

Having located the cross close to the heart of Paul's theology, Käsemann reflects on the ecumenical concerns of the 1960s, and identifies the theology of the cross firmly as polemical theology: "The catchword about the 'theology of the cross' loses its original meaning if it is used non-polemically. It was always an attack on the dominating traditional interpretation of the Christian message."[9] For Käsemann, theology which takes its starting point from the cross is always polemical theology because it challenges false ideology both inside and outside the church. While in general terms "hostility to the cross is the leading characteristic of the world",[10] specifically,

> it is clearly the legalistic piety of Jewish-Christian circles and the enthusiasm of the Hellenistic church which is the real object of his (Paul's) attack... According to him, there are actual enemies of Christ in the Christian communities in Galatia and Corinth, in Philippi and Rome and they are not to be found so much among the waverers as among the keenest and most devout church members.[11]

This point has been noticed and taken further by Ulrich Luz, who remarks that "the two great theologians of the cross in the New Testament, Paul and Mark, are both polemical theologians".[12] The theology of the cross, heavily influenced by Luther's polemical programme, has therefore often been seen within German theology as a particularly controversial kind of theology, not sitting harmlessly alongside other approaches, but maintaining a bold claim to be the test and touchstone of all true Christian theology.[13] It not only opposes the world outside Christian theology, giving that theology its own distinctive identity,[14] but it also addresses other forms of Christian theology which fail to take the cross with sufficient seriousness as the true heart of theology, merely relegating it to one theme among many.

Käsemann rightly identified Paul's theology as the foundation stone of subsequent theologies of the cross. His approach is however not without its critics. In particular, subsequent scholarship has highlighted two serious problems with his exposition.

THE LUTHERAN PAUL

Käsemann adheres pretty closely to the Lutheran interpretation of Paul.[15] He interprets Paul's *theologia crucis* in accordance with his well-known advocacy of justification by faith as the centre of Paul's theology,[16] in which Paul opposes humankind in its very religiosity and attempts at self-justification.[17] It is of course precisely this Lutheran Paul which has come under sustained and devastating criticism since Käsemann's article, especially in the work of Krister Stendahl and Ed Sanders.[18] This again places a question mark over the value of Käsemann's analysis of Paul, which needs to be addressed if the wider concerns of the essay, his attempt to establish the cross as a defining mark of Pauline theology, are to be upheld. Once we have learnt to take off our Lutheran spectacles when reading Paul, what can the theology of the cross mean for him? If it is not the symbol of justification by faith standing over against all human religion, then what is it? And why does Paul place the cross in such a central position?

The problem with the Lutheran interpretation of Paul was that it identified not so much "what Paul originally meant" but rather the application of Pauline ideas to a later context.[19] If we are to understand and reappropriate Paul's *theologia crucis*, and appreciate the way its dynamics have influenced subsequent theology, then we will need to understand the context into which it was spoken much more clearly than Käsemann did. This contextualisation is what Sanders has done for the issues of law, the place of Judaism and Jewish people, in his work on Palestinian Judaism. It needs to be attempted in connection with Paul's *theologia crucis* as well.

THE SOCIOLOGICAL PERSPECTIVE

Since Käsemann's article, extensive sociological study has been conducted on the New Testament in general and the Corinthian Church in particular.[20] This provides a valuable resource in reconstructing the state of affairs in the Corinthian church at the time of the letter.[21] We are as a result in a much better position than Käsemann was to reconstruct the sociological and cultural context into which Paul wrote.

The studies emerging from Germany in the 1960s and 70s all shared one characteristic. While identifying the theology of the cross as polemical theology, they failed to tie down with any great precision the target of Paul's polemic. Luther had a clear sense of the target of his polemical theology of the cross in various forms of late medieval scholastic theology, as we shall see in due course. Käsemann himself had a clear sense of the contemporary context into which his essay (and indeed all of his theological work[22]) was written. Yet when it comes to showing how Paul's own theology of the cross functions, the target of Paul's polemic, the other half of the conversation, is much more blurred. He simply asserts that behind Paul's Corinthian opponents lies some form of over-realised eschatology.[23]

This lack of concern for context is by no means limited to Käsemann. Hans Weder's *Das Kreuz Jesu bei Paulus* is an important and thoughtful account of the significance of the historical factuality of the cross for the question of the relationship between faith and history. In a close exegesis of 1 Cor.1, Weder assumes a background to the Corinthians' theology in Hellenistic Jewish wisdom speculation, a form of wisdom thinking which was more interested in the general and universal than in the contingent and particular. This effectively played down the significance of the cross as a *historical* event with definite eschatological implications. However, Weder simply assumes this background, bringing little evidence to substantiate it.[24] There is no scholarly unanimity on the question of the precise situation into which 1 Corinthians was written, and there are, as we will see, major difficulties with this particular theory about the background to Corinthian theology. It can therefore only be tendentious to presume this as the target of Paul's polemic, and it runs the risk of undermining the validity of what Weder is trying to do.

Again, more recently, Charles Cousar has provided an admirable survey of the different ways in which the cross operates in Paul's understanding, but again the book does not engage with these contextual questions. The early chapters of 1 Corinthians are examined, but only a brief discussion for half a page[25] is given to the question of the setting into which Paul delivers his theology of the cross, drawing only on the work of one commentator on the complex questions involved.[26]

The difficulty here is that theology which has quite clearly been recognised as polemical is being utilised without sufficient attention to the target of that polemic. The true nature of any polemical theology can come into focus, only as the opposite argument itself becomes clearly visible. *Polemical meaning can only be discerned contextually.* In other words, the significance and interpretation of Paul's theology of the cross must be controlled by an understanding of how it functioned in its original context. Without this contextual grounding, it may be possible to describe the character of this type of theology as dogmatic or systematic theology, but not strictly speaking as *polemical* theology, which as Luz has pointed out, is to miss the whole point of the theology of the cross. It is also to miss the precise way in which Paul's theology addresses bids for power within the church, as we shall see in due course.

WHY 1 CORINTHIANS?

Paul is not the only theologian of the cross in the New Testament,[27] and 1 Corinthians is by no means the only place where he expounds the influence of the cross of Christ on his thought and ministry. Philippians 2-3,[28] 2 Corinthians 10-13 and parts of Galatians[29] all display the influence of the cross on Paul's understanding of the Christian and apostolic life. 1 Corinthians however is a particularly important text for an exploration of the nature and role of this kind of theology for Paul for two main reasons.

Firstly, the language and ideas of chapters 1 and 2 have aroused fascination throughout the history of Christian thought. The daring themes of these chapters, such as the foolishness and weakness of God, and the hiddenness of God's revelation, have left a distinct mark on later theologians of many different traditions, some of whom we will examine subsequently.

Secondly, this passage can claim to provide a more considered and fuller exposition of Paul's theology of the cross than many others. There is much evidence to suggest that in chapters 1 and 2, Paul is using previously composed material, containing ideas which he had worked through with some care and consideration, well before the controversy with the Corinthian church.

In the 1930s, Louis Cerfaux suggested that an Old Testament *florilegium*, a collection of verses, lay behind 1:18-3:24;[30] since then Peterson has claimed that behind this passage lay a sermon Paul once preached in a synagogue setting[31]. More recently, while Wuellner argued that chapters 1-3 of the letter display the characteristics of a haggadic homily on the theme of divine judgement on human wisdom,[32] Bailey thinks the passage betrays the poetic structure of a piece originally written by Paul for an oriental audience (possibly the church in Greek/Syriac speaking

Antioch).[33] Branick suggests it contains a midrashic homily consisting of 1:18-31; 2:6-16, and 3:18-23, with the intervening sections being adaptations for the specific Corinthian context.[34] Taken at face value, these theories might suggest that and that a verse such as 1:26 was really written as a generalised statement for a sermon originally preached elsewhere. This would of course question the value of these verses in describing the exact nature of the church in Corinth, and seriously hinder our attempts to understand what this church was actually like.

The variety of these attempted reconstructions of the material behind the passage shows how difficult it is to pin down the precise form of any such pre-existent material. None of these hypotheses has been universally accepted. For example, despite the discovery of *florilegia* in Qumran, the main difficulty with Cerfaux's theory is that the Old Testament quotations in the passage diverge significantly from the LXX. This would be much better explained by Paul's quoting fairly freely from memory than from a fixed written collection of 'testimonies'.[35]

It is difficult to discern where the pre-existent homiletic material stops and material written specifically for the Corinthian situation starts,[36] while some deny the use of previously composed material at all.[37] There is a good deal to suggest however that Paul is using some kind of homily, whether haggadic or midrashic. The stylised use of Old Testament quotation noticed by Wuellner, the poetic structure identified by Bailey, the evidence for a freely used and remembered (rather than written) collection of OT texts, all suggest that Paul may well be using pre-existent material here, rather than writing entirely in an immediate response to the Corinthian situation. Branick's division of the passage is ultimately more satisfactory than Wuellner's theory because it takes into account the likelihood that 2:1-5 and 3:1-4 refer directly to the Corinthian church. To modify Branick's analysis of the passage, we would suggest instead that the homily (or selection from various homilies) consists of the material found in 1:18-25, and 2:6-16. Branick's account does not take into account the *ad hominem* nature of 1:26-31 and 3:18-23, which distinguishes these sections clearly from

1:18-25 and 2:6-16. This in turn aligns 1:26-31 and 3:18-23 more
with 2:1-5 and 3:1-17, sections which also have an *ad hominem*
character, and which Branick himself acknowledges are written to
adapt the homily for use in Corinth.

If this is correct, then two important consequences follow. Firstly,
it can be assumed that 1:26-2:5 does reveal Paul's impression of this
particular congregation and his encounter with them. This is
important for the task of reconstructing the social and economic
constitution of the church in Corinth, and what was actually going
on there at the time when this letter was written. Secondly, Paul's
meditation on Christ crucified in 1:18-25 must be given full weight
as a piece of carefully crafted and deeply considered theology.
Rather than something hastily thrown together in the heat of the
moment, and conditioned merely by the circumstances of the church
in Corinth, it becomes a piece of writing with more lasting
significance. Paul would presumably not have re-used such
previously composed material if he were less than happy with it, or
if it were merely a tangential and unimportant part of his thought.
The statement of Paul's Theology of the Cross in 1 Cor. 1:18-25 can
claim to have emerged from considered and lengthy theological
rumination, an important theme in Paul's theology, rather than an
occasional piece written for a transitory and contingent situation. At
the same time, it was theology which Paul felt particularly
applicable to the church in Corinth. These chapters offer us a text
from which we can hope to discover what was happening among the
Christians in Corinth around the middle of the first century, a task
which is vital if we are to discover more of the function and
meaning of Paul's theology of the cross.

Notes:

[1]For example, M. Kähler, *Das Kreuz: Grund und Mass für die Christologie*
(Gütersloh: C. Bertelsmann, 1911); A. Schlatter, "Das Kreuz Jesu unsere

Versöhnung mit Gott", Gesunde Lehre - Reden und Aufsätze (Velbert im Rheinland: Freizeiten, 1929).

[2]See R. Bauckham, *Moltmann: Messianic Theology in the Making* (Basingstoke: Marshall Pickering, 1987), 53-90, a chapter entitled 'The Crucified God and Auschwitz'.

[3]For example those translated and published in Int 24 (1970), 131-242.

[4]See F. Viering, *Das Kreuzetod Jesu: Interpretation eines theologischen Gutachtens* (Gütersloh: Gerd Mohn, 1967).

[5]Translated into English in Int 24 (1970), 151-77, and in E. Käsemann, Perspectives on Paul (London: S.C.M., 1971), 32-59. It is from the latter of these that quotations here are taken.

[6]C.B. Cousar, *A Theology of the Cross: The Death of Jesus in the Pauline Letters* (Minneapolis: Fortress, 1990), 9.

[7]Käsemann, "Saving Significance", 41.

[8]Ibid., 55-6.

[9]Ibid., 35.

[10]Ibid., 37

[11]Ibid., 38-9.

[12]U.Luz, "Theologia Crucis als Mitte der Theologie im Neuen Testament," Ev.Th. 34 (1974), 116-41. (Here 118).

[13]Luz, "Theologia Crucis", argues that the Theology of the Cross, rather than being a theological system in itself, brings into question and makes provisional all theological systems, including Paul's own: "Das Wort vom Kreuz ist aber gerade die permanente Krisis aller eigenen theologischen Versuche", 130.

[14]Cousar concludes that "the message of the cross functions as the norm and point of critique of the church's quest for identity". *A Theology of the Cross*, 183.

[15]Tom Wright suggests that Käsemann thinks that "radical historical critics like himself represent the genuine Lutheran tradition, protesting against a theologia gloriae, a theology of the church triumphant, of worthy devotional practices, of bourgeois religiosity". N.T. Wright, "A New Tübingen School? Ernst Käsemann and his commentary on Romans," *Them* 7 (1982), 6-16.

[16]E. Käsemann, "The Righteousness of God in Paul", *New Testament Questions for Today* (London: S.C.M., 1969), 168-82.

[17]"Paul appropriated the tradition which was already in circulation about Jesus' cross in the sense of his doctrine of justification based on the cross; and this is, conversely, his interpretation of Jesus' death." Käsemann, "Saving Significance", 42.

[18]Cf. in particular K. Stendahl, *Paul Among Jews and Gentiles* (Philadelphia: Fortress, 1976); E.P. Sanders, *Paul and Palestinian Judaism* (London: S.C.M., 1977).

[19]See E.P. Sanders, *Paul, The Law and the Jewish People* (London: S.C.M.,

1983), 154-60 for his critique of the 'legalistic' interpretation of Judaism, including a critique of Käsemann's position.

[20]This movement goes back to the work of A. Deissmann, *Light from the Ancient East: The New Testament illustrated by recently discovered texts of the Greco-Roman world* (London: Hodder, 1927) German original, 1923. It was taken up in the 1960s by several significant works by E.A. Judge, especially *The Social Pattern of Christian Groups in the First Century* (London: Tyndale, 1960). For more recent growth in this area of New Testament scholarship, see A.J. Malherbe, *Social Aspects of Early Christianity* (Louisiana State University: Baton Rouge, 1977), R. Scroggs, "The Sociological Interpretation of the New Testament: The Present State of Research", *NTS* 26 (1980), 164-79, and W.A. Meeks, *The First Urban Christians: The Social World of The Apostle Paul* (New Haven: Yale, 1983).

[21]Most of these take their cue from Gerd Theissen's ground-breaking work on 1 Corinthians, collected together in English in *The Social Setting of Pauline Christianity* (Edinburgh: T. & T. Clark, 1982). Other works will be cited in footnotes as they are considered in turn.

[22]"My questioning and my listening have never been directed exclusively to academic theology... it is for the very purpose of liberating the Church for decisive action that theology has to carry out its work of radical and critical questioning." *New Testament Questions of Today*, x.

[23]"...the cross could appear as a mere transit point on the way to the exaltation, and as a station which the exalted Christ left behind, and which had therefore merely historical relevance... This was apparently exactly the way the Corinthians looked at it." (55) "...the Corinthians were already taking shelter behind the proclamation of a resurrection reality mediated through the sacraments." (56)

[24]H. Weder, *Das Kreuz Jesu bei Paulus* (Göttingen: Vandenhoeck & Ruprecht, 1981), 128.

[25]Cousar, *Theology of the Cross*, 34.

[26]J. Schütz, *Paul and the Anatomy of Apostolic Authority* (SNTSMS 26; Cambridge: C.U.P., 1975).

[27]In recent years, Mark's gospel has increasingly been seen in these terms, e.g. R.H. Gundry, *Mark - A Commentary on His Apology for the Cross* (Grand Rapids: Eerdmans, 1993). See also Luz, "Theologia Crucis", 131-41.

[28]See W. Willis, "The 'Mind of Christ' in 1 Corinthians 2.16", *Bib* 70 (1989), 110-22, for an excellent account of the theological connections between 1 Corinthians 2:16 and Philippians 2:5-11.

[29]Notably Gal. 2:19-21; 3:1; 5:11; 6:14.

[30]L. Cerfaux, "Vestiges d'un florilège dans 1 Cor. 1.18-3.24?," *RHE* 27 (1931), 521-34.

[31]E. Peterson, "1 Korinther 1.18 und die Thematik des jüdischen Busstages," *Bib*

32 (1951), 97-103, argues that the passage contains a Christian interpretation of the synagogue readings for 9th Ab., namely Baruch 3:9-4.4, a wisdom theme which had already raised interest in the church in Corinth: "Verlockend wäre es, in diesem Text eine in der Synagoge von Paulus gehaltene Predigt zu sehen.", 103. C.K. Barrett, *A Commentary on the First Epistle to the Corinthians* (2nd ed.n; London: A. & C. Black, 1971), 51, also supports this conjecture.

[32]W. Wuellner, "Haggadic Homily Genre in 1 Cor.1-3," *JBL* 89 (1970), 199-204.

[33]K.E. Bailey, "Recovering the Poetic Structure of 1 Cor. 1:17-2.2," *NovT* 17 (1975), 265-96.

[34]V.P. Branick, "Source and Redaction Analysis of 1 Cor. 1-3", *JBL* 101 (1982), 251-69.

[35]See the discussion in H. Conzelmann, *1 Corinthians* (Hermeneia; Philadelphia: Fortress Press, 1975), 44. German original, Göttingen: Vandenhoeck & Ruprecht, 1969.

[36]For example, Wuellner suggests it is only 1:18 and 3:21 which operate as connecting verses tying in the homily to the Corinthian situation, whereas Branick identifies 1:17; 2:1-5 and 3:1-4 as the Corinth-specific material. Branick's analysis agrees with that of E.E. Ellis in two separate articles. "'Wisdom' and 'Knowledge' in 1 Corinthians," *TynBul* 25 (1974), 82-98, claims that 2.6-16 is a midrashic composition, while "Traditions in 1 Corinthians," *NTS* 32 (1986), 481-502, makes the intriguing suggestion that it was composed by a colleague in Paul's missionary group. He concludes: "On balance, 1 Cor.2:6-16 is probably a pre-formed piece that Paul has employed and adapted to its present context" (490).

[37]G. Fee, *The First Epistle to the Corinthians* (Grand Rapids: Eerdmans, 1987), 66-7, thinks the question is inconsequential: "Since it (the homily) is so thoroughly Pauline in its present 'adaptation', it is nearly irrelevant to suggest that it may have had prior existence." N. Richardson, *Paul's Language about God* (JSNT 99, Sheffield: Sheffield Academic Press, 1994), argues that Branick's case founders on "..the fact that 2:1-5 are firmly linked with the preceding verses both in theme and language, and, similarly, 3:1-4 are difficult to detach from both preceding and following verses" (97).

Two: Corinthian Divisions

Early on in Paul's letter to the church in Corinth, he mentions the rumour he has heard that the congregation has become divided over the various Christian leaders who had played an important role in the founding and growth of the group. This description in 1:12 of divisions within the church around Paul, Apollos, Cephas and Christ has of course long been regarded as a crucial point in the interpretation of the whole letter. A vast amount of scholarly ink has been spilt wondering why these four names are mentioned here, whether or not they refer to four distinct groups, and if they do, what their distinguishing marks were. Naturally, this argument over names also needs to be related to the other disputes mentioned in the letter. If, as has been argued in the previous section, it is important to understand the context into which Paul spoke his theology of the cross, then we will need to understand what is really going on at this point. More particularly, if we are to understand the dimensions of power operating in the church, and how Paul's theology responds to it, then this text is a vital piece of evidence which needs to be examined. A competitive atmosphere has clearly built up within the church, and competition suggests jostling for power. Paul's theology of the cross as expounded here in 1 Corinthians is addressed not just to disunity, but to power, and as a result, its elucidation requires a close look at the underlying dynamics of this rivalry.

CEPHAS

Some recent studies[1] have revived F.C. Baur's nineteenth century thesis that the basic struggle in Corinth is between a 'Paul party' and a 'Cephas party'.[2] This latter group is said to be the result of the influence either of Peter himself, who, it is suggested, had visited Corinth,[3] or of Jewish Christian missionaries connected with the Jerusalem Church who had been there and left behind a Cephas party, "who from then on, represented a nucleus of Jewish-Christian criticism of Paul in Corinth".[4] On this theory, the language in 3:10-15 is a veiled criticism of those who appeal to Peter as the 'rock' on whom the church is built (Mt.16.18),[5] and the references to Cephas in both 9:5 and 15:5 indicate Paul's sensitivity to the charge that he is an inferior apostle to Peter.[6] There are however a number of difficulties with this theory.

1.   A first major obstacle is the virtual disappearance[7] of Peter from Paul's argument between 1:13 and 4:7, where the polarity seems clearly to be between Paul and Apollos. Attempts to get around this sound awkward. Goulder suggests that Paul disguises his real argument with Peter by using Apollos's name in 4:6 to blunt the edge of his polemic against Peter for pastoral reasons.[8] This results in a curious and forced exegesis which claims that Paul *writes* Apollos, where he really *means* Peter. Goulder's Paul combines sourness towards Peter with a desire to avoid confrontation with him. This picture sits uneasily with the parallels Goulder himself adduces with the issues in Galatians 2. If pastoral sensitivity does not hold Paul back from stressing his public opposition to Peter in Galatians, why is he so coy about it before the Corinthians?

2. Besides this, there is no conclusive evidence that Peter ever visited Corinth. Lüdemann oversteps the evidence when he claims that 9:1-12 shows that Peter had claimed support from the church at Corinth. 9:5 assumes a knowledge of Peter's practice, such as would have been available to many in the networks of the early Christian world, in which many people travelled (such as 'Chloe's people' – 1:11?), passing on gossip between the different Christian centres. It does not require that Peter had visited the city himself.[9] To see the passage, as Lüdemann does, as a defence of Paul's apostolic authority against a challenge from followers of Peter is to miss the larger point he is making. The argument in chapter 9 revolves around Paul's decision not to make use of his right to financial support. In 9:1-12, Paul insists that he does have this right, along with the other apostles. The questions in v.1 are not defensive, but rhetorical; Paul is saying, "I am a free agent,[10] I am an apostle, with all apostolic rights to marry and receive support, but I have deliberately chosen not to exercise these rights."

This section forms part of Paul's wider rhetorical strategy in this part of the letter, putting himself forward as an example of the voluntary surrender of rights (9:18), the course of action he wants to recommend to the Corinthians.[11] It might be argued (and with some plausibility) that the vehemence of Paul's self-presentation in 9:1-12 shows evidence of a certain touchiness on his part. However this need not mean that the issue here concerns a challenge to Paul's apostolic status. Both Peter Marshall and Ronald Hock have shown in different but complementary ways that any opposition to Paul in chapter 9 fits naturally into the context of Greco-Roman conventions of friendship, enmity and class expectations.[12] The chapter defends Paul's apostolic practice, not his apostolic authority.

Although recourse to a theory of Petrine visits to Corinth is unnecessary, it must be said that the possibility of such a visit cannot be ruled out. However, if he did visit, it is unlikely that he stayed long, or that his visit had a major impact upon the community. If a figure as central in the early Christian world as Peter had spent a good length of time there, it would be hard to explain the relative paucity of explicit mention in the letter of

Peter's name and influence, compared to that of Apollos, whom we know had stayed with the church for some time.

For Lüdemann, Paul's claims in 15:3-11 to have seen the risen Christ, and to have worked harder than the other apostles, betray a similar defensiveness about his own apostleship compared to Peter and James.[13] However the passage reads more naturally, and makes more sense in its context as an assertion of the reality of the bodily resurrection of Jesus, and that the risen Jesus that Paul had seen was the same as the one seen in all the other resurrection appearances. The Corinthians are not so much questioning the validity of Paul's witness to the resurrection, as the feasibility of a general resurrection of the body, defined in physical terms, as we shall argue in due course. Again, the theory of disputes between Paul and Peter reads too much into the text, and looks like a theory read into the text, rather than an inference arising from it. Paul does show consciousness of the issues surrounding himself and the Jerusalem apostles, but references to these and to the law (e.g. 15:5, 7, 56) are quite plausibly, and more naturally read as Paul's awareness of these issues in the wider context of the previous few years, rather than evidence that they were particular problems for the Corinthians.

3. Furthermore, the letter does not show a great deal of interest in the major issues at stake between Jewish and Gentile Christians. In the early part of this century, Lütgert asked why there is no discussion of the Law in 1 Corinthians if Paul's opponents are Petrine Jewish Christians.[14] Goulder claims that there is veiled discussion of the law in chapters 1-4 because the σοφία discussed there really refers to "a way of life in accord with torah".[15] This must be highly unlikely when the Greek word for Law, νόμος, does not even occur in the passage, and when the discussion at this point of the letter concerns eloquent speech and wisdom, rather than circumcision, food regulations, law or promise. The whole argument seems to run along different lines, with different language and categories. Given that σοφία has a clear meaning in Greek thought, one is left with the nagging suspicion that Goulder has forced 1

Corinthians into the mould of his overall thesis of the New Testament as reflecting a Baurian division between Paul and Peter.[16]

Peter Richardson has argued that the absence of Jewish issues in the letter can be put down to Paul's desire to mediate eirenically between the two extremes of an Hellenistic Alexandrian Jewish approach focused on Apollos, and a more traditional, Palestinian group focused on Peter.[17] The argument has a number of difficulties, not least those attached to any argument from silence. He assumes a Jewish background to the food issues of chapter 8 and 10,[18] failing to account for the indications in 8:10 and 10:7, 14, 20-21 that at least one, if not the major[19] point of contention was the practice of believers dining at pagan temples, a practice most likely among Gentile Christians. In fact both sides in this dispute are more probably Gentile: the 'weak' are those "hitherto accustomed to idols" (8:7), and the 'strong' (although the word is not used in this context), are those who are tempted to be "at table in an idol's temple" (8:10).[20] Paul's references to Jews (e.g. 1:22-24 and 9:20) are again more naturally taken as statements of his general missionary strategy to Jews, rather than indicating any great tension on these issues within the congregation in Corinth. While Richardson claims that 10:32 refers to internal disputes, the verse actually seems to *distinguish* Jews and Greeks from 'the church of God'. As a summary of the argument of the previous section, it refers to relations with those outside as well as those inside the community.

4)   Other attempts to identify Peter as the main focus of opposition to Paul in 1 Corinthians depend on discerning a Jewish context for the ideas Paul refutes. Richard Horsley in a series of articles[21] has proposed that the theology current in Corinth is a type of "Hellenistic Jewish religiosity focussed on sophia and gnosis". The Corinthians' gnosis fits into a "pattern of religiosity" similar to that in Philo and the Wisdom of Solomon. Paul responds by replacing their sophia with Christ as the locus of divine revelation. Horsley therefore roots the conflict in Corinth within 1st century Jewish diversity. J.A. Davis[22] claims that Corinthian wisdom is a

Torah-centric form of Hellenistic Jewish wisdom. He notes the connection between Wisdom and Torah in Sirach, Qumran, the Wisdom of Solomon and Philo, and how in these traditions, the search for wisdom proceeds by way of the interpretation of the Torah as the locus of divine Wisdom. In Corinth, he sees a Torah-centric σοφία. Paul's response is to replace the Torah with the cross and to claim that the kerygma about the cross is the true locus of divine Wisdom.

It is questionable whether a Jewish background does provide a totally sufficient explanation of Corinthian theology. The main difficulties are these:

4.i) To be sure, the language of 1 Corinthians can often find parallels in Hellenistic Jewish writings. Wisdom 9:17, for example, links σοφία and πνεῦμα, as Paul does in 2:10-13. This latter argument is Paul's own, however, not that of his opponents, and merely shows that he has used the language of the first century Jewish wisdom tradition. It therefore tells us nothing about Corinthian theology. Elsewhere, terms are often used in significantly different ways. For example, the Wisdom of Solomon associates wisdom with noble birth (8:3), wealth (8:5) and power (6:20).[23] However, it is to the noble birth of Wisdom itself, not that of the wise that the text refers, and the wealth of which it speaks is not financial but spiritual riches bestowed by wisdom which are actually being contrasted with financial wealth. In each case the context and use of the term in the Wisdom of Solomon is so different from that of the Corinthian Church as to make the derivation highly questionable.

4.ii) Pearson's claim that the πνευματικός/ψυχικός terminology must derive from Hellenistic Jewish exegesis of Gen. 2:7 is also questionable. There is good reason to suppose that πνευματικός is Paul's word, not the Corinthians', as he uses it in a clearly positive non-polemical context in Gal. 6:1.[24] Much of this terminology has parallels also in the wider Greco-Roman culture, so that a derivation from *Jewish* Hellenistic sources is not conclusive. Davis' claim that

Corinthian wisdom is essentially Torah-centric also fails to come up
with a convincing answer to Lütgert's question as to why the
concept of *Torah* is absent from the main concerns of the letter.

4.iii) Paul does say that while Jews seek signs, it is *Greeks* who
seek wisdom. Again, while the cross is a σκάνδαλον to Jews and
μωρία to Gentiles (v.23), it is on the cross as μωρία that Paul
concentrates in the rest of the passage. Although σκάνδαλον does
not occur again in the letter, the word of the cross is said to be
μωρία in 1:18, 20, 21, 25, the word being taken up again in 2:14 and
3:18. It seems that Paul feels he has primarily to tackle the Gentile
perception of the cross as foolishness, rather than the Jewish
perception of it as a stumbling-block.

4.iv) Although there were Jewish Christians in Corinth, the church
appears to have been predominantly Gentile rather than Jewish.
There is no evidence that the Jewish community in Corinth was
particularly sizeable,[25] and much to suggest that Paul's mission to it
was less than an outstanding success.[26] Paul three times mentions
the pagan background of the Corinthians. 12:2 is the most clear-cut
example, but 6:9-11 and 8:7, 10 imply a largely pagan audience.[27]
In other places, the argument and language used is much better
explained by presuming a Gentile-Christian rather than a
Jewish-Christian audience. For example, in 10:18, Paul writes
"Consider Israel according to the flesh". This can be compared with
a similar shift of focus in an argument in 12:2, where he can simply
say "You know that when you were pagans…" In the latter, Paul
can quite clearly appeal to their knowledge of their own past, while
in the former he does not appear to be able to do so. As we have
seen, 10:14-21 suggests that some of the church still participate in
worship at pagan temples. This is less likely to have been a serious
temptation for people with a Jewish background, and implies that
Paul has a predominantly Gentile readership in mind.

In conclusion, while there was clearly a Jewish Christian element
within the church at Corinth, the evidence suggests that the majority

of the congregation was Gentile. If the Jewish section was in the minority, and the concerns Paul addresses seem to concern issues explicable within a Gentile Greco-Roman context, then the idea of a 'Cephas-party' of Jewish Christians as the root of the problems in Corinth is unlikely. Even if Peter did visit Corinth briefly, the terms of the debate seem very different from other accounts we have of Paul's tensions with Peter. If the main contention surrounded the competing claims of Paul and Peter, presumably 1 Corinthians would tackle the same kinds of issues faced in Galatians for example, yet the letters are very different.[28] Having said all of this, the evidence of 1:12 remains that some were using Peter's name in the Corinthian competition over apostolic figures. While these are probably not the main source of trouble for Paul in Corinth, and most likely represent a minority view, they still need to be accounted for. Our argument does not require the total absence of Petrine or Jewish influence in the Corinthian church, it simply suggests that such influence is not the major factor in the problems Paul faces as he addresses it.

APOLLOS

In contrast to Peter, we do know that Apollos stayed for some time with the church in Corinth (3:6). Acts 18 suggests that he arrived in Corinth at some point after Paul's departure, and pursued an active preaching ministry there. His ministry in Corinth, unlike that in Ephesus (Acts 18:26), was presumably conducted outside the synagogue. Although Acts tells us only of his ministry to Jews, by the time Apollos arrived it is likely that the Corinthian church's relationship with the synagogue was strained to say the least (Acts 18:12-17), and he is said to have confuted Jews "publicly" (Acts 18:28).[29] The verb used here, διακατελέγχομαι, a *hapax legomenon*, implies not so much that his ministry led to great numbers of Jews being converted, but that he was known (in Christian circles at least) to have been effective at refuting the Jewish opposition. It is by no means unlikely, especially as his speaking was so public, that many of those who entered the

Christian community through his preaching were Gentile, especially when we recall the strong arguments in favour of the predominantly Gentile constitution of the Corinthian church. It is probable, given 1:13, that Apollos also had baptised some at least of these converts.

Acts also describes him in carefully chosen words,[30] as both ἀνὴρ λόγιος, and ζέων τῷ πνεύματι (vv.24-5). These are presumably mentioned because they were memorable features of Apollos' style of ministry, and well-known in early Christian circles. Both of these have been understood in several different ways.[31] Although ἀνὴρ λόγιος can simply mean eloquence of speech, it most likely refers to specific rhetorical training and ability, perhaps from Apollos' background in Alexandria.[32] Apollos' Alexandrian origins have inspired much speculation, but little that is firm can be built on them.[33] Pogoloff's conclusion is apt: "Although any speculation about Alexandrian origins is risky, we are on much firmer ground when we assume that any educated Alexandrian was well trained in rhetoric."[34]

The meaning of the other phrase, ζέων τῷ πνεύματι, is also disputed. Its parallel in Romans 12:11 implies that it means more than just "enthusiastic". Most modern commentators agree with the common patristic interpretation that πνεύματι must be a reference to the Holy Spirit, due to its being paralleled by τῷ κυρίῳ in the same verse, and Paul's standard association of emotional language with the Holy Spirit .[35] As this phrase occurs only in the NT, and there only in these two places, it is likely to be a standard phrase "current in the language of Christian edification".[36] If so, it can be assumed to have a common meaning in Romans and Acts.[37] Apollos was most probably well known as a man "boiling over with the Spirit".

Two notable features of the Corinthian church seem to have been a love for rhetoric and a high valuation of ecstatic spiritual gifts. Paul acknowledges this pointedly at the very start of the letter (1:4-7) when he describes the church as "enriched with all speech and knowledge," and then as "not lacking in any spiritual gift" (χαρίσματος). He deliberately chooses these two characteristics to describe the church, and it is striking that they are the very characteristics for which Apollos' ministry was known.

Two objections are commonly raised against the thesis that Apollos is the main focus of the problems at Corinth. First, Paul clearly presents himself and Apollos as allies, not opponents, for example in both 3:5-7 and 16:12.[38] This is of course true, although Duane Litfin may well be right in seeing an implied gentle rebuke or warning to Apollos in 3:10-15.[39] The objection counts only against the thesis that Apollos was consciously stirring up opposition to Paul: it disappears if Apollos is seen as an unwitting focus of rivalry. Paul presumably thought that the problem was more to do with the Corinthians themselves than Apollos. Those claiming Apollos' name were doing so without his knowledge and against his will.[40]

Secondly, the imagery of building on a foundation in ch.3 has sometimes been seen as undercutting Peter, the 'rock' on which the church was to be built (Matt.16:18).[41] This again is doubtful on three counts. 1) The building imagery makes essentially the same point as the agricultural metaphor, namely that one ministry complements another. 2) The return to wisdom/foolishness language in 3:18ff implies Paul is still thinking of Gentile not Jewish wisdom, given the Hellenistic focus of the wise/foolish opposition in 1:22-23. 3) The clear implication of 4:6a is that each of the three images used in 3:1-4.5 (the farmer, the builder, the household manager) applies to Paul and Apollos, not Peter.[42]

While there are difficulties with the idea that Peter is the focus of discontent with Paul, Apollos has a much stronger claim to such a position, albeit against his own will. There are good reasons for supposing the 'Apollos party', however that is to be defined, as the other main grouping and the major focus of opposition to Paul.[43]

CHRIST

Does "I am of Christ" in 1:12 indicate the existence of a 'Christ-party' in Corinth?[44] Suggestions have ranged from describing this slogan as referring to a group of proto-gnostics,[45] *pneumatikoi* holding an exaltation Christology,[46] or an extreme Jewish-Christian group.[47] Others have suggested that the phrase refers not to another Corinthian group,[48] but to Paul's own response to the divisions, in parallel to the three names mentioned in 3:22-23,[49] or even that the phrase does not belong here, being a later interpolation by a rather over-spiritual scribe.[50]

It would certainly be odd and not a little unnatural for Paul to criticise those who say they belong to Christ, when he clearly considers they all *do* belong to Christ (3:23: ὑμεῖς δὲ χριστοῦ). On the other hand, the grammar of 1:12, especially the continuing μέν ....δὲ construction, favours 'Christ' as a rival centre of loyalty alongside Paul, Apollos and Cephas, there being no indication of any break between the third and the fourth clause.

The identification of Corinthian theology as gnostic or proto-gnostic, with the Christ-group as its proponents, always more popular in German than in English-speaking scholarship,[51] has largely been abandoned in recent years. There is an increasing consensus that the kind of gnostic Redeemer myth of 2nd century gnosticism is simply not there in 1 Corinthians.[52] To claim that aspects of Corinthian theology can be traced in later gnosticism[53] may say something about the future development, but very little about the origins of these Christians' beliefs. Witherington states the current position: "It is increasingly agreed that it is probably anachronistic to describe either the Corinthians' or Paul's views as gnostic in the second century sense of the term."[54] Although it is true that the Corinthians are concerned with γνῶσις,[55] this can be explained within the context of ·1st century Greek thought and culture, without having to anticipate the language of later gnosticism as we shall see in due course.

The lack of unambiguous evidence for such a group in the rest of the letter, the clear Paul-Apollos axis in 3:4-15, and the evidence that belonging to Christ is a position of which Paul himself approves, all make the existence of such a prominent 'Christ-group' unlikely. In fact, most of the positions indicated in the literature on this group link it with either the Peter group (e.g. Baur, Goulder), or the Apollos group (e.g. Sellin). Fee tentatively suggests that the 'Christ' group, while having no particular human leader to look to, have yet been caught up in "spiritual elitism", comparable to others in the congregation.[56] The implication of 12:12-26 is indeed that some in the congregation may have claimed superiority to others on the basis of their supposedly superior spiritual gifts.[57] As we shall see, one feature of the 'Apollos group' seems to have been a form of elitism over others in the congregation. To modify Fee's suggestion slightly, those who say "I am of Christ" are not necessarily a separate group from those loyal to Apollos, nor even to Paul, nor linked to them by conversion or baptism. It may simply be that some in either or both of these groups express their sense of superiority by a claim to belong to Christ in an exclusive way, as in: "we are the ones who *truly* belong to Christ." We will return to this slogan, but the evidence for there being a distinct 'Christ' group is slender.

PAUL

The 'Paul' slogan has surprisingly received much less treatment than the other three. The assumption is usually that this refers to Paul's supporters. It needs stressing at this stage that although some were loyal to Paul, *he does not appear to take their side*. This factor needs to be explained in reconstructing the Corinthian situation.

1 Corinthians gives us some clues as to the identity of the Paul group. Paul probably arrived in Corinth in AD 50,[58] and according to Acts 18:11 stayed approximately eighteen months. During that period, Acts tells us that he preached to both Jews and Gentiles (18:4). Those converted no doubt included Crispus, the ruler of the synagogue (Acts 18:8), Gaius, in whose home he wrote Romans (Rom.16:23), and Stephanas. These three he also baptised, either because they were the first of his converts (this was certainly the case for Stephanas – 1 Cor.16:15), or because they were especially close to him (it is clear that Gaius at least became part of his network of hosts, and Stephanas visited Paul at least once – 1

Cor.16:17).[59] Besides these, he most likely saw a number of others
converted, including Erastus (1 Cor16:23) the city treasurer,[60]
Quartus, who is also mentioned in Rom 16:23, and being known to
the Romans, had presumably travelled with Paul, Titius Justus (Acts
18:7), and perhaps Chloe (1 Cor.1:11) and Phoebe (Rom.16:1).

There is good reason to believe that most of these were relatively
wealthy, high-status people in Corinthian society. Crispus held
responsibility for maintenance of the synagogue buildings; Gaius
was the head of a large enough home to accommodate the 'whole'
church (Rom.16:23); Stephanas was a householder and probable
slave-owner;[61] Erastus was an οἰκονόμος (possibly also *ædile*?);[62]
Titius Justus was wealthy enough to accommodate Paul; Chloe was
also probably an owner of slaves.[63] It is hard to be certain that all of
these owed their Christian faith to Paul's ministry, but it is at least
likely that Paul's stay in Corinth resulted in some wealthy, high-
status people joining the Christian church in Corinth. Those
converted through him are all likely to have retained a certain
loyalty to Paul in any subsequent dispute, and there is no indication
in 1 Corinthians that Paul was estranged from any of those
mentioned by name. Some at least of these must have been
numbered among those 'of Paul', however Paul himself refrains
from automatically endorsing their point of view.

SUMMARY

As many have pointed out, the dynamics of chapters 1-4 suggest
an opposition of two main parties, not four.[64] This brief survey of
the options has led to the impression that the main difficulty which
Paul saw in Corinth came from a group claiming Apollos as a model
or champion, although this does not deny the likelihood that other
currents are present in the dynamics of the complex relationships in
the church at Corinth. These people are more likely than not to be
Gentile in origin, and to admire Apollos' rhetoric and spiritual
fervency, although Apollos himself has not consciously sought to

foment antagonism to Paul. If these Christians entered the church *after* Paul's time in Corinth, they would have known the content of his teaching only second-hand. While there may be some who claim allegiance to Peter or even to Christ, they are unlikely to be the main target of Paul's polemic in the letter. To identify a group of Apollos' admirers is not to say a great deal about what that group was like, and what they believed and valued. It is to that question that we turn next.

Notes:

[1] Notably G. Lüdemann, *Opposition to Paul in Jewish Christianity* (Minneapolis: Fortress Press, 1989), 64-80, and M. D. Goulder, "Σοφια in 1 Corinthians" *NTS* 37 (1991), 516-34.

[2] C.K. Barrett gave additional support to this theory in "Cephas and Corinth", *Essays on Paul* (London: S.P.C.K., 1982), 28-39. Originally published in: *Abraham unser Vater: Juden und Christen im Gespräch über die Bibel; Festschrift für Otto Michel* (Leiden: Brill, 1963), 1-12.

[3] C.K. Barrett, "Christianity at Corinth", *Essays on Paul*, 1-27, esp. 4. Cf. also "Cephas in Corinth" in the same volume, 31.

[4] Lüdemann, *Opposition,* 80; cf. also 94-7.

[5] Barrett, *1 Corinthians*, 87-8.

[6] Lüdemann, *Opposition*, 68-74.

[7] The only mention of his name comes in 3:22, where Cephas appears alongside Paul and Apollos, but with no mention of 'Christ'.

[8] Goulder, "Σοφια", 519. Barrett, "Cephas and Corinth", 31 tries to get around this by making 4:6 mean "I have made these things look as if they applied to Apollos and me (only)... though in fact the lesson really applies to a third party". This 'translation' reads far too much into a text (3:5-4:5) which at face value refers only to Paul and Apollos. It looks very much like special pleading!

[9] P. Bachmann, *Der erste Brief des Paulus an die Korinther* (Leipzig: A Deichert, 1905), 66, suggests that Petrine influence is accounted for by a group of Peter's Palestinian converts (therefore using the Aramaic form of his name Κηφᾶς), who had moved east to join the church at Corinth.

[10] "Am I not free?" in v.1. is paralleled by "I am free from all men" in v.19.

[11] See B. Witherington III, *Conflict and Community in Corinth* (Grand Rapids: Eerdmans, 1995), 203-6, *pace* Fee, *1 Corinthians*, 392-4.

[12]P. Marshall, *Enmity in Corinth: Social Conventions in Paul's Relations with the Corinthians* (Tübingen: J.C.B. Mohr, 1987); R.F. Hock, *The Social Context of Paul's Ministry: Tentmaking and Apostleship* (Philadelphia: Fortress Press, 1980).

[13]Lüdemann, *Opposition*, 72-3.

[14]Goulder, "Σοφια", 527. W. Lütgert, *Freiheitspredigt und Schwärmgeister in Korinth. Ein Betrag zur Charakteristik der Christuspartei* (Gütersloh: C. Bertelsmann, 1908), 49-52. 'Law' is mentioned in 15:56, but this appears to be a passing comment, arising more from Paul's developed theology of the law and its connection with sin and death, than from any controversy over the issue in Corinth. Referring to v.56b ("the power of sin is the law"), Fee claims: "The (second) statement belongs to the first one as a theological construct, not as an issue in this church." *1 Corinthians*, 806.

[15]Goulder, "Σοφια," 521.

[16]Cf. M.D. Goulder, *A Tale of Two Missions* (London: S.C.M., 1994).

[17]P. Richardson, "On the Absence of 'Anti-Judaism' in 1 Corinthians" *Anti-Judaism in Early Christianity Vol. I* (2 vols.), ed. P. Richardson and D. Granskou (Waterloo: Wilfred Laurier, 1986), 59-74.

[18]His attempt to read chs. 8-11 as a single unified section answering the problem of food is unconvincing.

[19]This appears to be the point at issue in ch. 8 (cf v.10). In ch. 10, the discussion revolves around the practice of εἰδωλολατρία (v.14), and partaking at τραπέζα δαιμονίων (v.21), in other words, still the practice of dining at pagan temples. Paul then enunciates his basic principle in vv.23-4, and offers two further applications of it, namely eating meat sold at the market in 10:25, and dining at a pagan's home in 10:27. This explains why Paul appears to offer conflicting advice in 8:13 and 10:21, from that offered in 10:25 and 27. Whereas in the former he is dealing with the more questionable practice of eating at pagan temples (which implies worship of those gods, 'provoking the Lord to jealousy' – 10:22), the latter concerns eating meat outside such temples, a practice on which Paul takes a much softer line.

[20]Thus contrary to C.K. Barrett, "Things Sacrificed to Idols," *NTS* 11 (1965), 138-53, and "Cephas and Corinth".

[21]R.A. Horsley, "'How can some of you say there is no Resurrection of the Dead?' Spiritual Elitism in Corinth", *NovT* 20 (1978), 203-31; "Gnosis in Corinth: 1 Corinthians 8:1-6", *NTS* 27 (1980), 32-51; "Wisdom of Word and Words of Wisdom in Corinth", *CBQ* 39 (1977), 224-39.

[22]J.A. Davis, *Wisdom & Spirit: An Investigation of 1 Corinthians 1.18-3.20 against the background of Jewish Sapiental Traditions in the Greco-Roman Period* (Lanham: University Press of America, 1984).

[23]G. Theissen, *Psychological Aspects of Pauline Theology* (Edinburgh: T. & T.

Clark, 1987), 353 n.1. cf. 1 Cor.1:26.

[24]Cf. Richardson, *Paul's Language,* 103. He concludes; "We should probably look to sources other than Jewish for the origin of Paul's conflict with 'the wisdom of this age'". The occurrence in 12:1 is best seen as recapitulating Paul's earlier teaching of the church about πνευματικοί, which the church has in turn picked up and used in ways which Paul had not intended.

[25]The well-known inscription found in Corinth in 1898 reading "...γωγη ἑβρ..." is undateable with great accuracy, although probably is much later than Paul's time (see ed. B.D. Merritt, *Corinth: Vol VIII part 1: Greek Inscriptions* (Cambridge, Mass.: Harvard University Press, 1931), 79. Contrary to what Meeks claims in *Urban Christians* 48, Philo's mention of Corinth (*Leg. ad Gaium,* 281) in a list of synagogues in the Eastern Mediterranean cannot be used to prove the existence of a *large* Jewish community there. The purpose of the reference in context is to demonstrate to Gaius how widespread the Jewish community is beyond Judaea, and how widely benefits given to Jews would be felt across the empire, were he to confer them. It is therefore in Philo's interest to include as many synagogues as possible, however large or small, significant or insignificant those communities might be.

[26]Acts 18:1-11 (especially v.6) gives the impression of a relatively unsuccessful Pauline mission to the synagogue (the conversion of Crispus and Sosthenes excepted), Paul fairly quickly turning to the Gentiles.

[27]6:9-10 shows signs of dependence on Jewish catalogues of Gentile vices: cf. P. Borgen, "Catalogues of Vices, the Apostolic Decree, and the Jerusalem Meeting," *The Social World of Formative Christianity and Judaism: Essays in tribute to H.C. Kee* (Philadelphia: Fortress, 1988), 131-3. That Paul uses this Jewish traditional form to refer to the Gentile past of his readers is made clear by the simple phrase καὶ ταῦτά τινες ἦτε (v11).

[28]Fee, *1 Corinthians*, 311, in connection with the reference to circumcision in 7:18, remarks how "the very lack of passion over this matter indicates that it is not an issue in the church at Corinth, as it was later to become in Galatia and Philippi... A Jew-Gentile struggle does not appear in this letter, not even in chs. 8-10, where one might most expect it".

[29]F.F. Bruce, *The Acts of the Apostles* (Grand Rapids: Eerdmans, 1990), 396, thinks this does not indicate a complete break with the synagogue. He perhaps underestimates the effect this incident, and the conversion of Crispus (Acts18:8; 1 Cor.1:14) would have had on synagogue-Christian relations in the city. Compare E. Haenchen, *The Acts of the Apostles* (Oxford: Blackwell, 1971), 539: "The scene with Gallio finally proves that Paul had broken with the Jews of Corinth"; also 551: "after the Corinthian congregation's breach with the synagogue (18:6) Apollos could no longer seek out the Jews there". Paul's reference to five beatings from the Jews in 2 Cor.11:24 may include his estrangement from the synagogue

in Corinth. Haenchen concludes concerning this whole account, that "we can view the report as a whole with confidence" (541). On the reliability of the account concerning Apollos in Corinth cf. also Bruce, *Acts*, 404.

[30]The language is especially carefully chosen if Acts does display ambivalence towards Apollos, as argued by E. Käsemann, "The Disciples of John the Baptist in Ephesus", *Essays on New Testament Themes* (London: S.C.M., 1964), 136-48.

[31]For references to the different views, see the footnotes in Haenchen, *Acts*, 550.

[32]Apollos has often been seen as a mediator of Hellenistic Jewish wisdom to Corinth. See Horsley, "Wisdom of Word". G. Sellin, "Das 'Geheimnis' der Weisheit und das Rätsel der 'Christuspartei' (zu 1 Kor. 1-4)", *ZNW* 73 (1982), 69-96, argues that the Christ party is strongly influenced by Apollos. Cf. also B.A. Pearson, *The Pneumatikos-Psychikos Terminology in 1 Corinthians: A Study in the Theology of the Corinthian Opponents of Paul and Its Relation to Gnosticism* (Atlanta: Scholars Press, 1973) and "Philo, Gnosis and the New Testament", *The New Testament and Gnosis: Essays in honour of Robert McLachlan Wilson*, eds. A.H.B. Logan and A.J.M. Wedderburn (Edinburgh: T. & T. Clark, 1983), 73-89. The reservations mentioned above about a Jewish origin to the ideas influencing the Corinthian church apply to these suggestions as well.

[33]See J. Munck, *The Church without Factions: Studies in 1 Corinthians 1-4* (London: S.C.M., 1959), 143-4.

[34]S.M. Pogoloff, *Logos and Sophia: The Rhetorical Situation of 1 Corinthians* (Atlanta: Scholars Press, 1992), 181.

[35]C.E.B. Cranfield, *The Epistle to the Romans* (ICC, 2 vols.; Edinburgh: T. & T. Clark, 1979), 2.633-4; C.K. Barrett, *The Epistle to the Romans* (London: A. & C. Black, 1957), 240; J.D.G. Dunn, *Romans 9-16* (WBC 38b; Dallas: Word, 1988).

[36]Käsemann, "Disciples of John the Baptist", 143.

[37]A. Oepke, "ζέω," *TDNT* 2.875-6 agrees that both usages have essentially the same meaning.

[38]E.g. Goulder, "Σοφια", 517-8.

[39]D. Litfin, *St. Paul's Theology of Proclamation: 1 Corinthians 1-4 and Greco-Roman Rhetoric* (Cambridge: C.U.P., 1994), 224-5. P. Richardson, "The Thunderbolt in Q and the Wise Man in Corinth", *From Jesus to Paul, Studies in Honour of Francis Wright Beare* (eds. P. Richardson & J.C. Hurd; Waterloo, Wilfred Laurier University Press, 1984), 91-111, oversteps the evidence in arguing for sharp theological divergence between Paul and Apollos. As a description of the tone of 3:5-15, Litfin's "veiled criticism" is much more appropriate than Richardson's "aggressively antagonistic passage".

[40]Cf. Fee, *1 Corinthians*, 824-5. Apollos may have refused to return to Corinth (16:12) because he was unwilling to be involved in opposition to Paul, preferring to steer clear of the situation altogether for the time being.

[41]e.g. Barrett, *1 Corinthians*, 87-92, on vv.11-17.

[42]See Witherington, *Conflict*, 136-7.

[43]J.C. Hurd, *The Origin of 1 Corinthians* (London: S.P.C.K., 1965), 97-8: "This position is attractive. There is considerable evidence in the text to support it." Witherington, *Conflict*, 78-9 and elsewhere, suggests that at this stage in the Corinthian correspondence, there is no opposition to Paul. 1:12 however does seem to imply that some Corinthian Christians felt Paul did not shape up to other apostolic figures, and 9:3 indicates that some 'examine him', making unfavourable comparisons with others.

[44]The various suggestions are helpfully laid out in Hurd, *Origin*, 101-6, and in Fee, *1 Corinthians*, 58-9.

[45]Lütgert, *Freiheitspredigt*, 76-80 calls them "libertinische Pneumatiker" (86). Cf. also W. Schmithals, *Gnosticism in Corinth: An Investigation of the letters to the Corinthians* (Nashville: Abingdon, 1971), 199-206.

[46]Conzelmann, *1 Corinthians*, 33-4.

[47]E.g. W.O. Fitch, "Paul, Apollos, Cephas, Christ", *Th* 74 (1971), 18-24.

[48]Hurd, *Origin*, 104-5 makes the telling point that the questions which follow would be meaningless addressed to a 'Christ-party', as they would clearly be able to answer in ways which furthered their own claims, whereas members of the other groups could not. J. Munck, *Church without Factions*, 142-3 also points out the paucity of evidence for the existence of such a group.

[49]K. Lake, *The Earlier Epistles of Paul: Their Motive and Origin* (London: Rivingtons, 1914), 127-8.

[50]J.Weiss, *Der erste Korintherbrief* (Göttingen: Vandenhoeck & Ruprecht, 1910), 17-8.

[51]See W. Schmithals, *Gnosticism in Corinth*, and "The *Corpus Paulinum* and Gnosis", *The New Testament and Gnosis*, 107-24; M. Winter, *Pneumatiker und Psychiker in Korinth: Zum religionsgeschichtlichen Hintergrund von 1 Kor.2:6-3:4* (Marburg: N.G. Elwert, 1975); U. Wilckens, *Weisheit und Torheit* (Tübingen: Mohr, 1959), and "Σοφία, σοφός, σοφίζω", *TDNT* 7, 465-528, esp. 509-22.

[52]Cf G. Macrae, "Gnosis in Corinth", *Int* 26 (1972), 489-91; G.W. Miller, "ΑΡΧΟΝΤΩΝ ΤΟΥ ΑΙΩΝΟΥ ΤΟΥΤΟΥ - A New Look at 1 Cor.2:6-8", *JBL* 91 (1972), 522-8; R. Scroggs, "Paul: Σοφος and Πνευματικος," *NTS* 14 (1967-8), 33-55.

[53]R.M. Grant, *Gnosticism and Early Christianity* (2nd ed.; New York: Columbia University Press, 1966), 157: "a movement like the one which later became Gnosticism was probably present in Corinth". See also, R.McL. Wilson, "How Gnostic were the Corinthians?," *NTS* 19 (1972), 65-74; also "Gnosis at Corinth," *Paul and Paulinism: Essays in honour of C.K.Barrett*, eds. M.D. Hooker and S.G. Wilson (London: S.P.C.K., 1982), 102-14. Neither discerns a full gnostic myth in Corinth, just the 'tentative beginnings' of what later became gnosticism.

[54]B. Witherington III, *Jesus the Sage: The Pilgrimage of Wisdom* (Edinburgh: T.

& T. Clark, 1994), 299. See also R.A. Horsley, "Gnosis in Corinth: 1 Corinthians 8.1-6," *NTS* 27 (1980), 32-51, esp. 32.

[55]Γινώσκω and γνῶσις seem to reflect Corinthian usage in 1:21; 2:8-16; 8:1-11; 13:2, 8-12; 14:6.

[56]Fee, *1 Corinthians*, 59.

[57]These may be those with links with the Dionysian mystery cults who over-value ecstatic speech.

[58]The date of Paul's arrival in Corinth (Spring AD 50) is one of the few reasonably fixed dates in most New Testament chronologies, due to its association with the Gallio inscription (Acts 18:12).

[59]E.A. Judge, "The Early Christians as a Scholastic Community", *JRH* 1.I (1960-61), 4-15, 1.II, 125-37 gives an account of Paul's supporters at Corinth, and explains the way in which his operation worked with a network of support across the empire.

[60]Perhaps the same as the ædile mentioned on the famous inscription found in Corinth? Theissen, *Social Setting*, 75-9, and A.D. Clarke, *Secular and Christian Leadership in Corinth: A Socio-Historical and Exegetical Study of 1 Corinthians 1-6* (Leiden: Brill, 1993), 46-56, agree that while the identification cannot be certain, there is a good chance that they are the same person.

[61]See below on the likely identity of Fortunatus and Achaicus (16:17) as slaves in Stephanas' household.

[62]Theissen notes the uncertainty about the social status of an οἰκονόμος, and comes down on the side of Erastus' high social status. *Social Setting*, 75-83.

[63]*Social Setting*, 69-96. Theissen's conclusion is that "The great majority of the Corinthians known to us by name probably enjoyed high social status... in all probability the most active and important members of the congregation belonged to the οὐ πολλοὶ σοφοὶ.. δυνατοι... εὐγενεις" (95). Cf. also Witherington, *Conflict*, 114-5.

[64]Goulder himself argues this on the basis of the dualistic structure between the wisdom of God and the wisdom of the world in 1:18-25, the singular ἄλλος in 3:10, and 4:6. For him, there are only two main groups in Corinth, although he sees them as Paul/Apollos vs. Peter/Christ. Cf. also N.A. Dahl, "Paul and the Church at Corinth according to 1 Corinthians 1.10-4.21," *Christian History and Interpretation: Studies presented to John Knox*, eds. W.R.Farmer, C.F.D Moule and R.R. Niebuhr (Cambridge: C.U.P., 1967), 313-35.

Three: The Apollos Factor

THE ISSUES AT STAKE

At significant points in the letter, the simple word τινες reveals a group within the congregation whom Paul has clearly in mind, and whose relations with him are clearly strained.[1] It is only "some" who are arrogant, thinking Paul will not return (4:18); it is only "some" of the congregation who "say that there is no resurrection of the dead" (15:12); there are "those" (τοῖς) who want to judge Paul (9:3) and by implication, others who do not. One group of people eats food offered to idols nonchalantly, leaving others defiled because they do so with a weak conscience (8:7). Paul addresses the man who has knowledge (γνῶσις), who eats with a clear conscience at a pagan table, asking him to consider the "weak man.., the brother for whom Christ died" (8:11). Some separate themselves from the rest of the congregation at the communal meal (11:17-22). Some feel themselves to be self-sufficient in the realm of spiritual gifts, having no need of others: χρείαν σου οὐκ ἔχω (12:21). Probably as a result of this, others are made to doubt their value to the body because they lack certain gifts (perhaps the σοφία and γνῶσις mentioned in 12:8), so they say οὐκ εἰμὶ ἐκ τοῦ σώματος

(12:15,16). One group separate themselves because they feel their spiritual gifting is superior, another group feel they do not belong because they do not come up to scratch.

Who are these people? If our impressions in the previous chapter were correct, that Paul is aware of two major groupings in Corinth, not four, primarily gathered around his own name and that of Apollos, we can begin to identify the characteristics of those who appeal to the latter by identifying the issues Paul raises in the letter. In general the issues appear to be the following:

RHETORIC

As mentioned above, at least some in the Corinthian church show a regard for rhetoric, which Paul does not wholly share (1:5; 2:4).

PAGAN WORSHIP

Some within the congregation[2] argue for the right to eat in pagan temples, possibly joining in the cultic meals in honour of idols (8:1-13; 10:7-33).[3]

SEXUAL CONDUCT

This group condones what Paul sees as sexual irregularity, namely a man sleeping with his stepmother (5:1), and men consorting with prostitutes (6:15-20). At the same time, there is evidence of sexual asceticism, even disparagement of sex (7:1-7). It is possible that the legal action referred to in 6:1ff. emerges out of the sexual disorder of 5:1. The whole sweep of chapters 5-7 concerns sexual behaviour, and it would make sense if the court case were connected to this issue.[4] Paul protests in 5:3-13 that they have not been able to discipline the one guilty of this crime themselves, but have allowed the dispute to spill over into the secular law-courts, an indication of how bitter some of the divisions were becoming.[5]

THE PLACE OF WOMEN

Paul is clearly uncomfortable with the conduct of some women in the church. Some pray with their heads uncovered (11:2-16), others perhaps interrupt the gathering by asking inappropriate questions at inappropriate times (14:34-36).[6]

SPIRITUAL GIFTS

Some are fascinated by spiritual gifts such as tongues, using them in such a way that some in the congregation are made to feel inferior (12:22-24), and the meeting becomes inaccessible to outsiders (14:23).

TREATMENT OF THE POOR

11:22 implies that one group in the congregation are guilty in Paul's eyes of separating themselves from "those who have nothing" when they gather for worship, humiliating the poorer members of the church.[7]

ATTITUDE TO PAUL

Paul is aware of some who do not expect him to show his face in Corinth again, and who can therefore safely ignore him (4:18). 9:3 may refer to some in Corinth who "examine" Paul, although it may simply refer to others outside who dispute his apostleship. Paul's practice of working with his hands as a tent-maker, and refusing to accept financial support from the Corinthians has, it seems, come in for some criticism, judging by Paul's vigorous response in chapter 9.

THE RESURRECTION

The views of some on the resurrection are significantly different from Paul's. Quite what those views were remains to be seen, but there is a serious theological divergence at this point.

A good deal of recent research on the letter has shown how many of these characteristics would have been associated with richer rather than poorer members of the congregation. A love for rhetoric was clearly associated with social status. Among the recent studies which have explored the rhetorical dimension of 1 Corinthians,[8] Pogoloff in particular highlights the link between rhetoric and social status.[9] Rhetorical ability was highly prized by the élite within Greco-Roman society, and was frequently seen as an indicator of high social status.[10]

The richer members of the church would also have been more likely to eat meat at pagan temples.[11] The issue of sexual irregularity is also likely to have involved the more wealthy in the congregation, raising sensitive issues of honour and shame. It has quite plausibly been argued that there were financial implications at stake here and the reason why this person had not already been expelled from the congregation was simply that he was of high social status.[12] This impression would be confirmed if the sexual misconduct had resulted in Christians going to court against one another. It has been shown conclusively how only the rich could afford and hope for success through litigation in a city such as Corinth.[13] Furthermore, Dale Martin has pointed out how in the context of a city such as Corinth, *glossolalia* were a sign not of irrationality or shame, but rather of social status.[14] Those who humiliate the poor at the community meal are most likely to be among the more wealthy, as Paul assumes they are home-owners (11:22a).[15] Those who criticise Paul for working with his hands do so presumably out of a sense of social superiority or wounded social pride.[16]

The cumulative force of these findings of recent scholarship has led to a consensus that Paul's opponents, as well as his supporters, are to be found among the richer members of the congregation. The 'Apollos group', if we can speak in such a defined way about them, are probably mainly well-off, higher-status people.[17]

THE SOCIAL STATUS OF THE CORINTHIAN CHRISTIANS

The question of the social status of the Corinthian congregation has been pondered for many years. In the 1960s, E.A. Judge initiated a new interest in the idea that the social context has a significant role in determining the way doctrine and ethics function in the New Testament.[18] He located early Christian groups in their urban context alongside other voluntary associations, the guilds, cults and philosophical groupings which met in all major Greek cities.[19]

Opinions on the social status of the church in Corinth have varied. Deissmann argued that most Corinthian Christians were relatively poor,[20] as more recently has Engels, who again thinks that the centre of gravity in the community is more towards the poorer end of Corinthian society.[21] Judge however stresses the relatively high social status of some in the community,[22] as does Wuellner.[23] Theissen makes out a good case for a wide range of social strata being represented within the Corinthian church,[24] a feature which distinguished it from other contemporary groupings, which tended to be more socially homogenous.[25] This conclusion was confirmed (with modifications) by Meeks.[26] Most scholars now stress the social mobility possible in Corinthian society since its refounding by Julius Caesar in 44 BCE, giving more opportunity for advancement in a society without the constraints of a long aristocratic tradition.[27]

Pogoloff claims that Apollos' supporters were not so much aristocratic, as *nouveaux riches*, aspiring to, but not yet arriving at, the top of the social pile. Paul's 'supporters', he suggests, were generally speaking of higher status than those loyal to Apollos.[28] This is an intriguing suggestion, and carries a good deal of merit. 1:26 does imply that while some of the congregation were wise, powerful and of noble birth, the majority were not, the inference being that it is fruitless to aspire to that social level. It is unwise to try to build too exact a demography of the Corinthian church upon this verse,[29] yet Paul presumably would not have used this language unless it reflected what he knew of the church in Corinth. While Meeks may be right that the extreme top and bottom of the social scale were absent, it is highly likely that the church did contain many from the lower strata of society, while a minority were higher-status upwardly mobile people, including those causing Paul most concern.

The "some" whom Paul addresses in the letter, are therefore, most likely Gentile, well-off, socially upwardly-mobile people. Moreover, they have kept many of their links with their pagan past.

THE 'WORLDLINESS' OF THE CORINTHIAN CHRISTIANS

Paul's first accusation is that there are ἔριδες among the church (1:11). This word has a particular nuance in Pauline terminology, generally occurring in lists of catalogues of pagan vices, probably taken from Jewish proselyte traditions.[30] In Paul's letters it regularly occurs in lists of characteristics of life in the world or the flesh (Rom.1:29; 2 Cor.12:20; Gal.5:20). 1:11 therefore suggests that this pattern of behaviour betrays worldly pagan attitudes. This impression is borne out by the evidence of the rest of the letter. The structure of 1:17-3:23 is clearly antithetical, between the wisdom of God and the wisdom of the world.[31] Paul accuses the Corinthians of being σαρκίνοι, of the flesh (3:1), the ἔριδες among them being a sign that they are no different from those outside the church, "behaving like ordinary men" (3:3). In fact in some cases they are worse than those outside the church (5:1). There are brothers who are acting in ways fitting only for outsiders (5:12). Litigation is being conducted through secular channels (6:1-11),[32] some are attending meals at pagan temples (8:10) and participating in pagan worship (10:14-21). In other words, one of Paul's major complaints about at least some of the Corinthian Christians is that they are blurring the distinctions between the church and secular society, God and the world; for Paul, they are behaving in a thoroughly 'worldly' fashion.

If Paul thinks the Corinthians are far too easily influenced by the surrounding culture, it is not only legitimate but even necessary to ask which parts of that culture influenced them the most. The sheer variety of culture, philosophy and religion on offer in a city such as Corinth should caution against generalisations about 'the influence of Greco-Roman culture' on the Corinthian church. If Paul's polemical response is to be understood, we will need to explore the various groups or ideologies which might have influenced the young church. Discerning that will provide the key to understanding the underlying nature and direction of Paul's polemic.

MYSTERY RELIGIONS

Richard Reitzenstein and subsequently Rudolf Bultmann maintained that the background to the church's language and practice should be found in the mystery cults entering Hellenistic society from the Near East,[33] especially in the Corinthian use of the term τέλειος. Since their time, this hypothesis has found occasional support, such as that of J. Painter[34] who claims the tongue-speakers in Corinth take their cue from ecstatic practice in the mystery cults.

More recently, the women worshipping with unbound hair in 11:3-16 have been regarded as mirroring the practice of the mystery cults. Elisabeth Schüssler Fiorenza suggests very plausibly that women at Corinth were wearing their hair unbound during the enthusiastic worship of the church, in a way similar to that in the mystery cults, where unbound hair was a sign of ecstatic endowment. Paul, wanting to play down their pneumatic role and curb orgiastic behaviour, tries to limit such a practice, lest the Christian group be mistaken for one of these "orgiastic, secret cults that undermined public order and decency".[35] This practice may also again reflect a wider tendency to status-conscious behaviour within the church.[36]

While acknowledging the plausibility of this suggestion, it is important not to take the evidence too far. Dionysiac worship provides a possible background to worship with unbound hair, one element of the complex relationship between the church and the surrounding culture in Corinth. It does not lead us to lay all the issues between Paul and these Corinthians at the feet of those

enamoured with the mystery cults. Although the πνευματικός-
ψυχικός terminology has sometimes been seen as evidence of the
influence of these groups, it is doubtful whether it reflects actual
usage in these cults.[37] There is also simply no evidence that the
mystery religions ever used the adjective τέλειος in the way it is
used in 1 Corinthians, and the sheer imprecision of the term
"mystery religions" makes it hard to build any substantial theory
upon it.[38] Although some influence may be discerned in the
behaviour of certain women in the church, the theory fails to explain
all of the factors in the Corinthian church.

POLITICAL PRACTICE

A number of scholars have sought to place the church in the
context of political forces in first century Corinth. Welborn[39] sets
the divisions over leaders against the background of political culture
in Hellenistic cities. Like Theissen, he sees class division as a vital
clue for interpreting the situation.[40] The divisions in 1:12 refer to
rich individuals creating division among themselves, claiming the
patronage of an apostolic figure, and attempting to gain support
from the poorer members of the congregation by patronage, using
material wealth and political rhetoric to do so, according to a
common pattern of political manoeuvring in such cities.[41] Paul
accuses them of secular worldly practice, and seeks to turn their
minds "from politics to theology."[42] Clarke takes this further to
argue that Paul's difficulties in Corinth stem from the adoption of
secular leadership practices in the church. These include personality-
cults around apostolic figures, boasting, self-display, over-valuing
of oratorical ability, and libertarian behaviour common in Greco-
Roman society.[43] Barton argues that the divisions in 1:12 are the
same as those in 11:18-19, in that they are basically divisions
between competing households or groups of households. Paul
addresses primarily the rich elderly male heads of these groupings.[44]
    These studies explain how such competitive behaviour might
arise within the church, and how such a group as we have been

trying to identify might have manoeuvred over against other groups. At times, these accounts are mutually incompatible. For example, if Theissen is right (as he surely must be - see 11:22) that the problem in chapter 11 is rich and poor Christians eating in different rooms and at different times at the Eucharist, it is not easy to see how the separate groups at the meal can consist of different households and rich and poor groupings at the same time. On Barton's theory, both rich (household heads) and poor (artisans, slaves etc.) would presumably be represented in each of the groupings, and the rich not eating together and separately from the poor, but apart from each other in their own households. Secondly, there are limitations in interpreting the letter purely in political terms,[45] and the evidence that the precise terminology of 1:12 should be interpreted in political terms is thin.[46] Political trends can explain some of the dynamics of the divisions within the community, but they do not account for the issues over which they divided, nor the kind of legitimisation given for divergence of behaviour.[47]

RHETORIC IN CORINTH[48]

Several recent works have explained the letter against the background of Greco-Roman rhetoric. Two major contributions are those by Pogoloff[49] and Litfin[50]. Both books cover similar ground in providing surveys of classical rhetoric, seem to have been written in ignorance of each other,[51] and reach similar conclusions about the role rhetoric played in Corinth, but disagree on Paul's response to it. Pogoloff's Paul is rhetorically sophisticated, appealing to the higher status members of the congregation, in contrast to Apollos' more popular style. This is doubtful. 2:4, and the clear implication that the weakness, fear and trembling of v.3 refer to his speech, would suggest that it was not the sophistication of Paul's rhetorical style which alienated some of the Corinthians, but rather its feebleness. These verses need to be read in the light of the persistent feeling about Paul in Corinth, expressed in the phrase λόγος ἐξουθενημένος (2 Cor.10:10), and his own candid admission in 2 Cor.11:6 that he was indeed ἰδιώτης τῷ λόγῳ.[52] Litfin's Paul deliberately chose not to use any form of rhetoric. Bearing in mind what Litfin himself says about the ubiquity of rhetoric in Greco-Roman culture, Paul would have to have been very naïve to think he could avoid all rhetoric whatsoever. 2 Cor.10:10 and 11:6 are not a disavowal of all rhetoric, but an admission that Paul is not very good at it. Chapters 1 and 2 actually reinforce Pogoloff's contention that Paul dislikes not rhetoric as such, but some of the social attitudes lying behind their admiration for it. Other studies such as those of Witherington[53] and Mitchell[54] have also pointed out Paul's conscious use of rhetoric in his letters, indicating familiarity with rhetorical practice and a certain skill in its use.

Whatever Paul's response, there is strong evidence that one of the elements in the group claiming allegiance to Apollos would have been a high regard for rhetorical aptitude, but it must be borne in mind that this was extremely common in any Greco-Roman city. Given Apollos' ability in this area mentioned in the previous chapter and Paul's probable lack of skill in *spoken* rhetoric, it is likely that this formed part of this group's preference for Apollos over Paul. Having said this, it is important not to think that σοφία λόγου is purely a matter of form. An important area of debate in classical rhetoric concerned the extent to which form and content could be separated. Was rhetoric just a technique to be admired, an end in itself (Isocrates), or was it a means of conveying truth (Plato)?[55] The σοφία λόγου Paul discerns in Corinth seems to consist of both.[56] The Corinthians admire rhetorical skill (this seems to be what Paul has in mind in 2:4-5), yet their wisdom also embodies a system of ideas, a philosophy. Wisdom is a means by which the world tries to know God (1:21), and is contrasted not with the style of Christian preaching, but rather its content, the cross (1:22-23) and Christ (1:30).

This therefore raises the question of the content of this wisdom, and how it is related to the concerns in the rest of the letter. To take an example, Litfin's study is sub-titled "1 Corinthians 1-4 and Greco-Roman Rhetoric". One major difficulty with the work is that it deals only with chapters 1-4 of the letter.[57] In other words, while rhetoric provides a useful background to the study of chapters 1-4, it is far from clear how its use relates to the numerous issues in the rest of the letter, such as marriage, food offered to idols, and differing views on the resurrection.

The relationship between chapters 1-4 and the rest of the letter has seldom been satisfactorily explained.[58] Those writing from a sociological, political or rhetorical perspective are quick (and correct) to criticise the imbalance shown by earlier scholars who assumed a doctrinal root to the problems at Corinth.[59] Most scholars now assume that there is a socio-economic dimension to the conflict, yet in fairness to earlier scholarship, these more recent approaches do not answer all the questions either. Specifically, they tend to ignore what earlier studies saw, namely the existence of real *ideological* divergence from Paul in Corinth. Chapter 15 reveals a clear difference of opinion between "some" (15:12) of the congregation and the apostle, which is not easily explained by the behavioural approaches of more recent scholarship. Many now agree that there is some form of disparagement of the poor by the rich in the church. Although Theissen has shown how this explains the divisions at the Eucharist in chapter 11, it is by no means obvious how this division between rich and poor relates to the divisions over leaders in 1-4, particularly as the same language occurs in both accounts (σχίσματα: 1:10, 11:18).

Paul's concern about the church in Corinth is not just that they are behaving inappropriately, but that they are both boasting in it, and trying to justify it ideologically. The various Corinthian slogans scattered through the letter indicate this ideological underpinning of behaviour by theology. Paul has to counter the theological justification of what he thinks is aberrant behaviour if he is to reform the church effectively. The reconstruction of the ideological framework of the Apollos-focused group in Corinth is therefore crucial to an understanding of the function of Paul's theology of the cross. We have argued that this group is made up of Gentile Christians still strongly influenced by their pagan past. The following chapter will explore one possible source for such influence.

Notes:

[1]This disagrees with Dahl's opinion in "The Church at Corinth" that Paul "deals with the church at Corinth as a unity" (328). According to Dahl, the whole church (perhaps excluding Stephanas and a few others) has rejected Paul's authority over them, and so 1-4 is essentially an apologetic piece, reasserting and justifying his apostolic authority. In a final footnote added to a 1977 edition of this essay, Dahl notes that he has changed his mind on this. He no longer sees it purely as an apologetic section for Paul's apostolic authority, because Paul is as critical of his "supporters" as he is of his "opponents", 1977, 61, n.50.

[2]That this is a group within the congregation is confirmed by the distinction made between those who eat at pagan temples without scruples, and the 'weak' whose conscience is more troubled by it. It is important to note that those who do eat meat offered to idols are not called the 'strong' here, as they are in Romans 15:1. The only place where the Corinthians are described as the 'strong' is 4:10, where the word used is ἰσχυροί. The word in Romans 15:1 however is δυνατός. This would suggest that the issues in 1 Cor.8-10:24 are different from those in Romans 14 and 15, where the issue at stake appears to be food laws rather than food specifically used in pagan worship.

[3]Both Witherington, *Conflict*, 187, 200, and Fee, *1 Corinthians*, 359-60, argue persuasively that the issue in ch.8 is linked to that of ch.10. The main issue is not that of eating meat bought in the marketplace, but the one addressed directly in 8:10, 10:14, 21, namely joining in with the common sacrificial meals in pagan temples which formed part of cultic worship in antiquity. See also R.A Horsley, "1 Corinthians: A Case Study of Paul's Assembly as an Alternative Society", *Paul and Empire*, ed. R.A. Horsley (Pennsylvania: Trinity Press International, 1997), 242-52, see especially 247-9.

[4]It is not necessarily the aggrieved father who has taken this man to court (J.H. Bernard, "The Connexion between the Fifth and Sixth Chapters of 1 Corinthians," *The Expositor* 7 (1907), 433-43, as cited in Fee, *1 Corinthians,* 195). Dispute over this sexual conduct may have heightened tension and confrontation in the congregation, which spilled into other areas, leading to different members of the congregation taking others to court: see below on the dispute between the Paul-loyalists and the Apollos faction.

[5]Was this the same man who was eventually disciplined by the congregation in 2 Cor.2:5-11?

[6]Although it is quite possible (even probable) that these verses are inauthentic. See the lengthy discussion in Fee, *1 Corinthians*, 699-705.

[7]See Theissen, *Social Setting,* 145-74. In is a well-argued analysis of this passage, Theissen shows how the variable beginnings of the meal (v.21a), different menus and different amounts of food and drink for different guests (v.21b) all reflect common Greco-Roman notions of social superiority, status and rank.

[8]M.M. Mitchell, *Paul and the Rhetoric of Reconciliation: An Exegetical Investigation of the Language and Composition of 1 Corinthians* (Tübingen: Mohr/Siebeck, 1991); Pogoloff, *Logos and Sophia*; Litfin, *Proclamation*; Witherington, *Conflict*.

[9]*Logos and Sophia*, chs. 5 and 7.

[10]D.B. Martin, *The Corinthian Body* (New Haven: Yale University Press, 1995), 50: "In the highly stratified Greco-Roman society... rhetorical education and ability were an indispensable status indicator."

[11]Theissen, *Social Setting*, 121-44 shows how a) the poor would have been likely to eat meat only at pagan festivals, and therefore would always have associated it with idolatry, and b) that such invitations to dine would naturally have come to the richer, rather than the poorer members of the congregation. Meeks, *Urban Christians,* 69-70, agrees, although denying that the 'strong' are therefore well integrated into the higher echelons of Corinthian society. He thinks their social status is more ambiguous.

[12]Clarke, *Leadership*, 82-3.

[13]B.W. Winter, "Civil Litigation in Corinth: the Forensic Background to 1Cor.6:1-8", *NTS* 37 (1991), 559-72.

[14]D.B. Martin, "Tongues of Angels and Other Status Indicators", *JAAR* 59 (1991), 547-89.

[15]Theissen, *Social Setting*, 48-5.

[16]Cf. Hock, *Social Context.* Marshall, *Enmity in Corinth,* argues that the major cause of Paul's difficulties with the Corinthians was his refusal to accept financial support from the wealthy in the church, thus rejecting their offer of 'friendship'. See esp. 216.

[17] D.G. Horrell, *The Social Ethos of the Corinthian Correspondence* (Edinburgh: T. & T. Clark, 1996), 121-3.

[18]Judge, *Social Pattern*, and "The Early Christians as a Scholastic Community".

[19]"There can be no doubt that... (Christians) were not distinguished in the public's mind from the general run of unofficial associations." Judge, *Social Pattern,* 44.

[20]Deissmann, *Light*, 6-7, 142.

[21]D. Engels, *Roman Corinth: An Alternative Model for the Classical City* (Chicago: University of Chicago, 1990), 114-6.

[22]"Far from being a socially depressed group... if the Corinthians are at all typical, the Christians were dominated by a socially pretentious section of the population of the big cities." Judge, *Social Pattern*, 60.

[23]"The Sociological Implications of 1 Cor.1:26-28 Reconsidered," *Studia Evangelica Vol. VI*, ed. E.A. Livingstone (Berlin: Akademie, 1973), 666-72: "Corinthian Christians came by and large from fairly well-to-do bourgeois circles with a fair percentage also from upper-class people as well as the very poor." (672).

[24]*Social Setting*, 69-119. Horrell, *Social Ethos*, 91-101, also stresses the wide

range of social strata represented in the Corinthian church.

[25]Judge, *Social Pattern*, 60, makes this point in general about Christian groups in the first century, while Theissen makes it in particular about the Corinthian church.

[26]*Urban Christians*, 72-3: "The extreme top and bottom of the Greco-Roman social scale are missing from the picture... The levels in between, however, are well represented."

[27]Theissen, *Social Setting*, 99-102; Meeks, *Urban Christians* 19-23; Engels, *Roman Corinth*, 67-74.

[28]*Logos and Sophia*, 197-212. People named in the letter all appear to be supporters of Paul, and as Theissen has shown, of high social status. This would fit with Pogoloff's suggestion. Likewise Witherington, *Conflict*, 114-5.

[29]As Wuellner, "Haggadic Homily Genre", and Branick, "Source and Redaction Analysis", have shown, and as argued in ch. 1 above, it is probable that Paul is using previously composed material here. W. Wuellner, "Ursprung und Verwendung der σοφός-, δυνατός-, εὐγενης-Formel in 1 Kor. 1.26", *Donum Gentilicum: New Testament Studies in Honour of David Daube*, eds. E. Bammel, C.K. Barrett, and W.D. Davies (Oxford: Clarendon, 1978), 165-184, also argues that although in itself unprecedented and unique to Paul, this formula has parallels in Hellenistic Jewish traditions. For these and (less plausible) grammatical reasons, Wuellner denies the picture of an impoverished majority in the church in Corinth here and in "Sociological Implications".

[30]Cf. Borgen, "Catalogues of Vice".

[31]See the helpful chart in Litfin, *Proclamation*, 175. He adds: "There is God's perspective and over against this there is another perspective comprising all the rest, the perspective τοῦ κόσμου." (176)

[32]Vv. 9-11 contrast especially clearly their past life and pagan behaviour with the new life and appropriate Christian behaviour. Paul uses traditional diatribal forms to emphasise the radical difference between the world's ways and those of the Christian community. See the commentaries of Conzelmann, 106, and Barrett, 140.

[33]For a useful account of these see H. Koester, *History, Culture, Religion of the Hellenistic Age* (New York: Walter de Gruyter, 1982), 183-204.

[34]J. Painter, "Paul and the Pneumatikoi at Corinth," *Paul and Paulinism: Essays in honour of C.K. Barrett*, eds. M.D. Hooker and S.G. Wilson (London: S.P.C.K., 1982), 237-50.

[35]E. Schüssler Fiorenza, *In Memory of Her: A Feminist Theological Reconstruction of Christian Origins* (London: S.C.M., 1983), 232.

[36]Cf. D.W.J. Gill, "Head-covering in 1 Corinthians 11.2-16", *TynBul* 41 (1990), 245-60.

[37]Pearson, *Pneumatikos-Psychikos Terminology*.

[38]"...at least in the Roman imperial period, the use of the term 'mystery' had

become so diversified that it is useless as a point of orientation." (Koester, *Hellenistic Age*, 197).

[39]L.L. Welborn, "On the Discord in Corinth: 1 Corinthians 4 and Ancient Politics", *JBL* 106 (1987) 85-111.

[40]"Ancient writers assumed that where there was discord, opposition between rich and poor lay behind." ibid., 96.

[41]See two articles on patronage in ed. Horsley, *Paul and Empire*: P. Garnsley and R. Saller, "Patronal Power Relations", 96-103; J.K. Chow, "Patronage in Roman Corinth", 104-25. The latter suggests that conventions of patronage may well lie behind some of the relational ties in the church, including the adherence to certain leaders.

[42]Welborn, *Discord*, 111.

[43]Clarke, *Leadership*. See the summary on page 89.

[44]S. C. Barton, "Paul's Sense of Place: an Anthropological Approach to Community Formation in Corinth", *NTS* 32 (1986), 225-46.

[45]See Pogoloff's criticisms of Welborn, *Logos and Sophia*, 88-9. Richardson, *Paul's Language,* is also concerned about the narrowness of this approach: "If there were no theological issues and the problem were simply a local power-struggle, why use the names of the apostles and of Christ at all?" (104).

[46]Mitchell, *Reconciliation*, 83-5, points out that Welborn has not produced, nor are there to be found, any examples of the precise formula used in 1:12 referring to allegiance to parties in ancient political literature.

[47]Although Clarke, *Leadership*, 107, is right to point out the imbalance of earlier commentators who assumed a theological core to the distinctions between the groups at Corinth, he leans too far in the other direction by tending to ignore the theological issues which underpin this inappropriate behaviour.

[48]Rhetoric has often been seen as the background to the language of e.g. 1:16, 20; 2:1, 4. See the summary in Litfin, *Proclamation,* 3, n.7. For a bibliography of recent rhetorical studies see Pogoloff, *Logos and Sophia*, 11, n.10; Witherington, *Conflict*, 55-61. This is of course counter to the views of, for example, Wilckens, "Σοφια, σοφός, σοφιζω", and "Zu I Kor. 2.1-16," *Theologia Crucis - Signum Crucis*, eds. C. Andresen and G. Klein (Tübingen: Mohr/Siebeck), 501-39, who interprets the language as gnostic, and R.A. Horsley, "Wisdom of Word", who sees it as the eloquence prized especially in Jewish circles by Philo and in the Wisdom of Solomon.

[49]*Logos and Sophia.*

[50]*Proclamation.*

[51]Pogoloff's book does not appear in Litfin's bibliography, even though it was published two years previously.

[52]Concerning Paul's embarrassment about his rhetorical ability, Pogoloff claims that "we must be careful not take his protestations too seriously", noting that self-deprecation was a common ploy among rhetors (136). The evidence of 2

Corinthians does seem to suggest, however, that more lies behind these statements
than false modesty. Paul appears to have felt particularly vulnerable at this point,
and that this inadequacy had become a bone of contention with some Corinthians.
[53]*Conflict.*
[54]*Reconciliation.*
[55]See Pogoloff, *Logos and Sophia*, 37-69.
[56]This differs from Pogoloff, who thinks Corinthian wisdom is mainly concerned
with style not content.
[57]Litfin acknowledges this, but doesn't seem too concerned by the problem: "..its
relationship to the rest of the epistle can for our purposes remain an open
question." *Proclamation*, 150.
[58]Cf. Dahl, "Paul and the Church at Corinth"; Richardson, "The Thunderbolt in
Q". Richardson's summary of the state of scholarship is acute: "no fully
satisfactory solution has yet been found, assuming the integrity of the letter, for
the relation of 1Cor.1-4 to 5-16... it is not so easy to describe the relation between
Paul's response to the oral information contained in Chapters 1-4 (plus 5-6?) and
his response to the written questions in chapters 7-16." He points out correctly,
that Dahl's opinion that the problems are mainly among the Corinthians
themselves, rather than with Paul, "underestimates.. the degree of polemic in 1-4".
(101). Litfin also acknowledges the lack of an adequate integrated solution:
Proclamation, 150-1.
[59]e.g. Clarke, *Leadership*, 89-90; Pogoloff, *Logos and Sophia,* 100-4.

Four: The Philosophical Background to Corinthian Theology

Over the past two decades the study of 1 Corinthians has seen intense interest in two areas already touched on: sociology and rhetoric.[1] Much of this seems to be a conscious or sub-conscious reaction against the tendency of earlier scholarship to assume a purely doctrinal root to the problems at Corinth.[2] There is no doubt that these studies have served to enrich our understanding of the letter, yet as with so many trends in New Testament research, there is a danger that babies may get thrown out along with bathwater.[3]

Most scholars now assume that there is some socio-economic dimension to the conflict reflected in 1 Corinthians, yet in fairness to earlier scholarship, these more recent approaches do not answer all the questions either. Specifically, there is a danger that a purely sociological or rhetorical approach can tend to ignore what earlier studies saw, namely the existence of real *ideological* divergence from Paul in Corinth. Chapter 15 for example reveals a clear difference of opinion between 'some' (15:12) of the congregation and the apostle, which is not easily explained by the approaches of more recent scholarship which concentrate on behaviour rather than ideas. Again, we have seen that there is some form of disparagement of the poor by the rich in the church. Although Theissen has shown how this explains the divisions at the Eucharist in chapter 11, it is by no means obvious how this division between rich and poor relates to other issues in the letter, for instance the divisions over leaders in chapters 1-4, particularly as the same language occurs in both accounts (σχίσματα: 1:10; 11:18).[4]

Paul's concern about the church in Corinth is not just that some of them are behaving inappropriately, but that they are boasting in such behaviour (5:6), and trying to justify it. The various Corinthian 'slogans' scattered through the letter reflect this ideological underpinning of behaviour by theology. Paul has to counter the theological justification of what he considers to be misguided behaviour if he is to reform the church effectively. For this reason, it is important that in our search for sociological and behavioural factors to clarify the situation, we do not forget the ideas which are intertwined with this behaviour, and which were used to justify it.

The theology of the Corinthian church can be elucidated by placing it alongside the ideas of another grouping, similar in many ways to the Christian church, which would have been present in first century Corinth: the followers of Epicurus. This chapter will suggest that the kind of ideas found in Epicurean circles provide a possible source of the ideological justification of 'worldly' behaviour which Paul encounters in the church,

The theory of Epicurean influence on Pauline churches is not new,[5] and was explored by Norman De Witt back in the 1950s.[6] While he made some useful observations, De Witt has generally been judged to have overstretched his point in seeing Epicurean influence lurking within most Pauline churches, even going so far as to suggest that Paul himself was heavily influenced by Epicureanism both before and after his conversion. These 'undisciplined'[7] proposals and the unfavourable reception they received have perhaps dissuaded others from exploring this aspect of the Greco-Roman context, and apart from a few passing remarks by other scholars, to some of which we will allude in what follows, the relationship between Christian and Epicurean groups has not been explored to any significant extent.[8]

EPICUREANISM IN CORINTH

Epicurus lived from 341-270 BCE, and his most well-known follower Lucretius from the early 90s to 55 BCE. Epicurean ideas appear not to have changed significantly over time however,[9] so both Epicurus' and Lucretius' writings can still be taken with some confidence as normative for 1st century Epicureanism. Howard Jones comments that "as the Roman Republic drew to a close, it was the Epicurean philosophy which held the field in Italy".[10] Even Seneca, although no Epicurean, gives grudging testimony to the widespread popularity of Epicurean teaching in the mid-first century.[11] In 45 BCE Cicero, despite his dislike for the movement, admitted that it was the most popular philosophy in Rome at the time.[12] It was, of course, just one year after he wrote this, in 44 BCE that Corinth was refounded as a Roman colony. It is therefore highly likely that colonists arriving from Rome would have brought Epicureanism (including the works of Lucretius) with them as a significant part of the philosophical and cultural environment in the new city-state.

Donald Engels' study of Roman Corinth points to the shift in ethnic and cultural identity from Roman (Latin) to Greek which took place in Corinth through the middle of the 1st century. He shows how the original social élite of the city, arriving in the new colony from Rome, tried to resist this process of hellenisation, wanting instead to preserve their Italian identity over against their new Greek cultural context as a mark of cultural and social distinctiveness, and no doubt to safeguard their sense of social and perhaps racial superiority.[13] Philosophies such as Epicureanism which they would have brought with them from Rome, would quite probably have formed an important part of this Italian identity. If so, then there would have been strong reasons why Epicureanism would have been actively maintained, especially among the social élite. If

Epicureanism was widespread in Greece and Asia Minor, there are good reasons for thinking that this was especially so in Corinth.

Epicureanism can be described as a philosophy where *knowledge* is closely linked to *power*. It claimed to offer true knowledge of the way things are. In fact, Epicurean ethics and philosophy are largely based upon its understanding of the physical structure of the universe.[14] The soul is made of fine particles which cannot exist outside the body; the soul simply disperses at death, the body returning to the primordial store of matter; all that happens is explained by the random movement of primary particles, and the gods are not concerned with human life. Once these essential physical principles have been grasped, the appropriateness of the Epicurean way of life becomes clear. All fear of death, the gods, and all dis-ease in life are shown to be irrational, and banished. Lucretius often makes the point that knowledge of the true nature of things is the key to happiness.[15] This knowledge leads to power over superstition, and often gave a sense of superiority or even disdain towards those who do not possess such knowledge. There is evidence to suggest that a significant group within the Corinthian congregation may have imported many of these principles uncritically into the church, and that much of Paul's theological argument is directed against these kind of ideas. At root, these Christians consider that their 'knowledge', better understood in Epicurean than Gnostic terms, gives them power over other Christians and over Paul. Paul's language in 8:1-3, and again in 13:8-12 suggests that in his own mind one of the most basic issues at Corinth was whether love or knowledge was foundational for Christian life. In Corinth, Paul combats what he sees as a theology of knowledge, possessed by some and not by others (8:1-7) which leads to an abuse of social and economic power wielded by some wealthy Christians. It has led to a sense of independence towards poorer members of the church and towards himself, bickering amongst these richer members, and away from inter-dependence, self-giving and unity. A pride in knowledge has combined with a desire for eloquence and social status to produce a group asserting its own power and superiority over against others in the congregation and in turn against the apostle. We turn first however to the evidence for these assertions, beginning with perhaps the most obvious theological issue over which there is disagreement between Paul and at least some Corinthian Christians, the Resurrection.

THE RESURRECTION IN THE CORINTHIAN CHURCH

From the slogan quoted in 15:12, it is clear that some in the congregation were saying ἀνάστασις νεκρῶν οὐκ ἔστιν. This has commonly been taken to imply an over-realised eschatology,[16] and until fairly recently this was often cited as the standard view.[17] However, there is nothing explicit in 1 Cor.15 to suggest that any of the Corinthians actually thought of themselves as already raised to resurrection life, or that the resurrection was past, or that they would not die.[18] Much of the case for over-realised eschatology has traditionally hung on the interpretation of 4:8,[19] and in particular on the single word ἤδη. Much depends on whether this word is to be taken in a strong eschatological sense, or in a weak sense such as Paul clearly intends in 6:7, where it just means 'really',[20] tinged with some irony. The context of 4:8 would suggest that Paul's criticism is not directed at their eschatology (it would be a very sudden change of subject at 4:8 if it were) but rather their arrogance. In 4:6-8 Paul has written of their being 'puffed up, one against another', and specifically mentions the verb καυχάομαι (v.7). After 4:8, Paul continues to speak of his own apostolic ministry and the arrogance of some (v.18). The context makes it plain that in ch.4 Paul is concerned not about their eschatology, but about their independence from and disparagement of him. It is 'without us' that they have been 'crowned' (v.8). The emphasis is not on eschatological dualism, but rather on their declaration of independence from Paul and the pattern of Christian life he models, setting themselves up as 'kings' rather than servants (cf. 4:1). The context therefore suggests the weaker sense of the word ἤδη, without the strong realised eschatology often read into it. The word is repeated in 4:8 merely to add ironic force to Paul's rhetoric.[21]

Anthony Thiselton has tried to show how 'over-realised eschatology' explains many other features of the letter besides 4:8 and ch.15.[22] The fact that at various points Paul urges the need for a future perspective by no means demands that the Corinthians believed themselves to have already fully arrived in the resurrection age. 1:7, 4:5, 8:2, and 9:25 do show Paul's concern that an eschatological balance be maintained, but they say much more about his emphases than those of the Corinthian church. Thiselton falls into the trap of mirror-reading, assuming that because Paul mentions something, it must be because his opponents believed the opposite.[23] On the contrary, surely it is unlikely, for example, that Paul would casually mention "...as you wait for the revealing of our Lord Jesus Christ" in his introduction (1:7) if this were a highly controversial point between him and the congregation. It sounds much more as if this is common ground he can assume with them. Thiselton's treatment of chapter 15 similarly claims rather weakly that the Corinthians "made too little of the future in their Christian outlook". (p.524). He ignores the much plainer statement of Corinthian concerns in 15:12 and 35, neither of which necessarily indicates over-realised eschatology.

Furthermore, at several points in the letter, Paul indicates that the Corinthians have indeed arrived at a kind of fullness. 1:5 suggests that they are rich, 3:22 claims that both the present and the future are in fact already theirs, and 2:7-10 indicates that God has already revealed his wisdom to them. It is surely unlikely that Paul would risk such language if the main problem in Corinth was faulty eschatology.[24] Instead, we need to look elsewhere to explain the beliefs which Paul criticises in chapter 15.

An important study by Abraham Malherbe examined the language of 15:32-34, concluding that it displays the characteristics of Cynic-Stoic diatribe, v.33 being a direct quotation from Menander's lost play *Thais*.[25] Malherbe explains Paul's reference to "beasts" in v.32 as "language used by the moralists of his day to describe the wise man's struggle against hedonism", and continues significantly, "His quotation from Isaiah 22.13 in this context would be reminiscent of the slogan attributed to the Epicureans and reflects the contemporary anti-Epicurean bias."[26] He goes on to remark how Plutarch uses this language specifically against the Epicureans.[27] He poses the question as to whether Paul has in mind a form of Epicureanism at this point, and although citing others who have wondered this,[28] simply notes that the idea "has never been developed".[29] In the end, he opts for a form of gnostic over-realised eschatology to explain the Corinthian view, but it is not clear on this understanding quite why Paul would choose to turn to this language to combat these opinions.[30]

If Paul does borrow anti-Epicurean rhetoric here, it may be because his target is similar to that for which this language was originally created. Faced with Epicurean-type ideas within the church at Corinth, it would be quite natural to utilise language and arguments which lay ready at hand, already crafted by other contemporary enemies of Epicureanism. This possibility is strengthened, as we shall see, when we recognise the similarity between Epicurean scepticism about resurrection and notions current in the Corinthian church on the same topic. If it is significant that Paul uses the language of anti-Epicurean polemic here, his choice of the quotation from Menander is also particularly apt. "Bad company ruins good morals" (φθείρουσιν ἤθη χρηστὰ ὁμιλίαι κακαί) may well refer to Paul's hunch that the Christians are indeed mixing with what he thinks are bad company, who indeed "have no knowledge of God" (v.34). Paul may be criticising too close an association with the kind of groups against which his language in vv.32-3 was commonly used, an association which was fast corrupting (as he saw it) their morality and beliefs.[31]

The Epicurean view of death was well known and distinctive. Put simply it was μηδὲν πρὸς ἡμᾶς εἶναι τὸν θάνατον: "death is nothing to us."[32] Epicureans claimed to have overcome the universal fear of death[33] by the simple argument that when death comes, we simply cease to be. As the soul consists of fine atoms which disperse at death, when death comes, sensation ceases, and where there is no sensation there is nothing to be feared.[34] For the Epicurean, it is not just the body that dies, but the soul as well. Fear of death is groundless, for as Epicurus wrote to Menoeceus, 'when we are, death is not come, and, when death is come, we are not';[35] in other words, fear of death is removed not by extending life, but by eliminating the yearning for immortality. The idea of the resurrection of the body would be nonsensical and foolish to an Epicurean,[36] and the consequence in Epicurean morality was commonly known.

The popular image of Epicureanism as unbridled hedonism[37] is of course a caricature, their position on pain and pleasure being much more nuanced. Epicurean physics taught that everything that exists consists of a mixture of matter and void.[38] The gods exist but have no concern for or interest in humankind,[39] being totally indifferent to them, "their peaceful homes unshaken by the gale".[40] Ethics is reduced to seeking a pleasurable life of tranquillity (ἀταράξια), measured not by intensity of ecstasy, but by absence of pain.[41] In fact, pleasure can be defined as the absence of pain.[42] Holding a thoroughly materialistic creed, Epicureans aimed at the satisfaction of simple bodily wants, "health of body and tranquillity of mind",[43] rather than excesses of indulgence. This insistence on seeking pleasure led to the popular perception that Epicureans simply wanted to "eat, drink and be merry".

The belief that there is no life beyond this one, that at death the soul simply disperses and the individual is no more, and therefore that this life is to be enjoyed and exploited for its own sake provides a striking resemblance to the ideas addressed in 1 Cor.15. The difficulty the Corinthians have with the idea of resurrection is not that it has already taken place, but that, given the corruptibility of the body, it just cannot happen.[44] The Corinthian Christians whom Paul addresses here simply believe that "the dead are not raised" (15:16). When Paul says, "if for this life only we have hoped in Christ" (15:19) he merely echoes what this group believe, that belief in Christ is indeed for this life only.[45] The slogan, "Let us eat and drink for tomorrow we die" is a caricature, but nonetheless not far away from what they are saying.[46]

Moreover, the question asked by Paul's imaginary interlocutor in 15:35 is a characteristic Epicurean concern. Questions about 'kinds of bodies' were a frequent theme of Epicurean apologetics. Book III of Lucretius' *De Rerum Natura* covers this issue at some length. He says concerning the *animus*: "Now I shall go on to explain to you, of what kind of body this mind is, and of what it is formed."[47] Lucretius delights in the putrid imagery of the decay of the body dissolving at death.[48] The soul is made out of fine matter, and cannot exist outside the body.[49] Therefore it is a natural Epicurean question to ask how the dead can possibly be raised, and what kind of body is envisaged for them once the body and soul have been destroyed: "For it is based on false reasoning to say that an immortal spirit is altered by a change of body; for that which changes is dissolved, therefore perishes. The parts of the spirit... perish at last one and all with the body".[50]

Lucretius even speaks of the "seeds (*semina*) of which we now are".[51] His view is that humankind comes from "celestial seed" which is dispersed at death.[52] Paul may well be picking up precisely such Epicurean imagery, but pressing it to another conclusion, that in reality, seeds do not just die but come to life again (15:36). Although Lucretius' argument is directed at a Platonic understanding of the soul as separate from and independent of the body, it can clearly be seen how, faced with Paul's teaching on the resurrection of the body rehearsed in 1 Cor.15, it would pose exactly the question asked in 15:35.

The Epicurean view of the fate of the body, which underlies chapter 15, would also explain the context of the argument in 1 Cor.6:13. If the Corinthian slogan commonly seen in this verse extends beyond the first phrase to include the second, i.e τὰ βρώματα τῇ κοιλίᾳ, καὶ ἡ κοιλία τοῖς βρώμασιν· ὁ δὲ θεὸς καὶ ταύτην καὶ ταῦτα καταργήσει,[53] Paul's reply proceeds with "the body is not meant for immorality..." It would surely be strange for Paul to argue for the destruction rather than the resurrection of the body, and if this is a Corinthian saying, then it would be further evidence to suggest that Epicurean ideas influenced the views underlying chapter 15, as it implies a belief in the disintegration of the physical body.[54]

Epicurean echoes are not only discernible in the discussion about the resurrection. They are heard also in several other arguments about Corinthian beliefs and practices.

SEXUAL MORALITY

The combination of sexual licence (5:1, 6:15) and asceticism (7:5) in the Corinthian church has proved hard to explain. The Corinthian argument Paul refutes in 6:12-20 suggests that as all things are lawful, there are no moral lines to be drawn. Since food is to be taken into the stomach and God will destroy both, the question of what we eat can have no great moral significance. Similarly, sexual intercourse is also a purely physical act and can have no moral significance. Sleeping with a prostitute causes no more harm than eating particular foods, because both sexual intercourse and eating are bodily functions outside the realm of morality.[55] Paul's argument is that the physical body belongs to Christ, and that sexual intercourse is a form of personal union with far greater spiritual and moral consequences than eating (vv.16-17). In tune with the Corinthians' libertarian approach to sex is tolerance of the man who lives with his mother-in-law (5:1ff). On the other side, however, sits an ascetic view, expressed in the letter to Paul and addressed by him in 7:1ff, where some are withdrawing from sexual relations within marriage. This too requires explanation.

According to Epicurus, the primary type of pleasure is *katastematic* pleasure, that which is associated with a settled condition, free from disturbance, a constant state of the absence of pain. Sex, however, is purely *kinetic* pleasure, in other words, something which "embellishes, titillates, or varies what is already a painless condition".[56] Sex in itself is not necessary, but is natural. Like eating particular kinds of foods, desire for sex with a particular person, or a particular kind of sex, is neither natural nor necessary.[57] Lucretius writes of sexual desire in purely physiological terms, distinguishing it clearly from romantic love (*amor*), so that for him, "sexual desire is merely a psychophysical reflex, which has nothing to do with Venus".[58] Two things become clear from this. One is that for the Epicurean, sex has no great moral significance.[59] If sensation is all, and is morally neutral,[60] then to have sex with a prostitute is not a moral issue, and could be indulged in without scruples. For example, a letter from Metrodus, an Epicurean, to one Pythocles, offers this advice:

> You tell me that the pricks of the flesh led you to overdo the pleasures of love. If you do not break the laws or offend in any way against accepted good manners, if you do not annoy any of your neighbours, exhaust your strength or waste your substance, give yourself without worry to your inclinations.[61]

Along similar lines, Epicurus is quoted as saying "I know not how to conceive the good, apart from the pleasures of taste, sexual pleasures, the pleasures of sound and the pleasures of beautiful form."[62] At the same time it is clear that Epicureans did not always recommend sexual activity without question. In contrast to the words mentioned above, Epicurus also wrote: "No one was ever the better for sexual indulgence, and it is well if he be not the worse."[63] The prized possession of Epicureans was ἀταράξια, a state of untroubled and pain-free repose. The difficulty with sex is that while it may be morally neutral, its passionate nature can disturb this calm, and so sex becomes problematic for the Epicurean. For both Epicurus and Lucretius, sex is a quite natural pleasure but no more. It is in fact, as Brown puts it, "too turbulent and overwhelming to be welcomed without reservation."[64]

Within Epicurean sources therefore we find conflicting advice on sexual activity. Sex can be recommended as morally neutral and harmless, yet at the same time there is a tradition of sexual asceticism within these same Epicurean communities, emerging from the view that sexual indulgence can disturb the Epicurean's calm ἀταράξια and complicate life unnecessarily. The Epicurean view of sex therefore provides a framework which would encompass both attitudes to sex among these Corinthian Christians. On the one hand, sex with a prostitute or with a close relation is justified as being as morally neutral as eating, yet on the other, some are inclined to withdraw from sexual activity altogether. This ambivalence towards sex is clearly paralleled in Epicurean attitudes.

IDOL WORSHIP

It seems that another Corinthian slogan was "an idol has no real existence" (8:4). It is probable that as a result some in the congregation felt free to attend worship at pagan shrines as it meant nothing (8:10; 10:14, 21). Epicureans did not deny the existence of the gods, but rather their involvement with earthly human life.[65] Consequently, both Epicurus and Lucretius can encourage participation in pagan worship, while at the same time warning that the gods "are not such as the multitude believe... Not the man who denies the gods worshipped by the multitudes, but he who affirms of the gods what the multitude believes about them is truly impious."[66] Although both groups believed in supernatural beings, the charge of atheism was levelled at both early Christians and Epicureans.[67] It is easy to see how disbelief in the active participation of the gods in human life, transposed to a Christian setting and allied to a Christian monotheism evidenced by the second half of 8:4 (οὐδεὶς θεὸς εἰ μὴ εἷς), would become the strident rejection of any objective reality to the gods in evidence here. If some Corinthians took particular pride in this knowledge which lifted them above others in the community, as seems to be the case in 8:1-13, then this would also echo the common Epicurean boast in knowledge of the true nature of the gods which frees them from superstition, and sets them apart from other people who remain in bondage because of lack of that knowledge.[68] In Epicureanism, as among this group of Corinthian Christians, such disparagement of the gods could co-exist with attendance at worship in pagan temples because again, such an action carried no great significance.[69]

SELF-SUFFICIENCY AND GROUP ISOLATION

Theissen has argued that in 11:17-22 one group of richer Christians are separating themselves from the poorer members at the common meal, and regarding themselves as socially superior to them.[70] We have already seen their sense of self-sufficiency from Paul. Epicureanism placed a very high value on friendship[71] and retirement from public life.[72] The Epicurean ideal was expressed in Epicurus' creation of the Garden just outside Athens in 306 BCE. It was the ideal of a quiet untroubled life away from public service or the common crowd:

> When tolerable security against our fellow men (ἐξ ἀνθρώπων) is attained, then on a basis of power sufficient to afford support and of material prosperity arises in most genuine form the security of a quiet private life withdrawn from the multitude.[73]

Epicurus is quoted as saying that "self-sufficiency (αὐτάρκεια) is the greatest of all riches",[74] and he suggests that its attainment leads to true freedom.[75] Critics of Epicureans quickly fastened on to what seemed to be a separatist and superior attitude.[76] This characteristic may explain part at least of this high-status group's sense of superiority and desire for separation. They may have seen the Eucharist along the lines of a funerary meal to remember the dead founder of the sect.[77] Epicurus had left commands that such a meal should be held annually in his honour,[78] and it would not be unusual for a group entering the Christian community from such a background or influenced by Epicurean friends to regard their new community's meal along similar lines. If this were the case, it would again help to explain how this group of Christians were treating the meal in an inappropriate (ἀναξίως) 11:27) fashion, along the lines of a Greek memorial meal, with all the social and culinary conventions described by Theissen,[79] and failing to see the distinctive nature of Christian participation in the new covenant.

WISDOM

It goes without saying that wisdom, as a virtue commonly sought after in Greek culture, was by no means confined to Epicurean groups. It is still worth mentioning that Epicurean texts show interest in the conduct and ideas of the σοφός. Diogenes Laertius' account of Epicurus' life includes a section depicting the wise man according to Epicurus' teaching.[80] Of particular interest to the study of 1 Corinthians are the claims that the Epicurean σοφός will overcome hatred, envy and contempt by the use of reason,[81] will not take part in public political life, instead withdrawing into the delights of friendship, yet will happily engage in litigation.[82] This is by no means to claim that the Corinthian delight in wisdom proves an Epicurean provenance for their ideas, but rather that, if on other grounds Epicurean influence provides a plausible setting, the σοφία material is quite at home here too.[83]

OTHER FACTORS

Some other features of first century Epicurean life are worth noting in passing. From 11:2-16, and possibly 14:34-6,[84] it seems that Paul felt that some women were speaking out of line in the congregation, and asserting a culturally inappropriate independence from their husbands. It is clear that women held an unusually liberated role in Epicurean groups, in that unlike other associations, Epicureans welcomed women, whether wives or courtesans as equal partners in Epicurean friendship.[85] There is some evidence of a particular veneration for individual leaders within Epicurean groups, which would help explain the tendency of this group within the church to latch on to leaders as guides and champions.[86] If, as Pogoloff has plausibly suggested, some of the congregation were *nouveaux riches*, aspiring to be, but not yet achieving the highest level of education and social status, this would fit evidence we have of Epicureanism's range of appeal.[87] Cicero accuses Epicureanism of appealing mainly to the unlearned (*indoctis*), and implies that its easily grasped principles gave it an instant appeal to those who were less philosophically sophisticated, yet wanted an easy entry into the arena of philosophical thought.[88]

A further comment concerns the relationship between Epicureanism and rhetoric. Regard for rhetorical skill was extremely common in the first century, and it can be taken for granted as immensely popular in a wide range of social groupings.[89] The likelihood that some Corinthian Christians had a liking for rhetoric simply shows they were still attuned to the social values of their day, not that they belonged or did not belong to any particular group within that society. It is true that Epicureans did not have a particularly strong reputation for rhetorical practice: Quintilian in particular discounts Epicurus as a useful ally in the search for good rhetorical practice, because he "bids his followers to fly from learning",[90] and disdains *disciplina*.[91] This does not mean however that Epicureans disavowed rhetoric. It perhaps says more about Quintilian's attitude to Epicurus than it does about the Epicurean attitude to rhetoric. The latter was such a widespread, commonly accepted virtue that despite not being known especially to cultivate it, Epicureans would have been as much able to appreciate and value it as any other group in first century Greco-Roman society.

CONCLUSION: CHRISTIANS AND EPICUREANS IN CORINTH

This brief survey has indicated a number of points of similarity between Epicurean beliefs and those held by at least some of the Christians in Corinth. Throughout I have hinted at ways in which these two groups may have been connected, and there are at least three possible ways in which the relationship could have worked. a) Some Corinthian Christians may have been converted from Epicureanism, and carried many of their previous beliefs uncritically into their new faith.[92] b) The group which causes Paul's disquiet may have kept close links with Epicurean groups, either through attending their dinner parties (10:27), or worshipping with them at pagan temples (10:14); they could well have held a similar view of such a practice as religiously insignificant, but socially desirable. c) A combination of these two may have seen a number of Epicurean converts to the Christian group retaining contact with Epicureans. It has occasionally been noticed how Christian and Epicurean groups were regarded in a similar fashion,[93] and would to some extent have been thrown together.[94] It would not be surprising if groups such as these which held a similar position in the social fabric of 1st century Corinth saw a good deal of transfer of personnel. It would certainly have been easier to move from one socially equivalent group to another, rather than shifting social registers altogether.[95]

It is impossible to settle this question without a high degree of speculation. It is possible though, to draw some more general conclusions. There are good grounds for believing that some Christians in Corinth were influenced by the ideas and practice of trends in Greco-Roman Corinth most strongly represented by Epicureanism. These trends provided an ideological foundation for a wide range of behaviour current in the Corinthian church. They viewed sexual activity as morally neutral, regarded the resurrection of the body as unnecessary and impossible, valued wisdom in the Greek sense of that word, and thought themselves superior to and separate from the poor in the congregation, and increasingly, those still loyal to Paul. In particular it gave them a sense of superiority and power over others in the church on account of their superior knowledge.

This is not to say that Epicurean influence explains everything within the church. It is probable that a number of other currents are at work, for example from the mystery religions, or from Jewish Christian sources. This is only to be expected in the cultural melting-pot of a city such as Corinth. It is important not to underestimate the effect of religious syncretism[96] and the degree of overlap between different philosophical schools.[97] It is also true that Epicureans themselves could hold allegiance to other religious movements, such as the mysteries.[98] All of this created an atmosphere of great fluidity of movement, where people could move from one movement into another, and where different influences were at play all the time on a small, young cosmopolitan group such as the Christian church. Nor does it exclude the role that interpretation of Paul's earlier teaching had upon the developing situation.[99] In fact, Paul's inherited teaching on freedom from the law, interpreted as freedom from ethical demands, and the breaking down of gender barriers, for example, may have had a particular appeal to those with Epicurean backgrounds. Nevertheless, it does suggest an ideological context for the ideas of those who disagree with Paul which arguably makes better sense of the evidence than other theories. It is also to suggest that Epicureanism has been underrated and insufficiently explored as a possible source of the 'worldly' attitudes Paul encounters in this church.

Our conclusions also help in understanding Paul's task in writing. The church at Corinth is still held together, however tenuously, by its faith in Christ, yet that unity is being stretched to breaking point as the community struggles to maintain its distinctively Christian identity, over against its largely pagan context and past. From afar, Paul suspects the intrusion into the Christian church of ideas and behaviour which do not belong there, an uncritical acceptance of notions which do not fit with the understanding of God which he sees revealed in Christ. The God who lies behind the Epicurean vision of life is uninvolved, and unconcerned. The ethic which follows lacks involvement in wider society and concern for the weak, and instead prizes self-sufficiency and ease. It fosters detachment, a sense of superiority, and has led to power-struggles within the church. The God who lies behind Paul's vision, the God of cross (ch.1) and resurrection (ch.15) is concerned for the "foolish" and "weak", and gives himself for them. The ethic which follows demands consideration for the poorer and weaker members, and values sacrifice and costly love. For Paul, the two visions are simply incompatible.

Notes:

[1]With some alterations, this chapter was originally published as "Christians and Epicureans in 1 Corinthians", *JSNT* 68 (1997), 51-72, and is reproduced here by kind permission of Sheffield Academic Press.

[2]E.g. Clarke, *Leadership*, 89-90; Pogoloff, *Logos and Sophia*, 100-4.

[3]Some sociological approaches have acknowledged this danger, e.g. Horrell,

Social Ethos, 119-23 who tries, albeit briefly, to suggest ways in which theological and sociological perspectives can be reconciled.

[4]The point here concerns the question of how the divisions over leaders expressed themselves in the Eucharist. The interpretations of Theissen (*Social Setting*, 54-7), and Horrell (*Social Ethos*, 101-17) imply that at the Eucharist, the rich met as a unified group separately from the poor, yet in chs. 1-4 they hold that the rich were actually divided among themselves over the question of which leader was the best.

[5]It was suggested for example by W.M.L. de Wette, *Kurze Erklärung der Briefe an die Korinther* (Leipzig: Weidmann, 1845), 129.

[6]N. De Witt, *St Paul and Epicurus* (Minneapolis: University of Minneapolis Press, 1954).

[7]Wayne Meeks' word in *The First Urban Christians: The Social World of the Apostle Paul* (New Haven: Yale University Press, 1983), 224. Concerning the relationship between Christian and Epicurean groups, Meeks does add: "The analogies would repay a more careful investigation than the present context permits." (84).

[8]Although see J.H. Neyrey, "The Form and Background of the Polemic in 2 Peter", JBL 99 (1980), 407-31, for a possible Epicurean background to views opposed in 2 Peter.

[9]J. Glucker, *Antiochus and the Late Academy* (Göttingen: Vandenhoeck & Ruprecht, 1978) comments that Epicureans were not marked for intellectual innovation: "Their lives were quiet and uneventful, and they offered no new doctrines or insights. Their function was to maintain the cult of Epicurus and to spread his doctrine of salvation". (371). A.J. Malherbe, "Self-Definition among Epicureans and Cynics," *Jewish and Christian Self-Definition* Vol 3, eds. B.F. Meyer and E.P. Sanders (London: S.C.M., 1982) also notes: "Epicureans are known for the conservatism with which they maintained the teaching of the master." (41).

[10]H. Jones, *The Epicurean Tradition* (London: Routledge, 1989), 62.

[11]Seneca, *Moral Essays*, viii.7-8, xxi.9. He notes that Epicurus is admired "not only by the more cultured, but also by the ignorant rabble." (Ep. Mor. lxxix.15).

[12]Cicero, *Tusculan Disputations*, IV,6-7.

[13]D. Engels, *Roman Corinth: An Alternative Model for the Classical City* (Chicago: University of Chicago, 1990), 73.

[14]Cf. *The Epicurean Philosophers* (ed. J. Gaskin; London: J.M. Dent, 1995), xxiii-xlii.

[15]See for example *De Rerum Natura* (henceforth DRN) 3.1071-5; 5.43-54; Lucretius also attacks contemporary scepticism at DRN 4.469-77.

[16]E. Käsemann, "On the Subject of Primitive Christian Apocalyptic," *New Testament Questions for Today* (London: S.C.M., 1969), 108-38; F.F. Bruce, *1 and 2 Corinthians* (New Century Bible; London: Oliphants, 1971), 48-9, 144.

[17]See e.g. the summary of scholarly opinion in O. L. Yarbrough, *Not like the*

Gentiles: Marriage Rules in the Letters of Paul (SBL 80; Atlanta: Scholars Press, 1985), 117-8: "according to the *communis opinio*, 1) there were some in the Corinthian community who claimed that they had already experienced the Resurrection; and 2) the individual problems Paul deals with in 1 Corinthians were somehow related to this belief."

[18]For a survey of different views on Corinthian beliefs about the resurrection see J.C. Hurd, *The Origin of 1 Corinthians* (London: S.P.C.K., 1965), 195-200. Since then, (and since Yarbrough's summary), with the arrival of more studies of the Greco-Roman social context, the 'defective eschatology' theory has receded a little, e.g. Litfin, *Proclamation*, 168-73. For him, Paul sets out "to admonish the Corinthians, not for an alleged misguided eschatology but for their misplaced values and false aspirations" (169). Litfin also has a useful summary of the literature in both sides of the debate in 168, n.28. See A. J. M. Wedderburn, "The Denial of the Resurrection in Corinth", *Baptism and Resurrection* (Tübingen: Mohr-Siebeck, 1987), 1-37, and D. Martin, *The Corinthian Body* (New Haven: Yale University Press, 1995), 105-8, for effective refutations of the "realised eschatology" view.

[19]This verse, as Martin points out, does not actually mention the resurrection. See also the comments in Litfin, *Proclamation*, 168-9.

[20]Arndt and Gingrich, 344: "in Matt.5:28 and 1 Cor.6:7 ἤδη approaches the sense really".

[21]Cf. E.E. Ellis, "Christ Crucified," *Reconciliation and Hope. New Testament Essays in Atonement and Eschatology Presented to L.L. Morris*, ed. R. Banks (Exeter: Paternoster, 1974), 69-75, esp. 73-4.

[22]A.C. Thiselton, "Realised Eschatology at Corinth", *NTS* 24 (1978), 510-26.

[23]See J.M.G. Barclay, "Mirror-Reading a Polemical Letter: Galatians as a Test Case", *JSNT* 31 (1987), 73-93, for the dangers of this practice.

[24]Cf. Martin, *Body*, 106.

[25]A.J. Malherbe, "The Beasts at Ephesus", *JBL* 87 (1968) 71-80.

[26]Malherbe, "Beasts", 77.

[27]"In hellenistic literature the libertinistic life popularly, if unjustly, associated with the philosophy of Epicurus is frequently summarized as φάγωμεν καὶ πίωμεν... In Plutarch's anti-Epicurean writings this becomes a formula for the sensual life." ibid., 76.

[28]E.g. E. B. Allo, *Saint-Paul, Première épître aux Corinthiens* (Paris: J. Gabalda, 1934), 417.

[29]Malherbe, "Beasts", 77.

[30]In *Social Aspects of Early Christianity* (Baton Rouge: Louisiana State University Press, 1977) 27, concerning the Corinthian church and Epicurean influence, Malherbe suggests that "further investigation of that church in the light of other contemporary conventicles such as the Epicureans may help us to better understand his (Paul's) letters".

[31]Paul's use of anti-Epicurean language does not of course prove that the idea he was opposing came from that source, but given traces of Epicurean influence in the rest of the letter, as shown below, such language assumes a greater significance.

[32]Diogenes Laertius, *Lives of Ancient Philosophers* Vol. II (Epicurus) X.124, from hence, DL. See also DRN III.830.

[33]DL X.125-6.

[34]DL X.63-9. Cf. J.C.B Gosling and C.C.W. Taylor, *The Greeks on Pleasure* (Oxford: Clarendon Press, 1982), 348-9.

[35]DL X.125.

[36]See DRN III.926-30 for the denial of resurrection in Epicureanism: "*quisquam expergitus exstat / frigida quem semel est vitai pausa secuta*".

[37]See for example Seneca, *De Vita Beati*, xii.4-xiii.3.

[38]DL X.39, also DRN I.420, 445.

[39]DL X.139.

[40]DRN III.19.

[41]See J.M. Rist, *Epicurus: An Introduction* (Cambridge: C.U.P., 1972), ch. 6.

[42]DL X.131-2.

[43]DL X.128.

[44]1 Cor.15:35, 42-4. See Witherington, *Conflict*, 306-7.

[45]This remained a problem in Corinth for some time. 1 Clement 23-27, written towards the end of the 1st century, presupposes disbelief among the Corinthian church in the possibility and relevance of a future resurrection from the dead.

[46]C.K. Barrett, *A Commentary on the First Epistle to the Corinthians*, 2nd ed.n. (London: A. & C. Black, 1971), 347, admits that on an initial reading, "one gains the impression that Paul's opponents were materialists, who denied any kind of life after death whatever". He draws back from this obvious conclusion however, asking, "could sceptics of this sort have been Christians.. at all?" These Corinthians seem to have believed in the resurrection of Jesus (15:4, 12), and thus had good claim to be Christians, but denied its relevance to the question of their own fate after death. Paul's tactic is to focus upon their failure to carry through the logic of Christ's resurrection to their own in 15:12-34.

[47]DRN III.177.

[48]DRN III.580ff, & 719-21.

[49]DRN III.603-6.

[50]DRN III.754-9.

[51]DRN III.857.

[52]DRN II.985-1022.

[53]Fee, *I Corinthians*, 253-4, shows how the structure of the sentence implies that the whole of the first half of the verse, up to καταργήσει represents the Corinthians' position, and the second half represents Paul's. See also J. Murphy-O'Connor, "Corinthian Slogans in 1 Cor.6:12-20", *CBQ* 40 (1978), 391-6.

[54]Witherington, *Conflict*, 168, interestingly agrees with this, suggesting also: "In view of this slogan and the Epicurean-sounding quotation in 15.32, one wonders if the strong in Corinth had been influenced by Epicurean philosophy." For the popular perception that the 'belly' was at the heart of Epicureanism, see Plutarch, *Moralia*, 1098, 1125.

[55]Fee, *1 Corinthians*, 254, states that their position on food has been "carried over to the body and sexual relations with prostitutes", and goes on to claim that "this is the view of the majority of commentators". Cf. also Barrett, *1 Corinthians*, 147.

[56]R.D. Brown, *Lucretius on Love and Sex* (Leiden: Brill, 1987), 104.

[57]Ibid., 108. Cf. also DL X.149.

[58]Brown, *Lucretius*, 64.

[59]For evidence of insinuations of sexual immorality among Epicureans see Plutarch, *Moralia*, 1097-8.

[60]DL X.31-2.

[61]Quoted in A.J. Festugière, *Epicurus and his Gods* (New York: Russell & Russell, 1955), 29. J.M. Rist, *Epicurus*, 125, states that there is "no concept of moral obligation in Epicureanism".

[62]DL.X.6. See Gosling and Taylor, *Pleasure*, 349 for a discussion of the issues surrounding this text.

[63]DL X.118.

[64]Brown, *Lucretius*, 67.

[65]See Rist, *Epicurus*, ch. 8; Festugière, *Epicurus*, ch. 4.

[66]DL X.123-4.

[67]Lucian, *Alexander*, 38: ἄθεος ἢ Χριστιανὸς ἢ Ἐπικούρειος. Cf. also Plutarch, *Moralia*, 1119.

[68]e.g. DL X.81-2, 123-4; DRN I.62-79, 6.50-79.

[69]Witherington, *Conflict*, 188, suggests that "perhaps some Corinthians had read Paul's monotheistic teaching through Epicurean glasses".

[70]Theissen, *Social Setting*, 145-74.

[71]DL X.148.

[72]A common complaint against Epicureans was their lack of any sense of public duty or wider responsibility beyond their own group: see Plutarch, *Moralia*, 135, 1125.

[73]DL X.143.

[74]*Epicurus: The Extant Remains* (ed. C. Bailey; Oxford: Clarendon Press, 1926), 136, lxx. See also 112, xliv.

[75]Ibid., 118, lxxvii: Τῆς αὐτάρκειας καρπός μέγιστος ἐλευθερία.

[76]See citations in Festugière, *Epicurus*, 50, n.81.

[77]Cf. Witherington, *Conflict*, 250.

[78]DL X.18.

[79]Theissen, *Social Setting*, 147-63.

[80]DL X.117-121.

[81]ὦν τὸν σοφὸν λογισμῷ περιγίνεσθαι. DL X.117.

[82]"take a suit to court" (δικάσεσθαι) DL X.120. Cf. 1 Cor. 6.1-8.

[83]Although there is no space to examine such views in detail, this suggests that 'wisdom' can be explained within a more purely Greek Gentile context, rendering the Jewish background suggested by e.g. M. Goulder "Σοφία" and Horsley, "Wisdom of Word" unnecessary.

[84]See the lengthy discussion in Fee, *1 Corinthians*, 699-705 on the question of the authenticity of these verses.

[85]Festugière, *Epicurus*, 29-30.

[86]Cf. N.W. De Witt, "Organisation and Procedure in Epicurean Groups," *Classical Philology* 31 (1936), 205-11.

[87]*Logos and Sophia*, 197-212. See also Witherington, *Conflict*, 114-5.

[88]*Tusc. Disp.* III.50-1, IV.6-7. Seneca also warns that someone who lacks experience and formal training, yet who "has good intentions and has made progress, but is still far from the heights... such a one falls into the chaos of Epicurus." *Ep. Mor.* lxxii.9.

[89]Litfin, *Proclamation*, 124-6. Pogoloff, *Logos and Sophia*, 129, writes of the "ubiquitous presence of rhetoric".

[90]Quintilian, *Institutio Oratoria*, XII.ii.24.

[91]Ibid., II.xvii.15.

[92]W. Schmithals, *Gnosis in Corinth*, 147, doubts whether Epicureans could have been converted without radically changing their view. They could however have been attracted to the Christian group despite its views on the after life, by other factors such as Apollos' rhetoric and spiritual fervency (cf. Acts 18:24-5), or by its teaching and practice of brotherhood and community (see below).

[93]Lucian, *Alexander*, 25, 38. Here Christians and Epicureans are both bracketed together for abuse from Alexander. Both were accused of atheism due to their disregard for the influence of the gods on human life.

[94]Malherbe, "Self-Definition", 47: "...both had highly organized communities, used oral propaganda, and sought to hold their scattered communities together by an epistolary literature." Also, in *Social Aspects*, 26: "From the standpoint of an outsider Christianity and Epicureanism appeared similar in many respects... They were considered to be atheistic, misanthropic, socially irresponsible and immoral." W.A. Meeks adds concerning Epicurean groups: "There is much in the life of these communities that reminds us of the Pauline congregations." (*Urban Christians*, 83).

[95]E.A. Judge, "Scholastic Community", 135 remarks on the social location Christian groups would have had, commenting that "the Christian faith, as Paul expounds it belongs with the doctrines of the philosophical schools rather than with the esoteric rituals of the mystery religions".

[96]See Koester, *History*, 164-7.

[97]W.A. Meeks, *The Moral World of the First Christians* (London: S.P.C.K.,

1987), 41, states that it is "debatable how distinctive the different schools were in Roman times". See Martin, *Body*, 108-17 for an account of views of death and the afterlife across the cultural and philosophical spectrum. Although a lack of belief in the afterlife was common to many groups, it was in Epicureanism that this trend was most clearly concentrated and explained.

[98]Festugière, *Epicurus*, 59. See also Plutarch, *Moralia*, 635, where the author returns from the Eleusinian mysteries with an Epicurean friend, to dine and converse about Epicurean philosophy. This also explains why the Corinthians' interest in ecstatic charismatic gifts should not count against Epicurean influence: if Epicureans could partake in ecstatic mystery cults, there is no reason why they would not also have been attracted by Apollos' charismatic gifting.

[99]J.C. Hurd, *Origin*, argues that this played a crucial role, Paul changing his mind after the Jerusalem decree towards more controlled expressions of faith, rather than the unrestrained freedom of his earlier teaching (see the summary, 289-95). See also D. Wenham, *Paul: Follower of Jesus or Founder of Christianity?* (Grand Rapids: Eerdmans, 1995), esp. 235-6, who sees many of the Corinthian disputes as arguments over the correct interpretation of Jesus' teaching. Our suggestion does not negate these: it merely suggests that Paul's earlier teaching was being viewed by one group through an Epicurean lens.

Five: Paul's Theology of the Cross in the Corinthian Church

Why then, did Paul focus on the cross when he wrote to the Corinthians? Why does he begin writing in such startling language about God? In the light of our explorations into the influences upon the Corinthian church, it should be possible to answer these questions with greater clarity and precision.

These themes have of course been examined before. Neil Richardson for example, has explored the theological significance of Paul's language in 1 Corinthians 1 and 2. His careful examination of Old Testament parallels[1] has shown that in ascribing weakness and foolishness to God, Paul has arrived at "not only new language about God, but also a new understanding of God".[2] He concludes: "Most important of all, the God who seems to be nowhere is in fact the ultimate reality which is the great subverter of the status quo."[3]

Although Richardson's conclusion is apt, it is hard to see precisely how it emerges from his own reading of the immediate problems of the church in Corinth. His suggestion is that the Christ-party so stressed the importance of Christ that they "marginalised belief in God"; in response, Paul emphasised the word Θεός to correct their defective eschatology. In fact, for Richardson, eschatology is the underlying issue at stake between Paul and his critics in Corinth. We have noted above some difficulties with using realised eschatology as a key to understanding the theology of the church in Corinth. If anybody's eschatology is realised here, it is Paul's, who claims that God has revealed his secret wisdom to him (2:9-10). Richardson's reconstruction faces other problems as well. 8:6 clearly states a *common* belief in the "one God the Father" between Paul and the Corinthians, and shows no hint of a 'marginalised' belief in God as such. Richardson's version reads too much into the frequency in the early section of the letter of the word Θεός, which is surely explained more by the rival claims to know the mind of God, than any 'Christomonism' on the part of the Christ-party. Moreover, if the problem were an insufficient Christology, why would Paul's answer emphasise the cross in particular, rather than the person of Christ in general? Again, in focusing on the Christ-party as the source of the trouble, Richardson underestimates the degree of internal dispute between different groups in the church, which from 1:10-12 appears to be the immediate cause of Paul's concern. Paul seems to focus on the cross not in order to correct the Corinthians' defective eschatology, but to oppose their internal power struggles, and the ideological justification which underlay the boastful behaviour which sparked it all off.

To choose a further example, R.S. Barbour arrives at a similar conclusion about Paul's language:

> 'Christ crucified' is 'wisdom of God', not by a simple identification in the processes of polemic, nor yet by the identification of Christ with an already-known pre-existent figure of wisdom, but in the process of asserting that the very heart of God's purpose is the cross of Christ; not just Christ but Christ crucified.[4]

Barbour thinks that the discussion in 1 Corinthians concerns "the secrets of the last days, on the model found in Jewish apocalyptic and at Qumran".[5] As we have seen, there are difficulties with the theory of a Jewish background for Corinthian theology, and there is little clear evidence that the Corinthian Christians claimed to be living in, or knew the secrets of, the last days. They simply did not put the issue in this form. Like Richardson, Barbour's conclusion is valid, but rests on uncertain foundations. Both in fact suggest that the main problem is theological, and that between these Corinthians and Paul there is primarily a clash of ideologies. However, the issues Paul confronts more directly are matters of conduct. He uses the cross to correct Corinthian behaviour rather than theology, although naturally there are some (perhaps unacknowledged) beliefs and pre-suppositions underlying that behaviour. The task is therefore to understand how the cross does act in this critical manner to counter these patterns of relationship emerging in the church.

In what follows, a reading of the events leading up to the writing of 1 Corinthians is described, which shows more appropriately how the cross, understood as a revelation of God, addresses that very conduct, and the social and philosophical context in which it developed. Paul's startling ascription of weakness and foolishness to God is in fact a specific counter to power plays being enacted in the Corinthian church.

THE GENESIS OF AN ARGUMENT

The ethical and doctrinal values of the 'Apollos group', influenced by Epicurean-style values and thinking, were markedly different from those who entered the church under Paul's ministry and teaching. If this were the case, it would not be surprising if the wealthy high-status leaders of the congregation who still looked to Paul as their spiritual father, on seeing this group behaving in the ways described above, began to protest and even to try to discipline these maverick new Christians. 5:9 indicates that Paul had written before, quite probably in response to an earlier complaint of some Corinthians that others within the church were behaving in an immoral fashion. The Corinthian request for advice referred to in 5:9 may well have come from the Paul-loyalists who objected to the worldly behaviour of this newly converted group.[6] This advice had been mistakenly interpreted (by the Paul group?) as advocating withdrawal from contacts with outsiders altogether (5:10), vindicating their opposition to these new Christians' over-friendly relations with pagan (perhaps Epicurean?) neighbours. This advice therefore simply gave rise to further dispute over what Paul really meant. The dialogue then degenerated into an argument over names, those still loyal to Paul claiming his authority, admirers of Apollos pitting his merits over against that of the founder of the church. In this atmosphere, it would also not have been surprising if some of the small number of Jewish Christians in the congregation started to claim partiality to Peter as well.

Subsequent to this, however, two factors in particular seem to have led to invidious comparisons between Paul and Apollos. One was Paul's lack of rhetorical skill, compared to Apollos' proficiency in this area. As suggested above, the most likely cause of the trouble was that Paul was considered by some in the congregation to be a bad speaker, or as Paul himself later put it, ἰδιώτης τῷ λόγῳ (2 Cor.11:6). This would naturally have become a bone of contention and an additional cause for contempt for a group who had specifically been attracted to the Christian church because of Apollos' rhetorical *skill*. Once their behaviour had been criticised in the name of Paul, the founder of the congregation, a natural response would be along the lines of: "Why should we take any notice of Paul, when he is so obviously inferior in σοφία λόγου to Apollos?"

The other bone of contention was Paul's decision to work at a trade rather than to exercise his right to financial support from the church, referred to in ch.9. Ronald Hock suggested that the issue here was Paul's means of support.[7] In order to distinguish himself from fraudulent Cynic teachers, and in contrast to the various options open to any travelling sophist, Paul chose not to exercise his right to enter a household, accept a patron and receive due financial support. Instead he chose to ply a common trade, making tents. Paul became a 'weak' figure in the social structure of Corinth in order to preserve his own freedom (9:1), and to enable him to offer the gospel 'free of charge' (9:18). Peter Marshall argued instead that it was not so much Paul's work, but his social obligations that were the key issue.[8] Marshall points out that Paul was happy to take financial support from the Philippians (Phil 4:14-20), so that it cannot be, as Hock claims, that Paul refused to claim support on principle. In fact, Marshall suggests, it was this very acceptance of support from Philippi that had caused the problem in Corinth. Paul refused offers of help from Corinth because he felt that to do so would put him under obligation to the group who had extended the offer, a politically sensitive point given the divisions in the community. Like Hock, Marshall agrees that Paul put himself in a socially disadvantaged position. Yet, in contrast to Hock, he argues that Paul does so not on principle lest the gospel should not be freely offered, but rather in order to shame the 'hybrists', those he criticizes for proud boastful behaviour, those in whose pocket he would have been, had he accepted their patronage. A third perspective comes from Dale Martin, who examines Paul's use of the metaphor of slavery, and highlights its often unnoticed complexity. To high-status people it implied voluntary condescension, but to lower-status people it implied the privilege of being a slave of Christ.[9] Martin argues that Paul refused to accept support from the Corinthians, not to avoid offending the rich but to avoid offending the poor, with whom Paul would have had little contact if he had taken up residence in the home of a rich Corinthian patrician.[10]

Paul's statement of his reasons comes in 9:22-3. Verse 23 suggests that he did not refuse payment and take up a trade out of a settled principle that he should preach the gospel free of charge: Marshall's point that Paul was happy to accept financial support elsewhere is entirely valid. Nor did he do it to avoid putting himself in the pocket of the wrong people in Corinth. The explicit reason given in the text is διὰ τὸ εὐαγγέλιον (9:23), and ἵνα τοὺς πλείονας κερδήσω (9:19). Paul chose to work with his hands to make the gospel available to the class of people he would meet while plying a trade, rather than the limited circle he would reach if attached to a household as resident teacher on the sophistic model.

When he claims that his reward for doing this is that he "may make the gospel free of charge" he means not restricting it to those who can pay to hear it. Hock's study showed how the obvious models for Paul's activity would have included charging fees and becoming the resident teacher at the home of a rich patron.[11] This would have restricted the gospel's appeal to the "rich, powerful and well-born" (1:26), and taken it out of the hearing of poorer, lower-status people, something Paul was not prepared to do.

This consequent loss of social status[12] was quite probably a major cause of disparagement of Paul among this status-seeking group. Paul was conscious as he wrote to the Corinthians of his 'weakness' in their eyes (2:1-5; 4:9-13; 9:22). It was at one and the same time their accusation against him, and his own deliberate boast.[13] This atmosphere of disdain towards Paul would have then extended into a critique of his views on the resurrection and various ethical matters. Theology influenced by Epicurean-style ideas fostered not only a distancing from the poor in the congregation, but from the founder of the church as well.

PAUL'S KNOWLEDGE OF THE CORINTHIAN DISPUTES

While this situation was developing in his absence, Paul received two separate pieces of information. First, an oral report came from "Chloe's people" (1:11), a message which concentrated not so much upon ethical irregularities as on divisions. Chloe's people used to be thought of as followers of Demeter,[14] but this view has little to commend it, and they should rather be seen as members of Chloe's household, either freedmen, or more probably slaves.[15] This report on the Corinthian church came most likely from the perspective of the poorer members of the congregation. Not surprisingly then, Chloe's people saw division only among the richer members, some claiming the name of Paul, some that of Apollos, and they duly reported this to Paul. From their perspective, the major problem at Corinth was this personality-based rivalry. It would appear that Chloe's people did not see themselves as part of this rivalry. This confirms the assumption that it was primarily the rich who were involved, on one side those converted by and still loyal to Paul, and on the other, those drawn into the church by Apollos' ministry.

Secondly, Paul received a letter (7:1), presumably delivered to him by Stephanas, Fortunatus and Achaicus (16:17). Stephanas it seems, despite being one of Paul's converts, had managed to stay clear of the argument.[16] He had perhaps acted as a mediator between the two main sides, delivering a letter informing Paul of the issues which had given rise to this rivalry (including asking for clarification on the question of what Paul had meant by his earlier advice not to associate with immoral men – 5:9ff). Fortunatus and Achaicus may have been rich householders like Stephanas,[17] yet more likely were Stephanas' slaves, perhaps senior members of his household travelling with him.[18] Coming from Stephanas, this written information emerged not from the perspective of the *poorer* members (as in the oral report from Chloe's people), but with full awareness of the issues which divided those at the higher end of the social scale in the church, namely the ethical and doctrinal problems Paul addresses in chapters 5-15.[19]

Basically, the poorer Christians see the problem as a squabble among the richer members over leaders, Paul's supporters see the problem as the behaviour of the 'Apollos group', and the Apollos group see the problem as their opponents' misguided adherence to Paul's authority. As Paul saw it, the worldly Epicurean-style 'wisdom' manifest in this group within the church which had begun to associate itself with the name of Apollos manifested itself as arrogance (καυχάομαι) and independence, both towards socially and charismatically inferior members of the congregation and subsequently and increasingly towards himself. This arrogance is based on the claim to *wealth, eloquence and knowledge*. Their attitude towards the others in the church, is expressed in 12:21: "I have no need of you". With regard to Paul, their boast is to be wise, filled, rich, kings, χωρὶς ημῶν (4:8). Others in the congregation, still loyal to Paul and his teaching, have been drawn into comparable attitudes of competition (ἔριδες) out of an initial unsuccessful attempt to correct these others, and in turn a small number of others have begun to express partiality to Peter.

Paul therefore had to tackle two problems, competition and boasting, both of which revolve around the use of *power*. The Apollos group's boasting was an assertion of superiority based on their knowledge, over the poor of the congregation, over those loyal to Paul and even over Paul himself. The resulting divisions of 1:10ff indicate a struggle for control of the congregation between those loyal to Paul and this 'Apollos group'. Paul's polemic in 1 Corinthians therefore needed to operate on two levels. In the foreground he addresses some major sections of the church which have become embroiled in a struggle for power. In the background he has to address this group whose social and theological arrogance has sparked the whole thing off. On both levels he confronted illegitimate struggles for power within the congregation, and had to develop a theology which counters such power-plays, whether on behalf of the 'Apollos group' or of his own supporters.

PAUL'S RHETORICAL STRATEGY

The two-dimensional nature of the problem at Corinth presented Paul with a delicate and difficult task. There was confusion over his role in the church, some claiming too much for him, others claiming too little. He wanted to defend his own authority and standing, yet without seeming to take sides, thus endorsing the divisions in the church and alienating even further a significant section of the congregation. He needed to combat arrogance without appearing arrogant, to combat division without being divisive. Paul's argument therefore weaves together a critique of both quarrelling and boasting. The direction of his attack constantly oscillates between the two, at times clearly addressing one (such as in 1:10-16), at times addressing the other (for example in 4:8-13), and at times combining an attack on both stances, revealing the underlying connection between them.[20] As Paul begins to address this complex situation, the cross is his central theological reference-point, so that 1:18-25 serves to introduce his counterpoint to their wisdom. In opposition to the Epicurean-influenced wisdom prized by some Christians, which has in turn led to the quarrelling outlined in 1:10-

12, and the desire for power which lies behind both, Paul puts forward the cross as the content of God's wisdom.

THE CROSS AS CRITIQUE OF CORINTHIAN QUARRELLING

Whether the 'Christ' slogan in 1:12 is a *reductio ad absurdum* of Corinthian quarrelling, or a phrase used by some within the Apollos group, Paul picks it up rhetorically to begin his response to the emerging cracks in the unity of the church. Paul's strategy is to redirect attention to their unity not in individual leaders, but in the Christ to whom they do in fact belong. Victor Furnish has argued persuasively that the motif of 'belonging to Christ' in 1 Corinthians functions as a key ethical grounding for paraenetic appeals.[21] Paul responds to their claim to belong to different apostolic figures by reminding them of the one to whom they *really* belong.[22] This impression is confirmed by an analysis of the following few verses.

The three rhetorical questions in 1:13 all expect a negative response. "Is Christ divided?" No, clearly not - Christ is One, and the basis for unity of *all* the church, regardless of which leader they prefer. "Was Paul crucified for you?" No - Christ was. Paul links Christ's crucifixion on their behalf to the fundamental unity of the congregation in Christ. For Paul, the unity of the church is grounded not just in Christ, but in Christ *crucified* for them. Christ's death for them places them in a relationship of belonging and interdependence to him and to each other.[23] This is reinforced by reference to baptism, their point of entry into the community. "Were you baptised in the name of Paul?" Clearly not, rather in the name of Christ. For Paul, the baptised are baptised into Christ's death (Rom. 6:4), and this act remains the fundamental basis of unity (1 Cor.12:13, Gal.3:27f.).[24] When Paul reminds them of their baptism into Christ, he refers them to the cross, the crucified Christ as the foundation stone of their unity as a congregation.[25]

By their focus on the leader who performed their baptism, the Corinthians have forgotten their baptism into Christ's death. For Paul, the new community, founded on the death of Christ, makes all the old divisions and oppositions irrelevant.[26] The cross is the decisive criterion of the church's unity and identity, and both are compromised by the behaviour of the Corinthian Christians, whether followers of Apollos or loyalists to Paul. This is of course why the dispute over who baptised whom would "empty the cross of its power" (1:17), because it denies the reality of the unity which the cross has achieved, and blurs the distinction between the church and the world.

Paul associates the cross and unity at two other points in the letter. One is at 8:11, where Paul apparently addresses those in the high-status 'Apollos group' who eat in pagan temples, without regard for the effect this might have on poorer, more conscientious members of the Christian community.[27] Paul's appeal to consider the weaker Christian is based on the fact that the latter is "the brother for whom Christ died". Paul again appeals to the cross as the basis of their common life and mutual belonging. Again at 15:3 the apostle rehearses the pre-Pauline tradition which he handed on to them. The context here also is that of an appeal to a common belief. This is the content of the original κηρυγμα which stood as the foundation stone of the Corinthian church. It begins of course with the clause Χριστὸς ἀπέθανεν ὑπερ τῶν ἁμαρτιῶν ἡμῶν (15:3). This teaching lies as the bedrock of the community's existence.[28]

The first part of Paul's answer to Corinthian quarrelling over leaders then, is found in 1:13, that is in his insistence that the unity of the congregation consists in the fact that Christ was crucified for all of them. They belong neither to him, nor to Apollos nor Cephas, but to the Christ who was crucified for them, who has "bought them with a price". (6:20). Paul is keen to distance himself from the possibility of becoming the focus of partisan loyalties, so he stresses the role he played in Corinth as evangelist, rather than as baptiser. He was chiefly the means by which they came to hear and accept the gospel of Christ crucified, rather than one who stands in a patronal relationship with them as their initiator into the community.[29] This tack is taken up again in 3:5ff., where again he examines the role that both he and Apollos played during their time in Corinth, minimising their significance over against "God who gives the growth". It makes no sense to claim himself or Apollos as identity-giving figures. They are merely "servants through whom you believed".

THE CROSS AS CRITIQUE OF CORINTHIAN ARROGANCE

While on the surface Paul has to deal with Corinthian division over apostolic loyalties, the deeper problem comes from a group of the congregation claiming Apollos as model, still strongly influenced by pagan Greek ideas and behaviour, and adopting a stance of arrogant withdrawal both from poorer members of the congregation and from Paul. This issue lies more hidden within the text for several reasons. The report of Chloe's people accused most if not all of the richer people in the church of breaking into factions. Paul can thus address that issue openly without appearing to take sides, adopting the position of the neutral observer. The other issue, the behaviour of the Apollos group about which his own supporters have rightly complained is more sensitive. Open criticism risks appearing to take the side of the 'Paul' group, thus invalidating his criticism of division over names of apostolic leaders. Criticism of this group and its behaviour therefore has to remain subtle and often indirect, naming no names,[30] woven into the more generalised criticism of the whole church.

Paul introduces the notion of wisdom in the transitional verse 1:17. As has been argued above, this is to be taken as in part an issue of rhetorical ability, and in part the ideal of σοφία behind it.[31] It is the 'wisdom' which values rhetorical skill (σοφία λόγου v.17) admires the δυνατος and εὐγενεις (v.26), boasts in its ethical freedom (5:1-2), disregards the scruples of the weak (8:9-11), looks down on an artisan apostle (2:3; 9:22), humiliates the poor (11:22) prides itself in superior knowledge (8:1) and spiritual endowment (14:37), and denies the resurrection (15:12).

Paul opposes this wisdom of the world (v.20) with the wisdom of God (v.21). In stark contrast, God's wisdom, or mind (νοῦς), is revealed in the scandalous 'choice' of a crucified messiah as the means of salvation.[32] God displayed the radically different character of his wisdom by choosing to save people through the word (λόγος v.18, κηρύγμα v.21) of the cross. Whereas Corinthian society prefers what is wise, strong and honoured, God chooses and values what is foolish, weak, low and despised. The central symbol of God's character-revealing wisdom is the historical cross of Christ as the means of salvation.[33] Paul illustrates this with two highly significant examples. First, (vv.26-31) he calls the attention of his readers to the poor in the community. God has by and large not chosen the highest level of society for his church; in fact he has often chosen those who are despised by the world. Κλῆσις in v.26 must refer to 'social standing',[34] and so Paul very deliberately brings into the discussion the presence of the poor of the congregation, τοὺς μὴ ἔχοντας (11:22). Paul's second witness to God's preference for the 'foolish' is himself. 2:1 introduces his own rhetorically unskilled, physically and spiritually exhausted persona into the discussion. God has chosen not only despised people for his church, he has chosen an unimpressive apostle as his messenger.

These two are chosen as examples precisely because they are the two targets of the Apollos group's disparagement. They humiliate the poor (8:11; 11:22) and they disregard Paul (4:18; 9:3). Paul's polemic is plain: *God has chosen what they have rejected*. Just as divisions in the community displays their failure to grasp the crucified Christ as the ground of their unity, so the arrogance of the Apollos group in an even more startling way displays their total failure to grasp God's wisdom, revealed in his scandalous choice of a crucified messiah as the means of salvation. To scorn the weak, poor and foolish is simply to reveal how wedded they are to the wisdom and values of the world which God will destroy (1:19). The cross therefore not only acts as the foundation of the congregation's unity, it also deconstructs the Apollos group's Epicurean-influenced theology of wisdom and knowledge. It counters not just competition for power within the church, but the underlying claim to independence and superiority over others.

THE APOSTLE AS MODEL OF THE CRUCIFIED

So far, Paul's polemic has been mainly destructive, showing how the cross destroys the wisdom of the world, setting up God's 'foolish' wisdom in its place. Paul moves beyond this critical stance to offer a positive model for the whole congregation to follow, and particularly those he thinks are guilty of arrogance or divisiveness. The cross in this text operates on another level still, as the emblem of Paul's own ministry, which they are still called to imitate (4:16), despite his reluctance to draw loyalty to himself (1:13). Paul's self-portrayal throughout the letter improvises yet again on the theme of the cross, indicating a correspondence between the pattern of his own ministry and that of Christ.

The argument of 2:6-16 has given rise to much speculation whether Paul had a secret wisdom teaching which he reserved for the mature (τέλειοι). Jean Héring considers it "a kind of Christian theosophy... reserved for a Christian élite amongst pagans",[35] while Robin Scroggs thinks this passage explains Paul's own secret teaching derived from the context of Jewish and Christian apocalyptic theology such as that found in Qumran and the Parables of 1 Enoch.[36] These views remain in the minority. Some see the difference between the τέλειοι and the νηπίοι as lying not so much in the content of the teaching they require, as in the perspective from which it is heard. In other words, the mature and the immature see the same thing in different ways because of their differing perspective.[37] The mysterious hidden wisdom of God of 2:7 is in all probability the same as the mysterious hidden wisdom of God revealed in the cross. Paul's thought is similar here to the idea expressed in 1:18. To "those who are perishing" the cross is simply foolishness. To "those who are being saved" it is the power of God.[38] This certainly makes much more sense of the context. Nowhere else can Paul convincingly be shown to have had a separate esoteric teaching for the élite, and the θεοῦ σοφία ἐν μυστηρίῳ of v.7 makes perfect sense as referring to the strange cruciform wisdom of God in 1:18-25. This is a mystery understood only by the τέλειοι and πνευματικοί, which are simply Paul's words for mature Christians who have grasped God's unexpected ways.

In this case, the purpose of 2:6-16 is to contrast those in the congregation who have understood the wisdom of the cross, in other words the τέλειοι,[39] and those who by their disparagement of both the poor and of Paul show that they do not have the mind of the Lord (2:16). God's wisdom is not generally known by the wise, powerful or well-born, that is the ἀρχόντες (v.8), a fact which they displayed by their failure to recognise Christ the Lord of glory when he fell into their hands thus also despising the cross. The mind or wisdom of God is known only by the Spirit and through revelation (vv.11-12), and Paul's remarkable claim is to "have the mind of Christ" (2:16). This phrase has received comparatively little attention, but W. Willis has helpfully pointed to the importance of Romans 12:2 and Phil. 2:5-11 for its interpretation.[40] As Willis explains:

> The 'mind of Christ' is not focused upon special wisdom or experiences, but community life... The intent of the whole section is a criticism of the internal strife at Corinth, manifested in their boasting about their apostolic heroes.[41]

The "mind of Christ" refers to the kind of self-lowering and humility recommended on the pattern of Christ's descent in Phil. 2, and it is this very attitude that Paul claims to display.

Paul illustrates his claim to have the mind of Christ by offering a self-portrait, focused in 4:14-16, climaxing in μιμηταί μου γίνεσθε. Paul sends Timothy to them specifically in order to remind them of "my ways in Christ" (v.17). The word ὁδοί (ways) is to be understood in its Old Testament sense, including both teaching and conduct, so that Timothy is sent as a faithful example of Paul's way of life as well as his doctrine. Paul's intention in this self-depiction is that the Corinthians in general and the Apollos group in particular should become imitators of him. This is, of course, a familiar rhetorical exercise,[42] yet Paul's use of it shows a variation on the normal pattern. Instead of the common appeal to follow the sage in the way of wisdom and philosophy leading to honour, he offers a call to imitation of his suffering and shame.[43]

Paul's self-portrayal in 2:1-5 deliberately highlights his weakness, fear and trembling. Twice he tells the Corinthians that they are to regard him and Apollos as servile inferiors. In 3:5, they are διάκονοι, and in 4:1, ὑπηρέται and οἰκονόμοι.[44] This is in deliberate contrast to the Corinthians' exaltation of them as leaders to be pitted against one another in intra-church rivalries. Paul includes Apollos in this servant-role, as he is anxious to present a united front with *both* himself and Apollos as servants. Whether members of the congregation remain loyal to him or claim Apollos as champion makes no difference - both are servants, and imitation of both will lead to servanthood.

As the chapter proceeds, the metaphor of servanthood is intensified to become that of the condemned criminal. Echoes of crucifixion abound here. The apostles appear as "men sentenced to death... a spectacle to the world" (4:9).[45] Besides the clear reference to the death sentence, the public aspect of the apostles' condemnation echoes Paul's consciousness of the public nature of Christ's crucifixion (cf. Gal.3:1). The apostles are μωροὶ, ἀσθενεῖς, ἄτιμοι, περικαθάρματα (4:10-13). J.T. Fitzgerald has shown how this catalogue of hardship echoes similar sophistic passages; the adjectives describing the Corinthians ironically in v.8 are all "qualities predicated of the sage".[46] In the sophistic tradition, these are trials through which the philosopher grows, proves his worth and then leaves behind. For Paul, they are the enduring marks of the apostolic condition. The purpose of the catalogue is not shame (ἐντρέπω) but exhortation (νουθετῶ – 4:14). Its aim is not criticism but encouragement.

Paul's weakness likewise has an unmistakably social and political connotation. Fools/wise (v.10) echoes the classic distinction common in sophistic circles between the philosopher and the common crowd. Honour/disrepute (ἔνδοξοι/ἄτιμοι v.10) again has a clear reference to social status.[47] The apostles are hungry, thirsty, ill-clad, buffeted and homeless. In particular the reference to Paul's freely-chosen artisan status[48] indicates the significance for Paul of his manual labour[49] for his social status.[50] 'Weakness' here is specifically linked to Paul's place on the social ladder of Greco-Roman society.

This self-depiction continues in chapter 9, where Paul again uses the language of slavery to describe himself. It is important to note the rhetorical structure of vv.19-23. The 'heading' as it were is the statement, "I made myself a slave to all, that I might win the more" (v.19). There follow several examples of his voluntary subjection to (strictly speaking) unnecessary conditions in order to win people. The "rhetorical goal of the list"[51] is becoming "weak to win the weak" in v.22. If the term 'weak' in the letter is a designation of the socially inferior, as both 4:9-13 suggests and Theissen has argued,[52] then this reference to becoming weak must refer to his becoming poor (an artisan labourer) to win the poor. The 'weak' cannot refer to Jewish Christians, as Paul has already mentioned Jews, and it would make no sense to say he needs to 'win' those who already have been 'won'.[53] Neither can it refer to non-Christians in general,[54] but rather, it is a conscious reference to his voluntarily adopted artisan status.

Paul decided to work with his hands in order to be in a position to reach the poorer levels of society in Corinth, rather than just the rich.[55] Paul's evangelistic reasons for this course of action have already been mentioned, yet he also gives another reason. Διὰ τὸ εὐαγγέλιον (9:23) has a double edge. It means partly the benefits of being able to reach a greater number and variety of people, but it also includes the idea that he might "share in its blessings". This tactic is in part an evangelistic strategy, but not purely so: it is also "soteriologically significant".[56] There is an inner dynamic in the gospel, that if Paul is to share in its benefits, he will need to take the same self-lowering path taken by the Christ who was crucified. Paul's adoption of an inferior social status is part of his response to the gospel (9:24-27). It is done "to win the more" (v.19) or to "save some" (v.22), but also in order that he, Paul, might "receive the imperishable prize" (v.25). And again the reason for recounting all this is to recommend this pattern of behaviour to them for imitation: "So run that you may obtain it" (v.24).

This discussion makes two things plain. First, Paul claims a correspondence between himself and the crucified Christ. 2:1-5 places his own ragged appearance in Corinth alongside God's choice of the poor in the city as examples of the divine cruciform wisdom. 4:9-13 picks up the language of public condemnation and shame, and 9:19-23 refers to Paul's self-chosen social humiliation as an artisan labourer. Secondly, this specifically takes the shape of identification with the poor of the church. 2:1-5, 4:9-13 and 9:19-23 all place Paul not alongside the higher social status members of the congregation (whether 'of Paul' or 'of Apollos'), but alongside the poor. He refuses to take sides between the groups claiming loyalty to himself or Apollos, but he does take sides in the social divisions in the congregation, because his *theologia crucis* tells him that God does.

The cross operates as the counter argument to both community infighting and worldly arrogance because it renders all "boasting" vain, whether boasting in leaders (3:21) or in one's own social, spiritual or intellectual superiority. Before the God who saves through a crucified messiah and chooses the foolish, weak and despised, no-one can boast about wealth, eloquence or knowledge, either his own or that of a human leader. Instead, Paul offers himself as a model of behaviour that corresponds to God's wisdom, the enslaved leader,[57] who lowers himself out of concern for his people. This for Paul is more than a political tactic. He does not commend himself as an example to follow because he has superior wisdom, rhetorical skill, charismatic gifting or access to a special knowledge unavailable to others. He offers himself as a model for imitation only in so far as his own apostolic career mirrors that of Christ crucified. In this way he can commend himself, and to a certain extent Apollos too, as an example in a fashion which undercuts claims to power based on "boasting" and which avoids taking sides in the personality dispute. Paul's answer to this complex theological and pastoral problem shows his theology of the cross as a central motif of his understanding of Christian belief and practice.

THE CROSS AND THE CORINTHIAN CHRISTIANS

The three examples of God's foolish wisdom, the crucified Christ, the poor, foolish and weak things of the world and the weak, trembling apostle stand in a carefully constructed theological relationship. The crucified messiah, scandalous to Jews and nonsensical to Greeks, is the starting point of Paul's reflections on God's strange wisdom. That wisdom is exemplified and expressed in his choice of the foolish, weak and lowly, rather than the wise, powerful and well born. For Paul himself, as the apostle of the crucified messiah, this then gives a practical and even political shape to the ministry he is called to perform. It too has to take the shape of the cross, which in social terms means taking up a position at the bottom of the social scale (4:9-13), along with the foolish, weak and lowly. For Paul there is a theological connection between the recognition that came at his conversion that the crucified Jesus was the messiah and his own experience of hardship and weariness in the apostolic life and manual labour. There is also a theological connection between the cross and the relatively low social standing of many in his churches. Yet there is a theological rupture between the cross and the kind of arrogant, self-satisfied power-seeking behaviour he encounters at Corinth.

The connection between the cross and the "low and despised in the world" means for Paul a life of social shame, hard labour, homelessness and misunderstanding. He presents a positive role model in his own self-lowering, which in turn is an imitation of the self-lowering of Christ to the cross (11:1). Yet he does not urge this precise form of social shame upon his city-dwelling churches. This extreme role he reserves for those in the apostolic calling.[58] For the Christians in Corinth, he uses the transitional concept of *servanthood*, the role in which he insists on being regarded by these Christians (3:5; 4:1). For them, the connection between the cross and the poor is to result ethically in love (14:1a, 16:14), the foregoing of ethical liberty for the sake of the poor (8:9)[59], edification rather than self-fulfilment (14:26), the renunciation of privilege for the sake of others.

In practical terms, this leads not to an anaemic 'love-patriarchalism',[60] but to a voluntary self-lowering to the role of servant, expressed in the attitude of love.[61] This is the purpose of chapter 13, coming as it does after material which indirectly accuses some in Corinth of feeling so superior to others in the congregation that they have no need of them. The true content of wisdom for Paul is not γνῶσις but ἀγάπη (8:1-3; 13:2-8). The wisdom which God prizes, and which enables one to discern the thoughts of God (2:11) does not consist of privileged knowledge of the nature of things,[62] but in an attitude of self-giving love towards one's fellow-believers, especially those who are poor. Paul appeals to the "certainty of agape as the ultimate 'norm' of social life".[63] It is this path he sees both in the crucified Christ, and in his own response to Christ's self-giving, in terms of his voluntary loss of social status. His *theologia crucis* possesses not merely soteriological implications, but ethical and ecclesiological ones as well. The true response to the God who saves through a crucified messiah is a life of voluntary servanthood, self-lowering, love, distinctly different from the attitude shown by his opponents, and even his supporters in Corinth.

CONCLUSION: PAUL, GOD, AND POWER

Paul's repeated appeal for imitation (4:16; 11:1) has been seen in some recent scholarship as a bid for power over the congregation. Elizabeth Castelli sees imitation ("mimesis") as an exaltation of sameness, a suppression of difference. In the light of Michel Foucault's understanding of power and oppressive models of patriarchy in antiquity, Paul's claim to be father of the church (4:15), and this call to imitate him are seen simply as an attempt to eliminate opposition and impose repressive hierarchical models of power.[64] Castelli's analysis however is another victim of the failure to contextualise Paul's discourse. She simply does not try to reconstruct the situation into which Paul writes, neither does she examine closely enough the nature of Paul's self-presentation. When it is understood that Paul is addressing not just theological disagreement, but competing claims to power within the congregation, the nature of his argument, as suggesting an *alternative* understanding of power becomes clearer.[65] Paul's appeal for imitation is in fact an appeal to imitate his voluntary *surrender* of relationships based on social, spiritual or intellectual power or privilege. It is precisely the opposite of the power-seeking discourse which Castelli finds in the text, and is enjoined precisely to protect the poor in the congregation who would otherwise suffer rejection and oppression. Paul is actually very happy to celebrate difference in chapters 12 and 14, passages which oppose the desire of some in the Corinthian church to impose 'sameness' by insisting that they do not need those who are different from themselves (12:21-24).[66] Paul's *theologia crucis* presents a vision of community life which resists claims to power by modelling itself on the self-giving and powerlessness of Christ, and the social self-lowering of his apostle.

Alexandra Brown has similarly drawn attention to the danger seen most clearly by some feminist critics that the theology of the cross, especially when seen in its Lutheran guise, can be used to glorify suffering and justify injustice.[67] Such a concern is well founded. The *theologia crucis* is vulnerable to misuse in this way, and Brown does suggest a defence of Paul's thought against this criticism. She does so by interpreting Paul's 'word of the cross' as mainly an expression of God's *love*. The difficulty here is that chs. 1-2 do not clearly focus on God's love as a central theme.[68] Instead, Paul sees the cross in these early chapters as primarily a revelation of God's *power* and *wisdom*, rather than his love. Strictly speaking, his concentration on ἀγάπη in the letter concerns more the love that Christians are to have for one another (cf. ch. 13) than that of God himself. However, Brown is clearly on the right lines, and her point can be developed in another way. In these chapters, Paul understands God's means of achieving salvation, the cross of Christ, as a paradigm for God's action in the world. In other words, God gets things done not by a conventional human use of power, by displays of force, impressive signs or sophisticated wisdom.[69] He achieves salvation through an act of what to human eyes is powerlessness on the cross; he chooses to dwell in Corinth[70] in a group of 'nothings' in the eyes of Corinthian society; he creates these new communities through the preaching of an unimpressive artisan tentmaker. The passage offers a vision of God's use of power through powerlessness. Through this apparent powerlessness, God achieves far more than human power ever could. In the light of this pattern, Paul appeals to these powerful Christians in Corinth not to conduct their business through the conventional means of human power, but through a kind of self-giving love for other Christians which surrenders privilege and may look like powerlessness, but which is much more in tune with the way God acts and achieves.

Brown is right in suggesting that Paul's *theologia crucis* does not sanction submission to injustice, but the point must be upheld on different grounds from those suggested by her. Read in context, the 'word of the cross' is addressed primarily to the wealthier, socially and economically powerful members of the church. It consists of an appeal to them to imitate Christ's and Paul's self-giving, to give the poorer brothers and sisters pride of place in their gatherings (cf. 12:23-4) and abstaining from attending meals connected with pagan worship when it offends other members of the church. It would be dangerously misused when addressed in the same way to the poor and victimised, to justify their continued exclusion and subjugation.

This *theologia crucis* presents an alternative understanding of power by grounding it in an understanding of God as one whose character and economy are revealed in the scandalous choice of the crucified Christ as the means of salvation. Paul claims that God's action in the cross is paradigmatic for his action in the present, in that just as God chose the weak suffering Christ, so also he chooses socially inferior people, and a weak suffering apostle. The cross therefore has theological significance for Paul, in that it reveals the way God works now, not just the way he achieved salvation in the past. Paul insists that the God who 'chose' the crucified Messiah also 'chose' the poorer Christians and a weak apostle. He works *now* in conformity with the pattern seen *then* on the cross: it is the God of the cross with whom the Corinthians now have to deal. As Richardson has seen, Paul's language in this letter implies a new understanding of God, rooted in OT perspectives,[71] of a God who always achieves his purposes through things which in the eyes of the world are weak and foolish. Our reading however provides a fuller picture of how this understanding of God meets the situation in the Corinthian church.[72]

As Paul seeks to counter the jostling for control of the congregation in his own name, or the claim to power based on superior knowledge, wealth, eloquence or spiritual gifts, the cross becomes for him the central polemical focus. The cross operates as a counter-ideology to the uses of power current within the church, fostering a regard for love rather than knowledge, the poor rather than the wealthy, their trembling apostle rather than the rhetorical ability of any 'rival', mutual upbuilding rather than spiritual showing-off. Theology that begins at the cross is for Paul the radical antidote to any religion that is a thinly veiled copy of a power-seeking culture.

Notes:

[1] Richardson, *Paul's Language about God*, 124-33.

[2] Ibid., 133.

[3] Ibid., 137-8.

[4] R.S. Barbour, "Wisdom and the Cross in 1 Cor.2.6", ed. C. Andresen and G. Klein, *Theologia Crucis - Signum Crucis; Festschrift für Erich Dinkler*, (Tübingen: Mohr/Siebeck, 1979), 57-71, here, 71.

[5] Ibid., 65.

[6] Hurd, *Origin*, 50-3, 77-83, 219-39, considers Paul's 'previous letter' and discusses the question of how Paul received the news of their misunderstanding. He concludes that "certainty is obviously not possible here, nor is it really necessary" (83). An additional question concerns why Paul raised the issue of immorality in his previous letter. Hurd suggests that the Jerusalem decree which appeared between the previous letter and 1 Corinthians has changed Paul's initial enthusiasm for wisdom and freedom into a more institutionalised and rigid moral stance (259-62). However, Paul only indicates that he wrote in that letter about the issue of associating with immoral men; the rest of Hurd's reconstruction of that letter is conjecture. It is more likely that this letter was written in response to a request from the Corinthians about how to deal with immorality in the congregation, Paul's words about avoiding those guilty of it being interpreted

differently by different groups in that congregation.

[7]R.F. Hock, "Paul's Tentmaking and the Problem of his Social Class", *JBL* 97 (1978), 555-64; *The Social Context of Paul's Ministry: Tentmaking and Apostleship* (Philadelphia: Fortress, 1980).

[8]Marshall, *Enmity in Corinth*, esp. 173. See also Chow, "Patronage in Roman Corinth", in ed. Horsley, *Paul and Empire*, 121-4.

[9]D.B. Martin, *Slavery as Salvation: The Metaphor of Slavery in Pauline Christianity* (New Haven: Yale, 1990), 73-8.

[10]"The point of 1 Corinthians 9 is that Paul takes on manual labour because of (not in spite of) his view that it is demeaning; he takes it on in order to gain the weak." ibid., 124.

[11]Hock, *Social Context*, 50-5.

[12]See A.C. Wire, *The Corinthian Women Prophets: A Reconstruction through Paul's Rhetoric* (Minneapolis: Fortress, 1990), 69-71 for some valuable comments on this.

[13]It is important not to overstate the opposition to Paul at this stage in the relationship. It has clearly not yet reached the open hostility evident in 2 Corinthians. Paul can still hope to transcend the divisions by an appeal to his example and status as founder of the church (see Witherington, *Conflict*, 203-4), although I would disagree with his claim that there is no opposition at all to Paul in 1 Corinthians.

[14]F.R.M Hitchcock, "Who are the 'People of Chloe' in 1 Cor.1.11?", *JTS* 25 (1923), 163-7.

[15]Theissen, *Social Setting*, 92-4; also Meeks, *Urban Christians*, 63.

[16]It is possible that Gaius and Crispus are embroiled on the 'Paul' side in the argument over apostolic loyalties, whereas Stephanas is not, which would explain why Stephanas' name is separated from theirs, and added almost as an afterthought in 1:14-16.

[17]Judge, "Scholastic Community", thinks they are. He also considers it "a likely guess that he (Stephanas) was leader of the Pauline faction" (130), but this remains no more than a guess.

[18]W. Bousset, "Der Erste Brief an die Korinther", *Die Schriften des Neuen Testaments Vol 2*, ed. J. Weiss (Göttingen: Vandenhoeck & Ruprecht, 1917-18), 72-161, here, 76; Theissen, *Social Setting*, 95, among others. See the useful discussion in Fee, *1 Corinthians*, 829-30, who inclines towards this conclusion, as their names are particularly common among slaves. In the absence of any indication that they were independent from Stephanas, the fact that vv.15-16 refers suddenly and approvingly to "the household of Stephanas", urging the church to be subject to such people, may indicate that these two men are members of that very household, either slaves or freedmen. Why otherwise would Paul mention Stephanas' οἰκία rather than just his name, if the delegation he had received were not from that very household? Paul's recommendation to 'recognise' these three

men clearly parallels the recommendation to be subject to the household of Stephanas, implying that all three belong to it.

[19]Perhaps the sexual and legal problems mentioned in chs. 5-6 were omitted from the letter, but reported to Paul by Stephanas et al. when they saw him?

[20]For example the verb καυχάομαι.shifts its orientation in the text. In 1:29 it seems to refer more naturally to boasting about one's higher status than others before God (i.e. to arrogance). In 3:21 however, its use is directed against quarrelling over leaders. The same is true of the verb φυσιόω, which in 4:6 clearly refers to divisions over leaders (quarrelling), but in 4:18; 5:2; 8:1; 13:4 shifts its reference towards arrogance and boasting in oneself.

[21]V.P. Furnish, "Belonging to Christ: A Paradigm for Ethics in 1st Corinthians", *Int* 44 (1990), 145-57: "(Paul's) counsels and appeals derive from the conviction that every member of the congregation has equal status by reason of who are whose they are: a community of sisters and brothers for whom Christ died." (154).

[22]The question of belonging is also raised in 12:15f. where the implication is that some are claiming not to need others because their spiritual gifts are different (superior?) to those of others. Likewise, these others feel they do not belong because their gifts are inferior. The issue here is belonging to each other in the community, alongside that of belonging to Christ in 1:12; 6:20 etc.

[23]Most probably he has in mind the idea of solidarity/incorporation in Christ's death as in 2 Cor.5:14; Gal.3:13. On this understanding, the death of Christ can act as the unifying centre for the Christian community. Christ died for all, and all died in Christ: the death of Christ is portrayed as unifying divided humanity in Rom.3:25; Phil. 2:2-8. Eph.2:16 also provides a recurrence of the idea.

[24]Both of these verses make the same point about unity in Christ despite cultural, gender and social background.

[25]Meeks shows how baptism in the Pauline congregations operated as a clear demarcation of the leaving of one life and the start of another, the "decisive point of entry into an exclusive community". *Urban Christians*, 150-7.

[26]Gal. 3:27-28. See J.L.Martyn, "Apocalyptic Antinomies in Paul's letter to the Galatians", *NTS* 31 (1985), 410-24.

[27]Cf. Theissen, *Social Setting*, 125-31.

[28]Although Ernst Käsemann attempted to distance Paul from the pre-Pauline atonement tradition, ("Saving Significance", 39-42), this would suggest that Paul, far from leaving that tradition behind, makes it the very foundation of his Theology of the Cross. Peter Stuhlmacher has criticised the Bultmann/Käsemann position on just this point: "In Paul, talk about the atoning death of Jesus is no traditional relic but the condition that makes the theology of justification and the cross possible!" ("Eighteen Theses on Paul's Theology of the Cross", *Reconciliation, Law and Righteousness: Essays in Biblical Theology* [Philadelphia: Fortress, 1986], 155-68, here 157). It is precisely because Paul came to understand the shameful death of the messiah as the locus of salvation

that it has such a central significance for him. Stuhlmacher links this discovery directly to Paul's experience of the risen Christ on the Damascus Road, revealing that the crucified one is now the "end of the law" (156).

[29]Conzelmann, *1 Corinthians*, 35, suggests that Paul wants to distance himself from the kind of relationship between baptiser and baptised in the mystery religions.

[30]Almost all of the names mentioned in connection with Corinth have some clear relationship with Paul, so are more likely than not to be his supporters. We get little if any clue as to the names of those ranged against him, those who think he will not return (4:18).

[31]The traditional distinction between form and content in classical rhetoric is hard to maintain, according to Litfin, *Proclamation*, chs. 4 & 5, and Pogoloff, *Logos and Sophia*, ch. 2.

[32]Martin Hengel, *Crucifixion* (London: S.C.M., 1977) shows the cultural and political significance of the scandal of crucifixion.

[33]See Weder, *Das Kreuz Jesu*, for a valuable discussion of the relationship between the cross as historical event and as symbol.

[34]This is the second of two meanings given by A&G (436).

[35]J. Héring, *The First Epistle of Saint Paul to the Corinthians* (London: Epworth, 1962), 15.

[36]R. Scroggs, "Paul: Σοφος and Πνευματικος", *NTS* 14 (1967), 33-55.

[37]T. Engberg-Pederson, "The Gospel and Social Practice according to 1 Corinthians", *NTS* 33 (1987), 557-84, W. Baird, "The Idea of Wisdom in 1 Cor.2.6", *Int* 13 (1959) 425-32. E.E. Ellis, "Traditions in 1 Corinthians", *NTS* 32 (1986), 481-502, sees this passage as a prior composition by one of Paul's companions inserted into the letter at this point. His case is less than convincing - the change to the first person plural at 2:6 simply widens the discussion from Paul's own appearance in Corinth to the content of his apostolic group's teaching. Otherwise, Ellis case rests on isolated variations from Paul's normal language, most of which can be explained by the context.

[38]This must also be the meaning of 2:14, where τὰ τοῦ πνεύματος τοῦ θεοῦ are foolishness to the ψυχικὸς, yet can be understood and appreciated by the πνευματικός.

[39]Perhaps these include Stephanas and his household among others, given Paul's positive estimation of them in 16:15-16?

[40]Willis, "The 'Mind of Christ'".

[41]Ibid., 119-20.

[42]Mitchell, *Reconciliation*, 42-6.

[43]J.T. Fitzgerald, *Cracks in an Earthen Vessel: An Examination of the Catalogues of Hardships in the Corinthian Correspondence* (Atlanta: Scholars Press, 1988), 205.

[44]Cf. Martin, *Slavery as Salvation*, ch. 1 for an account of the function of

οικονόμος in the Greco-Roman household.

[45]Conzelmann comments here that "the theologia crucis interprets the existence of the confessor in terms of exposing himself to death", *1 Corinthians*, 88.

[46]Fitzgerald, *Cracks*, 144.

[47]Cf. the account of the significance of honour and shame in the first century mediterranean world in B.J. Malina, *The New Testament World: Insights from Cultural Anthropology* (London: S.C.M., 1981), 25-50, esp. 47: "honor stands for a person's rightful place in society, his social standing. This honor place is marked off by boundaries consisting of power, sexual status and position on the social ladder." See also Witherington, *Conflict*, 154-5.

[48]κοπιῶμεν ἐργαζόμενοι ταῖς ἰδίαις χερσίν - v.12

[49]Hock, *Social Context*, 64: "Paul's tentmaking must be assumed as largely responsible for his humiliation."

[50]The question of Paul's social status has been debated for many years, from Deissmann, *Light*, who placed Paul along with most early Christians as among the poorer social classes, to Judge, *Social Pattern*, who claims that Paul "possessed an unusually well balanced set of social qualifications" (58). Cf. also R.F. Hock, "Paul's Tentmaking", and S.K. Stowers, "Social Status, Public Speaking and Private Teaching: The Circumstances of Paul's Preaching Activity", *NovT* 26 (1984), 59-82.

[51]D. Martin, *Slavery as Salvation*, 119. Martin also remarks that Paul does not claim to have "become strong to win the strong". This is not a generalised principle but a specific manoeuvre to target a particular group.

[52]Theissen, *Social Setting*, ch. 3.

[53]Barrett, who takes this view, suggests rather weakly that Paul "uses the word from force of habit, not noticing that it is inappropriate" to get round the problem (*1 Corinthians*, 215).

[54]D.A. Black, *Paul, Apostle of Weakness: Astheneia and its Cognates in the Pauline Literature* (New York: Peter Lang, 1984) says that in this context, "The weak are non-Christians, whether Jewish or Gentile, who are powerless to work out any righteousness for themselves" (118). This interpretation faces at least two major problems. Paul has already mentioned both Jew and Gentile as those he tries to win; it is not clear how the category of 'the weak' can add to this - if Black is right it simply repeats what Paul has already said. Secondly, it is hard to see how Paul can claim to have become 'powerless to work out any righteousness for himself' in order to win them! Besides these two points, the context of the passage, that of Paul's working for a living (9:4-18), weighs heavily in favour of 'weakness' as a sociological not a soteriological category.

[55] See Horrell, *Social Ethos*, 210-6. Horrell writes "His manual labour both prevents him from becoming dependent on and obligated to certain wealthy patrons and also enables him to become 'weak' like those he seeks to gain" 215.

[56]Martin, *Slavery as Salvation*, 129.

[57]The phrase is from Dale Martin who writes of the 'topos' of the enslaved leader as a characteristic, but threatening, figure to traditional political expectations in Greco-Roman society, *Slavery as Salvation*, ch. 3.

[58]Engberg-Pederson, "The Gospel and Social Practice", shows how on one level Paul presents the radical demands of the gospel, yet he adjusts his ethical demands to make obedience possible in the realities of the Corinthians' own social position.

[59]Horrell, *Social Ethos*, 149-50 draws attention to Paul's appeal to wealthier Christians that they give up their theological 'right' to dine with pagan friends if it causes offence among the poorer brothers and sisters. He recognizes the wide implications this has for the rich in their social interaction in wider Corinthian society.

[60]Theissen's phrase for Paul's ethical stance here. See the well-argued critique in Engberg-Pederson, "The Gospel and Social Practice", also Martin, *Slavery as Salvation*, 128.

[61]See Horrell, *Social Ethos*, 126-98 for an extended critique of 'love-patriarchalism' as a description of Paul's ethical teaching in 1 Corinthians.

[62]Note the careful and recurrent opposition of love to knowledge in 13:2, 8, 9, 12.

[63]Engberg-Pederson, "The Gospel and Social Practice", 567.

[64]E. Castelli, *Imitating Paul: A Discourse of Power* (Louisville: Westminster/John Knox Press, 1991).

[65]On Castelli's reading Paul would surely have endorsed the viewpoint of the 'Paul' group, who are advocating submission to his authority. In fact Paul refuses to do this.

[66]Castelli touches on this point (129-33), but says that in the end Paul is arguing for unity, which is still imposing a totalizing structure on the congregation. The argument suffers from her constant assumption (e.g. 98) that unity and 'sameness' are identical. Paul argues for unity in 1 Cor. 12 and 14, but not necessarily for 'sameness'.

[67]A.R. Brown, *The Cross and Human Transformation* (Minneapolis: Fortress, 1995), 150-7.

[68]Brown is conscious of stretching the point about the minor mention of ἀγάπη in 2:9c, see 122, n.43.

[69]The two types of power are interestingly placed side by side in 4:21: ἐν ῥάβδῳ ἔλθω πρὸς ὑμᾶς, ἢ ἐν ἀγάπῃ πνεύματί τε πραΰτητος;

[70] Cf the use of temple imagery in 2:16 and 6:19.

[71]O. Betz, "Der gekreuzigte Christus, unsere Weisheit und Gerechtigkeit (Der alttestamentliche Hintergrund von 1 Korinther 1-2)'" *Tradition and Interpretation in the New Testament: Essays in Honor of E.E. Ellis for his 60th Birthday*, eds. G.F. Hawthorne and O. Betz (Grand Rapids: Eerdmans, 1987), 195-215, claims that Paul reinterprets Old Testament texts such as Isaiah 43:3-23 and 52:13-53:12 to urge the principle and priority of an ethic of service on the Corinthian congregation. Brown, *Human Transformation*, esp. 80-97, also draws attention

to Paul's use of OT traditions (especially apocalyptic and prophetic) in his formulation of the 'word of the cross'. This Old Testament background is an important dimension of the origins of Paul's theologia crucis.

[72]E.g. H.K. Nielsen, "Paulus' Verwendung des Begriffes Δύναμις: Eine Replik zur Kreuzestheologie", *Die Paulinische Literatur und Theologie* (ed. S. Petersen; Aarhus: Vandenhoeck & Ruprecht, 1980), 137-58. Nielsen has correctly seen that Paul's *theologia crucis* concerns the use of power, but applies it only to the way God's power works: he fails to see its relevance to the power issues within the Corinthian church itself, and the way this theology counters such claims to power.

Part II

Luther's *theologia crucis* and
the Late Medieval Church

Six: Introduction

Luther's *theologia crucis* is not exactly virgin territory in modern theology. Ever since the Luther renaissance of this century, following the work of Karl Holl and his followers, and the rediscovery of important texts from Luther's early lectures, the theology of the cross has increasingly been recognised as a seminal theme in Luther's developing early theology. There remain however some intriguing questions connected with this important theme, not least concerning its sources and its use.

Despite the level of interest in the theme, the precise origins of Luther's theology of the cross remain obscure. Theo Bell has commented on how little research has been carried out into the sources of this theology in medieval theology and spirituality.[1] The origins of any trend in late medieval theology must be complex due to the sheer diversity of theological movements in the period, and the blurring of the lines between them,[2] yet this has remained a neglected area of study. The development of the idea against the background of late medieval theology has been well documented by Alister McGrath.[3] He shows how the *theologia crucis* gave Luther the theological method which, when applied to the issue of justification, produced the Reformation breakthrough. He also demonstrates convincingly the strong link between the *theologia crucis* and the subsequent theology of justification by faith. From this perspective, the theology of the cross is seen largely as a reaction against the soteriology of the *via moderna*, the particular school of late medieval theology in which Luther was trained, and a critique of medieval scholasticism in general. McGrath interprets this theology primarily as a repudiation of elements in the late medieval theological scene. Von Loewenich's book with the same title confined itself to an account of how the theme develops within Luther's own writings from the Heidelberg Disputation of 1518 onwards, a description and analysis of that theology, and a section on the influence of mysticism on the younger Luther. He mentions (only to refute) the older thesis that Luther's Ockhamism explains his *theologia crucis*,[4] but beyond this, not much attention is given to its earlier origins in Luther's background. McGrath traces the beginnings of the doctrine in Luther's early lectures on the Psalms, the *Dictata super Psalterium* of 1513-15, as the background to Luther's rediscovery of the Righteousness of God.[5] Although the last and briefest chapter of the book is entitled 'The Origins and Significance of the Theology of the Cross', McGrath's real interest lies in the relationship between this doctrine and the Reformation breakthrough, and Luther's intellectual background in the *via moderna*. As a result, there is little reflection on the sources of the doctrine other than this. The book describes the forces against which Luther's theology of the cross was in rebellion (i.e. Aristotelian scholasticism and the *via moderna*), but not where it found its weapons in the first place.

   This approach, which sees Luther's *theologia crucis* as a break from the late medieval theological tradition, is valid as far as it goes. It is potentially misleading however, if it is taken on its own. In this case, it might suggest that Luther's *theologia crucis* was purely a reaction to and repudiation of late medieval Catholicism. It needs to be supplemented by a different perspective, namely that his *theologia crucis,* while on the one hand representing a rejection of some elements of late medieval Catholicism, was at the same time a reassertion of other elements within that context. This is essentially what will be argued here. This section will in turn show how the *theologia crucis* was kept alive in aspects of popular devotion, apart from the controlling paradigms of theology, before Luther appropriated it into theological discourse. It will proceed to demonstrate how this theology resolved Luther's growing awareness of a fundamental contradiction between his own spiritual and theological origins, a dissonance between late medieval spirituality and theology which cried out for resolution.

Among the theological and spiritual influences which led Luther to his *theologia crucis* the Bible must of course take pride of place. Luther lectured on the books of Psalms, Romans, Galatians, and Hebrews during these early years, yet is has not often been recognised how much Luther turns to the passage in 1 Corinthians which we have just explored during these years as well. This resolution of Luther's theological and spiritual dilemma came at least partly through a reappropriation of the Pauline themes of 1 Corinthians 1 and 2, as we will hope to show in due course.[6]

Beyond the question of sources lies the notion of use. While the story of Luther's role in the emerging Reformation challenge to the papacy has been told again and again, the part which his theology of the cross played in his developing critique of the power of the papal church and the ideology which underlay it has not always been given the prominence it deserves. A final aim of this section will be to show how this "specific kind of theology"[7] served Luther in this task, and provided him with the resources for addressing not just his own dilemmas, but also the wider crisis of late medieval Christianity.

THE OUTLINES OF LUTHER'S *THEOLOGIA CRUCIS*

Before we proceed further with an investigation of the origins of Luther's theology of the cross, it as well to know what we are looking for, or at least how this theology looked in its developed form. This is not to pre-judge the issue, it is just to set down a marker which defines at least initially how this theology can be described.

Von Loewenich suggests that Luther's theology of the cross is marked by five features:

1.   The theology of the cross is a theology of revelation, as opposed to speculation.
2.   God's revelation is indirect and concealed.
3.   This revelation is recognised in suffering not in works.
4.   The God hidden in his revelation is known only by faith.
5.   God is known in the 'practical thought of suffering'.[8]

Useful as it is,[9] the drawback of such a list is that it fails to place these elements in relation to one another, or to give them any sense of sequence, whether logical or chronological. It also stresses heavily the theme of revelation, and fails to relate this to questions of soteriology, which were clearly so much on Luther's mind at the time this theology came into being. The theology of the cross is commonly thought to have received its most systematic expression in the 1518 Heidelberg Disputation,[10] and there are good reasons to turn there in order to construct an initial account of what this theology is for various reasons.[11]

First, the form of the Disputation, as opposed to Luther's exposition of Scripture lends itself to the clear, structured explanation of an idea, rather than allowing it to emerge incidentally from the study of Scripture. In Heidelberg, Luther was trying primarily to explain his theology, not to expound a text. Secondly, the historical circumstances of the event suggest that this was Luther's attempt to explain his ideas as clearly and persuasively as he could. This was a regular meeting of the chapter of the Augustinian Order, at which Luther as district vicar had to appear anyway. As such, it was a golden opportunity to present and test his theology further afield. Luther evidently saw it as a chance to spread Wittenberg theology beyond the university itself, and so attempted (with some success) to stimulate debate[12] and to win over a wider audience.[13] Thirdly, it comes as the climax of a number of works written between February and April 1518 which are permeated by the *theologia crucis*, the other three being the *Asterici Lutheri adversus Obeliscos Ecki*, the lectures on Hebrews,[14] and the *Resolutiones disputationum de indulgentiarum virtute*.[15] It therefore comes at the end of a period of sustained theological reflection on this theme, and invites us to treat it as a systematic explanation of Luther's *theologia crucis* in 1518.

Ole Modalsli read the Heidelberg theses as evidence of Luther's new understanding of the Righteousness of God, that God makes people righteous in Christ not progressively, but at once.[16] He claims that the distinction between law and gospel is the foundational structure of the work. While this is clearly an important theme in the theses, Modalsli does not consider nor account for the central theses 19-21, which most clearly oppose the *theologian of glory* to the *theologian of the cross*, an omission which leaves his account one-sided. While *iustitia dei* is not far from Luther's mind, the subtlety of his thought is not entirely captured by pressing it altogether into this mould.

At the heart of the theses are two parallel insights, one soteriological, the other epistemological.

1. The first is, as Modalsli implies, that *God condemns before he saves*.[17] The sinner must first be humbled, brought to a knowledge of his bankruptcy before God by the knowledge of his own sin, before God can begin to do anything with him.[18] The law is one of the prime ways in which God does this, and is dangerously misused if it is understood as a means of acquiring righteousness.[19] The experience of suffering and despair is the true teacher, not abstract speculation,[20] and suffering is to be preferred to works.[21] Humility therefore plays a crucial role in salvation.[22]

2. Related to this is the second insight, that *God chose to reveal himself at the Cross*, in humility, weakness and suffering.[23] God can be known only there,[24] yet this revelation is obviously the wrong way round. It is back to front, hidden, indirect and contrary to what might be expected. God's true virtues, his wisdom and justice, are now invisible to human eyes, hidden behind what he allows us to see, that is Christ's humanity, weakness and foolishness, expressed

most distinctly on the cross.[25] For this reason, faith, and not natural wisdom or reason is the only appropriate attitude towards God.[26]

When these two insights are combined, a reversal takes place: things are not what they seem, and appearance and reality are very definitely out of joint.[27] What seems to be weak, foolish and wasted, in reality is pricelessly valuable. The pathetic death of Christ on the cross is in fact the revelation of God, and the sufferings of the sinner under the judgement of God are God's mean of preparation for the reception of grace. Human goodness, wisdom, works and philosophy, which seem of such high value, are in fact worthless, empty, and even dangerous.

These two insights and the relationship between them will be explored more fully in due course. For the time being, they can be understood as the two fundamental structural principles behind the theology of the cross as it appears in the Heidelberg Disputation. In passing, it is worth noting at this stage the importance of the language and themes of 1 Corinthians 1:18-31 for Luther's development of these ideas. The themes of wisdom and foolishness, strength and weakness, and the paradoxical nature of the relationship between them in the light of the cross, are evident in Luther's presentation in Heidelberg, and resonate throughout the development of his *theologia crucis*.[28]

Luther had few pretensions to originality. He was conscious of standing in a long tradition of exegesis of Scripture and of reflection upon the cross. It is to that tradition that we turn next, to establish the theological background against which Luther's appropriation of the cross as a central theme of theology took place.

Notes:

[1]"...es wurde doch zu wenig nach den Quellen dieser Theologie in der mittelalterlichen Theologie und Frömmigkeit geforscht", T. Bell, *Divus Bernardus: Bernhard von Clairvaux in Martin Luthers Schriften* (von Zabern:

Mainz, 1993), 375.

[2]Cf. W.J. Courtenay, "Nominalism and Late Medieval Religion", *The Pursuit of Holiness in Late Medieval and Renaissance Religion*, eds. C. Trinkaus and H. Oberman (Leiden: Brill, 1974), 26-59, and A.E. McGrath, *The Intellectual Origins of the European Reformation* (Blackwell: Oxford, 1987), 1-31.

[3]A.E. McGrath, *Luther's Theology of the Cross* (Oxford: Blackwell, 1984).

[4]W. von Loewenich, *Luther's Theology of the Cross* (Belfast: Christian Journals, 1976), 65-77.

[5] McGrath, *Luther*, ch. 5.

[6]A.R. Brown, *Human Transformation*, 150-2, mentions in passing the role this passage played in the Heidelberg Disputation, but its influence in Luther's earlier work is less frequently noticed. See below.

[7]Von Loewenich, *Luther*, 19-22.

[8]Von Loewenich, *Luther*, 22.

[9]McGrath reproduces a similar list: *Luther*, 149-50.

[10]K. Bauer, "Die Heidelberg Disputation Luthers", *ZKG* 21 (1900), 233-68, 299-329.

[11] For a valuable contemporary account of the theology of the Heidelberg Disputation, see G.O. Forde, *On Being a Theologian of the Cross: Reflections on Luther's Heidelberg Disputation 1518* (Grand Rapids: Eerdmans, 1997).

[12]L. Grane, *Modus Loquendi Theologicus: Luthers Kampf um die Erneuerung der Theologie 1515-1518* (Leiden: Brill, 1975), 146.

[13]K. Bauer, *Die Wittenberger Universitätstheologie und die Anfänge der Deutschen Reformation* (Tübingen: Mohr/Siebeck, 1928), 53-7.

[14]For an account of the *theologia crucis* in the Hebrews lectures, see E. Ellwein, "Die Entfaltung der theologia crucis in Luthers Hebräerbriefvorlesung", *Theologische Aufsätze: Karl Barth zum 50. Geburtstag*, ed. E. Wolf (Münich: Kaiser, 1936), 382-404. He maintains that the *theologia crucis* runs "wie ein roter Faden" throughout the lectures (401).

[15]For a helpful examination of these four documents, see J. Vercruysse, "Luther's Theology of the Cross at the time of the Heidelberg Disputation", *Greg.* 57 (1976), 523-48.

[16]O. Modalsli, "Die Heidelberger Disputation im Lichte der evangelischen Neuentdeckung Luthers", (*LJB 47*, Göttingen: Vandenhoeck and Ruprecht, 1980), 33-9.

[17]Thesis 4: "*Dominus humiliat et perterrefacit nos Lege et conspectu peccatorum nostrorum*" (WA 1.356.37-8). Thesis 11: "*impossibile est in deum sperare, nisi de omnibus creaturis desperatur sciatque sibi nihil prodesse citra Deum posse*" (WA 1.359.20-2). Thesis 16: "*Sic opus alienum Die inducit tandem opus eius proprium, dum facit peccatorem, ut iustum faciat.*" (WA 1.361.4-5).

[18]Theses 18 and 24.

[19]Theses 1, 2, 3, 5, 7, 8, 9, 10, 23.

[20]Thesis 20, 22.

[21]Thesis 21, (WA 1.362.24).

[22]Thesis 4, WA 1.357.17: "*humilitas et timor Dei est totum meritum*". Thesis 8, WA 1.358.30-2; thesis 16, WA 1.360.38-361.5.

[23]Theses 19-21. e.g. "*voluit rursus Deus ex passionibus cognosci*". WA 1.362.6-7). Note firstly the perfect tense used, referring to God's historical revelation in Christ. Also, the LW (31.52) omission to translate *rursus* is misleading here: the text would surely be better rendered as "God wished to be known *backwards* in suffering."

[24]Thesis 21: "*Deum non inveniri nisi in passionibus et cruce.*" (WA 1.362.28-9).

[25]The 1519-21 *Operationes in Psalmos* would confirm this analysis. The most recent edition of Psalms 1-11(12) is *Operationes In Psalmos: Archiv zur Weimarer Ausgabe: Band 2, Teil 2*, eds. G. Hammer and M. Biersack (Köln: Böhlau, 1981). Quotations from these Psalms are taken from this edition (referred to here as AWA 2) and those from Psalms 12(13)-21(22) from Vol. 5 of the Weimar edition (WA 5). The *Operationes* are shot through with the *theologia crucis*. The dialectic between God's *opus alienum* and *opus proprium* is an essential part of its theological structure (Cf WA 5.503.26-8; AWA 2.97.20-4; 181.7-8; 300.2-4; 353.5-9; 559.20-1), it sustains a strong critique of appearance and the vital distinction between what is visible and what is invisible (AWA 2.106.28-107.13.), and gives an important place to experience in Christian theology (AWA 2.178.28-9. Cf. also AWA 2.317.7-9, 366.10-11, 559.4-5, WA 5.397.35-8).

[26]Thesis 25.

[27]Thesis 3 applies the divergence of appearance and reality to human works, thesis 4 to the works of God, thesis 21 to good and evil.

[28]For Luther's use of this section of 1 Corinthians, see for example in the *Dictata* WA 3.612.25-6, 646.23-4, 4.30-31. In the Romans commentary, WA 56.171.8-10, 173.21, 174.21, 371.26-7, 380.34-381.1, 393.7-8, 405.3, 471.13-14. In Hebrews, WA 57.122.15-19, 185.16-17, 210.18-19, 238.2-6. In Galatians, WA 2.544.23-25, 562.12-13. Examples of this usage will be explored further in due course, particularly in the later *Dictata*, and in the Romans commentary.

Seven: The Theology of the Cross in the Western Theological Tradition

Luther's theology of the cross emerged against a background of a long tradition of understanding of the cross in Western theology. Two central beliefs in that tradition combined to work against the development of a specific *theology* of the cross in the patristic and medieval periods: the impassibility of God, and the two natures doctrine in Christology. From a wide range of possibilities, three examples will suffice to illustrate this point.

TERTULLIAN

Tertullian was the first major theologian to speak of the '*Deus crucifixus*'. In *Adversos Marcianos* he writes:

> Our knowledge of God comes to us from the prophets and from Christ, not from the philosophers or from Epicurus... But well it is that Christians are allowed to believe that God has even died, and yet is alive forever... As you despise a God of that sort I wonder if

you do honestly believe that God was crucified *(nescio an ex fide credas deum crucifixum).*[1]

Tertullian thinks Marcion has an essentially Epicurean view of God, unmoved by anger or passion of any form, and this is the target of his polemic. He claims that God feels the passions of anger, love and so on, but not in the way that fallen human creatures do, in that he is not affected negatively by them as we are.[2] But does Tertullian really mean that God suffered and died? The reference to God dying in this passage is not picked up and developed, and in fact is incidental to the argument. Rather than the basis of a developed theology of the cross, it sounds much more like a rhetorical flourish to emphasise God's involvement through the incarnation in human experience. Marcion finds Tertullian's God unworthy, subject to too much passion. Tertullian asserts the opposite, that the incarnation speaks of the glory of God, as it was undertaken for the sake of human salvation. Marcion cannot bear the idea of a God who is so involved with humanity as to undergo death. Tertullian glories in it. Neither has significant implications for the knowledge of God.

The controversy with Marcion concerns the question of the nature of God, but while Tertullian can use this language it is clear that he ascribes the passion to God only by extension. Tertullian's statement[3] of the Christological problem has been described as that of "one living person, but two Things, possessing the attributes and displaying the activities of each several Thing, without confusion of the Things or division of him the Person".[4] Tertullian deliberately distinguishes between the humanity and the divinity in Christ,[5] and ascribes suffering to the human, not the divine nature, which can experience it only indirectly.

This point can be developed by an examination of Tertullian's employment of similar language in *De Carne Christi*:

Let them call it prudence that God was crucified *(deum crucifixum).* Yet wise you cannot be, except by becoming a fool in the world by believing the foolish things of God...
Your answer is now required... was not God truly crucified? *(nonne*

vere crucifixus est deus?).. did he not, as truly crucified, truly die?...

The Son of God was crucified: I am not ashamed - because it is shameful. *(crucifixus est dei filius: non pudet, quia pudendum est)* The Son of God died: it is immediately credible - because it is silly *(ineptum).*[6]

The view Tertullian addresses here is a form of Docetism which asserted Christ's flesh to be an illusion, and that therefore his sufferings were not real. In that case, Tertullian argues, Christian faith and hope would also become illusory and unreal. The function of the '*deus crucifixus*' terminology is not to assert suffering in God, nor to indicate that God works through weakness, but to establish the reality of Christ's sufferings, and therefore the reality of salvation. Salvation for Tertullian depends upon Christ's having assumed real humanity. For him the sufferings are crucial in that they demonstrate the reality of the human nature in Christ, which is essential if salvation is to be effective: "The powers of the Spirit of God proved him God, the sufferings proved there was the flesh of man."[7]

Tertullian uses startling and innovative language about God, but does not develop this language in any theologically significant way in his controversy with Marcion. He explicitly repudiates the idea of suffering in God in the dispute with patripassian Monarchianism. Praxeas is taken to task precisely because he 'crucifies the Father'. Tertullian replies with the assertion that "that which died was the nature which was anointed; in a word, the flesh... The Father was not associated in suffering with the Son."[8] Tertullian assumes without argument that God is impassible by nature. In reply to the Monarchian argument that the Father is a 'fellow-sufferer' with the Son, Tertullian replies: "Now if the Father is incapable of suffering, He is incapable of suffering with another."[9] Monarchianism was essentially an attempt to answer Christological and Trinitarian questions.[10] In his refutation of it, Tertullian also argues on Christological and Trinitarian grounds. He does so in the familiar patristic way by distinguishing the natures and ascribing suffering and weakness to the human side, not the divine. God is protected from the suffering of the cross, which as a result, has no particular *revelatory* function.

It may seem puzzling how Tertullian can imply suffering in God in the controversy with Marcion, but deny it so emphatically in the controversy with Monarchianism. The answer lies in his rhetorical training.[11] Barnes notes for example how when it suits him, Tertullian can stress the prosperity of the Roman world, yet at other times underline the gloomy hardship of life there.[12] This is what happens in his language concerning the cross. Against Marcion it suits him rhetorically to use such language as *deus crucifixus*; against the Monarchians, he avoids it. Out of the two, his understanding of God's involvement in the cross emerges more clearly in the anti-Monarchian language: suffering is the property of the human, not the divine nature.

ANSELM

The most influential of all medieval treatises on the cross was Anselm's *Cur Deus Homo*. Here, the cross is described primarily as satisfaction for sin, which is defined as the failure to pay God what is his due. God has humbled himself "because the human race - his very precious work - had utterly perished; and it was not fitting that God's plan for man should be completely thwarted".[13] The cross is the means by which Christ pays to God on behalf of humankind the satisfaction due to him after human sin. It effects the restoration of the original relationship with God.[14] It reveals little about the nature or character of the God who thus makes satisfaction. On the question of divine impassibility, Anselm is unequivocal:

> Without doubt we maintain that the divine nature is impassible (*impassibilem*)... when we maintain that God undergoes some lowliness or weakness, we understand this to be in accordance with the weakness of the human substance which he assumed, not in accordance with the sublimity of his impassible (divine) nature... We do not understand any abasement of the divine substance to

have occurred in the incarnation of God.[15]

Anselm here uses the familiar device of the patristic period, the attribution of the suffering of the passion to the human, not the divine nature. Any significant development here is in the realm of Anselm's understanding of the way the atonement works, not in the development of an understanding of God and his ways beginning from the cross.

This conclusion can be illustrated by a passage in Anselm's *Meditatio redemptionis humanae*, where he deals with the hiddenness of God in the passion of Christ.[16] Anselm considers Augustine's view that in the incarnation God concealed his divine power in order to deceive Satan.[17]

> But surely because it is disguised (*absconditum*) in weakness it is something hidden (*celatum*), because veiled in humiliation it is something concealed (*occultum*), because covered with contempt it is something inaccessible. O hidden (*abscondita*) might! A man appended to a cross suspends the eternal death impending over the human race... O concealed power!... O unseen strength!... Why did you veil such strength with such lowliness?[18]

Anselm argues on the contrary that God is no deceiver. The concealment of God is more apparent than real:

> For you did not assume a human nature in order to conceal (*operires*) what was known about you, but in order to reveal (*aperires*) what was unknown about you.. The hiddenness was unavoidable, not deliberate. The reason that the event occurred as it did was not in order to be hidden (*absconderetur*), but in order to be performed the right way.. If this event is called concealed (*occultata*), then it is called so only because it is not revealed to everyone.[19]

While the hiddenness of God in the passion of Christ becomes very significant for Luther's theology of the cross, Anselm sees no great theological significance in the notion. God has hidden his strength in the weakness of the cross purely because this was unavoidable in attaining the greater purpose of human salvation. The incarnation and crucifixion do not hide God in order to deceive Satan, as Augustine taught, nor was their intention to reveal anything significant about the way God relates to the world, as Luther later believed. For Anselm, God's hiddenness is not deliberate, whereas for Luther, it most definitely is. Anselm acknowledges the concept of the hiddenness of God in his work on the cross, but evacuates it of theological meaning.

AQUINAS

Moving from the 11th to the 13th century, Thomas Aquinas deals with the passion of Christ towards the end of his *Summa Theologiae*. The section entitled "The Passion of Christ" comes in the *Tertia Pars,* the section dealing with Christology, after the specifically theological concerns of the *Prima Pars*, and an analysis of the various aspects of the Christian life in the *Prima Secundae* and *Secunda Secundae*.[20] Already, this relegation of the subject to a comparatively late stage in the work, and firmly in the realm of Christology rather than theology, implies that the cross has no strong *theological* significance for Aquinas either. His understanding of the cross does not show very significant development from Anselm. In some ways their doctrines of the cross are very similar, particularly in their agreement as to the necessity of satisfaction for sin and the notion that dealing with sin was the prime reason for the incarnation.[21] Aquinas differs from Anselm however in two important respects.

First, God could conceivably have chosen ways of salvation other than the cross. Whereas for Anselm the death of Christ was *necessary* for the salvation of humanity, Aquinas stresses instead the freedom of God: "*Ergo non fuit necessarium Christum pati.*"[22] For Aquinas, the suffering of Christ was not necessary but fitting *(convenientius)*. It was fitting because it demonstrated the love of God for people, provided an example of obedience, humility and other virtues, merited justification (understood as the infusion of grace), was an incentive for refraining from sin, and lent humanity the dignity of the fact that a Man has overcome death and Satan.[23]

Because Aquinas sees the cross as merely contingent, it cannot play a theologically significant role in his thought. If God could have effected salvation in other ways, then the suffering of Christ is incidental rather than essential. It does not reveal anything about the nature or economy of God, but is instead a means to the greater end of salvation. Aquinas's reasons for the appropriateness of the cross concern its significance for people on the path of salvation, not its significance for an understanding of God. Even in the respect in which Aquinas differs from Anselm, he demonstrates no movement towards a theology of the cross.

Secondly, Aquinas does make limited use of the concept of the hiddenness of God in the passion of Christ.[24] When considering the question of whether Christ's passion should be attributed to his divinity, he deals more carefully than Anselm with the question of the divine/human nature of Christ. In line with his essentially Chalcedonian Christology,[25] he argues that "the passion is to be attributed to the divine person, not by reason of Christ's divine nature, which is impassible, but by reason of his human nature".[26] He goes on to cite Theodotus of Ancyra approvingly on the passion of Christ: "Hidden *(celabatur)* in it was that kingly WORD, by nature one who was born, and not merely uttered by man's tongue."

Aquinas does not share Anselm's embarrassment over the concept of God's concealment in the suffering of Christ, nor does he attribute the suffering solely to the human nature as Anselm does. Suffering pertains to the divine nature by virtue of its intimate union with the human nature. However, although Aquinas shows greater subtlety and more confidence than Anselm here, he still makes nothing of it theologically. There is no sign of an interest in the implications this might have for an understanding of God. While Denis Janz has emphasised the extent of agreement between Luther and Aquinas,[27] the presence or absence of the theology of the cross as a controlling factor in theological thought explains many of the differences between them, as we shall show in due course.

In these two major medieval understandings of the doctrine of the passion of Christ, there is no real interest in developing a theology of the cross. Both share the reticence of the patristic period in this area, due to an unwillingness to compromise the impassibility of God and the two natures doctrine of Christ which allowed the attribution of suffering to the human, not the divine nature.

The picture is similar through the late Middle Ages. Occasionally the subject is touched upon, but seldom developed. Hugolino of Orvieto in the Augustinian tradition at the beginning of the 15th century, for example, uses the phrase '*deus crucifixus*' in the course of his discussion of the *communicatio idiomatum* in his Commentary on the Sentences. He is clearly uncomfortable with it however, and does not enlarge upon it or employ it in a significant manner.[28] Medieval theology can be said to show as little interest in the theology of the cross as the patristic period.

This brief survey has shown that while from time to time patristic and medieval theologians showed interest in the *deus crucifixus*, yet they did not make a great deal of the theme theologically. Generally speaking, within the patristic and medieval theological tradition, the cross is contingent rather than necessary. There is a 'fittingness' about the cross as the means of salvation, but beyond that it has no particular significance for an understanding of God and how he works in the world. It is incidental for God's nature, not typical, characteristic or archetypal. Luther would have found little within this tradition to help him develop a *theology* of the cross. We turn now instead to traditions of spirituality and piety, which as we shall see, provided a much richer resource for his reflection.

Notes:

[1]Tertullian, *Adversus Marcionem* II.16, 27. (The translation here, and in all the sections quoted is taken from *Adversus Marcionem*, ed. and trans. E. Evans (Oxford: O.U.P., 1972).
[2]Cf. J.K. Mozley, *The Impassibility of God* (Cambridge: C.U.P., 1926), 37: "the divine nature *(substantia)* is free from all that is corruptible, and the divine feelings will have the same character."

[3]"Tertullian offers no 'solution' of the problem or mystery of the Incarnation, but merely a statement of it." E. Evans, *Tertullian's Treatise against Praxeas* (London: S.P.C.K., 1948), 74.

[4]Evans, *Tertullian's Treatise,* 74.

[5]*Adv. Mar.* II.16: "Discriminate between the natures, and assign to them their respective senses, which are as diverse as their natures require."

[6]All of these quotations from *De Carne Christi* V.

[7]*De Carne Christi* V.

[8]*Adv. Prax.* 29 (ANCL XV 402).

[9]*Adv. Prax.* 29 (ANCL XV 403).

[10]Modalist Monarchianism was "an attempt at a solution of the Logos-Christological problem". K. Baus, *Handbook of Church History Vol I: From the Apostolic Community to Constantine* (London: Burns & Oates, 1965), 256.

[11]T.D. Barnes, *Tertullian: A Historical and Literary Study* (Revised ed.; Oxford: Clarendon Press, 1985), 213.

[12]Ibid., 219: "Tertullian's erudition and technique can... both be viewed as a manifestation of the Second Sophist Movement."

[13]Anselm, *Cur Deus Homo: S. Anselmi Cantuarensis Archiepiscopi: Omnia Opera* (4 vols. ed. F.S. Shmitt; [Rome/Edinburgh: Nelson, 1938-6]) II.I.iv.8-10 (52).

[14]*Cur Deus Homo* book 1, (Anselm: Treatises Vol III, ed. & trans. J. Hopkins and H. Richardson, [Toronto: Edwin Mellen Press, 1976]), 130.

[15]*Cur Deus Homo* book I: *Omnia Opera* II,viii,18-28.

[16]Anselm, *Omnia Opera* III, 84-91.

[17]Cf. J. Hopkins: *A Companion to the Study of St. Anselm,* (Minneapolis: University of Minnesota Press, 1972), 190.

[18]Anselm, *Omnia Opera* III.,21-31.

[19]Anselm, *Omnia Opera* III.,36-42.

[20]3a. 46-52. The Latin and English translation together are found in *Thomas Aquinas: Summa Theologiae* Vol 54, ed. and trans. R.T.A. Murphy OP (London: Blackfriars/Eyre & Spottiswoode, 1965).

[21]Cf. B. Davies, *The Thought of Thomas Aquinas* (Oxford: Clarendon, 1992), 320-2.

[22]*Summa* 3a.46.1.

[23]*Summa* 3a.46.3.

[24]He also speaks of "the hidden plan *(occultam rationem)* of God's judgments" (*Summa* 3a.49.3), in allowing the devil to deceive men at certain times and places.

[25]Cf. R. Cessario OP, *The Godly Image: Christ and Salvation in Catholic Thought from Anselm to Aquinas* (Petersham, Mass.: St. Bede's, 1990), 19, 132-4. Also, Davies, *Thought,* 297-8.

[26]*Summa* 3a.46.12.

[27]D.R. Janz, *Luther on Thomas Aquinas: The Angelic Doctor in the Thought of*

the Reformer (Wiesbaden: Franz Steiner, 1989). See also D.R. Janz, *Luther and Late Medieval Thomism: A Study in Theological Anthropology* (Waterloo: Wilfred Laurier University Press, 1983).

[28]Cf. A.E.McGrath, "The Christology of Hugolino of Orvieto", *Schwerpunkte und Wirkungen des Sentenzkommentars Hugolins von Orvieto O.E.S.A.*, ed. W. Eckermann O.S.A, (Würzburg: Augustinus, 1990), 253-62, here, 261.

Eight: Luther's *Theologia Crucis* and Late Medieval Spirituality

Luther's *theologia crucis*, although original and startling in its love for paradox and hyperbole, still did not emerge out of thin air. As we have seen, there was not much promising material in the theological tradition behind Luther to encourage him in this direction. However it must always be remembered that before Luther was ever an academic, he was a monk, or more strictly, a friar. Luther grew up in the atmosphere of the extraordinary and wide-ranging array of late medieval piety, in both its lay and monastic forms. The century before Luther's revolt had witnessed not only the rise of a huge appetite for spiritual vitality among lay people, but also a good deal of millenarian speculation, interest in the prophetic and works of nationalist fervour, often with a marked anti-clerical tone, especially in Germany.[1] From the time of his schooling in Magdeburg, where he lodged with the Brethren of the Common Life,[2] through his experience at University in Erfurt, which was said to have housed over 800 monks,[3] on into his sudden entry into the Augustinian monastery in that city in September 1505, and his experience in that monastic house, Luther was surrounded by the atmosphere of the burgeoning spirituality of late medieval Europe.[4] The relationship between this outpouring of devotion and the Reformation movement is complex, and there is neither time nor space for an extensive inquiry into that relationship here.[5] Nevertheless, late medieval spirituality will naturally be an important area of investigation in the search for the origins for Luther's theology of the cross.

Late medieval piety cannot be understood apart from the increasing pace of social, economic, ecclesiastical and spiritual crisis in Europe from the 14th century onwards.[6] This of course resulted not only in the challenge to the papacy of conciliarism, but also in a range of movements impatient with the complex speculative theology of the 13th and earlier centuries. These movements often stemmed from a widespread and often Franciscan-inspired desire for the simplicity of an experience-centred Christian life as opposed to the seemingly fruitless disputes and confusion of authority in the Church of the Great Schism and Thomist theology.[7] In such movements, whether we have in mind the *devotio moderna*,[8] strands of mysticism such as represented by Eckhardt, Tauler or Gerson, or even in the spiritual writings of 'nominalists' such as Gabriel Biel, the ideal of *conformitas Christi*, understood as conformity to Christ's suffering pervades the piety of the period.[9]

LUTHER, BERNARD OF CLAIRVAUX AND THE CROSS

When commenting on Psalm 118(119):45 during his first set of Lectures on the Psalms, the *Dictata super Psalterium* of 1513-5, Luther introduced language which is reminiscent of his later writing on the theology of the cross:

> He crucifies and kills, so that he may revive and glorify. Thus he does a work that is foreign to him so that he may do his own work (*alienum opus eius ab eo, ut faciat opus suum*) (Is.28:21). As blessed Bernard correctly said, the divine consolation is delicate and is not given to those who grant access to an alien one. Therefore you must

be... found entirely in the cross and judgments on the old man if you want to walk at large according to the new man.[10]

This is one of the earliest references to the dialectic between God's own work (*opus suum*) and his alien work (*opus alienum*) in Luther's writings. He developed this contrast later in the context of his theology of the cross, and it is noteworthy that when he begins to explore these themes, Luther's mind turns to Bernard of Clairvaux.

On the shelves of the library in the Augustinian friary in Erfurt lay several works by Bernard of Clairvaux. The library carried at least a copy of the 1476-7 Augsburg edition of Bernard's *De Consideratione*, his sermons on the Song of Songs, and his *Sermones de tempore et de sanctis*.[11] Luther would have heard these works read over meals in the monastery,[12] most probably studied them himself in the library, and would have come across them again during his preparation for the priesthood, when reading Biel's *canonis missae expositio*.[13] In 1548 in his *Historia de vita et actis Lutheri*, Melancthon mentioned how an 'old man'[14] had counselled the anxious Luther by reminding him of a passage in Bernard's Sermon on the Annunciation, where he interprets the article in the Apostles' Creed on forgiveness to mean not general forgiveness of all men, but personal forgiveness of the individual's sins.[15]

Bernard of Clairvaux clearly exerted a significant influence upon Luther in his early years. It has frequently been pointed out that Luther saw in Bernard confirmation of many of the emerging themes of his theology, such as his growing distaste for the scholastic method, a close attention to scripture, and a critical evaluation of the papacy.[16] At times this influence has been overstated. The later Luther distanced himself from Bernard partly when Luther's Catholic opponents began to cite him in their favour,[17] and partly from a growing awareness of theological as opposed to spiritual differences between them, on issues such as monastic vows, the role of Mary, creation and justification, and the mass.[18] However, even the mature Luther continued to commend Bernard for his personal piety, even if he thought his theology lacking at various points.[19]

While the influence of Bernard on Luther has been explored in many different areas, the role of the Cistercian in the development of Luther's theology of the cross has seldom been examined.[20] It is nonetheless clear that Bernard's writings, especially his Sermons on the Song of Songs, from which Luther quotes frequently, played a significant role in Luther's increasing concentration on the cross as the central theme in theology in these vital early years. Four themes in particular can be identified in these sermons in particular which were important for Luther.[21]

1.   The sermons are full of a cross-centred piety. Echoing Augustine's view of the cross as both *sacramentum* and *exemplum*, the cross offers both forgiveness and an example to follow.[22] Meditation on the cross of Christ is highly beneficial, and the penitent is to meditate constantly on the cross of Jesus,[23] especially when troubled or anxious.[24]

2.   Sermon 61 refers to Exodus 33:22-23, where God denies Moses a sight of his face, but instead allows him a glimpse of his back as he passes by.[25] For Bernard, God's "back" represents his love shown on the cross, which sinners are allowed to see, rather than his glory and splendour, a vision of which is not permitted yet. In similar vein, God's anger hides his mercy.[26]

3.   The church is not to attempt to mimic God in his glory and majesty, but instead, in his humility and lowliness in Christ.[27] God has revealed himself in this particular form, and as such provides the precise example which the church and the Christian are to follow.[28]

4.   Bernard's spirituality stresses heavily the importance of humility in the Christian life. It is the virtue most prized by God,[29] emerges from the self-knowledge without which no-one can be saved,[30] and reaches its most perfect expression in the crucified Christ.[31] God sends the experience of humiliation and suffering as his means of bringing humility, which in turn brings grace,[32] and it is clear that for Bernard, God takes the initiative in humbling the proud.[33]

It is striking how many of these themes recur in Luther's developing theology of the cross. Luther's preoccupation with the cross in the years 1515-19 echoes Bernard's cross-centred piety. Bernard's idea that God reveals himself primarily in the weakness and suffering of the cross rather than in the glory and splendour of creation or wealth or power, and that the church and the Christian are to take the former as their model for imitation prefigures Luther's opposition of the *theologus crucis* to the *theologus gloriae* which we have noted in the Heidelberg Disputation. Bernard's citation of Exodus 33:22-3, the 'back' of God is a close parallel to Luther's use of the passage both in a gloss on Psalm 79(80):5[34], and more famously in the Heidelberg Disputation itself.[35] As we shall see, humility plays a central part both in late medieval monastic spirituality as a whole, and also in Luther's own early thinking, and Bernard would have provided a significant source for Luther's thinking about the topic, especially by his particular tendency to stress the divine initiative in humbling the sinner. In Bernard of Clairvaux's spiritual theology, the younger Luther found much that was congenial to his developing thought, not least some important themes connected with revelation. The ideas that God revealed himself primarily through the cross, carried out his work of salvation through the experience of suffering, humiliation and God's anger, and that the Christian is to be conformed to the image not of the glorious resurrected Christ but the suffering Christ, all fed Luther's emerging theology of the cross. They did so however in the context of a wider concentration on the cross in late medieval piety, to which we now turn.

THE CROSS IN LATE MEDIEVAL SPIRITUALITY

The Augustinian friars, whose monastery Luther joined in Erfurt in 1505 shared the widespread interest in meditating upon the sufferings of Christ.[36] This practice of meditation on the passion left behind a residue in a large number of printed works on this theme in 15th century religious literature. These recount the story of the passion in various forms, including imaginary conversations between Christ and his mother, interpretations of Old Testament stories as prefiguring the crucifixion, meditations inviting the penitent to picture the wounds of Christ in graphic detail, or the representation of the passion in visual terms on canvas, woodcuts or on church walls. In their theology, these meditations embody standard scholastic teaching on the necessity of Christ's death for salvation.[37]

Martin Elze emphasises features which these late medieval passion meditations have in common, while attempting to show how Luther differs from them.[38] He compares Jordan of Quedlinburg's (d.1370/80?) *De Passione Christi*, Ludolf of Saxony's (d.1378) *Vita Christi*,[39] and Aelred of Rievaulx's (d.1167) *De Institutis Inclusarum*. He draws attention to the way in which all these works presuppose a distinction between the inner and outer parts of human personality. The inner man is conformed to the suffering of Christ by *compassio,* while the outer man is conformed by *imitatio*.[40] The sufferings of Christ are seen almost exclusively as example (*Vorbild*) to be contemplated and followed.

In a similar vein, Berndt Hamm has described the prevalence of a type of spiritual theology (*Frömmigkeitstheologie*) at the beginning of the 16th century in Europe which, compared to scholastic theology, was more reflective and instructive in intention, aiming to shape the inner and outer life of the reader through its choice of themes and style.[41] This type of theology sought to reform Christian life as much as thought, and tried to bridge the gap between popular piety and academic scholastic theology, against which so much of 14th-15th century thought and piety was in revolt.[42] The centre and focus of Christian doctrine in this tradition was the question of the right and proper *vita Christiana*. A move such as the one the young Luther made in 1505 from the University into the monastery was therefore characteristic of the time.[43] Such theology was addressed either to the laity at large or to simple priests, preachers or confessors.

Hamm identifies two different strands within this tradition.[44] The first, which he calls '*der Weg nach Außen*' is represented by

Johannes von Paltz, whom, as we have seen, was a close contemporary of and known to Luther. The other, '*der Weg nach Innen*' is represented by Johannes von Staupitz, Luther's early mentor and immediate superior in the Augustinian order at Erfurt. The first of these strands, also identified in some of Luther's later Catholic opponents such as Tetzel, Wimpina and Prierias,[45] counters late medieval insecurity about salvation by directing the penitent to the objective guarantees of the sacramental life of the church. Ecclesiastes 9:1[46] was used frequently in late 15th century works of spirituality, because it expressed the difficulty of knowing whether one has done enough, or is properly penitential enough to be sure of salvation.[47] In face of this uncertainty, von Paltz wants to lead the sinner away from subjective guarantees towards what he sees as the firmer ground of the Papal church. The sinner has to begin by doing what lies within her, by her own natural powers, flee to the sacraments, and the institutional guarantees of the church will do the rest. This all rests on the *facere quod in se est* of the soteriology of the *via moderna*.

Biel and von Paltz are more agreed than is sometimes thought on the question of what this *quod in se est* consists of,[48] and they have no obvious disagreement on the question of the smallness of the movement required. The penitent must flee to the sacraments of the church which are able to fan the flame of this weak love for God into something stronger and more robust. This is perfectly in line with Biel's soteriology where an initial good act produced without the help of grace is accorded merit *de congruo*, according to the covenant (*pactum*) which God has ordained *de potentia ordinata*. This grace then enables a person to perform acts which are meritorious on their own terms, worthy of merit *de condigno*.[49] This confirms both von Paltz's agreement with Biel, and the prevalence of such spiritual theology in the circles inhabited by von Paltz's young colleague in Erfurt from 1505-1507, Martin Luther.

Besides their soteriology, when it comes to meditation on the passion of Christ, von Paltz and Biel share many features in common, particularly in the sacramental focus of such meditation.[50] Biel's understanding of the cross, like that of von Paltz, stresses its objective character as satisfaction. As Oberman puts it: "There is with Biel also a theology of the cross but this is limited to a discussion of the objective work of Christ through his self-sacrifice and his victory over the devil."[51] Biel's understanding of the passion of Christ and how it works in the life of the Christian is summarised in his *Sermones de festivitatibus Christi*: "To heal the wounds inflicted by our sins, He, through the effusion of his blood, earned efficacy for the sacraments."[52] The death of Christ effectively wins the remission of sins, which is channelled to the Christian through the sacraments. As Oberman has shown, while keeping within an Anselmian framework, Biel pictures the passion of Christ not so much in its Godward direction as an offering to God by Christ on behalf of men, but rather as an offering from God to men of a path leading to the goal of salvation. His pastoral advice consisted of: "*Nullum cruce christi contra diaboli insidias compendiosius et efficacius antidotum*".[53] Oberman points out how the cross here is understood in the sense of *Christus Victor*: if the believer meditates on and comes to imitate the obedience of Christ in his suffering, he will in turn share the benefits of Christ's victory over sin, the devil and hell. Like von Paltz, Gabriel Biel's passion meditation is sacramentally anchored and focused.

The other strand which Hamm describes, associated with von Staupitz, Johannes Lang, Karlstadt, Wenceslaus Linck, Spengler and even Luther himself, is less interested in the objective guarantees of the institutional church, but concentrates more upon the unmediated subjective relationship of the individual soul to Christ. The interiorisation of the process of penitence and forgiveness stems from Gerson and the *devotio moderna*, and stresses the internal experience of penitence, grace and forgiveness without the necessity of aid from the institutional church. This naturally has affinities with the picture of passion meditation which Elze has painted, in the sense that the passion works in a direct manner upon the individual, rather than indirectly through the sacraments. Aelred of Rievaulx, for example, towards the end of his treatise on guidance for a female recluse, while recommending contemplation of, among other things, Christ's life and sufferings, extols the benefits of meditation, particularly on the cross:

> ...meditation will arouse the affections, the affections will give birth to desire, desire will stir up tears.. until you appear in his sight and say to him... "My Beloved is mine and I am His."[54]

The purpose of meditation on the passion is this arousal of feeling leading firstly to inner compassion, which in turn leads to an external conformity to Christ.[55] In other words, Christ died in order that people might contemplate him, imitate him and become like him. This kind of meditation on the cross was common across Europe, from the standard piety of late medieval England[56] to the early 15th century *De Imitatione Christi* of Thomas à Kempis, within the tradition of the *devotio moderna*. Here again, Christ is said to have "died for you, so that you too should carry your cross, and long for a death on the cross".[57] Christ's offering of himself in the mass is to be met with the disciple's offering of himself to God in return. Such a spirit of self-offering is to be evoked by the careful meditation of Christ's self-offering on the cross.[58] The point was to arouse an emotional involvement with Christ's sufferings, to weep for them along with the first century disciples: "Christ's wounds and anguish are magnified in order to evoke the believer's compassionate response to the agonies he endures."[59]

When we turn back to the Augustinian monastery in Erfurt, it is clear that both of these types of meditation on the passion were found there. Both von Paltz and Staupitz were influential figures in the Erfurt Augustinian house during Luther's time there, so he would have been aware of both of these types of devotion, both focusing upon the cross as their central theme. Incidentally, this must make us cautious about speaking of one single Augustinian 'school' or 'theology' of which Luther was an automatic inheritor.[60] Staupitz's influence on Luther is a clear signal of the type of meditation Luther was drawn to, but it is clear this was not the only or automatic choice for him.[61]

From this discussion, two points can be made.

First, despite the differences between these approaches to spirituality, both leant heavily upon the practice of meditation on the cross of Christ. For Staupitz, the experience of suffering could be made profitable only by meditation on the suffering of Christ, so that the whole life of the Christian could be described as an imitation of the composure *(Gelassenheit)* of Christ in his sufferings. The centre of this spirituality of imitation was contemplation of the cross, so that the Christian was intended to recapitulate in his own life the events of Christ's passion.[62] Staupitz's pastoral advice to Luther recommended the value of focusing attention upon the wounds of Christ in the experience of temptation and anxiety.[63] Staupitz saw the effect of meditation on the crucified Christ as working directly on the believing soul, bringing consolation and relief.

Von Paltz urged similar meditation on the suffering of Christ as a daily practice.[64] Unlike Staupitz or Ludolf of Saxony's *Vita Christi* however, he did not urge meditation on the suffering of Christ with the aim of arousing imitation of Christ's sufferings in the inner life of the believer; his was the more objective approach. By contemplating the soteriological efficacy of the passion, mediated by the sacraments of penance and absolution as well as through indulgences, the believer was to be reassured as to the value of those very sacraments. The sacraments were a means of moving the believer towards the crucial goal of a true penitence. The passion of Christ did not have a direct impact on the soul, but worked effectively through the objective use of the sacraments.[65]

Secondly, if we can speak of a widespread interest in meditation on the suffering of Christ throughout late medieval piety, we must at the same time speak of a variety in the uses to which such meditation was put. For some, it was a way of approaching the sacraments in the right spirit, for others it directed the believer to the objective efficacy of the institutional church's penitential system. For others again it was commended as having a direct effect upon the soul, and to that extent might operate quite independently of the 'external' guarantees of the Papal Church.

We may in fact speak of two broad types of passion meditation. One had its focus in the death of Christ as achieving objective satisfaction for sins, represented by, for example von Paltz and to a certain extent in the *Christus Victor* sacramental theology of Gabriel Biel. In this kind of meditation, the passion of Christ was to be contemplated in order to strengthen faith in the efficacy of the sacraments. It therefore had a specifically ecclesiastical focus, and in a sense, led people back to the safe haven of the institutional papal church, as the guardian and dispenser of the sacraments through which grace came. It was frequently linked to a 'nominalist' type of soteriology which utilised the *facere quod in se est* familiar in the *via moderna*. This type could be called *Objective Sacramental Meditation*.

The other kind was that found for example in Aelred of Rievaulx in the 12th century, Jordan of Quedlinburg, Ludolf of Saxony, the *devotio moderna* in the 14th century, and Johannes von Staupitz at the beginning of the 16th century. This had as its primary function the imitation of Christ by the arousal of internal *compassio* for the sufferings of Christ followed by external *imitatio* of his patience and forbearance. Christ died that we might follow his example. This tended to operate in conjunction with but not so closely tied to the official sacramental life of the church. This type might be termed *Subjective Imitational Meditation*.

LUTHER AND MEDITATION UPON THE CROSS

On March 13th 1519, Luther wrote to Spalatin that he was "planning a treatise dealing with meditation on Christ's passion".[66] The letter gives a glimpse of Luther's frantic busyness in lecturing and preaching in this period of his life, so much so that he did not have time to translate his exposition of the Lord's Prayer into Latin. He did make time however to plan this treatise on meditation on the Passion, which perhaps shows how important he felt it was.

Finally published on 5th April of the same year, this became the *Sermon von der Betrachtung des heyligen leydens Christi.* The work surveys the different styles of contemporary passion meditation, from the type which concentrates on blaming the Jews, to those which use mementoes of the passion (crosses, pictures, relics etc.) as talismans to protect the faithful from harm. More significantly, Luther writes of those who "feel pity for Christ, lamenting and bewailing his innocence".[67] Luther complains of the excessive length and tedious quality of these exercises, and he clearly has in mind the "subjective imitational" style of meditation identified above. He goes on to mention those whose meditation directs them to the mass as an end in itself, which again sounds like a distinct reference to the "objective sacramental" type of meditation. Not surprisingly, given the variety of styles of meditation on the cross he would have experienced at Erfurt and elsewhere, Luther shows awareness of these different types of meditation, before suggesting how such meditation should be carried out. For Luther meditation on the passion is meant to impress upon the sinner the gravity of his sin which sent Christ to the cross. It is meant to "terrify", crucifying the old self, and as such, Luther suggests, is an immensely valuable exercise. He writes how "this meditation changes man's being and almost like baptism, gives him a new birth".[68] Significantly, Bernard of Clairvaux is cited as an example of one whose contemplation of Christ on the cross brought home to him the depth of his own sin.[69] Rather than the usual route of entry into the labyrinth of the medieval penitential system, Luther now recommends simply casting those sins upon the crucified Christ, firmly believing the words of promise that they are paid for by Christ's sufferings. From there, the believer is to pass on from meditation on the cross, to contemplate the loving heart of God in Christ. The final stage is when the sinner's passive and helpless submission to God is replaced by the active modelling of life upon the cross of Christ, a constant awareness of the triviality of human sufferings compared to those of Christ, and a willing and cheerful endurance of such sufferings.

Around this period, of 1518-19, Luther's writings mention meditation on the passion several times. In the Hebrews Lectures, probably in the early months of 1518, he again writes of those who meditate on Christ's passion, in a way which is critical of contemporary practice, insisting instead that the purpose of such exercises is the increase of faith that Christ's blood was shed for one's own sins.[70]

In two Good Friday Sermons,[71] probably to be dated in 1518[72] Luther again turns to the right way to meditate upon the cross.[73] Here again, Luther heartily approves of meditation on the cross if it leads to a firmer sense that Christ's sufferings were undertaken 'for me', not just as *exemplum*, but also as an objective *sacramentum*, to use Augustine's terms.[74] Sorrow and sympathy is directed not at Christ's sufferings, but for one's own sin. Passion meditation is the art of "reading oneself in Christ".[75] Rather than the contrast between the *affectus* (inner) and the *effectus* (outer) aspects of his type of piety, commonly to be found in such works, Luther contrasts the *affectus* with the *intellectus*,[76] favouring an inner emotional engagement with the sufferings of Christ over a dry objective intellectual detachment. Here, Luther's view of passion meditation develops into a critique not just of late medieval patterns of piety, but also of scholastic theology which for him, failed to feel the effect of the cross pressing home a sense of sinfulness and unworthiness.

Thus Luther shows how he thinks Passion meditation should work. He certainly does not reject its use, but he does want to rethink its purpose. When he considers current practice, Luther approves of its concern for emotional engagement with the passion of Christ and its stress on the objective value of what Christ has done on the cross, but these two are re-directed. The emotion generated by meditation on the cross is not to take the form of sorrow for Christ or anger at his enemies. Rather it is to lead to a profound sorrow for one's own sin which placed him there. Similarly, the objective achievement of the cross is not to direct the penitent to the mass as an end in itself. Instead it is to lead to faith in the word which tells that the death of Christ is the payment for sin, and offers forgiveness. It culminates eventually in thankfulness and joy for God's grace, and a life conformed to the bearing of suffering like Christ.

Luther's familiarity with such types of meditation has clearly led him to some important themes in his developing theology, and in particular to his theology of the cross. The work of the cross as provoking despair over one's own sin, the value of suffering, the preference for experience over speculation (*affectus* over *intellectus*), the need for identification with the sufferings of Christ, the role of faith as the appropriate mode of knowledge of God, all of these are key ideas in the emerging theology of the cross. Each of these three texts appears to have been on Luther's mind in and around 1518-19. The "Meditation on Christ's Passion" was being planned in March 1519, and appeared in print just before Luther's *Operationes in Psalmos*, a work permeated by the theology of the cross.[77] The Hebrews lecture was probably given in early 1518, and the two Good Friday sermons preached on April 2nd 1518. Luther set out on foot for the Heidelberg Disputation, in which he explains the theology of the cross most clearly, just a week later. This is a period in Luther's life when the theology of the cross crystallised in his mind, and it is precisely this period in which he brings to mind memories of the practice of passion meditation. Such meditation reminded him of the significance of the cross in providing satisfaction for sin, and the importance of emotional, not just academic appreciation of Christ's sufferings. In the emergence of the theology of the cross, this feature of late medieval spirituality clearly played a vital role.

JOHANNES VON STAUPITZ

Besides the traditions we have been exploring, several other influences are often mentioned as shaping Luther's early theology of the cross. Luther himself frequently indicates his debt to Staupitz, his superior in the Augustinian order in connection with the significance of the cross and suffering,[78] and the elder man's practical-spiritual theology clearly affected Luther's thinking.[79]

David Steinmetz, in two significant works,[80] has drawn attention to the importance Staupitz placed on predestination focused in the wounds of Christ, as the pledge of the fidelity of God to his promises.[81] For Staupitz, sufferings come from God as he permits Christians to fall into sin, leading to despair of self and imitation of the *'Gelassenheit'* of Christ on the cross.[82] Luther seems to have found several aspects of Staupitz's teaching particularly consolatory,[83] namely the idea that true penance begins rather than ends with the love of God,[84] that one needs to avoid trust in one's own natural powers, the usefulness of temptation and *Anfechtung*,[85] and in particular the value of turning to the crucified Christ when suffering anxiety over election.[86] Steinmetz concludes that Luther shows a large degree of independence from his teachers and superiors, and that Staupitz's influence upon him was primarily pastoral, rather than theological.[87] Staupitz was, alongside general late medieval passion-centred piety, clearly a seminal figure in turning Luther's mind to the cross as the central theme of consolation within the structure of a theology that was at once academic and pastoral.

GERMAN MYSTICISM[88]

Traces of the emerging *theologia crucis* have often been discerned in various strands of late medieval mysticism,[89] especially in the works of Johann Tauler, whom Luther frequently quotes favourably from around 1516 onwards.

Earlier scholars saw Luther as an enthusiastic advocate of German mysticism, although more recently this has been increasingly questioned. Instead it is more commonly thought that while Luther used mystical terminology, he clearly filled that language with his own meaning. He reinterpreted mystical language to such an extent that it no longer counts as properly 'mystical'.[90] Others still argue for strong connections between the early Luther and German Mystics.[91] Oberman sums up the argument: "Reformation scholarship has reached no consensus concerning whether or not Luther ought to be called a mystic."[92] The comparative lateness of Luther's contact with the German mystics would suggest they were a confirmation rather than a source of the theology of the cross.[93] Luther encountered Tauler relatively late in the early stages of his career.[94] Luther discovered German mysticism as a forgotten but rich backwater of medieval thought. It is unlikely however, that it took much part in his theological training much before 1516.[95] Moreover, recent studies have emphasised how the motivation behind events such as the publication of the *Theologia Deutsch* in 1516 and 1518 was as much political as it was spiritual. Luther was keen to show that the developing Wittenberg theology had roots in genuinely *German* piety, and was therefore continuous with a long and respectable German tradition.[96] As will be argued below, much of Luther's theology of the cross was in place towards the end of his first lectures on the Psalms in 1515. When compared to Bernard of Clairvaux and the monastic piety of Luther's youth, German mysticism simply arrives too late to have had a decisive influence on the origins of his theology of the cross. Luther simply found congenial ideas in these mystics, a theology which stressed experience, the need for self-abandonment before God's will, the initiative of God, passive suffering, and the hiddenness of God. For Luther, such mystical language however always had a strictly *Christ*ological, rather than *theo*logical meaning, as it did for the German mystics. It referred not to the being of God, hidden in mystery, but to the hidden form of his revelation in Christ.[97]

CONCLUSION

The theological tradition represented by Tertullian, Anselm and Aquinas, while occasionally using language which indicated the significance of the cross for the understanding of God, held back from developing a full *theologia crucis*. It is not to these theological traditions that we must look for the origins of Luther's theology of the cross, but rather to late medieval popular and monastic spirituality, particularly the personal piety of Bernard of Clairvaux and the practice of meditation on the passion of Christ. Hitherto, studies on the theology of the cross have tended to concentrate on its theological sources, or at least those theological trends against which Luther was reacting.[98] Luther's training in the soteriology of the *via moderna* under his nominalist tutors in Erfurt, Jodocus Trutfetter and Bartholomäus Arnoldi von Usingen has been described well in these works.[99] In comparison, the important role that more popular spiritual and religious traditions played in the emergence of this theology has gone relatively unnoticed. While it is correct to stress Luther's emerging theology as a break from late medieval theology, it must also be remembered that this theology emerged from these more popular spiritual traditions as well. The *theologia crucis*, and the Reformation theology which emerged from it, was not a complete repudiation of the late medieval scene, but flowered from particular elements within it.

Popular and monastic piety, the spiritual air which Luther breathed, was a distinctive form of cross-centred spirituality which prized humility above all virtues, and emphasised direct emotional engagement with the crucified Christ. In the common practice of passion meditation and the monastic theology of St. Bernard, Luther learnt that God directs the sinner to meditation on the cross and the 'back' of God, that suffering works the purposes of God in humbling the sinner and producing constant repentance, and that God often works in an unexpected way to achieve his final purpose of salvation.

This chapter has shown how many of the elements of Luther's *theologia crucis* lay within these late medieval spiritual traditions. It has also begun to shed light on the beginnings of the process by which he came to question commonly accepted notions. As we saw above, a distinction between piety and theology is helpful at this point. What Luther gained from late medieval monastic and popular Christian life was not so much theology, but spirituality. Luther's increasing divergence from *theological* aspects of these traditions, whether in the practice of passion meditation, Bernard or mysticism, shows that division very clearly.

From time to time in these early years, Luther would describe a sense of being at war within himself.[100] This internal conflict was at least in part, a conflict between this late medieval popular spiritual tradition and the theology which co-existed alongside it. On the one hand, the kind of piety learnt from Bernard and the monastic life taught Luther to examine his sins constantly, to despair of himself, and to value suffering as God's way of making him humble. The cross was primarily an example of this humility and penitence. On the other hand, the theology he had learnt from Gabriel Biel among others,[101] taught him to value works of contrition, penance, indulgences, masses and confession. It taught him to view his humility as an active virtue, on the basis of which God would supply grace, as he tried to love God above all else, in other words, doing *quod in se est*. As a result, inside the young Luther, a spirituality of self-accusation lived uneasily alongside a theology of self-justification. What his spirituality told him to accentuate, his own helplessness before God, his theology told him to deny. It has sometimes been suggested that it was Luther's individual and abnormal experience which sparked of his disagreement with the church and theology of the late middle ages.[102] More probably, it was the spirituality which he had learnt from Bernard and meditation on the cross which was at odds with the theological resources available to interpret it. Due to this conflict, theological notions such as *iustitia dei*,[103] the penitential system,[104] even the idea of cross as an example to be followed, which were intended as consolatory, became terrifying to him.[105] Luther found in them only uncertainty and despair over his ultimate salvation, rather than the security he craved, because they set before him a standard of holiness which his spirituality taught him he could never achieve. Luther found himself caught between a spirituality and a soteriology which he increasingly felt to be mutually incompatible.

One of these had to make way, and it was the soteriology of the *via moderna* which was finally cast aside. Yet Luther was no uncritical adherent of this cross-centred piety. He resolved this conflict by a *theological reworking of late medieval spirituality*. Some elements of this spirituality were rejected, yet other elements, as we have seen, helped him to move beyond it. In reworking these spiritual traditions and practices, he took them far beyond both the *via moderna*, and even the *via antiqua* of the Thomists, who had held the line against the synergistic soteriology of much late medieval theology. This response was in fact the development of the theology of the cross. Luther's *theologia crucis* can therefore be understood in part at least, as a revolt of popular and monastic piety against the dominant privatised speculative theology of late medieval scholasticism. His theology of the cross, which is closely related to his Reformation breakthrough, was indeed a break from, yet at the same time in an important sense continuous with significant elements of popular late medieval religion. How it emerged and in which ways it developed the distinctives of that tradition is the subject of the next chapter.

Notes:

[1] For an account of this type of literature in the century before Luther, see A.G. Dickens, *The German Nation and Martin Luther* (London: Fontana: 1976), 1-20.
[2] M. Brecht, *Martin Luther: His Road to Reformation 1483-1521* (Philadelphia: Fortress, 1985), 15-17.
[3] Ibid., 26.
[4] For a fine one-volume account of this on its own terms, which represents it as "vital and progressing" (342) on the eve of the Reformation, see R.N. Swanson, *Religion and Devotion in Europe, c.1215-c.1515* (Cambridge: C.U.P., 1995).
[5] See G. Lottes, "Luther und die Frömmigkeitskrise im Spätmittelalter", *Luther in seiner Zeit*, ed.s M. Greschat and G. Lottes (Stuttgart: Kohlhammer, 1997), 13-28, for an exploration of the relationship between these two phenomena.
[6] A useful account of these changes and the state of religious life before the Reformation are found in F. Oakley, "Religious and Ecclesiastical Life on the Eve of the Reformation", ed. S. Ozment, *Reformation Europe: A Guide to Research* (St. Louis: Center for Reformation Research, 1982), 5-32.
[7] See for example H.A. Oberman, "Fourteenth Century Religious Thought: A Premature Profile", and "The Shape of Late Medieval Thought", in *The Dawn of the Reformation: Essays in Late Medieval and Early Reformation Thought* (Edinburgh: T. &. T. Clark, 1986), 1-38. Also, A.E. McGrath, *Intellectual Origins,* 9-28.

[8]On this, see R.R. Post, *The Modern Devotion: Confrontation with Reformation and Humanism* (SMRT 3; Leiden: Brill, 1968).

[9]A more detailed treatment of some of the themes in this chapter is found in G. S. Tomlin, "The Medieval Origins of Luther's Theology of the Cross", *ARG* 89 (1998), 22-40.

[10]WA 4.331.13-18. (LW 11.451)

[11]J. Matsuura, "Restbestände aus der Bibliotek des Erfurter Augustinerklosters zu Luthers Zeit und bisher unbekannte eigenhändige Notizen Luthers", *Lutheriana: Zum 500. Geburtstag Martin Luthers von den Mitarbeitern der Weimarer Ausgabe* (AWA 5; Köln: Böhlau, 1984) 318, 324, 326. Cf. also Bell, *Divus Bernhardus*, 28.

[12]B. Lohse, *Mönchtum und Reformation: Luthers Auseinandersetzung mit dem Mönchsideal des Mittelalters* (FKDG 12; Göttingen: Vandenhoeck & Ruprecht, 1963), 137ff.

[13]Bell, *Divus Bernhardus*, 31; Oberman, *Harvest*, 5, 141.

[14]Perhaps Staupitz, or even Johann von Grefenstein, Luther's confessor in the monstery, see H. Boehmer, *Martin Luther: Road to Reformation* (Cleveland: Meridian, 1946), 40-1.

[15]Cf. E. Kleineidam, "Ursprung und Gegenstand der Theologie bei Bernhard von Clairvaux und Martin Luther", *Dienst der Vermittlung. Festschrift zum 25-jahrigen Bestehen des philosophisch-theologischen Studiums in Priesterseminar Erfurt*, eds. W. Ernst, K. Feiereis and F. Hoffmann (Leipzig: St. Benno, 1977), 221-47. Cf. also Bell, *Divus Bernhardus*, 33.

[16]See A.H. Bredero, *Bernard of Clairvaux: Between Cult and History* (Edinburgh: T. & T. Clark, 1996), 173-4.

[17]T. Bell, "Pater Bernardus. Bernard de Clairvaux par Martin Luther", *Citeaux* 41 (1991), 233-55.

[18]B. Lohse, "Luther und Bernhard von Clairvaux", *Bernhard von Clairvaux: Rezeption und Wirkung im Mittelalter und in der Neuzeit*, ed. K. Elm (Wiesbaden: Harrassowitz, 1994), 271-301. The article clarifies some of the differences between the mature Luther and Bernard, and includes a useful bibliography of work on the relationship between the two.

[19]Ibid., 294.

[20]For example, F. Posset, "Divus Bernardus: Saint Bernard as Spiritual and Theological Mentor of the Reformer Martin Luther", *Bernardus Magister: Papers presented at the Nonacentenary Celebration of the Birth of Saint Bernard of Clairvaux*, ed. J.R. Sommerfeldt (Spencer MA: Cistercian Publications, 1992), 517-32, points out several areas where Luther's thought has been touched by Bernard's, but fails to identify his influence on the Reformer's theology of the cross.

[21]For more detail on the following, see Tomlin, "Medieval Origins", 31-6.

[22]Sermon 43.(III).4, Vol.II (223). The quotations in this section are taken from the English Translation of the sermons, *Bernard of Clairvaux: On the Song of*

Songs (Cistercian Fathers Series No. 7; trans. K. Walsh OCSO; Kalamazoo: Cistercian Publications, 1976). The numbers in brackets are page numbers from this edition.

[23]Sermon 61.(III).7, Vol.III (146).

[24]Sermon 43.(III).5, Vol.II (224). Cf. also Sermon 62.(IV).6,7, Vol.III (157-8).

[25]Sermon 61.(III).6-7, Vol.III (146).

[26]Sermon 42.(II).4, Vol.II (213). Cf. also Sermon 23.(V).14, Vol.II (38), and 23.(VI).16, Vol.II (40).

[27] Sermon 62.(III).4-5. Vol III, (155-6).

[28]*De Gradibus Humilitatis et Superbiae*, ET VII.21, (48-50)

[29]Sermon 42.(VI).9, Vol.II (218).

[30]Sermon 37.(1), Vol.II (181).

[31]Sermon 42.(V).8, Vol.II (216).

[32]Sermon 34:4, Vol.II (163).

[33]Sermon 34.1, Vol II, (161).

[34]WA 3.604.34-9: *"Et sic Christum ut hominem videre est posteriora seu dorsum eius videre. Ut deum autem, est faciem eius videre"*. The same idea is present in WA 3.617.9.

[35]Thesis 20, WA 1.354.19-20.

[36]M. Nicol, *Meditation bei Luther* (FKDG 34; Göttingen: Vandenhoeck & Ruprecht, 1984), 32-3, notes that von Paltz's *Coelifodina* cites the use of such meditation in the Order. Von Paltz lived in the Erfurt Augustinian house with Luther for two years, before moving on to become prior of Mühlheim in 1507.

[37]K. Ruh, "Zur Theologie des mittelalterlichen Passionstraktats", *ThZ* 6 (1950), 17-39.

[38]M. Elze, "Das Verständnis der Passion Jesu im Ausgehenden Mittelalter und bei Luther", *Geist und Geschichte der Reformation: Festgabe H. Rückert*, eds. H. Liebling and K. Scholder (Berlin: Walter de Gruyter, 1966), 127-51.

[39]This work was first printed at Strasbourg and Cologne in 1474 and soon became very popular. Thus it provides a good example of the kind of passion meditation in circulation on the eve of the Reformation.

[40]Ruh, *Passionstraktats*, confirms the basic aim of these meditations as *compassio* and *imitatio*.

[41]B. Hamm, *Frömmigkeit am Anfang des 16. Jahrhunderts: Studien zu Johannes von Paltz und seinem Umkreis* (BHT 65; Tübingen: Mohr/Siebeck, 1982), 133.

[42]Martin Elze also draws attention to this kind of *Frömmigkeitstheologie* in "Züge spätmittelalterliche Frömmigkeit". In particular he stresses how distinct this was from the mystical path: "Man muß jedenfalls von einer Einwirkung der spämittelalterlichen ganz unmystischen Frömmigkeit sprechen." (395).

[43]Hamm, *Frömmigkeitstheologie*, 139.

[44]Ibid., 222-47.

[45]Ibid., 246.

[46]"But all this I laid to heart, examining it all, how the righteous and the wise and their deeds are in the hands of God; whether it is love or hate man does not know."

[47]Ibid., 224 and H.A. Oberman, *The Harvest of Medieval Theology: Gabriel Biel and Late Medieval Nominalism* (Cambridge, Mass.: Harvard, 1963) ch. 5.

[48]Hamm suggests that von Paltz's understanding of *facere quod in se est* is not quite the same as that of Gabriel Biel. While according to Biel, it comprises contrition and a love for God above all other things, von Paltz reduces this to a minimum, indicating that the smallest movement of the heart in love towards God is enough to meet this requirement *Frömmigkeitstheologie, 253-7.* Oberman suggests however that Biel also holds to a similar view that even the smallest motion of love towards God is enough, so that Hamm's distinction between them at this point is questionable: *Harvest*, 158.

[49]The best account of Biel's soteriology remains H.A. Oberman, *Harvest*, (especially chs. 5 and 6). See also B. Hägglund, *The Background of Luther's Doctrine of Justification in Late Medieval Theology* (Philadelphia: Fortress, 1971) first published in *LuthW* 8 (1961), 24-46.

[50]Although Biel concentrates more on the incarnation than the death of Christ, particularly in relation to pastoral consolation.

[51]*Harvest*, 233.

[52]Gabriel Biel: *Sermones de festivitatibus Christi, Hagenau 1510,* in "De Circumcisionis Domini, Sermo II in ordine 14". ET: H.A. Oberman, *Forerunners of the Reformation: The Shape of Late Medieval Thought* (London: Lutterworth, 1967), 166.

[53]Quoted in Oberman, *Harvest*, 270

[54]Aelred of Rievaulx, *De Institutis Inclusarum* 33. ET in Aelred of Rievaulx: *Treatises, The Pastoral Prayer*, ed. D. Knowles (Kalamazoo: Cistercian Publications, 1982).

[55]The idea is simply and briefly expressed in many works of popular piety of the time, for example this typical English lyric of c.1390:

The mynde of thy swet passion, Jesu -
Teres it tolles
Eyene it bolles
My vesage it wetes
And my hert it swetes.

ed. D. Gray, *A Selection of Religious Lyrics* (Oxford: Clarendon, 1975), 31.

[56]For an account of this kind of piety in England, see E.M. Ross, *The Grief of God: Images of the Suffering Jesus in Late Medieval England* (Oxford: O.U.P., 1997).

[57]"*Et mortuus est pro te in cruce, ut tu etiam portes crucem et mori affectes in cruce.*" *De Imitatione Christi*, 2:XII.12, ed. T. Lupo (Vatican: Libreria Editrice Vaticana, 1982), 121. For the significance of the cross in this work, see esp. 2.xi, xii; 3.lvi.

[58]*De Imitatione Christi,* 4.VII and VIII (Lupo, 327-331).

[59]Ross, *The Grief of God,* 6.

[60]The question of Luther's relationship to the *Schola Augustiniana Moderna* is still uncertain. Heiko Oberman argued in "Headwaters of the Reformation: Initia Lutheri - Initia Reformationis", *Dawn of the Reformation,* 39-83, (first published 1974), that it played a large part in Luther's theological growth. D.C. Steinmetz, *Luther and Staupitz: An Essay in the Intellectual Origins of the Protestant Reformation* (Durham, N. Carolina: Duke University Press, 1980), 27-30, cast doubt on Oberman's conclusion, arguing that Staupitz's Augustinianism comes not from any *Schola Augustiniana Moderna,* but from Augustine himself. McGrath, *Luther,* 63-71, also maintained that the relationship was more complex than Oberman allowed and that the theologians who had especially influenced Luther in Erfurt such as Johannes Nathin and Bartholomäus Arnoldi von Usingen cannot be said to be representatives of this school.

[61]Hamm argues that von Paltz was not an extremist in the Augustinian order, but a true representative of it. Von Paltz, looks back to Dorsten and Proles, authoritative figures in the theological tradition of the order, in his combination of features of the soteriology of the *via moderna* and a characteristically Augustinian stress on the objective guarantees of the church (329).

[62]Cf. D.C. Steinmetz, *Misericordia Dei: The Theology of Johannes von Staupitz in Its Late Medieval Setting* (Leiden: Brill, 1968), 164-71.

[63]Steinmetz, *Luther and Staupitz,* 31-4, has a useful discussion of Staupitz's advice to Luther.

[64]Hamm characterises von Paltz's theology as *"nichts anders als theologisch reflektierte Passionsfrömmigkeit".* (262).

[65]B. Hamm, *Frömmigkeitstheologie,* 262-3.

[66]WA Br 1.359-360 (LW 48.114)

[67]*"haben sie eyn mit leyden mit Christo, yhn zu clagen und zu beweynen als eynen unschuldigen menschen".* WA 2.136.21-2.

[68]LW 42.11.

[69]WA 2.137.37ff.

[70]WA 57.209.16-21 (LW 29.210-1).

[71]"Duo sermones de passione Christi", WA 1.335-45.

[72]The Editors of the Weimar edition date them to 1518. Martin Elze, "Das Verständnis der Passion Jesu im Ausgehenden Mittelalter und bei Luther," *Geist und Geschichte der Reformation: Festgabe H. Rückert,* ed. H. Liebling and K. Scholder (Berlin: Walter de Gruyter, 1966), 127-51 disagrees, dating them earlier. The Weimar editors are probably right: see Tomlin, "Medieval Origins" 27-8 for a discussion of the issue.

[73]The sermons (especially the first) have also been examined in Nicol, *Meditation,* 117-50.

[74]WA 1.339.17-9. Luther also uses this idea in the lectures on Galatians: WA 2.501.34-37.

[75]*"se ipsum in Christo legens"* (WA 1.388.35).

[76]*"Scriptura quoque nos hortatur magis ad affectum passionis Christi quam intellectum." (WA 1.343.28-9). "Ideoque intellectus non potest capere nec lingua dicere nec littera scribere, sed tantum affectus percipere, quid sit Christum passum esse: omina enim absorbet infinitum."* (WA 1.344.9-11).

[77]On the theology of the cross in the *Operationes*, see H. Blaumeiser, *Martin Luthers Kreuzestheologie: Schlüssel zu seiner Deutung von Mensch und Wirklichkeit; eine Untersuchung anhand der Operationes in Psalmos 1519-1521*, (Paderborn: Bonifatius, 1995)

[78]WA 43.461; TR 2.1820; TR 1.2654a, b.

[79]D.C. Steinmetz, *Misericordia Dei: The Theology of Johannes von Staupitz in Its Late Medieval Setting* (Leiden: Brill, 1968), 154ff.
Steinmetz, *Misericordia Dei*, 154ff.

[80]See also D.C. Steinmetz, *Luther and Staupitz: An Essay in the Intellectual Origins of the Protestant Reformation* (Durham, N. Carolina: Duke University Press, 1980).

[81]e.g. TR 2.1490-1532.

[82]Steinmetz, *Misericordia Dei*, 164-71.

[83]For a summary of Luther's debt to Staupitz, see Steinmetz, *Luther and Staupitz*, 31-4; also U. Saarnivaara, *Luther Discovers the Gospel: New Light upon Luther's Way from Medieval Catholicism to Evangelical Faith* (St Louis: Concordia, 1951), 19-22.

[84]WA 1.525-27, esp. 525.11-14.

[85]H. Appel, *Anfechtung und Trost im Spätmittelalter und bei Luther* (Leipzig: M. Heinsius Nachfolger, 1938), 102-4.

[86]WA 43.461.11-16.

[87]Steinmetz, *Luther and Staupitz*, 141-4.

[88]See G.A. Benrath, "Luther und die Mystik - ein Kurzbericht", *Zur Lage der Lutherforschung Heute*, ed. P. Manns (Wiesbaden: Franz Steiner, 1982), 44-58, for a survey of scholarship on Luther and mysticism.

[89]E.g. K.W. Eckermann, "Luther's Kreuzestheologie. Zur Frage nach ihrem Ursprung", *Catholica* 37 (1983), 306-17.

[90]This was the approach taken by H.A. Oberman, "Simul Gemitus et Raptus: Luther and Mysticism", *The Dawn of the Reformation*, 126-54, as well as by K-H. zur Mühlen, *Nos extra Nos: Luthers Theologie zwischen Mystik und Scholastik* (Tübingen: Mohr/Siebeck, 1972), 175, 198-203. S. Ozment, *Homo Spiritualis: A Comparative Study of the Anthropology of Johannes Tauler, Jean Gerson and Martin Luther (1509-1516) in the Context of their Theological Thought* (Leiden: Brill, 1969), also argues for radical differences between Luther and both Tauler and Gerson in the area of anthropology.

[91]E.g. M. Brecht, "Randbemerkungen in Luthers Ausgaben der 'Deutsch Theologia'", (*LJB* 47; Göttingen: Vandenhoeck & Ruprecht, 1980), 11-32.

[92]H.A. Oberman, "The Meaning of Mysticism from Meister Eckhart to Martin Luther", *The Reformation, Roots and Ramifications* (Edinburgh: T. & T. Clark, 1994) 77-90 (here, 88).

[93]For a useful account of Luther's initial encounter with German mysticism, see M. Brecht, *Martin Luther: His Road to Reformation*, 137-43.

[94]Cf. J. Ficker, "Zu den Bemerkungen Luthers in Taulers Sermones (Augsburg 1508)," *THStKr* 107 (1936), 46-64.

[95]A letter from Luther to Spalatin dated December 14 1516 (WA Br 1.77-9) recommends Tauler to the latter, but implies that Luther's discovery of Tauler *post*-dates his discovery of the gospel.

[96]W. Zeller, "Luther und die Mystik", *Theologie und Frömmigkeit. Gesammelte Aufsätze 2,* ed. B. Jaspert (Marburg: N.G. Elwert, 1978), 35-54; S. Ozment, "Mysticism, Nominalism and Dissent", 67-92.

[97]H. Bandt, *Luthers Lehre vom verborgenen Gott* (Berlin: Evangelische Verlagsanstalt, 1958), ch. 2, shows clearly how Luther's understanding of the hiddenness of God (at least at this early stage) is always grounded in the incarnation and the cross as the hidden form of divine revelation.

[98]e.g. von Loewenich and McGrath.

[99]McGrath, *Luther*; Oberman, *Harvest*.

[100]For example in the Romans commentary, while discussing his former difficulties with scholastic theology: "*non potui intelligere, quomodo me peccatorem similem ceteris deberem reputare et ita nemini me preferre, cum essem contritus et confessus.... Ita mecum pugnavi..*" WA 56.274.2-11.

[101]L. Grane, *Contra Gabrielum: Luthers Auseinandersetzung mit Gabriel Biel in der Disputatio contra scholasticam theologiam 1517* (Copenhagen: Gyldendal, 1962), has shown how Luther's target in this work is Biel's theology and soteriology.

[102]For example, the extended critique of Luther and the normative estimation of his personality and experience in J. Lortz., *Die Reformation in Deutschland*, 4th ed. (Freiburg: Herder, 1982 - first published 1939), 381-437.

[103]WA 54.185.12-186.21.

[104]WA 1.525.6-10.

[105]J. von Rohr, "Medieval Consolation and the Young Luther's Despair", *Reformation Studies: Essays in Honour of R.H. Bainton*, ed. F.H. Littell (Richmond: John Knox, 1962), 61-74. Von Rohr helpfully points out how the standard forms of late medieval consolation were of little use to Luther, but still suggests that Luther's own *experience* was at odds with the means offered to soothe it. He underestimates the extent to which the very monastic spirituality of Luther's early life had contributed to that experience. The disjunction lies more between Luther's spirituality and his theology than between his experience and late medieval consolation.

Nine: The Emergence of Luther's *theologia crucis* (i)

THE THEOLOGY OF THE CROSS IN THE *DICTATA*

The theology of the cross begins to emerge in Luther's first set of lectures on the Psalms, the *Dictata super Psalterium* of 1513-15. It is commonly agreed that Luther's earlier works (mainly the marginal notes to Augustine and Lombard of 1509-10) follow more or less straightforwardly the standard concerns of a late medieval theologian within the *via moderna*.[1] During these lectures on the Psalms, Luther begins to develop many of the themes of the theology of the cross, and towards the end of the work, he makes a significant step from the late medieval *spirituality* of the cross in the direction of a *theology* of the cross.

The earlier consensus of scholars following Holl,[2] held that the *Dictata*, and the notion of humility they contained were already fully reformatory. Vogelsang suggested the decisive Reformation breakthrough took place during Luther's work on Psalm 71:2,[3] while Hirsch preferred Psalm 31:2.[4] The 1950s saw a number of challenges to this generally accepted version of events. Saarnivaara[5] identified Luther's breakthrough with his departure from Augustine on Justification, and dated it towards the end of 1518, denigrating all his previous work as "pre-Reformation and sub-Reformation".[6] Most well known was Ernst Bizer's dramatic reversal of the consensus in his 1958 *Fides ex Auditu*,[7] which dated the decisive event in the winter of 1517-18. Bizer thought that the whole of the *Dictata* and even the 1515-16 Romans commentary were pre-reformatory, because they taught only the accusing, not the gracious word of God. The *humilitas*-theology of the *Dictata* is nothing more than the standard old monastic virtue, which is sometimes called faith. This is in time replaced by the theology of God's gracious Word of justification, which faith simply accepts and believes.[8]

More recently, the tide has turned again. Not long after Bizer's sortie into the field, Heinrich Bornkamm criticised his methodology,[9] and Regin Prenter dated the breakthrough even before the *Dictata*.[10] Prenter argued that Luther's theology of humility was simply an expression of his full *iustitia dei passiva*, "..if this *Humilitas* is pre-Reformation, then probably the whole of Luther is pre-Reformation!"[11] Oberman could even claim in 1967 that "all scholars involved emphasise that in Luther's first lectures on the Psalms, humility can no longer be meant as the medieval monastic virtue".[12] Damerau's major study on Luther's understanding of humility agreed that over the course of the *Dictata*, his perception of humility changed decisively,[13] while Steinmetz concluded that by 1515 Luther has come to deny that humility is a virtue, or a preparation for grace, and that justification comes by faith alone.[14] More recently, while agreeing with Bizer over against Vogelsang that neither Psalm 70 (71) nor 71 (72) shows any significant advance on the early theology of humility, McGrath has suggested that somewhere towards the end of the *Dictata*, Luther does make a significant break with the soteriology of the *via moderna*. The new theology is clearly in place in the Romans commentary, and a significant breakthrough is to be dated in 1515.[15] The present climate of opinion tends to date significant changes earlier, rather than later. If anything, it leans more towards the opinion that Luther's breakthrough took place gradually rather than suddenly, despite what the later Luther would sometimes like us to believe.[16]

Whatever is decided about Luther's reformation breakthrough, it is noteworthy how many of the themes of his theology of the cross already appear in the *Dictata*. In the *Scholia* on Psalm 76(77), he writes:

> You have now become visible and appear in weakness, and you do your works in humility, and so you are not known by the proud; you are not working in majesty and power, but from a hidden strength. Therefore your footsteps are not known, nor for that reason, are you, that you are God. Your works are veiled in humility, so that they are not believed to be yours, but those of some weak man. But even now, how often the Lord comes to meet us... and we do not know enough to greet him because we do not recognise his footsteps.... For just as divinity was veiled under the flesh of weakness, so his works were veiled in the weakness of suffering.[17]

God's self-revelation comes in the form of humility and suffering, not strength and glory. The hiddenness and obscurity of that revelation means that human understanding is unable to recognise God under the veiled form of his revelation. Luther compiles a list of the achievements of Christ's Passion, and continues:

> Who would have thought that the cross and suffering would achieve such incalculable results...? Faith understands that the devil has been conquered, death killed and heaven opened, but reason does not know it. He has veiled these works under the weakness of suffering, as he has his deity under his humanity so that by faith he might also veil reason and make foolish the wisdom of the world.[18]

Because God's revelation contradicts the expectations of human reason, faith is required as the only appropriate mode of perception. Christ, he continues, was not recognised by the Jews, because they were unable to recognise him in "*humilitas, afflictio, angustia et iudicium et damnatio*".[19] In accordance with the tropological sense of Scripture, this is then applied not just to Christ but also to the believer:

> ...any righteous man, and the whole human nature, seeing his wretchedness and filled with remorse, cries to the Lord for deliverance.[20]

God then hears these cries, and answers with the gift of bringing him *in statum salutis*, to which the believer responds in praise of God's wonderful works. But, Luther adds, concerning God's wonderful acts,

> He does not do them in a person unless He first humbles and afflicts him, and brings him to remorse.[21]

As an example of what he means, Luther turns directly to the story of Augustine's conversion in the *Confessions*. Luther obviously feels uneasy at this point, as he does not feel himself to be experiencing the kind of remorse Augustine felt:

> Hence one who has not experienced this remorse and meditation cannot be taught this psalm with any words. It is difficult for me, too, because I am outside of remorse and yet speak about remorse. No one can worthily speak or hear any Scripture, unless he is touched in conformity with it, so that he feels inwardly what he hears and says outwardly and says, "Ah, this is true."[22]

This whole passage shows Luther's thought being shaped increasingly by the theme of suffering and the cross. Because God reveals himself in weakness and suffering, only faith (not reason) can recognise it. God first humbles and condemns before he saves, and it is therefore the experience of *compunctionem* that teaches the sinner to see God aright. Yet at the same time, the hiddenness of God is focused not so much in the cross as in the incarnation. Luther uses the traditional notion of Christ's divinity hidden under his humanity rather than the more radical form of the hiddenness of God in the directly contrary form of the cross. Earlier in the *Dictata*,

the theme of God's hiddenness is present, but not specifically
related to the cross. At his exposition of Psalm 17(18).12 he lists
five senses in which God is hidden from humankind, in faith, in
unapproachable light, in the incarnation, in the church or the blessed
virgin, and the Eucharist. The cross does not even get a mention.[23]

Luther is part of the way there. When he writes on Psalm 91(92)
the themes of God revealing himself in a contrary form, the
hiddenness of God's work, and the consequent need for faith
coalesce:

> Christ's work and creation, the church, does not appear to be anything
> outwardly, but her entire structure is inward in the presence of God,
> invisible *(intus coram deo invisibilis)*. It is no wonder that the senseless
> do not know, because these counsels and ways in which God works are
> veiled altogether under the appearance of the opposite *(que in illis deus
> facit omnino contrariis speciebus)*. Behold in the spirits and in the inner
> man God produces glory, salvation, riches, beauty and inestimable
> strength. But on the outside nothing of this appears; indeed everything
> appears as the opposite *(immo contraria omnia apparet)*. He abandons
> them in disgrace, weakness, lack of riches, contempt and filth, yea even
> unto death... The thoughts of God are understood only by faith, which
> comes from the Spirit. So then, when the saints inwardly receive these
> magnificent gifts of God, they receive the opposite on the outside.[24]

Clearly evident is the dialectic between the visible and the
invisible,[25] and therefore the need for faith as the only possible
attitude if God's ways are to be understood. So also is the idea of
theology as a critique of appearance:[26] *"que lateat, non que
pateat"*.[27] God's ways are hidden under a contrary form.[28] Even the
theme of God's *opus suum/opus alienum,* which we have already
encountered and which is usually associated with Luther's later
work, is developed explicitly in the *Dictata*.[29] The necessity of
suffering is also stressed throughout, as the teacher of the *vera
theologia*.[30] The embryonic *theologia crucis* has even begun to be
used as a polemical device. Although the target at this point is not
scholastic or mystical theologians but rather the more traditional

"jews and heretics", the argument used against them is the same. They try to look for God outside of his revelation in Christ, to "dwell in God nakedly".[31] They avoid the place where God has made himself known, the suffering of the cross (called here God's 'shadow'), and want to be directed by God at first hand *(immediate a deo)*. Luther claims that on the contrary such "face to face" knowledge of God is impossible. The inevitable and significant conclusion, strongly reminiscent of the later *theologia crucis* is: "if you want to dwell, if you want to be saved, behold, go to His secret place, behold, go to His shadow".[32]

While many of Luther's characteristic later thoughts are evident here, what is less clear is the extent to which these have reached a fully reformatory form. We have seen that two central themes of late medieval spirituality were humility and the cross. Luther's understanding of these and the relationship between them in the *Dictata* sheds light both on the emerging theology of the cross, and on the impending *initia reformationis*.

HUMILITY IN LUTHER'S THOUGHT: 1513-15

It has sometimes been thought that towards the end of the *Dictata* or later Luther changed his mind on the question of how humility comes about. It is claimed that at the start of the *Dictata*, he held that humility is initiated from the human side, as the first stage in the process of justification, so that self-humbling is necessary for salvation. Luther later comes to believe that God initiates it: God does the humbling, and God alone moves people to repentance and humility.[33] There is a measure of truth in this but it does need some clarification and modification. Luther indeed moves towards the idea that God alone is active in salvation, while the sinner is purely passive. The problem with this suggestion as it stands is that in subsequent years Luther keeps referring to the possibility of self-humbling and the necessity of self-accusation. Such language does not disappear from his terminology, as one would expect if this were the crucial shift in his thought. It occurs towards the end of the

Dictata,[34] continues in the Romans commentary[35] (in the Romans lectures, Luther even suggests that forgiveness follows self-humbling as a consequence,[36]) through the lectures on Galatians,[37] and into his second set of Lectures on the Psalms of 1519-21.[38] It is even present in the Heidelberg Disputation.[39] Conversely, at a very early stage of the *Dictata*, Luther can quite easily talk about humbling as something God does rather than man,[40] while at the same time defining it as *accusatio sui.*[41] From 1513 through to 1521 and beyond, whether God humbles the sinner, or the sinner humbles himself, as Luther says in his lecture on Ps. 17(18), "souls must be bowed and humbled, for he gives his grace and light only to the humble".[42] Luther's understanding of humility differs from late medieval spirituality not so much in its origin as in its nature, as we will see shortly.

Damerau's survey of the notion of *humilitas* before Luther shows how most of the medieval tradition understood humility and grace as an ascending scale: the more humility is acquired, the more grace is given.[43] Common to much medieval teaching is the Benedictine concept to be found even in Bernard of Clairvaux, of humility as a ladder up which the believer ascends towards perfection. Despite what Damerau suggests about Luther however,[44] it is surprising how seldom these concepts are found even in the early stages of the *Dictata*. Luther can, it is true, give the impression that humility is a preparation for grace.[45] While expounding Psalm 68(69), Luther writes of humility in a way reminiscent of common medieval treatments of the subject: "the more deeply a person has condemned himself and magnified his sins, the more is he fit for the mercy and grace of God".[46] Similarly, he can speak of humility along with the traditional monastic virtues of poverty and patience,[47] and even use *pactum* language beloved of the *via moderna*[48]. Overall, however, the humility he has in mind is very different from the synergistic kind Damerau has described.

For example, during his exposition of Psalm 10 (11), Luther seems at first sight to include humility in a traditional list of virtues.[49] The point he is making though, is quite different from what might be expected. Humility, along with poverty, chastity, abstinence is a *privative*, rather than *positive* virtue. Rather than an actual quality which the soul can be said to possess, it denotes instead the absence of something. Humility is associated with language of emptiness,[50] nothingness,[51] despising of self. Luther does not think of *humilitas* as a positive quality or *habitus* to be offered to God as a precondition for first grace. Humility as a positive quality is in fact useless for salvation: it is not the one who seems to possess humility who is justified, but he who condemns himself.[52] Steinmetz[53] is correct when he indicates that Luther denies the idea of merit from an early stage,[54] and insists on election through grace without merit.[55] Luther's *pactum* terminology is not the same as Biel's. For Luther, all the sinner can do is to "accuse and damn himself",[56] and trust in the faithfulness of God to his covenantal promise. Luther uses the idea of covenant here not to imply that the sinner can contribute his humility to his salvation, but to drive home the point that on their own, faith and humility can do nothing. God's faithfulness to his promise is the only foundation of salvation.[57]

Luther's language and that of late medieval spiritual theologians overlap. Gabriel Biel, for example, firmly wedded to the idea of *facere quod in se est* as the first step to salvation, prizes humility above all[58] and speaks of humility as self-accusation, self-denigration and self-humiliation.[59] All the same, he clearly understands it as a human work, produced without grace as part of "doing what lies within you". Although Luther can occasionally imply that humility is a positive virtue[60] which grows and progresses within the soul,[61] he is increasingly at pains to point out the emptiness of humility, its essentially negative quality. Toward the end of the *Dictata* and beyond, potentially ambiguous language about the *pactum*, or describing humility as a positive quality or virtue grows less frequent, and stronger language is used to press the point home.[62] Humility is a passive acceptance of God's verdict on the sinner.[63] No human virtue counts before God, but only Christian virtue,[64] in fact human virtue, understood as a positive quality is no less than a vice before God,[65] By the time of the 1519-21 *Operationes in Psalmos,* the language is even stronger. In contrast

to pride, the source of all heresy, only humility teaches rightly.[66]
Nothing can please God unless it is done in humility.[67] Humility is
unambiguously divorced from the *pactum* soteriology and the *facere
quod in se est*:

> Thus despairing of himself and all that is his, and taking hold of this
> remedy alone, that he flees to the throne of mercy, confessing his secret
> sins. By this humility alone will he be saved.[68]

Humility is the despairing of one's own powers, a naked honesty
before God as to the absence of any soteriological resources, and it
becomes the place where one must simply wait for God's gift of
grace. To make this clear, Luther adds,

> What do our sophists mean, when under the pretext of an invincible
> ignorance, they speak of offerings, oblations, making a first motion,
> doing what lies within you?[69]

Humility here is by no means a work done as part of the *quod in
se est*, something offered either in or outside of a state of grace as a
human part of the bargain with God. Instead it is a confession of
emptiness,[70] the active rejection of all claim upon God, and a
becoming passive before God as far as salvation is concerned. Just
as Christ was made passive on the cross, so must we be made
passive before God:

> Not the active life *(activa vita)*, but the passive *(passiva vita)* is pure and
> works hope and glory. All must be stripped away from us, to leave us
> with God alone.[71]

As shown in the previous chapter, much late medieval piety saw
the Christian life as a matter of progress, a journey towards a
destination or climbing a ladder or mountain towards perfection.
Increasingly, Luther prefers a very different image: that of a potter
working with clay.[72] Traditional metaphors have humankind as the
active mover, always the *viator* on the way to perfection. Luther's

metaphor has men and women as entirely passive in the hands of the potter: the image speaks of no progress, no climbing of ladders, but rather on the human side sheer passivity, while being shaped by the divine hands.[73] To be humble is to stop acting, working, trying to contribute anything to one's own salvation. It can be described with the sinner as the active party, but in this case it is always an active passivity, a becoming passive.

The really significant move Luther has made is not in denying the possibility of self-humbling, but to define humility passively, not actively, privatively, not positively. It does not so much concern the question of how humility comes about, as what humility is. The process can be described with either God or the sinner as the subject, but the result is the same: a becoming empty, passive before the God who alone can save. By 1527, Luther can distinguish his understanding of humility quite clearly from that which he imbibed in his days in the monastery at Erfurt:

> Therefore our humility is not the monastic kind, which is a pride and a humility in itself, not in Christ; it is the pretence of humility. Those who are most humble are in fact the most proud. But your humility should be the kind which does indeed have very great gifts but nevertheless fears God, because he judges in a wondrous manner.[74]

This survey of Luther's early understanding of humility leads to three conclusions.

1.   Despite his disclaimers, Luther's theology would not have taken its distinctive shape without the monastic concentration on humility. Luther began his spiritual journey within a piety which held humility as the chief of Christian virtues. The development of his thought is a change in his understanding of what humility is rather than a rejection of that humility-centred spirituality.

2.   Although he clearly owes a debt to this tradition of monastic humility, Luther also shows from an early stage a surprising independence from it. His language does not show evidence of a

total *volte face* over this issue, but it becomes clearer and less ambiguous over the period 1513-21. From early in his first Lectures on the Psalms, he views humility privatively not positively, passively not actively. Luther reworks the late medieval understanding of humility, which used the language of self-accusation, but often understood it as a human contribution to the process of salvation.

3.   Luther's understanding of humility is closely linked to his understanding of salvation. He is convinced that this is the way God saves people, by first humbling them, bringing them to despair over themselves and reducing them to nothing.

In these lectures then, we find one of the two major themes of the theology of the cross plainly visible. God condemns before he saves. God humbles before he lifts up. Humility is a precondition for salvation only in the sense that the cross is a precondition for the resurrection. Luther has taken up the common late medieval virtue of humility and refashioned it to prepare for the emergence of the theology of the cross. Moreover, his understanding of humility moves away from the notion that it is a possession of the believer which earns merit, towards the position that it is merely the absence of all pretence to merit, the realisation of powerlessness before God. In late medieval theology, there was no disagreement that grace was needed for salvation. The only question was about the proper preparation for grace. While the theologians of the via moderna argues that it was to do *quod in se est*, Luther came to realise at a relatively early stage, that there is nothing a sinner can do to prepare for grace. Sinners are entirely passive in salvation, not active. In fact what stands in the way of our receiving grace is precisely the idea that we can prepare ourselves by confessions, penance, indulgences and masses. The only true preparation for grace is to be brought to the realisation that we can do nothing to prepare for it! Instead it is God who does this through the experience of *Anfechtung*. He humbles the sinner, making him aware of his sin, weakness, a troubled conscience, and his bankruptcy and powerlessness before

God. This will become a significant theme in Luther's critique of the late medieval church, as he extends this principle beyond the individual's relationship with God into the way the church functions.

Notes:

[1]On their conventional teaching on humility, see R. Damerau, *Die Demut in der Theologie Luthers* (SGR 5; Giessen: Wilhelm Schmitz, 1967), 53-8; on monasticism, Lohse, *Mönchtum und Reformation*, 213-26; on mysticism and scholasticism, K-H zur Mühlen, *Nos extra Nos: Luthers Theologie zwischen Mystik und Scholastik* (Tübingen: Mohr/Siebeck, 1972), 1-25. Several scholars suggest that although these remarks are largely conventional, Luther is either preparing to divest himself of Ockhamistic ideas, e.g. Saarnivaara, *Luther Discovers the Gospel*, 53-8; H.J. McSorley, *Luther Right or Wrong? An Ecumenical-Theological Study of Luther's Major Work, the Bondage of the Will* (Minneapolis/New York: Newman, 1969), 218-20; J. Wicks, *Man's Yearning for Grace: Luther's Early Spiritual Teaching* (Washington: Corpus, 1968), 25-40.

[2]K. Holl, *Gesammelte Aufsätze zur Kirchengeschichte Vol 1: Luther* (Tübingen: Mohr/Siebeck, 1921), 155-203, esp. 193-7.

[3]E. Vogelsang, *Die Anfänge von Luthers Christologie nach der ersten Psalmenvorlesung* (Berlin: Walter de Gruyter, 1929), 57-61.

[4]E. Hirsch, "Initium Theologiae Lutheri", *Lutherstudien II* (Gütersloh: Bertelsmann, 1954), 9-35. This assertion explained 27-33.

[5]Saarnivaara, *Luther Discovers the Gospel..*

[6]Ibid., 126.

[7]E. Bizer, *Fides ex Auditu* (Neukirchen: Kreis Moers, 1958).

[8]For a useful analysis and critique of the history of research up to this point see K. Hagen, "Changes in the Understanding of Luther: the Development of the Young Luther," *ThSt* 29 (1968), 472-96.

[9]H. Bornkamm, "Iustitia Dei beim jungen Luther", *Der Durchbruch der Reformatorischen Erkenntnis bei Luther,* ed. B. Lohse (Darmstadt: Wissenschaftliche Buchgesellschaft, 1968), 115-62.

[10]R. Prenter, *Der Barmherzige Richter: Iustitia dei passiva in Luthers Dictata super Psalterium 1513-1515* (Copenhagen: Universitetsforlaget I Aarhus, 1961).

[11]Ibid., 140.

[12]H.A. Oberman, "Wir Sein Pettler. Hoc est Verum. Covenant and Grace in the Theology of the Middle Ages and Reformation", *The Reformation: Roots and*

Ramifications (Edinburgh: T. & T. Clark, 1994), 91-115 (here 94). First published as: "Wir sein pettler. Hoc est verum. Bund und Gnade in der Theologie des Mittelalters und der Reformation", *ZKG* 78 (1967), 232-52 .

[13]R. Damerau, *Die Demut*.

[14]*Luther and Staupitz*, 78-95.

[15]McGrath, *Luther*, 119-47.

[16]As for example in the famous autobiographical fragment of 1545 (WA 54.185.12-186.21). Oberman suggests the helpful image of "a series of successive waves, one tumbling over the other", in "Headwaters of the Reformation: Initia Lutheri - Initia Reformationis", *The Dawn of the Reformation* (Edinburgh: T. & T. Clark, 1986), 39-83 (here, 40). See also W.D.J. Cargill Thompson, "The Problem of Luther's 'Tower Experience' and its Place in his Intellectual Development", *Studies in the Reformation: Luther to Hooker*, ed. C.W. Dugmore (London: Athlone Press, 1980), 60-80, on some problems with the 1545 account. McGrath also writes: "The essential thesis of the present study is that Luther's theological development over the period 1509-19 is a continuous process, rather than a series of isolated and fragmented episodes", (*Luther*, 176).

[17]WA 3 547.14-25.

[18]WA 3.547.25-548.9.

[19]WA 3.548.22-3.

[20]WA 3.548.38-549.1.

[21]"*Verum non facit in quoquam, nisi eum prius humiliet, affligat et in compunctionem ponat.*" (WA 3.549.20-1).

[22]"*Unde qui non est expertus hanc compunctionem et meditationem: nullis verbis potest hunc psalmum doceri. Inde enim et mihi difficilis, quia extra compunctionem sum et loquor de compunctione. Nullus enim loquitur digne nec audit aliquam Scripturam, nisi conformiter ei sit affectus, ut intus sentiat, quod foris audit et loquitur, et dicat 'Eia, vere sic est'*"(WA 3.549.30-5).

[23]WA 3.124.29-39.

[24]WA 4.81.11-35.

[25]Although here it is linked to the internal/external distinction. This note is missing in the later *Operationes*, where it becomes two alternative ways of looking at the world. Cf. e.g. zur Mühlen, *Nos extra Nos*, 91: "Die Unterscheidung von homo interior und exterior wird... immer weniger im Sinne zweier Teile der menschlichen Natur als vielmehr existential-theologisch im Sinne zweier alternativer Existenzweisen verstanden."

[26]e.g. WA.3.104.31-4, 455.23-4; WA.4.82.17-8: "*dat sub contrariis, et discordat signum a signato.*"

[27]WA 4.245.2.

[28]WA 4.77.37-8. This refers to the thoughts of God, which "*non tantum abscondita et profunda sint, sed etiam nimis profunda, quia sub contrariis apparent latere*".

[29]e.g. WA 3 246.19-20; *"dum opus eius alienum est ab eo, ut faciat opus suum".* (WA 4 87.24-5): *"Sic alienum opus eius ab eo, ut faciat opus suum".* (WA 4.331.14). This occurs in the immediate context of a quote from Bernard along the same lines (331.13-18).

[30]e.g. WA 3.104.27-9, 345.29-30, 432.26-9, 613.15-16, 614.28-30; WA 4.88.11-12, 108.39-40.

[31]*"nude in deus se habitere presumerunt"* (WA 4.64.28).

[32]LW 11.209: *"si vultis habitare, si salvare: Ecce absconditum, Ecce umbraculum eius subite"* (WA 4 64.28-65.1).

[33]See for example M. J. Harran, *Luther on Conversion: The Early Years* (Cornell University Press: Ithaca, 1983). 69f., 100. She concludes: "From initial uncertainty regarding humility as preparation for grace and conversion, Luther gradually realised that God Himself works the necessary preparation in man. It was only in the works of 1518 and 1519 that he united this insight with the perception that perseverance in conversion is also God's work in man", 189. Also McGrath, *Luther*, 128-33.

[34]WA 4.88.11-12.

[35]WA 56.17.16-18.19, 252.17 (*"nos oportet humiliari"*), 416.7-8.

[36]*"qui autem sic timuerit et humiliter confessus fuerit, dabitur ei gratia, ut Iustificetur et dimittatur peccatum."* (WA 56.252.27-9 [on Romans 3:22]).

[37]WA 2.490.9-13, 538.19-21, 591.36, 597.16-17, 614.13.

[38]AWA 2.573.1-17; WA 5.565.14-6, 660.16-9.

[39]*"Fit autem deformitas illa in nobis vel a Deo flagellante vel a nobis ipsis accusando"* (WA 1.357.13-4), *"quantum nos accusamus, tantum Deus excusat"* (WA 1.359.29-30).

[40]WA 3.90.10-1. (on Psalm 9:3).

[41]WA 3.26.24; 29.16-27 (on Psalm 1:6).

[42]*"oportet inclinari et humiliari, quia humilibus solis dat gratiam et lucem sui"* (WA 3.125.20-1).

[43]R. Damerau, *Demut*, 9-53, esp. 29-32.

[44]Ibid. 110-8.

[45]WA 3.429.9-10, WA 3.458.3-5: *"Sed nunc iustitia dei est tota hec: scilicet sese in profundum humiliare. Talis enim venit in altissimum: quia descendit in profundissimum prius."*

[46]LW 10.368. *"quanto enim quis se profundius damnaverit et peccata sua magnificaverit, tanto aptior est ad misericordiam et gratiam Dei"* (WA 3.429.9-10).

[47]WA 3.32.7-9.

[48]WA 3.289.1-4: *"Immo et fides et gratia, quibus hodie iustificamur, non iustificarent nos ex seipsis, nisi pactum dei faceret. Ex eo enim precise, quia testamentum et pactum nobiscum foecit, ut qui crediderit et baptisatus fuerit, salvus sit, salvi sumus."*

[49]WA 3.95.4-7: "*Ideo iste omnes virtutes sunt privative, scilicet paupertas, castitas, abstinentia, humilitas, &c. Ille autem positive, ut fortitudo, magnanimitas, &c.*"

[50]WA 3.42.25, 28-30: "*Utinam vacuus ita fuisset et humilitate plenus, sicut publicanus, qui veritate plenus non erat vacuus coram domino.*"

[51]WA 3.283.8, 4.130.3.

[52]WA 3.290.31-32: "*Igitur Non qui sibi humillimus videtur, sed qui sibi fedissimus et turpissimus videtur, hic est speciosissimus coram deo.*" WA 3.465.5-7: "*Et est proprie humilitas immo humiliatio. Quia non qui se humilem putat, iustus est, sed qui se detestabilem et damnabilem reputat in oculis suis.*"

[53]Steinmetz, *Luther and Staupitz*, 78-95. Cf. Oberman, "Wir Sein Pettler", 111-3.

[54]e.g. WA 3.42.16-20, 200.14-16; WA 4.19.25-30. Steinmetz concludes that in the *Dictata* Luther is in agreement with Staupitz that "humility is not a virtue prior to justification". *Luther and Staupitz*, 93.

[55]WA 3.116.1-2, 25-26, 179.26-180.1.

[56]WA 3.288.30 (i.e. 12 lines before the passage about the *pactum* quoted above).

[57]WA 3.289.5: "*In hoc autem pacto deus est verax et fidelis et sicut promisit, servat.*" (this immediately follows the quotation on the *pactum* above at WA 3.289.1-4.

[58]See Oberman, *Harvest*, 352.

[59]Cf. Damerau, *Demut*, 47-51.

[60]WA 3.95.4-5; WA 4.155.30-3.

[61]WA 3.26.19-36.

[62]WA 56.259.18-20, 404.1-3.

[63]E.g. WA 3.111.20-1; WA 4.241.30-1.

[64]WA 56.195.7-9, 237.14-15, 403.23-405.6.

[65]WA 57-3.110.11-13.

[66]AWA 2.222.9: "*sola humilitas recte docet*".

[67]AWA 2.251.18-19: "*Ita nihil deo placet potest, nisi quod in humilitate geritur.*"

[68]WA 5.565.14-16.

[69]"*Quid audent nostri Sophistae, qui praetextu ignorantiae invincibilis, obicis, oblati, primi, motus faciendi, quod in se est...?*" (WA 5.565.23-5)

[70]WA 5.660.16-19.

[71]AWA 2.302.6-15.

[72]WA 56.376.25-7, 386.10-11, AWA 2.320.18-22.

[73]For Luther's thought on the believer as *viator* in relation to the medieval and mystical traditions see S. E. Ozment, "Homo Viator: Luther and Late Medieval Theology", *The Reformation in Medieval Perspective*, ed. S. E. Ozment (Chicago: Quadrangle, 1971), 142-54.

[74]WA 25.23.32-24.3.

Ten: The Emergence of Luther's *theologia crucis* (ii)

While Luther's developing understanding of humility is an intensification rather than a repudiation of earlier themes in the *Dictata*, he does appear to arrive at a new appreciation of the role of the cross in Christian theology during the writing of these, his first lectures on the Psalms.

LUTHER'S INTERPRETATION OF PSALM 4

This conclusion is confirmed by a comment he makes towards the end of his *scholia* on verse 4 of Psalm 92(93). Luther considers the way God saves the Psalmist, while allowing him to go through all kinds of troubles. This theme reminds him of 1 Cor.2:2, and the ubiquity of the cross in the Scriptures. He then recalls his earlier exposition of Psalm 4, which had obviously left him dissatisfied:

> Hence, because we remember Ps. 4 and were not sufficiently understanding *(non satis intelligentes)* when we explained it and many, seeking to understand it apart from the cross of Christ *(extra crucem Christi)*, had difficulty in explaining it, recall that he says, 'When I

called' (Ps.4.1). By this very word he already confesses that he bears the suffering of Christ.[1]

Luther suggests that when he first interpreted Psalm 4, in August 1513,[2] he too understood it *extra crucem Christi*, whereas now he sees things in a different way. This incident clearly stayed in Luther's mind, as he implicitly refers to it again in the course of his exposition of Psalm 4 in his second set of lectures on the Psalms, the *Operationes in Psalmos*, about six years later.[3] By the time he is working on Psalm 92(93) in the *Dictata*, Luther has come to think that Psalm 4 concerns the sufferings and cross of Christ, God's habitual pattern of bringing low in order to raise. Likewise in the *Operationes*, he sees it as an "exhortation to the work of God, that is to suffering and the cross". Between his first and second attempts at interpreting Psalm 4, Luther considers he has made a significant development in his understanding, a development which is related to viewing the cross in a new light.

In these early years, Luther expounded Psalm 4 at least four times. After the scholia on Psalm 92(93) in the *Dictata*, he proceeded to give a short revised exposition of Psalm 4, according to his new understanding in the light of the cross of Christ.[4] Unfortunately for us, Luther's dissatisfaction with his first attempt at Psalm 4 was so great that at some stage, according to Boehmer, he revised the earlier exposition in September or October 1516, inserting a new version which we now have at WA 3.39-60.[5] To try to make a complicated picture a little clearer, we can arrange the four versions chronologically as follows:

A: The first exposition in the Dictata, later revised and now lost (c. August 1513)
B: The short exposition during Psalm 92(93) in the *Dictata* (late 1514?)
C: The revised text at WA 3.39-60. (Sept./Oct. 1516)
D: The exposition of Psalm 4 in the *Operationes*. (1519?)

Luther's revisions mean that we are unable with entire confidence to read version C as evidence for Luther's understanding of Psalm 4 in 1513 (A), interpreted *extra crucem Christi*. However, Luther's revisions of earlier work during this busy period were not always very thorough,[6] and there are traces within version C of what might well have been in version A. For example, as we have seen, Luther later reads the Psalm as an exhortation to suffering and the cross. Version C retains the statement that "the best way to lift the mind up to God is to acknowledge and ponder past blessings. Therefore one must begin with thanksgiving and confession."[7] This seems very different from the exposition of the same verse (v1) in version B, which begins not with past blessings but with "*tribulatione, persecutionis, compunctionis.*"

More notable still are Luther's comments on verse 3. In version B, Psalm 92(93):4, and especially the phrase "Wonderful (*mirabilis*) is the Lord on High"[8] reminds Luther of Psalm 4:3 which contains a similar phrase: "Know that the Lord has made his Holy One wonderful."[9] He interprets both as referring to Christ. In version C, Luther's 1516 revision, the phrase is interpreted in terms of the incarnation. God has made Christ *mirabilis* in the sense that "he is the Lord, and the Lord is with him, and the Father is in the Son."[10] It refers to Christ's miracles, and to his being both God and man.[11] God is hidden in Christ's incarnation.[12] The phrase in version B, written during the exposition of Ps. 92(93), however, refers to the pattern of cross and resurrection: "he hands him over to every kind of suffering and death and tribulation and saves him at the same time."[13] The former, sounds very much like a remnant of version A, written *extra crucem Christi.* When Luther first expounded the Psalm (version A), he thought God makes Christ *mirabilis* by endowing him with the divine nature, in version B, he sees that God does it by crucifying and raising Christ. God rescues the one he abandons.

Luther's understanding of God's ways with Christ and the believer have changed. Now, in the light of the cross, Luther understands the pattern of descent and ascent, suffering before glory, condemnation before salvation. Now that Luther understands the phrase in this way, it becomes a notion which includes, rather than excludes the believer. Before, God's glorification of Christ set him apart from sinners. He alone is the Son of God, he alone is both God and man. Now, this pattern, that God condemns before he saves, *includes* the believer, in that God works in exactly this way to save sinners. Luther, in fact, for the first time introduces the idea of God's proper and alien work in this context.[14] The cross and resurrection are not just the means of salvation, but have become a paradigm of salvation. What God has done to Christ he does to us. The way God treated Christ is the way he treats us. The anguish of the sinner who knows he needs God's help takes on a new significance as the *"crucem et passionem Christi"*,[15] in other words, it places him at exactly the same point as Christ on the cross, waiting for the deliverance of God. God's salvation works through suffering and death, whether in the cross of Christ or in the crucifixion of the sinner in anguish and despair.

Between version A, which Luther eventually rejected, and version B, this principle has becomes of paradigmatic importance for Luther. God saves *"per stultitiam crucis"*,[16] so that this becomes a foundational hermeneutical principle for the exposition of Scripture. The cross is found everywhere in Scripture for those who have eyes to see it,[17] and wherever salvation is mentioned in Scripture, this principle (the cross) is present.[18]

The true theologian, the one who understands the ways of God and whom Luther will later call the "theologian of the cross" views everything according to the paradigm of the cross. The disciples in Luke 24:26 are prime examples of those who fail to understand this principle:

> The cross of Christ is found everywhere in the Scriptures. Then, finally, when He foretold his suffering and resurrection, they understood nothing and the word was hidden from them. For they hoped he would reign according to the flesh apart from all trouble. Therefore when his cross was seen and his death perceived, they all failed and despaired. For they did not yet savour the Spirit and did not know that the Lord has made his Holy One wonderful, that he would save him even under suffering.[19]

Luther's point is that the disciples did not understand God's work in Christ because they were looking in the wrong place, for Christ's reign in power. They were not expecting him to be found in trouble and death, or on a cross.

This discovery of the cross as the key hermeneutical principle in understanding Scripture introduces a whole series of paradoxes into Luther's mind. If God condemns in order to save and kills in order to raise, all kinds of expectations are reversed:

> He shows you good things, but only through evils. He is wonderful in that he shows good things especially when he shows evil things.[20]

> We do not seek what they seek, for we have been instructed and enlightened by you. It is not good things that we seek, but rather evil... we accept evils so that we may cry to you and you may hear us, that you may make us wonderful while you show us good things when you show evil.[21]

> When you see me most downcast, then I will be most accepted, and when, according to the folly of your mind you will think me accursed by God, then I will be most blessed.[22]

Suffering is the constant state of the Christian: "How good it is always to be in trouble",[23] and speaking of judgement and tribulation: "In it all who are Christ's must always be."[24] Salvation begins not with a consideration of past blessings but with being brought into tribulation, because only then will a person cry out genuinely in a sense of total powerlessness before God.

There are two sides to this hermeneutical principle.[25] On the one hand it insists that the Scriptures be interpreted in the light of God's ways with Christ, the pattern of condemning in order to save.[26] Yet on the other hand, this is for Luther far more than an abstract criterion of technical hermeneutics. It means that the Bible is read rightly and understood properly only from the position of anguish, powerlessness and suffering.[27] The true theologian seeks evil and suffering in all his dealings with God, because he knows that while they will lead him to cry out to God and be heard, prosperity and good fortune will lead to a sense of independence from God and

pride which "consumes and melts away all the inner parts".[28] Only
from the perspective of enduring evil and suffering will a person be
heard by God, see him aright and understand his ways: "only he who
is in anguish cries out."[29]

THE *THEOLOGIA CRUCIS* IN 1517

Luther makes this point repeatedly in the following years, and
comes to play a vital role in the important developments of 1517. In
the Spring of that year, Luther's first publication under his own
name, *Die Sieben Bußpsalmen* is shot through with the
consciousness of waiting passively upon God.[30] Luther indicates that
it is the experience of distress and despair which alone enables a
reader to know God[31] and to understand the Psalms.[32]

The 95 Theses, posted or published in October 1517, strike
similar notes.[33] The document is framed by statements which set the
theological and spiritual tone underlying the critique of indulgences.
The first four theses insist that the whole life of believers consists
of both inward and outward penitence, not just when performing
penitential acts. The last four, theses 92-95, contrast the false
security offered by indulgences, not so much with faith or the Word,
but directly with the cross and suffering, following Christ "through
penalties deaths and hells". Heaven is entered "through many
tribulations rather than through a false assurance of peace". These
opening and concluding remarks indicate the perspective from
which Luther writes, that indulgences mislead the faithful because
they lead them to the wrong place. Indulgences encourage a trust in
human works and words rather than a passive penitence and "hatred
of self", which according to Thesis 4 is "true inner repentance".
Indulgences are found wanting because they do not accord with "the
piety of the cross" (Thesis 68).

Luther's "Explanations of the 95 Theses", planned in late 1517, but
published only in August 1518 make it clear how much the theology
of the cross lies behind Luther's contribution to the indulgence
controversy.[34] The distinction between God's alien and proper work,
an idea which lies at the heart of the *theologia crucis*, and which has

already been developed in the *Dictata*, is employed prominently. In explaining thesis 7 he writes:

> When God begins to justify a man, he first of all condemns him; him whom he wishes to raise up, he destroys, him whom he wishes to heal, he smites, and the one to whom he wishes to give life, he kills... He does this however when he destroys man and when he humbles and terrifies him into the knowledge of himself and of his sins... However this consternation is the beginning of salvation... in short, God works a strange work (*opus alienum*), in order that he may work his own work (opus suum).[35]

Such an infusion of grace certainly does not feel like one. In fact it is "hidden under the form of wrath".[36] Indulgences and the contemporary penitential theology which underlies them, persuade the sinner to place confidence in the forgiveness offered by the word of the pope rather than the word of God. The explanation to Thesis 23 remarks that God "has decided that all men should conform to the image of his Son, that is to the Cross".[37] Luther repeats these ideas and even uses the phrase *"theologia crucis"* during an important section of his explanation of Thesis 58.[38] Scholastic theology has silenced the theology of the cross, and the *theologus crucis*, "who speaks of the crucified and hidden God" values sufferings as the best relics Christ has left behind. The *theologus gloriae* on the other hand despises suffering and weakness, and instead "defines the treasury of Christ as the removing and remitting of punishments", in other words, the very things offered in an indulgence. At this stage, Luther clearly did not see this as an attack on the papacy as such: under pressure from Tetzel, Wimpina, Cajetan and Prierias in the aftermath of the Indulgence controversy, and especially Eck in Leipzig, this inference became clear even to Luther.[39] The beginnings of his argument with the papacy are embedded in the theology of the cross. It was in the name of this type of theology that Luther objected to the abuse of indulgences, and in turn to the whole practice of indulgence-selling. In turn, this protest was to lead to the Reformation itself.

The same theology undergirds Luther's thought over the next few years, on into the 1520s.[40] The cross, understood as the experience of desperation, crying out of a sense of helplessness to God for help and mercy, is the only vantage point from which God can properly be known. To read the Scriptures *extra crucem Christi* is to miss the pattern of God working out his purposes through evil and suffering, through the cross. It is to fail to understand God's characteristic way of working. It is to fail to understand God.

LUTHER AND 1 CORINTHIANS

Just before he turns back to Psalm 4, during his exposition of Psalm 92(93), Luther turns to 1 Cor.2:2:

> God saves the more by the foolishness of the cross, and very many are offended (*schandalisantur*) at him. Therefore you see the sufferings and cross of Christ depicted everywhere, so that we are well able to say with St. Paul that we know nothing except Jesus Christ and him crucified.[41]

This citation draws attention to a more general pattern in these later parts of the *Dictata*, namely the increasing use Luther makes of the themes and vocabulary of these early chapters of 1 Corinthians. It is significant that as the Dictata proceeds and the *theologia crucis* comes increasingly into focus, so these verses crop up with increasing regularity. Luther's exposition of Psalm 83 (84), for example, returns to this passage four times, firstly to indicate God's choice of humble, insignificant things,[42] then with reference to the double offering of Christ and then ourselves on the cross, rejoicing in sufferings and therefore "making foolish the wisdom of the world".[43] In expounding verses 5-6, Luther again turns to 1 Cor.1:23-24,[44] and at the end of the Psalm, 1 Cor.1:27 expresses his thought on wanting to bear reproach with Christ. No other passage outside the Psalms is referred to as often.

Luther refers to these chapters again in Psalm 84(85),[45] and when he reaches Psalm (90)91 and beyond, the occurrences come thick and fast. Psalm (90)91 turns his mind to the passage,[46] as do Psalms

(91)92 (in the course of an extended meditation on the hiddenness of divine wisdom and the alien form in which it appears),[47] 92 (93) as we have seen above, 93(94) (twice),[48] 95(96),[49] 97(98),[50] 101(102)[51], 103(104),[52] 111(112),[53] 113(114) (twice),[54] 115(116),[55] and at least eight times in 118(119).[56]

If Luther did made a notable advance in his thinking about the cross as a key hermeneutical principle around this time, it is also significant that it coincides with an increasing interest in this Pauline passage. A typical example of this comes in Luther's exposition of Psalm 91(92), where he engages in a lengthy meditation on the word *profunde* in v.(6)5. The 'deepness' of God's thoughts refers to their hiddenness *sub aliena specie*.[57] The passage bristles with paradox, and the sense that God's revelation in Christ was hidden under "*confusio, mors, crux, infirmitas, laguor, tenebre et vilitas*".[58] The passage is typical of much of Luther's tone at this stage in the *Dictata*, and significantly, it is to 1 Cor.1:21 that Luther turns to express the essence of this paradoxical alien wisdom of God.[59] God's means of saving the humble and condemning the proud through the weakness and foolishness of the cross expresses precisely the insight we have been describing, that is, that the cross represents the pattern of God's working in the world.

One more significant example of the use of this Pauline passage in the establishment of Luther's early theology comes in the "Explanations of the 95 Theses" published in 1518. In the lengthy explanation of Thesis 58 mentioned above, Luther explicitly discusses the differences between the theologian of the cross and the theologian of glory. He then asks, "who will be the judge of these two?" His answer comes in the form of two biblical quotations, one from Isaiah 66:4, and the other from 1 Cor.1:27. In the light of this verse he continues:

> But if one should accept this judgment as true, there is nothing for us to do, if we should wish to speak the truth, but confess that the treasures of indulgences are the greatest harm that can be done, if they are understood.. as the remission of all punishments.[60]

For Luther, Paul's teaching in 1 Corinthians that God uses what is weak to shame the strong, and what is foolish to defeat what was wise, came as an important confirmation, and also as a significant stimulus in developing the theology that would eventually challenge the papacy and attempt to reform the church.

In conclusion, while the theological tradition before Luther generally regarded the cross as contingent and incidental, and neither necessary nor typical of God's action, towards the end of his first set of lectures on the Psalms, at some point in early 1515, Luther made a significant break from that tradition, understanding the cross as necessary and typical of God.[61] The cross now *reveals* God and his characteristic way of dealing with believers. Luther arrives at this insight partly through the kind of meditation on the cross we have seen in late medieval spirituality and in Bernard of Clairvaux, but also under the influence of this particular passage in 1 Corinthians. The spiritual tradition before Luther held the cross at its centre, and encouraged emotional involvement with it, but due to soteriological and theological restraints, failed to work this through to its full theological consequences. It was in the light of Paul's teaching of the cross as representing the wisdom of God, folly to unbelievers, yet wisdom to believers, that Luther was able to 'theologise' this spiritual tradition. It enabled him to see the cross not just as central to Christian piety, but as a revelation of God and his ways. This new understanding of the cross was in due course applied to the medieval practice of passion meditation as we have seen above, particularly over the period 1517-19. More famously still, it was applied to the question of indulgences and their place in the church and the Christian life. This theology of the cross thus became the seedbed of Luther's revolution, directed at the heart of an unsuspecting church.

Notes:

[1]WA 4.87.39-88.3 (LW 11.237).
[2]H. Boehmer, *Luthers erste Vorlesung* (BVSAW 75.1; Leipzig: S. Hirzel, 1923), 38.
[3]AWA 2.162.1-2
[4]The later version of Psalm 4 is printed in the Weimar Edition at WA 3.61.26-64.25, immediately after the earlier version, although, as a note at the bottom of the page makes clear, originally it was located after Psalm 92(93).
[5]Boehmer, *Luthers erste Vorlesung*, 37-8. Boehmer arrives at this conclusion by means of an examination of different paper types, colours and watermarks, as well as handwriting in the Dresdner Scholia of Luther's first lectures on the Psalms. H. Wendorf, "Der Durchbruch der neuen Erkenntnis Luthers im Lichte der handschriftlichen Überlieferungen", *Historische Vierteljahrschrift* (1932) accepts these conclusions, as cited by G. Rupp, *The Righteousness of God* (London: Hodder, 1953), 130.
[6]As for example, a comparison between the 1517 and 1525 editions of Luther's *Die Sieben Bußpsalmen* shows. See the editor's comments at WA 18.467-9.
[7]WA 3.42.1-3, 6-7.
[8]*"Mirabilis in altis dominus"*.
[9]*"quia mirificavit dominus Sanctam suum"*.
[10]WA 3.52.5: *"quod sit dominus, et dominus cum eo et pater in filio."*
[11]WA 3.52.10-29.
[12]WA 3.52.39-40.
[13]WA 4.87.21-2.
[14]*"Sic enim mirabile (secundum Isaiah 28.) fecit consilium suum, dum opus eius alienum est ab eo, ut faciat opus suum"* (WA 4.87.23-5).
[15]WA 4.88.2-3.
[16]WA 4.87.34.
[17]*"Vides igitur ubique passiones et crucem Christi depingi"* (WA 4.87.35).
[18]*"ubicunque in Scripturis exauditio, liberatio, salus ponitur, mox ibi ante esse crucem est passionem intelligitur"* (WA 4.88.18-9).
[19]WA 3.63.1-7 (version B).
[20]WA 3 64.5-6: *"Ostendit vobis bona, sed non nisi per mala. Mirabilis enim est, quod dum mala ostendit, maxime bona ostendit"* (version B).
[21]WA 3.64.21-5 (version B).
[22]WA 3.63.13-15 (version B).
[23]WA 3.62.21-2.
[24]WA 3.62.6-7.
[25]The first of these bears significant resemblance to the convergence in the *Dictata* on the tropological sense of Scripture, highlighted by E. Vogelsang, *Anfänge*. The second corresponds to the existential character of Luther's theology, explored

among others by L. Pinomaa, *Der Existentielle Charakter der Theologie Luthers* (Helsinki: Suomalainen Tiedeakatemia, 1940).

[26]*"Quo concluditur, quod ubicunque in Scripturis exauditio, liberatio, salus ponitur, mox ibi ante esse crucem, est passionem intelligitur"* (WA 4.88.17-19 - at the end of the exposition of Ps. 92(93), just before version B in the original manuscript).

[27]"Das Evangelium nur von dem Angefochtenen richtig verstanden wird", Pinomaa, *Existentielle Charakter*, 190.

[28]WA 3.62.14-15.

[29]WA 3.63.10-11: *"non autem clamat nisi qui in maxima angustia est."* Cf. also WA 3.62.3-4.

[30]WA 1.208.21, 209.13 etc.

[31]WA 1.172.1-3, 176.26-7, 207.31-8, 216.32.

[32]*"ja nit mueglich zuvorsteen, dan den, die es fulen unnd erfaren"* WA 1.206.30-1. Luther left this point unchanged in his revision of this work for publication in 1525 (WA 18.517.3-4), indicating how it remained as a crucial principle during the following years.

[33]The Latin text of the Theses is found at WA 1.229-238, an English translation at WA 31.25-33.

[34]The Latin text is at WA 1.525-628, the English translation at LW 31 83-252.

[35]WA 1.540.8-19 (LW 31.99).

[36]WA 1.541.16-17 (LW 31.101).

[37]WA 1.571.35-6 (LW 31.153).

[38]WA 1.613.21-614.20 (LW 31.225-7).

[39]D. Bagchi, *Luther's Earliest Opponents: Catholic Controversialists 1518-25* (Minneapolis: Fortress, 1991) shows how Luther's opponents made the connection for him between the attack on indulgences and an attack on the papacy.

[40]For example in his second set of Lectures on the Psalms of 1519-21, the Operationes super Psalterium. For example, *"nam experientia opus est (ut saepe diximus) ad intelligenda verba dei"* (AWA 2.178.28-9). *"Vexatio enim (ut Is.28.19 dicit) sola dat intellectum auditi, id est, verbum dei fit intelligibile insensatis, si bene vexati fuerint passionibus. Crux Christi unica est eruditio verborum dei, theologia sincerissima."* (AWA 2.389.13-16). See also AWA 2.54.25-7, 162.1-7, 180.8-10, 296.8-11, 317.7-9, 325.1, 341.15, 366.13-4, 379.35-8, 559.4-5.

[41]WA 4.87.34-7.

[42]WA 3.645.10-1.

[43]WA 3.646.33.

[44]WA 3.648.31-2.

[45]WA 4.10.25.

[46]WA 4.72.38-9.

[47]WA 4.82.24-5.

[48]WA 4.97.17, 98.7-8.
[49]WA 4.111.25-6.
[50]WA 4.122.25.
[51]WA 4.153.27-8: *"Ego non intelligo usquam in Script. nisi Christum crucifixum."*
[52]WA 4.182.17.
[53]WA 4.252.36-253.2.
[54]WA 4.261.5-6, 16-17.
[55]WA 4.268.15-16.
[56]WA 4.328.6, 332.38, 354.33, 366.18, 22, 377.40, 387.24, 382.31-2.
[57]WA 4.83.14.
[58]WA 4.8.32.34-5.
[59]WA 4.82.24-5: *"Sic enim placuit deo per stultitiam crucis salvare credentes et per sapientam salutis damnare incredulos."*
[60]WA 614.28-31
[61]Cf. G. Rupp, "Luther's 95 Theses and the Theology of the Cross", *Luther for an Ecumenical Age: Essays in Commemoration of the 450th Anniversary of the Reformation* (St. Louis: Concordia, 1967), 67-81: "It seems clear to me that in 1516 some new experience of the gospel lay immediately behind him and finds its expression in a series of utterances about the peace and joy of the Christian gospel." Rupp links this new experience to the emergence of the theology of the cross which he dates to 1516.

Eleven: The Theological Foundations of Luther's Revolt

In contrast to much of the theological tradition before him, humility was for Luther no longer an active meritorious quality of the soul, nor a virtue which could be possessed. Instead, the truly humble person was one who had become passive, empty-handed, aware of powerlessness before God. This powerlessness cannot be a virtue, simply because it is nothing, the absence of self-justification. If the sinner comes to God with hands full of virtues, works, indulgences to offer to God, God cannot fill them with his righteousness. He can do so only if the sinner comes with empty hands to receive. God therefore dashes from human hands the things we would offer him; he destroys human righteousness, works, and wisdom, in order to prepare his creatures for himself. The cross demonstrates exactly this pattern. God kills before he raises. Luther picks up Paul's identification of the cross as the central criterion of a Christian understanding of God and his ways, as well as his language of wisdom and foolishness, power and weakness. Just as God acted in Christ, reducing him to shame, weakness, powerlessness and the foolishness of the cross, only to raise him from death, so he acts towards sinners, destroying in order to create.

Luther claims that the cross is the central point of God's self-disclosure. Yet, this theology has not emerged out of thin air. In Luther's creative hands, two central themes of popular and monastic spirituality, humility and the passion of Christ, have been recrafted into the *theologia crucis*.

SALVATION AND REVELATION

But what of Luther's early experience of conflict between his monastic spirituality and nominalist soteriology? How did this new understanding of the cross help to resolve this dilemma? All the contrition, self-accusation and awareness of sin which late medieval spirituality evoked in Luther, seemed to him a barrier to his acceptance by God. This spirituality taught him to magnify his own unworthiness, his distance from God. If he had nothing he could offer to God, how could it help him to be told *facientibus quod in se est infallibilite Deus infundit gratiam*, however small the movement required? This new understanding of the cross as the revelation of God's ways with sinners taught him a new meaning to his experience of despair about himself. Far from a disqualification from grace, it became the only qualification for it. As Anders Nygren put it, for Luther we have "fellowship with God on the basis of sin".[1] God only saves sinners, only teaches the stupid, only enriches the poor, and only raises the dead.[2] Therefore to be saved we must become sinful, foolish, poor, helpless, exactly what his spirituality had led Luther to acknowledge himself to be.

Another way of expressing this conflict is that revelation and salvation were sundered. The way God had revealed himself in Christ bore no particular relation to the way he acted towards people in the present. Christ's life, death, suffering were past actions which could arouse emotional sympathy or validate the sacraments, but which were quite definitely past. Because Christ had suffered, there was no great need for the sinner now to suffer. God had acted one way in Christ and another in Luther. For Christ, God was saviour; for Luther, he was judge.

As we have seen, Luther's theology in 1518 at the Heidelberg

Disputation centred upon two theological assertions: that God condemns in order to save, and reveals himself at the cross. At the core of Luther's theology lies the connection he makes between these two insights. The way God saves people in the present and the form in which he has revealed himself historically are joined at the cross. The vital clue for understanding the way God works is always the cross: God works and is to be found in suffering and weakness, not strength and glory, whether in Christ or the Christian, in the first century or the sixteenth. God's activity in the present is always continuous with his revelation in history. Luther's *theologia crucis* is therefore an assertion of the unity and continuity of God's action in history and in the present, in revelation and in salvation.[3] He is not one God in Christ and another God for us. This is why Luther insists that to know God is to know him in Christ alone, or in the words of the Heidelberg Disputation, *"in Christo crucifixo est vera Theologia et cognitio Dei"*.[4] To know him now, one must look to his revelation in the past. The theology of the cross roots God's present action in his revelation in history, and refuses to sever the two. Luther's Christology therefore asserts in the strongest possible way the faithfulness of God to his promise and his revelation. It also brings together God's revelation in the past and his revelation in the present. As God revealed himself in the suffering Christ then, he reveals himself in the suffering of the Christian now. The *theologia crucis* preserved the actuality of revelation in a way which on the one hand did not render it arbitrary and speculative, and which on the other did not confine it irrevocably to the past.

In this unity of past revelation and present salvation, Luther found great comfort. Without it, the common late medieval experience of despair and uncertainty could only be a disqualification for salvation. With it, that experience became the one supreme qualification for salvation. In the shadow of the cross, understood as the revelation of God's characteristic manner of dealing with people, Luther's experience of temptation, fear and anguish could be interpreted not as condemnation but as salvation. Condemnation, God's alien work, is done only in order to produce salvation, his proper work. He also found in it a sober realism. If God shows his love for his Son by allowing him to be crucified, so that he might be raised, God will do the same for the believer today. Because God acts in this way, he can be known only when there is a correspondence between the sinner and the form of God's self-revelation. Luther reasserts the theme of *conformitas Christi*, not in the medieval sense of sharing his virtues, but in sharing his suffering and passivity on the cross. Because God reveals himself *in* the cross of Christ, he can be known only *from* the cross of the Christian. Luther has sometimes been accused of making salvation too easy, by insisting that it is simply a matter of faith alone. Such a charge entirely misunderstands him. In fact he accuses late medieval scholasticism of having made it too easy by suggesting all that is needed is one tiny momentary act of merit![5] Instead, true faith means abandoning all conventional wisdom, being stripped of all pretension and pride, and leaving aside trust in anything but God's word in Christ.[6] Salvation in nominalistic scholasticism involved the suffering of Christ but did not involve the suffering of the Christian, because it had lost sight of "Christ alone", the unity and continuity between revelation and salvation.

For Luther both soteriology and epistemology must be understood from exactly the same standpoint, namely the cross, and they therefore become inseparable. To know God is to be justified by him, and to be justified by him is to know him aright, and both begin with the humbling of the sinner. In this way, the cross becomes the central motif of true theology.

These insights led in turn towards polemics. Two aspects of this can be highlighted here: Luther's critique of wisdom and power, both in the philosophy of scholasticism (particularly the influence of Aristotle),[7] and then in the power of the papacy.

THE CROSS, FAITH AND PHILOSOPHY

In the *Operationes*, Luther criticises the traditional understanding of faith as a *"habitus* or as *actus elicitos"*.[8] He goes on to define his view of faith both negatively and positively: "For faith is not, as they say, a *habitus* which lies dormant, snoring in the soul, but is a

constant turning towards God".[9] The pattern here is similar to
Luther's evolving view of humility. As there, faith is no longer a
positive quality in the soul, a *habitus* or virtue, but just as humility
is the correct orientation towards oneself, faith becomes the correct
orientation towards God. It means turning away from oneself and
concern for one's own sins and spiritual progress, to fasten on to the
Word which promises forgiveness.[10] Faith, from the later stages of
the *Dictata* onwards is always orientated away from the visible
towards the invisible, and is defined by that opposition, in that
God's hidden presence is discerned only by faith which leaves
behind the visible and clings to the invisible word.[11] The church, for
example, is not known to physical but to spiritual eyes[12] The
thoughts of God, because veiled *(velata)* and hidden under the
appearance of the opposite)[13] are understood only by faith.[14] Faith
takes on this whole new meaning as the ability, or even the
determination, to see beyond what is apparent, to the hidden reality
behind it.

Luther attacks any attempt to know God directly, outside of his
revelation in the cross. This refers to Jews and heretics,[15] to mystical
theologians,[16] and Aristotle,[17] but is chiefly directed at
scholasticism. Luther's wide-ranging critique of scholastic
theology[18] falls generally speaking into two parts, epistemological
and soteriological.[19] The speculative Aristotelian approach built its
knowledge of God upon what was visible, and failed to reckon with
the God who reveals himself on a cross, hidden behind a contrary
form.[20] Appearances therefore deceive,[21] and the sign does not
necessarily conform to the thing signified.[22] In the realm of
salvation, scholastic theology looked to faith as a *habitus*, a
possession of the sinner, whereas Luther increasingly looked for an
external righteousness *(extra nos)*.[23] Luther's *Disputatio contra
scholasticam theologiam* of 1517[24] is a direct challenge to
Aristotle's ethical teaching, which had been taken over into most
forms of scholastic theology.[25] The whole piece, with its stress on
the bondage of the will, the necessity of grace for the performance
of any good work opposes the idea that salvation can be based upon
anything within the sinner. Such a teaching sought righteousness in

virtues nurtured and possessed by the human agent. We become righteous by doing righteous deeds. Instead, love for God means not becoming more virtuous, but more hateful in one's own eyes, a process which takes place through suffering,[26] not the acquisition of merits.[27] Luther stands apart from what he saw as the Pelagian theologians of the *via moderna*,[28] who thought God would reward with condign merit works done without the help of grace. He even distances himself from Thomists who denied this, and held to God's initiative in giving grace for a first act. For Luther, both looked to human righteousness rather than Christ's, a righteousness which was internal, not external. Both ignored God's intention to empty sinners of all that their own, before he can replace it with all that is Christ's. For Luther, neither understood the wisdom of the cross.

In brief, Luther's criticism was that as a *theologia gloriae*, scholasticism failed to grasp the necessity for the personal experience of suffering and humiliation. It missed this because it failed to understand the cross of Christ as the paradigmatic revelation of God and his ways.[29] Scholastic theologians are simply too detached, and 'academic', dabbling in theology, with no experience of the things of which it speaks.[30] They do not write their theology from the perspective of temptation, guilt and despair.[31] Luther memorably complains that their chief problem is that "they do not know what anger and lust are"![32]

This insistence that the Scriptures are read from the cross, within the experience of humiliation and suffering, leads directly to Luther's critique of scholasticism, starting with the theologians of the *via moderna*, and especially from the *Disputatio contra scholasticam theologiam* onwards, extending to Thomist scholastics as well.[33] Denis Janz strikes exactly the right note when he concludes that the main methodological difference between Luther and Thomas Aquinas was in the role of experience. Luther's, he says, was 'existential' theology, Aquinas's was 'sapiental'.[34] A large part of the reason for this however, which Janz does not mention, was Luther's insistence on the cross as the paradigm for God's dealings with sinners. For Luther, faith always included the experience of being humbled and brought to the point where the sinner must learn not to rely upon his own wisdom, but instead, to have faith in the word of promise.

Scholastic theology had ignored the importance of the experience of temptation, despair and suffering which provided the only sure perspective from which God can be understood and known. The church which it legitimised had thus become disjointed from the deeper currents of the spirituality of humility, as well as the concentration on the cross within elements of late medieval popular piety. It had failed to see the connection between God's action in Christ and God's action in the present, and sought power rather than the cross. Luther urges that God's way with Christ must be God's way with the church now. A purely historical knowledge of Christ's death and sufferings is soteriologically useless, without the corresponding experience of death and suffering in the present, as the essential prelude to grasping the significance of that death *pro se*: "it is living, or rather dying and being damned that makes a theologian, not understanding, reading and speculating."[35]

THE CROSS, FAITH AND THE CHURCH

Luther's critique could not remain purely at the theological level. It began to be focused increasingly against the power, prestige and wealth of the papal church. If God can be known only when there is a correspondence between the sinner and the form of God's self-revelation on the cross, the same holds true for the church. It too must conform to the image of the crucified Christ if it is to be true to the God of Jesus Christ. Thus, the *theologia crucis* plays a vital role in Luther's growing critique of papal wealth and power. This reaches its full clarity in the 1520 Reformation treatises, especially *An den christlichen Adel deutscher Nation von des christlichen Standes,*[36] yet its origins can be traced in these earlier texts as stemming from Luther's new understanding of the cross,[37] and in his appropriation of the ideas and language of 1 Corinthians. In the *Dictata*, Luther often borrowed Bernard of Clairvaux's idea that there are three ages of church history.[38] The first age was marked by persecutions, the second by heresy, the third by ease and comfort, preceding the imminent end of the age,[39] and Luther applies this analysis to his own day in the light of 1 Cor.1:27-8. The peace, wealth and security enjoyed by the church are signs not of its success, but of its demise: the church is in greatest danger when it is rich, well-fed and powerful, and most blessed when it is poor, persecuted, and tempted. The *Dictata* several times expand on these to urge the salutary effect of sufferings for the church, and how Christians should prefer the company of the poor over the rich of this world.[40]

Again in 1515, Luther makes a similar point in his comments on Romans 1:16-20, crucial verses of course for his developing Reformation theology. Throughout this section, Luther clearly has 1 Cor:1-2 in the back of his mind, as he explicitly refers to the passage several times in the space of just few pages of text.

Firstly Luther claims that the power of God, referred to in Rom. 1.16 is to be contrasted with the power of men, which God has *"evacuavit per Christi Crucem"*,[41] a clear verbal parallel to the Vulgate text of 1 Cor.1:17. Luther goes on to claim that "the rich and the powerful do not receive the gospel. Therefore they do not receive the power of God."[42] He then quotes 1 Cor.2:14, referring to the apparent insignificance of the Word, compared to the power and influence and number of his audience.[43] Luther continues:

> Thus we arrive at the conclusion: He who believes in the gospel must become weak and foolish before men so that he may be strong and wise in the power and wisdom of God as 1 Cor.1.25-27 tells us.... For this reason the life of the princes of this world, of lawyers, and of all those who have to maintain their position by power and wisdom is threatened by the gravest dangers.[44]

The passage is shot through with language of power, wisdom, righteousness, and foolishness, in other words, the language of 1 Cor.1-2. Commenting on Romans 1:19 shortly afterwards, he quotes 1 Cor.1:25, in contrasting the foolishness of God with the "strength and the power and wisdom of men".[45] Romans 1:18 is then interpreted as polemic against worldly wisdom and power:

> The apostle directs his chief attack against the powerful and the wise of
> the world... because they have opposed the Gospel and the word and the
> life of the cross of Christ, and have incited others against it.... To no one
> does the preaching of the cross (*predicatio crucis* - cf 1 Cor.1.18) appear
> so foolish as to philosophers and men of power because it is completely
> contrary to them and to their sensitivities.[46]

Romans 1:20 leads him directly to 1 Cor.1:21, where the wise of
this world fail to perceive the createdness of the world.[47]

At this point, Luther's polemic is against Aristotelian philosophy
and the wealthy in general. It is only a step away from a radical
critique of the church's wealth and power, such as develops in
Luther's writings over the next few years. Three things are notable
about this passage:

First, Luther's critique of power and the abuse of wealth grows
out of the ideas of 1 Corinthians 1 and 2 about the cross, wisdom
and foolishness, power and weakness. The language and themes of
this passage have directly informed and shaped both his emerging
theologia crucis and now his increasing sense of unease about the
reigning philosophy and attitudes to power within the late medieval
church. This passage has not only given him a vocabulary to express
his ideas, it has provided a framework into which the contemporary
ecclesiastical situation can be interpreted.

Secondly, all of this centres around the opposition between a
cross-centred theology and those in power who reject it. For Luther,
the cross is God's way of working over against those who depend on
human power and wisdom, a description which he increasingly
applies to his own contemporaries.

Thirdly, the polemic is conducted on two fronts at once, at the
wise and the powerful, against "*philosophis et principatibus*". For
Luther, the two fed off one another, and the indulgence controversy
of 1517 was a prime example of this very symbiosis. A theology of
works and human power had legitimised an oppressive, avaricious
practice, which served only to increase papal wealth, and as Luther

was to discover, papal power served to endorse the theology which underpinned it.

In December 1518, Luther criticised the bishops, and especially the pope for exploiting their power to ensure the submission of all the whole church, failing to take the form of a servant, the form of Jesus Christ.[48] Scott Hendrix has shown how Luther's growing doubts about the papacy developed from his conviction that instead of feeding the flock of Christ as it should have done, the bishops and the popes had used their power to dominate and oppress and starve the people of God.[49] Given the theology of the cross which underlay it, what began as a theological dispute within German universities, or between groups of Augustinian and Dominican monks, could not remain just that. It had to spill over into a critique of a church which as Luther saw it, had taken the path of human power not the cross, and had thus lost the true power of God. In the *Operationes*, he recalls the old story of the pope who boasted to the emperor in the words of Acts 3:6, "We can no longer say 'silver and gold have I none'", to which the emperor replied 'Yes, but neither can you say get up and walk!" The story makes his point exactly.[50]

When Luther comes to attacks the papacy openly in 1520,[51] one of the main strands of his theological critique concerns the abuse of power in the papacy, and its failure to accord with Christ crucified. The main charge levelled at the papacy is that of tyranny over the people of God.[52] The papacy and the papal curia have failed in their task to teach and shepherd God's church, and have instead set themselves up in tyrannical rule over it, demanding submission to human rule rather than to Christ. In the context of criticism of papal extravagance and claims to power, he proposes a very different model of the papacy:

> He is not the vicar of Christ glorified but of Christ crucified. As Paul says, 'I was determined to know nothing among you save Christ, and him only as the crucified' (1 Cor.2.2).... Or again in 1 Corinthians 1.23, 'We preach Christ, the crucified.' Now the Romanists make the pope a vicar of the glorified Christ in heaven.[53]

Again, the ideas, and here even the text itself, of the first two chapters of 1 Corinthians have shaped Luther's critique of the contemporary church. If God's action in the present is continuous with his action in Christ, then the papacy needs to model itself upon the weakness and poverty of the cross, rather than on images of imperial power. The papacy's failure to do that simply betrays not just its moral deficiency, but its theological misunderstanding.

In June 1520, *Exsurge Domine*, the papal bull threatening Luther with excommunication was finally issued, After Luther's burning of the bull outside Wittenberg in December, the further bull which actually excommunicated him was issued on January 3rd of the next year. Luther lost no time in replying, issuing his *Assertio omnium articulorum M. Lutheri per bullam Leonis X*, rebutting the bull's criticism of his theology of penance point by point. Towards the end of the work, during the defence of his denial of both free will and the proposition that "whoever does *quod in se est* sins mortally", Luther's attack on the papacy reaches a crescendo. It is in this context, that he explicitly and directly links the attack on the papacy to the theology of the cross:

> This theology, which condemns whatever the pope approves, and makes martyrs, is of the cross. For the cross is soon replaced by pleasure, poverty by opulence, ignominy by glory…. I have no stronger argument against the kingdom of the pope than that it rules without the cross.[54]

Luther's critique of the papacy, was essentially an attack on its spiritual tyranny, its abuse of its position of power and responsibility to teach the gospel, and its departure from the spirit of the crucified Christ. His revolt against the papacy, as well as his earlier attack on scholastic theology, stemmed from his theology of the cross. Both theology and the ecclesiastical politics of the time came under the judgement of this theological reworking of popular and monastic spirituality. Against the cross, and the God who acts now in the way he acted in Christ, both speculative scholasticism and papal absolutism of the late Middle Ages were found wanting. The *theologia crucis* can therefore rightly be called a spiritual theology, a recognition of the theological strength which lay within aspects of popular piety, and therefore a revolt of that piety against the abuse of power. The theology of the cross, learnt from and developed from St. Paul, St. Bernard and the tradition of passion-centred piety proved again its ability to challenge notions of power within the Christian church, which Luther considered to have betrayed its very identity.

Notes:

[1] Quoted in B.A. Gerrish, *Grace and Reason; A Study in the Theology of Luther* (Oxford: Clarendon, 1962), 114.

[2] WA 56.427.3-4 (Romans commentary).

[3] So Erich Vogelsang, *Anfänge*, 54, puts it well: "Der Grundsinn alles Handelns Gottes ist darin offenbar, wie Gott an Christus in seinem ganzen Leben, Leiden und Auferstehen handelt... und so durch Christus das gleiche an uns tut wie an Christus selbst... Christus in seiner geschichtlichen Person offenbart das Handeln Gottes."

[4] Thesis 20, (WA 1.362.18-9).

[5] Luther speaks of those (in the context, clearly Gabriel Biel) *"qui uni momenantio actui meritorio tribuunt dignitatem meriti aeternae gloriae"*. (AWA 2.583.2-7).

[6] AWA 2.318.12-3.

[7] Thesis 28. This theme is of course continuous with Luther's *Disputatio contra scholasticam theologiam* of September 1517 (WA 1.221-8) aimed at Gabriel Biel, as Grane, *Contra Gabrielem* has shown.

[8] WA 5.394.24-5.

[9] *"Non enim, ut illi somniant, fides est habitus in anima subiectus et stertens, sed perpetuo et directo intutu in deum versus."* (WA 5.460.9-10).

[10] See B.A. Gerrish, "By Faith Alone: Medium and Message in Luther's Gospel", *The Old Protestantism and the New: Essays on the Reformation Heritage* (Edinburgh: T. & T. Clark, 1982), 69-89, for an excellent treatment of this aspect as central to Luther's mature understanding of faith.

[11] Cf. H. Bandt *Luthers Lehre*, ch. 2.

[12] *"in intellectu et fide cognoscuntur"* (WA 4.81.11-16 [on Ps.91(92)]).

[13] *"que in illis deus facit omnino contrariis speciebus"*.

[14] *"qui fide tantum, que ex spiritu venit intelligentur"* (WA 4.81.25-35 [on Ps. 91(92)]).

[15] WA 4.64.9-30.

[16]WA 56.299.28-300.3; AWA 2.296.8-11, 318.12-13.

[17]WA 1.613.17-27.

[18]L. Grane, "Luther and Scholasticism", *Luther and Learning: the Wittenberg University Luther Symposium*, ed. M.J. Harran (Selinsgrove: Associated University Presses, 1985), 52-68, provides a useful account of the main course of Luther's campaign against scholastic theology.

[19]S. Ozment, "Luther and the Late Middle Ages: The Formation of Reformation Thought", *Transition and Revolution: Problems and Issues of European Renaissance and Reformation History*, ed. R.M. Kingdon; Burgess, Minneapolis: 1974), 112-28, points out how Luther opposed scholasticism in the realms of reason/revelation and salvation.

[20]For a bibliography on the *deus absconditus* in Luther, see A.E. McGrath, *Luther*, 164, n.44. Controversy still surrounds the two senses of God's hiddenness in Luther, within and behind his revelation. See especially H. Bandt, *Luthers Lehre*, who argues persuasively that the early Luther really knows only of God hidden *within* his revelation, and B.A. Gerrish, "To the Unknown God: Luther and Calvin on the Hiddenness of God", *JRel* 53 (1973), 263-92, who is more pessimistic about Luther's ability to reconcile the two.

[21]*"Aliter habet quam apparet"* (AWA 2.425.11).

[22]WA 4.82.17-18.

[23]Zur Mühlen, *Nos extra Nos*, 49, 129-40.

[24]Latin text in WA 1.220-28, English Translation at LW 31.9-16.

[25]Theses 40-45, 50, 51.

[26]Thesis 25.

[27]Thesis 30, 95.

[28]WA 56.503.1-5.

[29]*"Theologus vero gloriae (id est qui non cum Apostolo solum crucifixum et absconditum deum novit, [1 Cor.2.2] sed gloriosum cum gentibus, ex visibilibus invisibilia eius..."* (WA 1.614.17-19).

[30]WA 5.497.18-31.

[31]*"peccatum, quid esset, ignoraverunt, nec quid remissio"* (WA 56.275.17-18).

[32]WA 5.497.34.

[33]Grane, *Contra Gabrielem*, 369ff; Janz, *Luther and Late Medieval Thomism*, 24-7.

[34]Janz, *Luther on Thomas Aquinas*, 78-80. Janz notes how Luther complained of the complete absence of the experiential dimension in Thomas' speculative theology, which rendered it incapable of reaching the inner depths of (at least Luther's) personal life and experience (14-16).

[35]*"Vivendo, immo moriendo et damnando fit theologus, non intelligendo, legendo aut speculando"* AWA 2.296.8-11.

[36]WA 6.404-69.

[37]Rupp, "Luther's 95 Theses and the Theology of the Cross", shows how the

theologia crucis is the structural principal behind Luther's Explanations of the 95 Theses, as a protest against the cheap grace of Indulgences.

[38]Luther mentions it at WA 3.416ff. and 420.14ff. during the exposition of Ps. 68(69).

[39]This idea is found in Augustine as well as Bernard. Bernard thought the end was to come soon, if it had not already broken through. (Bell, *Divus Bernhardus*, 46).

[40]E.g. WA 3.432.26-9, 4.112.34-7.

[41]WA 56.170.10.

[42]WA 56.170.22-3.

[43]WA 56.171.5-6.

[44]WA 56.171.8-21.

[45]WA 56.173.21-4.

[46]WA 56.174.4-10.

[47]WA 56.174.21-2.

[48]WA*Br* 1.270.82-6

[49]S.H. Hendrix, *Luther and the Papacy: Stages in Reformation Conflict*, (Philadelphia: Fortress, 1981)

[50]AWA 2.472.7-15.

[51]Hendrix, *Papacy*, 78-112, shows how Luther came out into open opposition to the papacy only after the Leipzig Disputation of 1519, and in the Reformation Treatises of 1520.

[52]Of Luther's treatise *"On the Babylonian Captivity of the Church"*, Hendrix writes: "the charge of tyranny resounds throughout the work" *Papacy*, 100.

[53]WA 6.416.7-12.

[54]WA 7.148.23-9.

Part III

Blaise Pascal's Theology of the Cross

Twelve: Introduction

PASCAL AND THE CROSS

Our final example of the doctrine of the cross as polemical, subversive theology brings us to Blaise Pascal and seventeenth century France. Pascal mentions Luther twice in his most famous unfinished work, the *Pensées*. In an assortment of various thoughts collected under L954,[1] the references are as brief as they are dismissive: "Luther: completely outside the truth... Luther, anything but the truth."[2] A clue to what Pascal had in mind in these enigmatic sentences lies in a third oblique reference in L733. In the course of a discussion of the Eucharist, he presents the Catholic belief in transubstantiation as an example of holding together two apparently opposing beliefs. He then concludes:

> Modern heresy, unable to conceive that this sacrament contains at once the presence and the figuration of Jesus Christ... believes that one of these truths cannot be admitted without thereby excluding the other.[3]

The manuscript of this fragment shows that Pascal originally followed the word *L'hérésie,* with *"de Luther"*. He then crossed them out, replacing them with *"d'aujourd'hui"*.[4] Pascal clearly associated Luther's name with disputes in Eucharistic theology. He seems to have believed that Luther was responsible for the denial of transubstantiation and the Real Presence, and for the belief that the Eucharist is purely *"figuratif"*. He seems completely unaware that while Luther denied transubstantiation, he quite famously held to the doctrine of the Real Presence in his disputes with Zwingli and other Swiss reformers over Eucharistic doctrine.[5] Ironically the position Pascal attributes to Luther is far closer to that of Zwingli than to that of the German reformer.

In the absence of other references to Luther, and in the light of this one instance of ignorance of Luther's actual thought, it is highly unlikely that Pascal ever read Luther. Pascal was born only 77 years after Luther's death, yet they inhabit very different worlds. While the great Lutheran question was "Where can I find a gracious God?", Pascal's intellectual world was dominated by Montaigne's *"Que sais-je?"*. In the light of scientific discoveries, Cartesian philosophy and the growth of sceptical thought in the early years of the seventeenth century, the focus had shifted from soteriology to epistemology.[6] Not only are Pascal's questions different from Luther's, so also are his opponents. The scholastic theology against which much of Luther's early polemic was directed declined steadily through the seventeenth century in France, both in intellectual and devotional circles.[7] Pascal's thinking took place instead against the background of Pyrrhonist, Cartesian and Jesuit ideas and in some cases, opposition. Although at the time, those associated with Jansenism were commonly accused of being crypto-Calvinists, it has been increasingly recognised in recent years that the movement needs to be located squarely within the Catholic Counter-Reformation, the wave of reform which swept through the Catholic church in the sixteenth and seventeenth centuries.[8]

It is all the more remarkable then that these two thinkers, separated by time, language, rhetorical context and confession, display interest in very similar themes. In particular, they share an exclusive Christocentric doctrine of revelation, and the notion of the hidden God. Furthermore, as we shall argue, their theologies both take the cross as a key reference point, adopting Paul's language and ideas in 1 Corinthians 1-2, the characteristically Pauline themes of the weakness, foolishness and hiddenness of God. As Pascal had evidently not picked up these themes from Luther, he provides a further example of the influence of these Pauline themes, now mediated through another strand of the Christian tradition.

THE CROSS IN THE *PENSÉES*

Pascal's sister Gilberte Périer, remarking on her brother's poor health in her *Vie de Monsieur Pascal* mentions how:

> ...he often used to say... that a Christian finds value in everything, and especially in sufferings, because there he comes to know Jesus Christ crucified, who must be the entire sum of the knowledge of a Christian, and the sole glory of his life.[9]

This impression of cross-centred spirituality and thought is borne out by evidence from Pascal's writings, particularly in the *Pensées*. Several of the fragments give a prominent place to the foolishness of the cross. For example, L291 states how despite all the signs and proofs which Christianity possesses, "none of this can change us and make us capable of knowing and loving God, except the virtue contained in the folly of the cross".[10] The Christian religion is frequently said to be simultaneously wise and foolish,[11] as is the doctrine of original sin.[12] The cross appears to play a significant role in the origin of faith. As L842 puts it: "What makes them believe is the cross."[13] God is described as "a God humiliated even to death on the cross"[14] and Christian morality is said to have at its head *"un Dieu crucifié"* (L964). The theme of the hiddenness of God is sufficiently well known to make an exhaustive list of occurrences unnecessary.[15] These various statements seem to play an important role in Pascal's projected Apology for the Christian religion;[16] it remains to be discovered how they function within it.

Pascal's explicit references to the cross fall into three types. One set of texts speaks of the cross as enabling belief. Fragments L291 and L842 just quoted fall into this category. The cross, as opposed to proofs, is said to be the element in Christian faith which is capable of bringing about spiritual change in a person, giving the ability to know, love and believe God. In a similar fashion, a Latin section of L834 juxtaposes the cross and signs, quoting 1 Cor.1.22 to make the same point, that although Christian faith possesses many signs and proofs, its true proponents point instead to the cross as its centre:

> For the Jews require a sign, and the Greeks seek after wisdom, but we preach Christ crucified
> But full of signs and full of wisdom.
> But you preach Christ not crucified and a religion without miracles and without wisdom.[17]

L808, an important fragment concerning the way belief comes about, describes how the crucial stage of *inspiration* occurs. We must open our minds to the proofs of Christianity, confirm it through habit, "offering ourselves through humiliations to inspiration, which alone can produce the real and salutary effect, *Lest the cross of Christ be made of none effect.*"[18] The quotation from 1 Cor.1:17 in this context could refer either to the *humiliations*, or to the *inspirations*, a question to which we shall return later. At this stage it is enough to point out how here again Pascal uses Paul's language about the cross in thinking about the process of coming to believe.

Secondly, the cross is a symbol of the obscure and indirect nature of human knowledge. L253, entitled *Figures,* refers to two great revelations given in the Scriptures. One is that "Everything happened to them in figures", and the second is that of "a God humiliated even unto the cross".[19] The reference to "two comings" (*deux avènements*) contrasts the first coming of Christ in obscurity with the second in clarity. Pascal's picture of the humiliated God as a revelation indicates the obscure, figurative nature of that initial revelation, compared to the unmistakable clarity of the second.[20] L268 bears the same heading, and after asserting that "Everything happened figuratively", Pascal gives examples of this general principle: "Christ had to suffer – a humiliated God – this is the cipher St. Paul gives us."[21] L241, although from a slightly different angle, seems to point in the same direction. *"Un Dieu humilié et jusqu'à la mort de la croix"* is, along with the two natures of Christ, the two comings of Christ, and the two conditions of man's existence, a "source of contradictions".[22] It stands for the sense of contradiction or paradox which lies at the heart of Pascal's understanding of Christian faith, and points to the indirect, figurative nature of human knowledge of God. In L964, one of the more untidy fragments in the collection, Pascal writes: "it is strange that there is no means of giving them any idea of religion." Attached to this in the manuscript is the brief comment "A crucified God" (*Un Dieu crucifié*). This bold statement of the identification of God with the suffering of Christ, is again a sign for Pascal of the obscurity of the Christian religion to those outside it, the impossibility of understanding the religion of a crucified God from a position of neutrality.

A third range of meaning understands the cross as representing a pattern of the Christian life. L271 declares how Jesus came to teach that people would be delivered from their blindness and sin, and that this would happen "by men hating themselves and following him through his misery and death on the cross".[23] As already mentioned above, Pascal sees Christian morality as symbolised by "a crucified God" ("*un Dieu crucifié*" - the first of two occurrences of this phrase in L964). Behaviour is to be shaped by the cross. This point is clarified by a remark made by Pascal in the letter sent from Clermont on the 17th October 1651 to his sister and brother-in-law on the occasion of his father's death:

> It is one of the great principles of Christianity, that everything which happened to Jesus Christ must happen both in the soul and the body of each Christian; that just as Jesus Christ suffered during his mortal life, died in this mortal life, was raised to a new life, ascended to heaven, and sat on the right hand of the Father; in the same way, the body and the

soul must suffer, die, be raised, ascend to heaven and sit on the right hand.[24]

Christian life is to take on a Christomorphic pattern, dominated in this life by suffering and death after the example of Christ. Towards the end of his life, Pascal increasingly returned to the theme of imitation of the cross and the adoption of suffering in his own personal piety.[25]

This brief survey has indicated how frequently Pascal picks up the language and themes of 1 Corinthians 1-2 in his analysis of conversion, revelation and Christian behaviour. The role of the cross in relation to the wisdom and foolishness of Christianity in Pascal's theology remains an aspect of his thought which has seldom been examined in any great detail. Sellier, for example, comments on the centrality of Christ and the cross for Pascal: "*Sans cette croix, pas de salut.*"[26] His reference to the cross concerns only the sinners' need for salvation, however. As we shall show, while this is certainly part of what Pascal has in mind when he mentions the cross, it has a much wider range of meaning, and forms an important structural theme in his theology and apologetics, defining his position between dogmatism and scepticism. Again, David Wetsel touches on the centrality of the cross for Pascal, but only in a short section in the conclusion of his study.[27] Otherwise, studies of Pascal's theology have generally neglected to examine this strand of his thought in the *Pensées*.[28] We have here an important theme for Pascal which has not attracted the attention it might have done. Pascal's thought is highly complex and interconnected, made more intricate and difficult to disentangle by the notorious textual problems associated with the form of the *Pensées*. As a result, his references to the cross are often linked to other related themes. The place of the cross in Pascal's theology can be understood only by placing it in the wider context of his theological and apologetic thought, and seeing the role it plays there. This task will be attempted in the chapters that follow.

Notes:

[1]I will refer to the *Pensées* as numbered in the Lafuma edition from *Pascal: Œuvres Complètes* (Paris: Editions du Seuil, 1963). English translations are mostly taken from ed. A. J. Krailsheimer, *Pascal: Pensées* (Harmondsworth: Penguin, 1966), where the numbering also follows the Lafuma edition.

[2]"*Luther tout, hors le vrai... Luther (tout hormis le vrai)."*

[3]"*L'hérésie d'aujourd'hui ne concevant pas que ce sacrement contient tout ensemble et la présence de Jésus-Christ, et sa figure... croit qu'on ne peut admettre l'une de ces vérités sans exclure l'autre, pour cette raison."*

[4]*Le manuscrit des Pensées de Pascal 1662*, ed. L. Lafuma (Paris: Les Libraires Associés, 1962), 249.

[5]Cf. B. Hall, "*Hoc est Corpus Meum*: The Centrality of the Real Presence for Luther", *Luther: Theologian for Catholics and Protestants*, ed. G. Yule (Edinburgh: T. & T. Clark, 1985), 112-44.

[6]See E.J. Kearns, *Ideas in Seventeenth-Century France* (Manchester: Manchester University Press, 1979), 1-31, for a summary of some of these developments, although it should be noted that Kearns does underestimate the importance of theological ideas in the period.

[7]A. Sedgwick, *Jansenism in Seventeenth Century France: Voices from the Wilderness* (Charlottesville: University Press of Virginia, 1977), 9, notes how figures as different as Montaigne and Saint-Cyran both rejected the scholastic method, the former because it failed to establish truth, the latter because it encouraged speculation rather than spirituality. T.H. Aston, *Crisis in Europe 1560-1660: Essays from Past and Present* (London: Routledge & Kegan Paul, 1965), 104, comments that this age marks "the end of Aristotelianism".

[8]R. Briggs, *Communities of Belief: Cultural and Social Tensions in Early Modern France* (Oxford: Clarendon, 1989), 341, remarks how modern scholarship has shown how Jansenism was "an integral part of the great movement for reform within the Gallican church. Practically every one of their individual views can be found in authors of unquestioned orthodoxy."

[9]*Vie de Monsieur Pascal, Œuvres*, 21.

[10]"*rien de tout cela ne peut nous changer et nous rendre capable de connaître et aimer Dieu que la vertu de la folie de la croix.*" The manuscript of this fragment confirms the impression that Pascal's thought at this point centres around the folly of the cross. The original piece seems to end with "...*mais la croix et la folie*" (the last five words in slightly larger letters implying emphasis). The next sentence of the fragment is written in much smaller letters, perhaps added later, again leading up to "... *la vertu de la folie de la croix*". The final two clauses ("*sans sagesse...*" and "*ainsi notre religion...*") are both written in small letters to one side, implying they are afterthoughts to help explain the main idea which consists of the folly of the cross as the heart of Christianity.

[11] L458, 808, 842.

[12] L 695. See also L131 for the same idea.

[13] *"Ce qui les fait croire est la croix."*

[14] L241: *"un dieu humilié et jusqu'à la mort".*

[15] *A Concordance to the Pensées*, (eds. H.M. Davidson and P.H. Dubé (Ithaca: Cornell University Press, 1975) lists all the occurrences, although there is a concentration of these in the fragments between L439-48.

[16] I take it that the *Pensées* were written in preparation for an Apology. See the robust defence of this position in D. Wetsel, *Pascal and Disbelief: Catechesis and Conversion in the Pensées* (Washington D.C.: Catholic University of America, 1994), 16-24.

[17] These are most probably the Jesuits, as we shall see in due course.

[18] *"s'offrir par les humiliations aux inspirations, qui seules peuvent faire le vrai et salutaire effet,* ne evacuetur crux Christi".

[19] *"Un Dieu humilié jusqu'à la croix".*

[20] See L261 for a fuller treatment of this idea.

[21] *"Il fallait que le Christ souffrît - Un Dieu humilié - Voilà le chiffre que saint Paul nous donne."* The manuscript again offers some clarification here: the words *"voilà le chiffre qui Saint Paul nous donne"* are inserted above the three other previous clauses, indicating that it refers to all three, not just to the last. This makes it clear that the *chiffre* does not refer just to God's humiliation in the incarnation, but to the Christ's passion, alluded to by *"il fallait que le Christ souffrît".*

[22] *"source [de] contrariétés".*

[23] *"en se haïssant soi-même et en le suivant par la misère et la mort de la croix".*

[24] *"C'est un des grands principes du christianisme, que tout ce qui est arrivé à Jésus-Christ doit se passer et dans l'âme et dans le corps de chaque Chrétien; que comme Jésus-Christ a souffert durant sa vie mortelle, est mort à cette vie mortelle, est ressuscité d'une nouvelle vie, est monté au ciel, et sied à la dextre du Père; ainsi le corps et l'âme doivent souffrir, mourir, ressusciter, monter au ciel, et seoir à la dextre".* (*Œuvres*, 278).

[25] e.g. according to Mme Périer, Pascal insisted on the necessity that the believer *"hait soi-même et qu'on aimait la vie mortifiée de Jésus-Christ"* for the correct understanding of Scripture (*Œuvres*, 23).

[26] P. Sellier, *Pascal et Saint Augustin* (Paris: Armand Colin, 1970), 295.

[27] D. Wetsel, *L'Ecriture et le Reste: The Pensées of Pascal in the Exegetical Tradition of Port-Royal* (Columbus: Ohio State University Press, 1981), 218-21. For an analysis of this argument, see below.

[28] e.g. J. Russier, *La Foi Selon Pascal* (2 vols.; Paris: Presses Universitaires de France, 1949); J. Miel, *Pascal and Theology* (Baltimore: John Hopkins Press, 1969).

Thirteen: Pascal's God

Pascal was one of many in seventeenth century France seeking to defend what he considered to be orthodox Christian faith from its detractors. Pascal's originality within this apologetic tradition has been interpreted in various ways. Julien-Eymard d'Angers's extensive study discerned three types of earlier apologists, Thomists who appealed primarily to rationality, Humanists who appealed equally to reason and *sentiment*, and Augustinians who recommended submission of reason to the authority of the Church and the Bible. In relation to these, the *Pensées*, while broadly following much of the Augustinians' theology, departed from them in significant ways. According to d'Angers, Pascal's unfinished apologetic contains three distinct marks of originality: a sophisticated and novel interpretation of the old argument of the wager, a more penetrating psychology which focused not on scholastic proofs but on evoking a dramatic sense of religious anxiety, and the dialectical method, seeking to bring the unbeliever to his knees to make way for the ultimate synthesis in the gospel.[1] Patricia Topliss divides 17th century apologists into just two types, "optimistic rationalists & pessimistic Augustinians",[2] placing

d'Angers' Thomists and Humanists into one category. While Pascal
again sides firmly with the Augustinians, for Topliss his originality
lies not so much in the ideas he uses, as in the rhetorical skill which
he displays in expounding them. The notions of the wretchedness of
man without God, the dual nature of humanity as both glorious and
wretched and its explanation in the fall, the wager, the arguments
from prophecies and miracles are all fairly common in contemporary
apologetics.[3] Pascal's originality lay more in rhetoric than in ideas.
Jean Mesnard again places Pascal among the Augustinian tradition,
but claims his originality lay in applying Augustinian principles, not
normally associated with persuasion and appeals to believe, to the
science of apologetics.[4]

PASCAL AND THE IDENTITY OF GOD

While other apologists mostly take the question for granted,
Pascal has an intense interest in the question of the *identity* of God.
In one particularly important fragment, L449, he argues that much
of the contemporary argument against Christianity does no harm at
all to the Christian God, but merely undermines the God of Deism.
Pascal is quite clear what Christianity is NOT. It is by no means

> worshipping a God considered to be great and mighty and eternal, which
> is properly speaking deism, almost as remote from the Christian religion
> as atheism, its complete opposite.[5]

Instead, Pascal depicts the true God of the Christians, the God of
the Bible. Using the motif of the God of the Patriarchs, as in his
famous *Mémorial*, Pascal's God, far from being merely the "author
of mathematical truths and the order of the elements",[6] is one who
fills the soul and heart, directly invading the interior emotional life
of men and women to bring about a sense both of their own *misère*
and his mercy. He is a God who desires intimacy with us at the
deepest level of the soul, a jealous God who instils in those whom
he possesses an insatiable and exclusive desire for himself. In place
of the impersonal creative force of Deism, or even of Cartesianism,[7]

Pascal evokes an intensely personal, passionate God who desires an exclusive intimacy with his human creation at the most profound level of its being. Pascal's God is not object but subject, the Augustinian God of love and consolation. This passage is in effect an exposition of the *"Dieu sensible au coeur, non à la raison"*, God perceived by the heart, not by the reason[8] (L424), a God apprehended in an entirely different way from the God of the Deists, pagans or Epicureans, and at an entirely different level of human cognition. God is known in this radically different way because he is a radically different kind of God.

These themes are of course characteristically Augustinian and Jansenist.[9] They are by no means original to Pascal, but are nonetheless foundational for him. For Pascal, in common with the Augustinian tradition, God is known through love. A vital theme both within and beyond the *Pensées* is that of the *deux amours*, love for God[10] and self-love.[11] The theme is explained in Pascal's letter to M. and Mme. Périer from October 1651:

> God created mankind with two loves, one for God, the other for himself; but under this law, that love for God should be infinite, that is to say, without any other end but God himself, and that love for oneself should be finite and related to God... Since sin arrived, mankind has lost the first of these loves.[12]

In the Fall, love for God was replaced by self-love. This exchange has infected all human existence, including the ability to reason and to know.[13] Truth without love cannot come from God,[14] lack of love for God leads to loss of understanding, an inability to recognise the hand of God;[15] to depart from love is to depart from God.[16] In turn, self-love is the one thing which prevents a person from finding God, and which eventually destroys the soul.[17] Humankind is therefore now blind due to self-love, which prevents both knowledge of and love for God.[18] To know God rightly it is necessary to be able to love him, something which only God can bring about by an act of grace.[19] This God is known through love, not speculation.

Pascal's concern with the identity of God lies at the heart of the *Mémorial*, the autonomous and highly personal document found sewn into Pascal's coat by an alert servant a few days after his death.[20] The content and nature of Pascal's experience on his 'night of fire', 23 November 1654 are disputed. Suggestions have ranged from an initial impetus to search for God which leads to a fuller conversion in due course,[21] to the arrival at a sense of certainty about God,[22] to an assurance of his own personal predestination which he had doubted before,[23] to a discovery of the humanity of Jesus which both resolved tensions and led him to the limit of the reasoning he had previously valued.[24] Very often the interpretation of the *Mémorial* is determined by other subsequent texts. If we examine purely the text itself, the content and nature of the experience can be identified with greater clarity.

After the precise timing of the experience, and the single word *Feu* the text begins with the famous distinction between the God of the Patriarchs, and that of the philosophers and scholars, the *"philosophes et savants"*. It proceeds to the double mention of *"Dieu de Jésus-Christ"*, again making a clear distinction between the God of Jesus Christ and any other type of God. Pascal's use of the biblical quotation from Ruth 1:16, "Your God will be my God" could refer either to the God of Jesus Christ, or more likely the God of Port-Royal, the Jansenist community near Paris. After all, part of Pascal's resolution on that night was to submit to the guidance of a spiritual director at the community.[25] In either case the line implies the adoption of a *particular* God, *"ton Dieu"*, and a departure from another God, presumably that of the *"philosophes et savants"*. Pascal has a profound sense of privileged initiation into the intimate knowledge of a God whom the world has not understood: "O righteous Father, the world had not known you, but I have known you." Several lines indicate further the Christocentricity of Pascal's experience of God:

He can only be found by the ways taught in the gospels…
"This is eternal life, that they might know you, the only true God, and the one you have sent"

Jesus Christ
Jesus Christ…
He can only be kept by the ways taught in the Gospel.[26]

Pascal's account of this experience is shot through with the sense of discovery of this different God, the God of Jesus Christ, the God found only in the ways taught by the gospels. It is a God from whom Pascal has turned in the past (*"fui, renoncé, crucifié"*), yet who now gives him a taste of joy, peace and certainty. The basic structure of the fragment implies that at least part of Pascal's experience was a turning away from a false God to discover, or perhaps rediscover the true God. This crucial distinction between the false and the true God runs through the document like a refrain. It has often been suggested that this experience ended a period of spiritual aridity at the nadir of Pascal's 'worldly period'.[27] 1654 had seen the intensification of the dispute surrounding Port-Royal over Jansenius's controversial Augustinian theology. Cardinal Mazarin had forced through a synodical condemnation of the Five Propositions, an alleged summary of Jansenius's teaching on the 9th March, and on the 29th September, Pope Innocent X had confirmed to the French bishops his condemnation of Jansenius. Pascal can hardly have been unaware of these developments, and the growing polarisation between the theology of Port-Royal and that of the Sorbonne. On the 27th October, less than a month before the 'night of fire', Pascal had quietly and rather abruptly withdrawn from his investigations with Pierre de Fermat on *La Règle des Partis,*[28] implying a certain weariness with such mathematical games. A decision in favour of "total submission to Jesus Christ and to my director"[29] (who was in time to be Singlin, one of the *Solitaires* at Port-Royal-des-Champs), could hardly be anything other than a commitment to Port-Royal and its theology, in opposition to that of its opponents. The earlier myth of Pascal's complete abandonment of the world after his 'worldly period', founded on Mme Périer's account of her brother's life and fostered by Chateaubriand, has now largely been discredited. It is clear, as we shall discuss in due course, that Pascal's rejection of the world was by no means total. On the 23rd November 1654, Pascal turned away not from all worldly activity as such, but from the God of the philosophers, to rediscover the God of Port-Royal, the Augustinian God of love and consolation, the God of Jesus Christ, the God as he now saw it, of Christianity.

LE DIEU CACHÉ

Pascal's most celebrated description of this particular God is that of the *Dieu caché*, the hidden God. Although not an uncommon idea in Jansenist literature, it has a prominence and sharpness in Pascal not shared by any other writer in this tradition. For example, Pierre Nicole could claim that God hides the truth among falsehoods, the right way among wrong ways,[30] and Antoine Arnauld, that God hides his future plans.[31] This same idea in Pascal's hands, becomes the notion of the God who hides *himself*, not just the truth about himself.

The *Pensées* frequently emphasise the impossibility of a direct knowledge of God though nature.[32] Instead for Pascal, the observation of creation (*l'ordre du monde*), proves "neither the total absence, nor the manifest presence of divinity, but the presence of a God who hides himself".[33] This God is at the same time accessible, yet inaccessible through nature. While it is impossible to perceive a full face-to-face vision of God, what can be perceived is, as it were, the space God has left behind, his absence.[34] Pascal does have a kind of natural theology, but it is a negative natural theology, teaching that God is hidden, inaccessible, absent, a *Dieu perdu*.[35] Outside faith and revelation, there is no certainty at all as to whether humankind was created by a good God, an evil demon or simply by chance,[36] and we can know neither goodness nor justice.[37] There is enough in nature to provide hints, signs of a God, but not enough to convince conclusively.[38] Observation of fallen nature provides not answers but questions, and the confusion of the simultaneous presence and absence of God.[39]

The relationship of the *Dieu caché* to the rest of Pascal's theology has often been questioned. It has been seen by some as a tactical move on Pascal's part to divert awkward questions and resolve difficult contradictions. As Henri Gouhier pointed out, for Pascal, hiddenness is part of God's will rather than his essential nature.[40] Pascal does not think of God as hidden in the humanist sense that he is transcendent and so high above puny mankind that they cannot attain to knowledge of him, but rather that he is hidden because he has chosen to hide himself. This can seem to imply that the hiddenness of God is a secondary and provisional theme for Pascal rather than something which goes to the very heart of God's nature. David Wetsel suggests that it gives a theological framework for the existence of figures, and constitutes a device used to explain why not everyone has acted upon the proofs of Christianity;[41] Patricia Topliss goes so far as to call it a "polemical subterfuge".[42] Is the Hidden God simply an apologist's device, or does it reveal something about the very nature of Pascal's God? Is it part of Pascal's rhetoric or his theology?

Pascal's Augustinian understanding of God demanded that he be known by love not speculation, by the heart and not reason. God's hiddenness is intimately linked with this understanding of God. If God cannot be known apart from love, it is not surprising that all speculative attempts to perceive him, to establish his existence, or relate to him without the prior desire to love him are doomed to failure. Faced with the Fall, the turning away from God to self-love, this God will always hide himself from those who will not seek him through the heart, but try to examine him through reason. God hides himself deliberately in order to divide those who love him from those who do not, the single most important distinction Pascal makes between people.[43]

The hiddenness of God is a theological expression of human blindness brought about through the concupiscence which possesses fallen people. It is the other side of the coin of human sin. In the classic Augustinian tradition, men and women are blind on the one hand because they have chosen self-love rather than love for God, and their minds have become darkened. Pascal expresses the other side of this dynamic in the idea of the God who hides himself. They cannot see God because God has hidden himself from them, to prevent any possibility of a presumptuous knowledge of himself by those who have no desire to love him.[44] Pascal has no problem in harmonising these two ways of speaking about the same thing. His first *Ecrit sur la Grâce* for example, is an extended explanation of how salvation and damnation can be ascribed both to God and to humankind at the same time. God's hiddenness is the counterpart to self-chosen human darkness, his response to a fallen world, and to creatures who want to know him on their own terms, without loving him. He hides from those who tempt him (*tenter*), but reveals himself to those who seek him (*chercher*).[45] He is partly hidden, and partly revealed in order to impress upon humankind both their corruption and yet also their capacity to know and love him.[46]

God's hiddenness is therefore a direct expression of his character as a God knowable only in love, not speculation, by the heart, not by reason. Despite appearing at times to be a secondary part of Pascal's polemic, the hiddenness of God is a necessary part of his argument not rhetorically but theologically. The idea of the *Dieu caché* is far more fundamental to Pascal's thought than is sometimes understood: it is an expression of the character of the God Pascal came to experience on the 'night of fire', the God who can be approached only in love, not curiosity. It is a kind of anti-revelation of God's character. By a deliberate act of concealment, God defines himself negatively, demonstrating that he is *not* the God who can be examined objectively within nature, and therefore pointing away from speculation or the observation of nature as the route by which he can be known.

Any attempt to prove or disprove this God through the observation of nature is doomed, because it founders on the rock of the ambiguity of the post-Fall created order. It is driven to ignore either the presence or the absence of God in nature in a desire to find a totalizing answer to the question of God's existence. It cannot live with the ambiguity which is inherent within the order of creation. As a result, it is bound to lead either to despair (with the conclusion that God can never be known), or to pride (with the conclusion that God is everywhere apparent, and can be known by human powers of reasoning). If it does claim to lead to knowledge of God, it merely leads to the knowledge of the wrong God, the God of the *"philosophes et savants"*. Contemporary Christian apologists may swallow this, but the truly perceptive searcher will not.[47] Instead, he will remain suspended between belief and unbelief, unable to decide between them.[48]

LE DIEU CRUCIFIÉ

While the observation of nature leads to uncertainty, several fragments in the *Pensées* indicate the place where God can be known, namely in Jesus Christ.[49] We have already noted the Christological focus of the *Mémorial*, and a study of other texts of the same period both reinforces this impression, and highlights a focus on the crucified Christ within Pascal's Christology.

Robert Nelson has noted the "fervent, pious self-abnegation" of the four texts written around the time of Pascal's 'night of fire' (The *Mémorial, Sur la Conversion du Pécheur, Le Mystère de Jésus,* and the *Abrégé de la vie de Jésus-Christ*).[50] This mood stands in stark contrast to the value placed on rationality, scientific knowledge and intellectual power in his letter to Christina, Queen of Sweden, sent to accompany his calculating machine in June 1652. For Nelson, the key factor for the newly devout Pascal, post-November 1654 is a rediscovery of the incarnation, the real humanity of Jesus. This theme recurs throughout these texts, and reverberates back into Pascal's own self-consciousness: "Jesus in his passion is equal to God, Pascal in his agony is equal to Jesus."[51] Nelson's analysis is acute and perceptive, but a close reading of these texts allows us to take this incarnational concentration even further.

1.   First, the reading of the *Mémorial* suggested above shows that Pascal's interest goes beyond the incarnation *per se* to the God who lies behind it. His newly kindled interest is not merely in Jesus Christ but the *God* of Jesus Christ. Nelson is quite right to emphasise Pascal's new interest in the real humanity of Jesus, but Pascal does not stop there. He goes on to ponder the implications of the revelation of God in this precise form for the identity of God himself.

2.   Pascal shows a particular interest in the sufferings and death of Christ during this period. *Le Mystère de Jésus*, probably composed early in 1655 only a few months after the 'night of fire' is in effect an extended meditation on the sufferings of Christ, in particular the scene in Gethsemane. On the one hand Christ suffers on behalf of sinners, praying for them while they sleep, the disciples literally, the elect spiritually. In this sense, Pascal envisages only a great gulf between the sinner and the Redeemer.[52] On the other hand, the meditation envisages conformity of the sinner to Christ's sufferings:

> Jesus tears himself away with his disciples to enter into his agony; we must tear ourselves away from those who are nearest to, and most intimate with us, to imitate him… I must add my tears to his and join with him, and he will save me in saving himself.[53]

Christ's sufferings are to be mirrored in the life of the sinner if he is to be saved. The gulf between God and the sinner is to be crossed by Christ's atoning death, followed by a conformity of the sinner to Christ, in particular by sharing his sufferings.

In the *Abrégé de la Vie de Jésus-Christ*, Pascal returns constantly to this theme. The Preface to the work begins with a brief account of Christ's life, death, resurrection and ascension, and the focus lies on the cross:

> He conversed with men, was stripped of his glory, taking on the form of a slave, and passed through many sufferings until his death on the cross, on which he carried our sorrows and our iniquities, and destroyed our death by his own.[54]

While the bulk of the *Abrégé* consists of an account of the passion, the events of Christ's life, his resurrection and ascension all receive much briefer attention. Even the *Entretien avec M. de Saci*, (the conversation which it records took place probably in early 1655) although not directly tackling the same themes as the previous two works, still shows Pascal using bold language to describe the Christian gospel promises, "which are nothing less than the ransom paid by the death of God".[55] The Christ of whom Pascal thinks in these intense early months after his so-called 'second conversion' is first and foremost the crucified Christ, both God and man, bearing the sins of the world, and the sins of Pascal himself. This accounts for Pascal's daring language about God as the "*Dieu crucifié*" and "*un dieu humilié*".[56] While Pascal's God is hidden in nature, he still points to the crucified Christ as the place where God can uniquely be known.

It does not follow, however, that while God lies hidden in nature, he is openly visible in Christ. For Pascal, God's revelation in Christ and in the Scriptures is equally ambiguous and hidden.[57] The prophets' message was that the messiah, when he came, would be hidden, unrecognisable as a revelation of God, mistaken by many.[58] The first coming of Christ was always meant to be hidden, quiet and ambiguous, recognisable only by those who looked for him, in contrast to his second coming, which would be plain to all, even his enemies.[59] In fact his presence was so obscure that historians of the time hardly even mention him.[60] Jesus came both to blind and to sanctify[61] at the same time, and even his miracles (like all miracles) are ambiguous.[62] God hides himself, even in the act of revealing himself.

The fourth of Pascal's letters to Mlle de Roannez in October 1656, is an important explanation of the theme of the *Dieu caché*, and gives a history of God's hiddenness. He was first of all "hidden under the veil of nature, which hid him from us until the Incarnation". In the incarnation itself, "he is still more hidden by covering himself in humanity", and since then he has been hidden in the elements of the Eucharist.[63] Hiddenness is therefore a constant within God's relationship to the world. More precisely, it is a constant within his relationship to a *fallen* world. Only Adam has experienced a state of glory, knowing God and salvation directly,[64] and only Christ's second coming, which will undo the effects of the Fall, will be clear and unambiguous to all.[65]

To the unbeliever, God remains hidden, both in nature, and even in Christ and the cross. There seems then no way through from a fallen world to knowledge of God, or possession of truth. Yet,

Pascal claims, the very obscurity of God's central act of self-disclosure gives the vital clue to the knowledge of God. The suffering Christ, the *Dieu humilié* is precisely the *chiffre que saint Paul nous donne.*[66]

LA RÉVÉLATION DE CE MÊME DIEU [67]

A number of fragments clarify what Pascal means by this enigmatic line of thinking. L192 explains how the knowledge of God through Christ points the way beyond pride and despair, both of which can only be partial solutions. It is because we find in Christ both *"Dieu et notre misère"*. L449 explains this at greater length. Pascal notes the general principle that "if there is a true religion upon earth… it ought to be... the goal and centre towards which all things lead".[68] In other words, it must be capable of comprehending and explaining all things. Sceptical critics argue that because the existence of a *Dieu considéré comme grand et puissant et éternel* is by no means obvious from observation of the world, Christianity cannot explain all things, therefore God does not exist, and religion is fruitless. Pascal agrees with them concerning the ambiguity of the evidence for the existence of God, but as we have seen, this is an argument not against Christianity, but against Deism. He proceeds to assert that the true "object towards which all things lead" is not the existence of this powerful and eternal God as such, but Jesus Christ: *"Jésus-Christ est l'objet de tout, et le centre où tout tend."* Jesus Christ explains all, and the observed order of the world actually points towards Jesus Christ. These are difficult ideas, though, and need some explaining!

Pascal has already indicated in this fragment what he considers are the two central points of Christianity: "that there is a God, of whom men are capable, and that there is a corruption in nature which makes them unworthy".[69] Human *grandeur* and *misère*, the infinite capacity to know God and the fall from that knowledge, are the two fundamental principles which it is vital to grasp, and to understand in balance with one another. Without that balance, one is led either into arrogant deistic pride or resigned atheistic despair.

Jesus Christ is the centre of all things because in him these two fundamental principles are united:

> Let us go on to examine the order of the world, and see whether all things do not tend to establish the two main tenets of this religion: Jesus Christ is the object of all things, the centre towards which all things tend. Whoever knows him knows the reason for everything… it is not possible to know Christ without knowing both God and our wretchedness alike.

Jésus-Christ here is a kind of shorthand for the church's teaching about Christ. It includes in its range the whole Christian message that there is a God, that men are fallen, and that God has sent a redeemer to rescue them.[70] Once these simple principles are understood, everything falls into place, and the obscurity of creation is explained:

> For my part, I confess that as soon as the Christian religion reveals the principle that men are by nature corrupt, and have fallen away from God, this opens one's eyes so that the mark of this truth is everywhere apparent: for nature is such that it points at every turn to a God who has been lost, both within man and without, and a corrupt nature.[71]

It is in this sense that Christ is the centre of everything, and explains everything.[72] Once Christ and the cross, the act of reconciliation between man and God are understood, both God and human sin, both human *grandeur* and *misère* are understood. When this dualism is understood, with all that it implies about both the reality of God, yet human inability to see him, the reason for the obscurity of God behind creation is understood. In the light of Christ, (and this principle of creation and fall understood within him), everything in creation now "resounds with proofs of these two truths". Without him, all remains confusing. To grasp that Christ was crucified for the sins of the world is to confess one's own weakness, and the obscurity in one's own mind. It is to understand that failure to see God clearly in creation is not caused by the fact that he is not there, but by human blindness which can only partially glimpse truth. Christ crucified therefore becomes the key which unlocks the mysterious ambiguity of nature.

CONCLUSION

This chapter has argued that one significant distinguishing mark of Pascal's apologetics was his insistence on the identity of God. Many 17th century apologists such as Antoine Sirmond, Pierre Charron, Jean de Silhon and Yves de Paris had tried to prove God or the immortality of the soul.[73] The attempt had failed, thought Pascal, not so much because it chose the wrong methods, as because it aimed to prove the wrong God, a God not susceptible to proof. Especially after the 'night of fire', Pascal identified God as the God of the Augustinian tradition represented in his own day by Jansenism. This God can be approached only by love, not speculation, through moral and spiritual reorientation, not rational deduction. This God therefore hides himself from human attempts to find him through objective observation: the hiddenness of God is a direct result of his belief in the Jansenist God. Pascal's world is not the neat Thomist world where God gives clear indications of his existence and nature, but the deeply ambiguous fallen Augustinian world which speaks simultaneously of God's presence and absence. For human creatures to know this hidden God will involve a much more radical solution than contemplating obvious proofs in nature. It will involve an engagement with God not just as object but an encounter with him as subject. The key to this puzzle lies in the crucified Christ, who for Pascal represents the dual principle of God and human sin.

We may conclude this chapter by pointing out two important implications of this argument for the study of the *Pensées*.

PASCAL, THEOLOGY AND SCIENCE

In the *Préface sur le Traité du Vide* completed in 1651, Pascal distinguishes carefully between the methodology for establishing truth in theology and in science. However, this is not to suggest that these two were in separate and unrelated compartments in his mind. For Pascal, observation of the natural world leads neither to belief in God nor atheism. Instead it provides "too much to deny and too much to prove".[74] It leads towards the inability to decide between the simultaneous presence and absence of God, to the *Dieu caché*. Pascal identifies this hidden God with the crucified God, with Christ himself. Therefore for Pascal, there is no inherent contradiction between the results of scientific observation of the natural world, and his belief in Christ: both, if anything point in the same direction: to the presence of the hidden God. God lies hidden in the natural world which gives hints of God's presence, but not enough to convince. This God is the same as the God he sees in Jesus Christ.

There is for him no essential contradiction between his existence as a scientist/mathematician, and his existence as a Christian and a theologian. God's self-revelation in Christ is in perfect harmony with his self-revelation in the natural world, in fact it is the only thing which makes sense of it. Both nature and Christ point not to the absence or manifest presence of God, but to the *Dieu caché*, the *Dieu perdu*. Pascal's empiricism has often been noticed, especially in contrast to Descartes's method of logical deduction from first principles.[75] The new science, far from disproving God, in fact supports Pascal's argument.[76] Like God's revelation in Christ, nature teaches not the clearly manifest powerful God of the philosophers, but the hidden God of Jansenism.

Likewise, his readers have sometimes wondered how Pascal was able to ally himself to the world-denying theology and spirituality of Port-Royal, yet avoid the path taken by his sister Jacqueline, the *Solitaires* of Port-Royal-des-Champs and the Barcosian faction of Jansenism, namely leaving the world behind for the solitary or monastic life. The answer lies in Pascal's insight into the *Dieu caché* as uniting both theological and scientific existence. His spiritual experience, theological meditation and scientific observation all harmonised into this vision of the hidden God, so that for him at least there could be no contradiction between them. All in turn point to the same God: one who hides himself within his very revelation. Hiddenness, obscurity is even the distinguishing mark of the Christian God.[77] It becomes for Pascal also the mark of true religion: any religion which asserts otherwise is manifestly false, and the religion which asserts a hidden God bears the mark of truth.[78] While the Thomist God of contemporary apologetics just does not 'fit' with the emerging scientific view of the world, Pascal argues that only the Augustinian God, hidden within a fallen creation, who reveals himself in hidden form, can both make sense within, and make sense of the observable created order. In the new empirical scientific age, to use the words of a much later theologian, "only a suffering God can help".[79]

THE *PENSÉES*, JANSENISM AND APOLOGETICS

It is uncertain how far the *Pensées* should be understood as a Jansenist text.[80] Pascal's rhetoric rather than his theology is often considered their most original feature. Leszek Kolakowski, for example, suggests that while Pascal's doctrine is Jansenist, all that is striking in the *Pensées* is not Jansenist: for him, Pascal writes an apology for Christianity, not Jansenism.[81] It is true that the distinctive colouring Pascal gave to these Jansenist doctrines makes his apology stand out from others, but it must not be forgotten that without his belief in the Jansenist God, the Augustinian God known by love not speculation, the apology would not be what it was. The Thomist God of much 17th century apologetics does not hide himself, but rather reveals himself in nature. Therefore Thomist apologetics proceeds from an entirely different starting-point, seeking to display the evidence for this God visible within nature. For Pascal however, God's self-concealment[82] is a direct result of the particular identity of this Jansenist God, who hides himself within a fallen world, in order that he may be found only by those who acknowledge their own weakness and sin[83] and who seek God with their whole heart. While Pascal goes beyond contemporary Jansenism in his attempt to write apologetics, the originality of that Apology derives from the very fact that it is Jansenist.[84] His whole approach to persuasion is founded on the identity of God as knowable by love not speculation, and consequently on an understanding of the way in which he can and cannot be found. It is vital therefore not to minimise the significance of Jansenism in the question of Pascal's originality, as Kolakowski is in danger of doing. What is original about Pascal's Jansenism is that he writes apologetics, what is original about Pascal's apologetics is that it is Jansenist.

This Jansenist cast of thought inevitably involved Pascal in polemics, due to the controversial character of the movement, and Jesuit-inspired attempts to subdue it. Pascal's discovery of this *Dieu crucifié* had political as well as spiritual implications, and drew him into questions of power and its operation in the controversies of seventeenth century France. This is clearly the case in the *Lettres Provinciales* but is less often noticed in the *Penseés*. How this understanding of God shapes Pascal's Apology and enables him to engage in these polemics will be explored in the next chapter.

Notes:

[1]J-E d'Angers, *L'Apologétique en France de 1580 à 1670: Pascal et ses Précurseurs* (Paris: Nouvelles Editions Latines, 1954), esp. 239-41.

[2]P. Topliss, *The Rhetoric of Pascal: A Study of His Art of Persuasion in the 'Provinciales' and the 'Pensées'* (Leicester: Leicester University Press, 1966), 130.

[3]See J.K.Ryan, "The Argument of the Wager in Pascal and Others", *TNS* 19 (1945), 233-50, for the occurrence of this argument in other writers of the period.

[4]J. Mesnard, *Pascal* (Connaissance des Lettres; 5th ed.; Paris: Hatier, 1967), 177-80. Also, *Les Pensées de Pascal* (Paris: SEDES, 1976), 136-69.

[5]"*l'adoration d'un Dieu considéré comme grand et puissant et éternel; ce qui est proprement le déisme, presque aussi éloigné de la religion chrétienne que l'athéisme*".

[6]"*auteur des vérités géométriques et de l'ordre des éléments*".

[7]Pascal's attributed criticism of Descartes, that he treats God merely as a *chiquenaude* to start the world off, places Cartesianism under the same critique as Pascal applies to Deism (L1001).

[8]L424.

[9]R. Taveneaux, "Jansénisme et vie sociale en France au XVIIe siècle", *Jansénisme*

et Réforme Catholique (Nancy, Presses Universitaires de Nancy, 1992), 17-33, argues that the *deux délectations* were the pivot of the whole Jansenist system.

[10]Cf. L205, 287, 380, 453.

[11]Cf. L44, 153, 368, 373, 380, 427, 432, 460, 617, 764, 978.

[12]*Œuvres*, 277,

[13]L491: "*Nature corrompue. L'homme n'agit point par la raison qui fait son être.*"

[14]L926: "*la vérité hors de la charité n'est pas Dieu.*"

[15]L834: "*Ce qui fait qu'on ne croit pas les vrai miracles est le manque de charité.*"

[16]L948: "*On ne s'éloigne qu'en s'éloignant de la charité.*"

[17]L460.

[18]L149: "*nous sommes plein de ténèbres qui nous empêchent de la connaître et de l'aimer.*"

[19]L149.

[20]The *Mémorial* was not part of the proposed Apology, but is classified in the Pensées as L913.

[21]J. Miel, *Pascal and Theology*, 119-22.

[22]H.M. Davidson, *The Origins of Certainty* (Chicago: University of Chicago Press, 1979), 133; P. Sellier, "'*Sur les fleuves de Babylone*': The Fluidity of the World and the Search for Permanence in the Pensées", *Meaning, Structure and History in the Pensées of Pascal* (Biblio 17; ed. D. Wetsel; Paris: Papers on French Seventeenth Century Literature, 1990), 33-44.

[23]J. Calvet, *La Littérature Religieuse de François de Sales à Fénelon* (Paris: J. de Gigord, 1938), 176-7.

[24]R.J. Nelson, *Pascal, Adversary and Advocate* (Cambridge Mass.: Harvard University Press, 1981), 119-44.

[25]Although it has been suggested that this line is a later addition.

[26]"*Il ne se trouve que par les voies enseignées dans l'Évangile...*
Cette est la vie éternelle, qu'ils te connaissent seul vrai Dieu et celui que tu as envoyé J-C.
Jésus-Christ.
Jésus-Christ...
Il ne se conserve que par les voies enseignées dans l'Évangile."

[27]e.g. J.H. Broome, *Pascal* (London: Edward Arnold, 1965), 35-6.

[28]See Pascal's letter to Fermat dated 27 October 1654 in the *Œuvres*, 49.

[29]The phrase occurs in the *Mémorial*.

[30]"*Il (Dieu) a caché la véritable religion dans la multitude des fausses religions, les véritables Prophéties dans la multitude des fausses Prophéties, les véritable miracles dans la multitude des faux miracles, la véritable piété dans la multitude des fausses piétés, la voie du ciel dans la multitude des voies qui conduisent en enfer.*" Nicole: *Œuvres Choisies*, ed. H. Brémond (Paris: Bloud, 1909), 44.

[31]L. Goldmann, *The Hidden God: A Study of Tragic Vision in the Pensées of Pascal and the Tragedies of Racine* (London: Routledge & Kegan Paul, 1964), 160-3. (French original, Paris: Gallimard, 1959).

[32]e.g. L199, 429, 905.

[33]L449: "*ni une exclusion totale ni une présence manifeste de divinité, mais la présence d'un Dieu qui se cache*". Cf. L471: "*La nature est telle, qu'elle marque partout un Dieu perdu.*" Cf. L429.

[34]L148: "*un véritable bonheur, dont il ne lui reste maintenant que la marque et la trace toute vide*".

[35]L471.

[36]L131.

[37]L148.

[38]L429.

[39]L260, 265, 448.

[40]H. Gouhier, "Pascal et les humanismes de son temps", *Pascal Présent* (ed. Faculté des lettres de Clermont; Clermont-Ferrand: G. de Bussac, 1962), 77-104 (here, 101).

Wetsel, *L'Ecriture et le Reste*, 161.

[42]Topliss, *The Rhetoric of Pascal*, 235.

[43]L427: "*je fais une extrême différence de ceux qui travaillent de toutes leurs forces à s'en instruire, à ceux qui vivent sans s'en mettre en peine et sans y penser.*" Cf. also L160.

[44]L149: "*Il n'était donc pas juste qu'il parût d'une manière manifestement divine et absolument capable de convaincre tous les hommes, mais il n'était pas juste aussi qu'il vînt d'une manière si cachée qu'il ne pût être reconnu de ceux qui le cherchaient sincèrement. Il a voulu se rendre parfaitement connaissable à ceux-là, et ainsi voulant paraître à découvert à ceux qui le cherchent de tout leur cœur, et caché à ceux qui le fuient de tout leur cœur il a tempéré.*"

[45]L444.

[46]L446: "*S'il n'y avait point d'obscurité, l'homme ne sentirait point sa corruption; s'il n'y avait point de lumière, l'homme n'espérerait point de remède. Ainsi, il est non seulement juste, mais utile pour nous que Dieu soit caché en partie, et découvert en partie.*"

[47]L781.

[48]L199 is the classic statement of this idea: "*incapables de savoir certainement et d'ignorer absolument*", and of course the Wager takes the unbeliever through a similar inability to decide.

[49]L189: "*Nous ne connaissons Dieu que par J.-C.. Sans ce médiateur est ôtée toute communication avec Dieu*". Cf. also L417.

[50]Nelson, *Adversary and Advocate*, 144.

[51]Ibid., 131.

[52]"*Il n'y a nul rapport de moi à Dieu, ni à J.-C. juste. Mais il a été fait péché pour*

moi."

[53]*"Jésus s'arrache d'avec ses disciples pour entrer dans l'agonie; il faut s'arracher de ses plus proches et des plus intimes, pour l'imiter... Il faut ajouter mes plaies aux siennes et me joindre à lui et il me sauvera en se sauvant."*

[54]*"il a conversé parmi les hommes, dénué de sa gloire et revêtu de la forme d'un esclave, et a passé par beaucoup de souffrances jusqu'à la mort de la croix, sur laquelle il a porté nos langueurs et nos infirmités, et a détruit notre mort par la sienne".*

[55]*"qui ne sont autre chose que le digne prix de la mort d'un Dieu".*

[56]L220, 241, 253, 268. L241 in particular makes it clear that the *dieu humilié* is a direct reference to the cross: *"Source des contrariétés. Un Dieu humilié et jusqu'à la mort de la croix.... Un Messie triomphant de la mort par sa mort."*

[57]L389 shows a distinct awareness of this question.

[58]L228: *"Que disent les prophètes de J-C? qu'il sera évidemment Dieu? non mais qu'il est un Dieu véritablement caché, qu'il sera méconnu, qu'on ne pensera point que ce soit lui..."*

[59]L261.

[60]L300, 499.

[61]L237.

[62]L835.

[63]Pascal also mentions in addition God's hiddenness in the figurative sense of Scripture: 4th Letter *aux Roannez*, October 1656, *Œuvres*, 267.

[64]L392, 431.

[65]L261.

[66]L268.

[67]L485.

[68]*"s'il y a une véritable religion sur la terre... elle doit être tellement l'objet et le centre où toutes choses tendent".*

[69]Cf. L192 above.

[70]L427: *"La foi chrétienne ne va presque qu'à établir ces deux choses: la corruption de la nature, et la rédemption de Jésus-Christ."* See also L431: *"Tout ce qu'il nous importe de connaître est que nous sommes misérables, corrompus, séparés de Dieu, mais rachetés par Jésus-Christ."*

[71]L 471. See also L232 for a similar thought.

[72]L449: *"Qui le connaît connaît la raison de toutes choses."* See also L417.

[73]For the works concerned and more extensive lists of contemporary apologists, see d'Angers, *Pascal et ses Précurseurs*, 35-46.

[74]*"trop pour nier et trop pour m'assurer"*. L429, cf. L471.

[75]Mesnard, *Pascal*, 187-8 speaks of the *"primauté de l'expérience"* for Pascal in both science and theology. See also Mesnard's *Les Pensées*, 95-7, and A.J. Krailsheimer, Studies *in Self-Interest from Descartes to la Bruyère* (Oxford: Clarendon Press, 1962), 117-24.

[76]Cf. S. Melzer, *Discourses of the Fall: A Study of Pascal's Pensées* (Berkeley: University of California Press, 1986), 104ff.

[77]L427: "*Mais puisqu'elle dit, au contraire, que les hommes sont dans les ténèbres et dans l'éloignement de Dieu, qu'il s'est caché à leur connaissance, que c'est même le nom qu'il se donne dans les Ecritures,* Deus absconditus."

[78]L242: "*Dieu étant caché toute religion qui ne dit pas que Dieu est caché n'est pas véritable... La nôtre fait tout cela.* Vere tu es deus absconditus."

[79]D. Bonhoeffer, *Letters and Papers from Prison* (London: S.C.M., 1953), 122.

[80]e.g. L. Kolakowski, *God Owes Us Nothing: A Brief Remark on Pascal's Religion and the Spirit of Jansenism* (Chicago: University of Chicago Press, 1995), 118-25.

[81]Ibid., 194.

[82]Kolakowski himself acknowledges that the hiddenness of God is "the dominant theme of the Pensées". 143.

[83]L189: "*Ainsi nous ne pouvons bien connaître Dieu qu'en connaissant nos iniquités.*"

[84]Thus I would agree with the older conclusion of Calvet: "le charactère janséniste des Pensées est donc indéniable". J. Calvet, *La Littérature Religieuse de François de Sales à Fénelon* (Paris: J. de Gigord, 1938), 242.

Fourteen: The Cross in Pascal's Apologetics

The originality and effectiveness of Pascal's apologetics in the *Pensées* is rarely disputed. It is less clear however how that apologetic works, or how Pascal thinks the unbeliever is to be brought to faith. Most often, the Wager is seen as the crucial manœuvre, the turning point of the whole exercise.[1] Sara Melzer, for example, argues that for Pascal, the Fall involves a fall from truth into language. The inescapably rhetorical nature of language means we can have no access to certain truth. The classical tradition, confident that language can convey truth, represented in Pascal's own time by Descartes, had reached a dead end. The Wager as the gamble of faith is Pascal's way out of this 'aporia', pointing to a type of meaning which can be found only in the "a-textuality of the heart".[2] On the other hand, David Wetsel points to Pascal's pre-modern belief in the historical accuracy of scripture as the key to his argument: "the whole force of the Apology is based on the premise that Christianity is historically demonstrable."[3] The Bible provides "convincing proofs" (L149) such as prophecies and miracles, which are enough to indicate God's existence to those ready to seek for him. For Wetsel, the historical accuracy of the Bible is therefore fundamental to Pascal's argument, and a major principle of his apologetic appeal. Melzer and Wetsel therefore propose different approaches to the question of how Pascal's apologetic works. The question turns around the place of 'proofs': do they convince the unbeliever who has begun to search, as Wetsel implies, or do they enable the believer to make sense of the world from a new perspective? Although there is clearly no single chronology of conversion for Pascal, are the proofs designed primarily for unbelievers or believers?

The previous chapter suggested the centrality of the theme of the cross in Pascal's theology, encapsulating the gravity of human sin, and the provision of a redeemer. This chapter goes further to show the vital role the cross plays within Pascal's apologetics.

PERSPECTIVES ON THE CROSS

Within the *Pensées* the cross is approached from various different angles, which in turn lead to different estimates of its value. To pick up on a theme touched on in the last chapter, the cross both reveals and conceals God. Two fragments in particular explain this dynamic. Using the language of 1 Corinthians 1:18-25, fragments L842 and L291 of the *Pensées* both speak of the simultaneous wisdom and foolishness of Christianity. It is wise in that it can lay claim to many miracles, proofs, prophecies etc., and foolish in that it does not actually offer these to the unbeliever, but instead offers the apparent absurdity of the cross. On the one hand Christianity, the religion of the cross, turns people away by its folly. On the other, the cross is the way to make people believe:

> None of this can change us and make us capable of knowing and loving God, except the virtue contained in the folly of the cross.[4]

> This is a good enough reason for condemning those who do not believe, but not for making those who do belong believe. What makes them

believe is the cross. *Lest the cross of Christ should be made of none effect.*[5]

One fragment which sheds light on these is L381, one of a number of pieces[6] which discuss simple Christians who have come to believe without reading the Bible, or without knowledge of proofs, prophecies and compelling reasons. They do so, Pascal explains, because they have an inner disposition which prepares them for the Christian gospel. That disposition, placed in their hearts by God, makes them feel that there is a God, that they wish to love him and hate themselves, yet sense that they are incapable of doing this themselves, of reaching out to God, unless he first comes to them. Having this disposition, when they hear the gospel, that "God became man to unite himself with us", this so matches their desire and inner sentiments that they believe it immediately. Feeling the need for a mediator, someone to lift them to God and enable them to love him, this inner orientation fits exactly with the content of the message.[7]

Pascal adds significantly, that having heard this simple message about fall and redemption, "it takes no more than this to convince men whose hearts are thus disposed and who have such an understanding of their duty and incapacity".[8] In other words, all that is needed to convince someone in this state is the simple foolish message of God come to man, the message of Jesus Christ, and in particular his death on the cross. Once this disposition is in place, the coming of Christ can be seen to be the very thing which meets the deepest need of humanity.

This sheds considerable light on the meaning of L842. What convinces those who are inclined to believe is simply the message of the cross, Christ come to die for the sins of the world. L291 also fits into this pattern: it is not convincing proofs or signs, but the message of the cross which is able to change a person and make them capable of loving God, once that person is inclined to believe. Although L381 describes the 'simple' Christian, the same process has to happen for all who come to believe. Whether conversant with all the arguments for and against Christian faith or not, "we shall never believe, with an effective belief and faith, unless God inclines our hearts, and we shall believe as soon as he does so."[9]

L291 concludes with an important distinction: "*Ainsi notre religion est folle en regardant à la cause efficace et sage en regardant à la sagesse qui y prépare.*" This is not an easy statement to interpret, but can perhaps be paraphrased in the following manner: The "*cause efficace*" of Christianity (Christ and his death on the cross) appears foolish from the outside. However, regarded from the perspective of the *sagesse qui y prépare*, the 'wisdom which prepares for it', that is, a proper awareness of one's own weakness, sin and need for God, it appears as the wisest and most satisfying of all religions.

The cross, as both the wisdom and foolishness of God, both shuts and opens the door to belief. The key factor which decides whether the message of the cross enables faith or confirms indifference, is the disposition of the person looking at it, or in other words, the perspective or standpoint from which it is regarded, whether from a state of indifference towards God, or a deep sense of distance from and need for him.

Pascal often writes of this sense of perspective in the *Pensées*. He remarks how "things are true or false according to the perspective from which we look at them".[10] As a revelation of God, the cross is by no means unambiguous, and Pascal is profoundly aware of how strange it is. The *Pensées* show an acute consciousness of the paradoxical nature of the atonement, as is evident in the juxtaposition of normally unrelated terms *(un Dieu humilié, crucifié* etc.) and in the irony of Death defeated by a death.[11] Christianity, and in particular its central feature, the crucified Christ, appears true or false depending on the angle from which one looks at it. Pascal often notes how the Jews failed to recognise the messiah on the cross.[12] The tomb of Christ divides people in a similar way. In the fragment entitled *Sépulchre de Jésus,* Pascal notes how Jesus' enemies ceased tormenting him, as they thought that was the end of the story, whereas he was buried by saints, and only saints went into the tomb. Here too, the saints grasp the significance of the dead Christ, whereas his enemies miss the point.

By revealing himself in such an ambiguous and obscure way, it would seem then that God has condemned mankind to a thoroughgoing relativism, torn between contradictory interpretations and conflicting viewpoints, with no independent standpoint from which to decide between them. Not even Scripture is immune from this relativism: "each man finds in these promises what lies in the depths of his own heart".[13] This has profound implications for Pascal's apologetic method. In fact it could be said that this sense of different perspectives is the key structural principle underlying the Apology towards which the *Pensées* were to lead.

LA FOLIE DE LA CROIX

Pascal sometimes remarks on the difference between his own apologetic method and that of other contemporary apologists. In L781, he outlines the content of a preface for the second part of the proposed Apology, presumably the part following the explanation of the *misère* of man, moving into the explanation of the Redeemer sent by God.[14] Having established the weakness of man's reason and inability to recognise God, he will proceed to recommend faith in God and his Son Jesus Christ. At this point, he clearly intends a discussion of attempts to argue for the existence of God, including presumably those of contemporary apologists. Pascal eschews all of their techniques, even the approach taken by Augustinian apologetics. L820, for example, opposes two ways of inducing belief: reason and authority. As d'Angers showed, Humanists and Thomists tended to take the former, Augustinians the latter. Pascal distances himself from both. He refuses to take the option of recommending belief purely on the basis of the authority of the Bible or the Church. Interestingly, for someone whose theology is so thoroughly Augustinian, he prefers the method of persuasion by reason, but in a crucial caveat, qualifies the reasons he is able to give for Christianity: "but these are feeble arguments, because reason can be bent in any direction".[15]

Pascal's Apology refuses to begin where others do, with proofs of the authority of the Church or Bible, or even of God himself. L781 considers those who do begin with proofs of God, who try to "prove the existence of God from the works of nature".[16] The problem with this for Pascal is not that there are no proofs, nor that they are ineffective. The difficulty is that not only do they end up proving the wrong God, as we saw in the previous chapter, but they are also addressed to the wrong people. Again it is a matter of perspective. To offer these proofs to those who already believe would make sense, but for those who not, this method is unconvincing, and leads only to disdain of Christian faith. For these, God is not open to scrutiny, but a God hidden from their eyes. Instead of starting with the clarity and plainness of God's self-revelation, Pascal's Apology begins with its obscurity. Rather than beginning with an explanation of how Christianity makes sense, he begins by explaining how it does *not* make sense. Unembarrassed by the lack of proof of Christianity, he delights in it. Christians are happy to submit to folly, not because it is intrinsically valuable, but because God has decreed that with purely human understanding, men and women should only see folly in God's self-revelation.[17] The sceptical accusation that Christianity is obscure carries no weight at all, for that is precisely what we should expect, if God is of such a kind that he wishes to hide himself from those who have no desire to love him.[18] Pascal refuses to offer rational justification even for the doctrine of original sin, accepting that

> ...nothing is more shocking to our reason than to say that the sin of the first man has implicated in its guilt men so far from the original sin that they seem incapable of sharing it. This flow of guilt does not seem merely impossible to us, indeed most unjust.

Pascal puts the issue in the starkest form he can, pointing out the distance in time from Adam, and the injustice of damning an innocent child for a crime committed 6,000 years (sic) ago.[19] Pascal deliberately stresses the sceptic's case, because for him, it is crucial to emphasise the obscurity of Christianity to the unbeliever. The truth of religion lies in its very obscurity, our lack of understanding of it, and even indifference towards it.[20] It is in fact these very contradictions which are the key to understanding Christianity: "All those contradictions which seemed to take me furthest from the knowledge of any religion are what led me most directly to the true religion."[21]

The point made here is vital: Pascal does not stress the obscurity of Christianity out of brazen fideistic anti-intellectualism, nor as a prelude to refuting each of these arguments in turn, nor simply to make an arbitrary virtue out of an intellectual necessity. On the contrary, his whole approach depends upon it. If Christianity is intellectually demonstrable to the idly curious, it actually destroys Pascal's argument, because that argument is based upon the supposition that God has hidden himself from those who do not search for him with all their hearts, which in turn is based on the very nature of God as knowable only through love. Pascal insists on the obscurity of Christianity to demonstrate that from the perspective of indifference, the true God, the hidden God of Jesus Christ can never be found, however many convincing proofs are put forward in his favour.

The cross in this context acts as a sign of the foolishness of Christianity. Looking again at L291 and L842, the cross is placed in opposition to proofs. The Christian religion is rich in signs and proofs, yet "it rejects it all and says that it offers neither wisdom nor signs, but only the cross and folly". (291) Pascal makes a crucial distinction between *convaincre* and *convertir*. Proofs convince (i.e. change the mind), but only the cross converts (i.e. changes the will)[22]. Because Saint Paul came to convert, not to convince, he claims to come "with neither wisdom nor signs". To convert, now using the language of L291, is to "change us and make us capable of knowing and loving God". In his sense, the cross stands, as we noticed before, for the Fall/Redemption dialectic, which is nonsense to the unbeliever, offending both reason and justice. To the unbeliever who understands neither the effects of the Fall nor the need for redemption, the cross is unnecessary and incomprehensible. It therefore expresses the foolishness of Christianity, its opacity to those who do not have the 'holy desire' to know and love God. Pascal's apologetics begin with the cross, as a barrier to a speculative, rational approach to the knowledge of God. The unbeliever has to be shown that Christianity offends his reason and sense of justice, as a prelude to the apologist's explanation of why this is so.

For Pascal, the problem lies not in the inherent irrationality of Christian faith, but in the reasoning powers of the unbeliever, not in the observed, but the observer. If Christianity makes little sense from the perspective of indifference, then that perspective itself is open to question, and lacks both the stability and neutrality which it claims to have. The very rationality which judges Christianity to be foolish is itself one among many equally subjective and relative viewpoints. Pascal's deconstruction of reason has two foci, the first attacking its instability and infinite flexibility. A great number of fragments are devoted to the process of "constant swing from pro to con" (*renversement continuel du pour au contre*),[23] whereby the apologist plays the role of a perennial devil's advocate, reacting against whichever point of view is taken up by his reader or interlocutor.[24] The function of this process is to show that reason unaided can be used to prove anything,[25] can find no firm ground upon which to rest and is notoriously fragile and unreliable.[26] Reason is in itself rootless, and needs grounding in first principles which can be apprehended only by the heart, and not by reason.[27] Hence Pascal argues that so much of what we consider to be natural is merely customary,[28] again depending on the perspective from which one views it.

The other point Pascal makes about reason is that it is by no means unified. He is acutely aware of the way in which opposing propositions can not only be defended, but be shown to be right on their own terms.[29] While his age was one which saw the rise of claims for a single infallible rationality which could explain and understand everything, there are for Pascal different rationali*ties*, all based on different starting points and perspectives, all possessing their own inner logic, but which fatally cannot co-exist with one another.[30] This is the essence of Pascal's line of thinking in the *Entretien avec M. Saci*. Montaigne's sceptical arguments are on their own terms highly effective,[31] as are those of the more confident

Epictetus. In fact these two systems are "the only ones that conform to reason".[32] Their problem is that neither can account for the other. Montaigne, aware as he is of the weakness of the human will and understanding, cannot explain the traces of man's original dignity which Epictetus has seen. Epictetus, with a clear vision of human greatness, cannot account for what Montaigne has grasped of human frailty. Neither the Stoicism of Epictetus nor the pessimism of Montaigne can provide a fixed point, because both sets of arguments cancel each other out.[33] The instability and anxiety created by this uncertainty can be resolved only by the discovery of a firm place, "*une assiette basse et sûre*",[34] a perspective which comprehends and understands all other viewpoints. To use Pascal's own image, what is required is not just another ship which gives the illusion that all other ships are moving while our ship remains still, but the harbour, which gives a sure standpoint, and from which the relative movement of all the ships can be seen.[35]

Both of these criticisms of reason are united by this sense of shifting perspectives.[36] Pascal tries to create within his reader a sense of instability, a lack of confidence in one's footing, a constant shifting of position, so that from whichever angle a question is examined, he shows how, seen from elsewhere, the view is entirely different. This effect is heightened of course by the fragmentary nature of the *Pensées*, where fragments are scattered out of their intended context, so that it is often difficult to work out who is speaking, and from which angle, belief or unbelief.[37] The final form of the Apology might have clarified some of these difficulties, but would surely have kept this feature of shifting perspectives, so crucial as it is to Pascal's enterprise. The *Pensées* maintain constant restlessness, movement and energy, "*le mouvement perpétuel*".[38] This is part of the human condition: "Our nature lies in movement, complete rest is death."[39] Reason shifts constantly, always deceived by changing appearances.[40] Human consciousness never finds a place to rest between the many dualisms Pascal describes, such as the infinite greatess and smallness of the natural order, man's *grandeur* and *misère,* figure and truth, Christ's humanity and divinity, scepticism and dogmatism, God's hiddenness and visibility. The dualistic character of Pascal's thought[41] on the one hand reinforces this sense of shifting perspectives, and on the other cries out for resolution, for firm ground upon which to build.

This feature of Pascal's Apology is expressed most clearly in the fragment *Disproportion de l'homme*, where the imagery of floating on an endless sea combines with that of building upon unsure ground to emphasise the sense of instability and constant movement:

> Such is our true state. That is what makes us incapable of certain knowledge or absolute ignorance. We are floating in a medium of vast extent, always uncertain and floating, blown from one place to another; whenever we think we have a fixed point to which we can cling and make fast, it shifts and leaves us; if we follow it, it eludes our grasp, slips away, and flees eternally before us. Nothing stands still for us. This is our natural state and yet the state most contrary to our inclinations. We burn with desire to find a firm footing, an ultimate, steady base on which to build a tower rising up to infinity, but our whole foundation cracks and the earth opens up into the depths of the abyss.[42]

Although the theme of *inconstance* was common in baroque literature,[43] Pascal presses it home more radically than most. For Yves de Paris, one contemporary apologist, reason is able to appreciate the light of the eternal Word shining through creation, so that it provides a fixed point, a means of resolving contradictions.[44] For Pascal, even reason is included in this constant movement and instability, even there, no fixed ground is found.

Pascal's evocation of instability is not so much an apologetic ploy as a theological necessity. The assumption is often made that Pascal chose a different approach from other apologists because he was more aware of what would and would not work with the likes of his *libertin* friends Damien Miton and Antoine de Méré.[45] In this view, Pascal's apologetic method is determined by his addressees. However, it seems more the case that Pascal's Apology starts with the deconstruction of rationality (including Christianity) rather than proofs for God, not so much because of the identity of his audience, but rather because of the identity of his God. It has often puzzled commentators that Pascal rarely deals in detail with objections to

Christianity in current libertine thought. René Pintard suggests that
this is because he aims to convert not philosophical *libertins*, but
those for whom *libertinage* was an excuse for a easy life.[46] Jean
Mesnard thinks that to argue against the detailed criticisms of the
sceptics would have been to fight the battle on their territory,
whereas Pascal wants to undermine their entire confidence in
reason.[47] Wetsel's recent study outlines the variety of people Pascal
has in mind as he writes.[48] These contain some truth: as we have
indicated above, there is much to suggest that Pascal writes for the
indifferent, those who allow *divertissements* to distract their minds
from more serious questions. These arguments, however, do not
explain all of Pascal's reasons for this strategy. He is more
concerned about the identity of the God he wants them to discover
than the identity of those for whom he writes. Pascal denies the
validity of reason, condemning his readers to endless wandering in
search of unattainable truth, not primarily because those readers
cannot be convinced that way, but because God cannot be
approached that way. God has closed off that route to himself.
Known only through love, he hides himself from those who test
him, and can be approached only through an acknowledgement of
sin and acceptance of the necessity of Christ's sacrifice on the cross.
The God who thus reveals himself in such an oblique and
ambiguous fashion clearly intends that his human creatures will not
discover him through human means. Pascal is always more
concerned with the universal problem of human sin and consequent
epistemological blindness than he is with particular types of
readership. The question of Pascal's readership, while of historical
interest, is of less relevance to the content of his Apology than has
sometimes been thought.

The first part of Pascal's apology therefore aims to lead the reader
to admit that it is not the incoherence of Christianity, but the
perspective from which it is seen which prevents it from being
recognised as true. The real issue is not a matter of intellectual
reasoning, but of the passions which blind and corrupt knowledge.[49]
As a result, apologetics must begin with the obscurity of
Christianity, with the cross, rather than with manifest proofs. For

this first section of Pascal's projected Apology, the theme of the cross is central, standing for the foolishness of Christianity, the first point which needs to be established in the journey to faith.

SAGESSE INFINIE

For the believer, Christ, the cross, prophecies, miracles all make sense, and add up to a convincing set of proofs of Christianity.[50] The message of the cross, the dialectic between Fall and Redemption, made sense for Pascal of scientific observation of the natural order, explaining the curious obscurity of God in creation. From the perspective of faith, the greatness of the historical Jesus is seen beyond the humility of his appearance;[51] from the perspective of love, truth can be recognised.[52] The question left hanging by this first part of the Apology concerns how one can bridge the gap between these two worlds, how this shift of perspective can take place. Pascal, insistent on the foolishness of Christianity, contends that there is no direct intellectual route from the human side. If Christianity is included within the general relativistic picture of human knowledge, if it makes no sense to unbelievers, how can they be expected to find a fixed point there?

The problem is intensified when we notice Pascal's belief that this shift of perspective is an act of God.[53] While he knows this shift cannot be manufactured by human means, at the same time, he is able to identify what this change or conversion looks like. L808 explains his ideas on the process of conversion. The three ways of believing (reason, custom and inspiration), while not a formal 'doctrine' of conversion,[54] all play a part in the process.[55] Reasoned proofs can satisfy the mind, custom can confirm and establish this belief, but inspiration, the divine touch of grace, is necessary to be a *vrai enfant* of the Christian religion.

In one sense this inspiration is a sheer gift of grace, and nothing can be done to earn or evoke it. In a notable return to the language of 1 Corinthians 1:17, Pascal does however indicate one way of preparing for this grace: "offering ourselves through humiliations to inspiration, which alone can produce the real and salutary effect. *Lest the cross of Christ be made to none effect.*"

To prepare for this inspiration which alone can bring about love for God within the heart, the sinner can only humble himself before God (*s'anéantir devant cet être éternel*). Without the inspiration which makes one aware of one's own need, the cross makes no sense, and is evacuated of meaning. When a person becomes existentially aware of their own need of God and redemption, the cross, the heart of the Christian message, begins to be understood.

The required "*disposition intérieure*" is "hatred of self" (*la haine de soi-même*), an awareness of one's own *misère*. The unbeliever must become aware of his weakness and sin, sense his need and cry out for a redeemer. Only when he becomes aware of the extent to which his passions cloud his reason will he abandon the attempt to approach God by that route. That is when the message of the cross becomes the beginning of wisdom, as it encapsulates the twin principles of God and human sin which explain the ambiguity in himself and in creation. From any other angle, the cross makes no sense. Once it is understood from the perspective of an awareness of sin, it can be seen that it *includes* all other rationalities, and it becomes an interpretative framework which resolves the contradictions in human existence. The test of its ability to provide a fixed point is whether, unlike Epictetus and Montaigne, it can explain and interpret others.

From the outside, however, the cross remains obscure and incomprehensible. These two perspectives are still far apart. Pascal has yet to explain how the sinner can shift perspectives and gain this fixed point, when from the outside it appears just as incoherent, if not more so, than any other.

THE CROSS AS MORAL REORIENTATION: THE WAGER

Bernard Howells has argued convincingly that the famous 'Wager' (*Pari*), rather than an argument demonstrating the profitability of faith, aims instead to reveal the unbeliever's hostility to truth, even when it can be shown to be to his advantage. It is "part of an overall strategy to bring an ultimate irrational resistance out into the open".[56] The notion of foolishness, central to the first part of the apology, plays a significant part in the *Pari*. Pascal begins with an argument for agnosticism about God's existence and nature. Reason is impotent before these fundamental questions upon which eternity depends, and on which neutrality is impossible.[57] Pascal emphasises the foolishness of Christianity as he has done many times before:

> Who then will condemn Christian for being unable to give rational grounds for their belief, professing as they do s religion for which they cannot give rational grounds? They declare that it is a folly, *stultitiam*, in expounding it to the world, and then you complain that they do not prove it." If they did prove it, they would not be keeping their word.[58]

As Howells shows, the key part of the fragment is not so much the mathematical argumentation designed to prove the benefits of faith, but the conversation which occurs after it. Pascal's point is precisely this:

> at least understand that your inability to believe comes from your passions. Since reason leads you to believe and yet you cannot do so, concentrate then not on convincing yourself by arguments for the existence of God, but by diminishing your passions.[59]

The conclusion Pascal wants his friend to reach is that "even if it could be shown that belief was the more profitable option, *he would still not want to believe*".[60] The Wager is designed to blow the myth of neutrality out of the water, by demonstrating that any betting man, looking purely at the odds, and the smallness of the stake, compared to the size of the prize to be won, would be bound to accept the wager of belief. As such, "it is not an invitation to bet, but an attempt to show that *the libertin has already bet*".[61] No-one stands outside of all perspectives on a firm bedrock of unassailable reason, every position is relative to others, and every person has taken up a position. The unbeliever, looking at Christian faith from his perspective refuses to bet on Christianity, this *sottise*, but as

Pascal has shown by the argument of the Wager, this perspective is in itself irrational, unstable and unjustified. Pascal has brought his interlocutor to realise that he is an unbeliever not because Christianity is inherently implausible, but because he simply does not want to believe. It is not lack of proofs, but a deeply irrational distaste for the foolishness of Christianity which prevents his conversion. The unbeliever protests that he cannot help this: "my hands are tied, and my lips are sealed. I am being forced to wager and I am not free; I am held fast, and I am made so that I cannot believe." Pascal, perhaps surprisingly, agrees ("*Il est vrai*"), but he has reached his intended goal. He simply drives home the lesson, that "your inability to believe derives from your passions", rather than from any intellectual difficulty. The real origin of this decision not to believe is not solid intellectual objection, or the inherent irrationality of Christianity, but an irrational and unfounded prejudice, based on an inability to see the truth of Christian faith. The problem is not lack of evidence but sin. To the person who acknowledges this, but yet remains unconvinced by Christianity, his advice is simply to act as if he was convinced, (*faisant tout comme s'ils croyaient*), submitting to religious patterns of behaviour, which will in turn bring about a settled pattern of faith.

While Howells is quite right to say that the *Pari* is designed to show the unbeliever that he has already bet, he does not do full justice to Pascal's argument when he claims that the fragment does not invite the *libertin* to bet. Pascal does seem to recommend a wager. He mentions those Christians who "were once bound like you, and who now wager all they have", and predicts that his interlocutor will discover, after deciding to believe, that "you have wagered on something certain and infinite for which you have paid nothing". Pascal does not merely point out that the unbeliever has already bet, already taken up a perspective and on completely irrational grounds at that. He goes on to invite the unbeliever to change perspective, to wager on Christian faith.

In this context, Pascal suggests the strategy of acting as if you believe, and adds the notorious phrase "*cela vous abêtira*", subject to a wide variety of interpretations. *Abêtira* has often been interpreted etymologically to refer to becoming like an animal.[62] Howells argues persuasively that Pascal goes beyond this precise meaning, using the word in a provocative rhetorical way. He deliberately aims to shock, stressing the sacrifice of intellectual sophistication and integrity which will be involved in the decision to believe. The word was originally understood as shocking, otherwise the Port Royal editors of the first 1670 edition would not have taken care to omit it altogether.[63] The word deliberately picks up the theme of foolishness, *stultitiam*, from the earlier part of the fragment.[64] The process of coming to believe begins with the recognition that Christian faith is foolish to those outside it, and ends with a willingness to become foolish with it.

A further insight into the word comes in an unpublished article by Richard Parish, who argues that the word should be read in the light of the relationship between the automatic action of the sacraments *ex opere operato*, and the requirement for the correct interior disposition for their efficacy. *Abêtira* refers to the required state of passivity needed for the sacraments to have their effect: "the only spiritual state required of the interlocutor in the Wager consists of a passive disposition to benefit from the mercy of God and the prayers of the Church, in order to obtain the light of faith".[65] Alongside the sense of 'becoming foolish', the word also carries the nuance of 'becoming passive'.

The force of *abêtira* then, is to suggest that acting in this way will make one stupid enough to believe this 'foolish' message, and passive, ('docile')[66] enough to receive the gift of faith. To believe involves a submission of will and of reason, an acknowledgement of the relativity of one's own standpoint, and the willingness to adopt another. It involves a willingness to lay aside one's own powers and autonomy, to adopt a belief in the crucified Christ, and all that implies, which seems ridiculous, stupid, foolish,[67] and to submit oneself to be the passive recipient of the prayers of the church and the mercy of God. The unbeliever is to submit to the folly of Christianity, to become passive before God and the church, to change perspectives.

Pascal's point in all of this is that perspectives are not changed intellectually, but morally. Because the *libertin,* like everyone else, has adopted his perspective for largely irrational, moral reasons, then a change of perspective also has to happen non-rationally and morally. What is required is not more effective proofs, but *"la diminution de vos passions".* To begin to do this, to begin to take holy water, have masses said, will begin to impress upon the soul a sense of its need for God.[68] This decision in itself is evidence for Pascal of God's grace acting upon the soul. The *Ecrits sur la Grace* make it clear that Pascal's resolution of the problem of grace and free will involves the ascription of the same action to both divine and human wills at the same time, though with God's as the dominant will.[69] The seeker's choice to act as if he believed is evidence of God's inclination of his heart to believe.[70] The main conclusion of the Wager is then, that fundamental perspectives which determine how the world is seen are taken up for largely irrational and moral reasons. Adopting a new perspective will therefore involve moral change before intellectual change, taking the path of crucifixion of one's own *amour-propre,* self-will and reason: Christ's salvation comes "by hating oneself, and in following him through his misery and death on the cross".[71]

Henri Gouhier has defined Pascal's understanding of conversion as "a love for God that excludes all others, and manifests itself in the hatred of oneself".[72] This is the Jansenist picture of God which was so important for Pascal at the time of his second conversion. Faith is a *'saint désir',* a taste for God, and a distaste for oneself.[73] Within the structure of the *deux amours* it is a turning away from self-love.[74] It is axiomatic for Pascal that God can be known only by those in whom he has placed a spark of love for himself. Conversion therefore inevitably involves a moral choice before an intellectual one, precisely because of the nature of Pascal's God. It means a turning away from self-love, a crucifixion of one's own understanding, rationality and pride:

> True conversion consists in self-annihilation before the universal being whom we have so often vexed and who is perfectly entitled to destroy

us at any moment, in recognising that we can do nothing without him and that we have deserved nothing from him but his disfavour. It consists in knowing that there is an irreconcilable opposition between God and us, and that without a mediator, there can be no exchange.[75]

In the previous chapter we saw how the cross expresses the identity of God in a fallen world. Conversion, the process of coming to believe in that same God, is also shaped by the cross. It involves a personal and existential recognition of sinfulness, which is the real reason for the failure to believe; it involves a realisation of the need for a mediator to die for sins, and then this radical crucifixion of self. It requires the crucifixion of Christ and the crucifixion of the sinner, by passive submission to daily habitual patterns of behaviour which will reinforce the truth of Christianity in the soul, truths which cannot be appropriated or understood without this moral and spiritual submission. *S'anéantir*,[76] *haine de soi*,[77] *abêtir*,[78] *soumission de la raison*,[79] *suivre par la croix*:[80] all are aspects of the same thing, and indicate what Pascal himself had experienced on 23rd November 1654: "Sweet and total renunciation... Total submission to Jesus Christ and my director."[81]

SUMMARY AND CONCLUSIONS

The cross shapes Pascal's apologetics in three distinct ways:

1. The cross hides God from unbelievers, as a sign of the foolishness and obscurity of God's revelation. This aspect is all that can be seen from the perspective of indifferent unbelief. It thus closes the door to an abstract speculative knowledge of God.
2. The cross reveals God as the one who rescues from sin, the principle of fall and redemption. From the perspective of faith, it explains the ambivalent revelation of God in creation, and enables all other rationalities to be comprehended.
3. The cross represents the only way in which the transition is made between these two perspectives, the way of crucifixion of one's own

self-will, the moral and spiritual reorientation which is evidence of God's touch of grace.

CONVINCING PROOFS?

How then do these conclusions help us understand the place of the "proofs" of Christianity to function in Pascal's Apology?

David Wetsel claims that access to God's existence is possible via signs of divinity which he has placed in the world. The "*preuves convaincantes*" to which Pascal refers in L149 are "the only exception to the rule that God has hidden himself from the sight of men".[82] The historical proofs of Scripture, prophecies and miracles are "the ultimate argument upon which he intended to rest his case."[83] Our survey of Pascal's use of the themes of foolishness and wisdom has suggested however that Pascal allows no exceptions to the rule of God's hiddenness to those who do not seek him with all their heart.[84] All rationality, all perspectives are relative, including the revelation of Scripture. As Pascal himself writes in L835: "the prophecies, even the miracles and proofs of our religion, are not of such a kind that they can be said to be absolutely convincing, but they are at the same time such that it cannot be said to be unreasonable to believe in them".[85]

The obvious sense of this is that Pascal does *not* expect these proofs to convince in the strong sense that Wetsel implies. The argument leads not towards compelling the unbeliever to believe, but (as in the Wager) to make him realise how it is his passions not his intellect which keep him back from faith. Wetsel builds much of his case on an analysis of L149, yet his case is far from clear-cut. Even in the very paragraph in which Pascal writes about the convincing nature of these proofs, he concedes: "you cannot yourself know whether they are true or not". Rather than pointing the unbeliever towards proofs, Pascal's aim here seems much more modest. Having pointed out the need for a solution which explains "*les grandeurs et les misères de l'homme*", he simply invites the unbeliever to look within to see whether or not this inner contradiction exists: "Observe yourself, and see if you do not find the living characteristics of these two natures." This is the heart of his apologetic appeal to the unbeliever: it urges examination not of proofs of religion, much less of God himself, but a look within to grasp the fallen nature of human self-understanding, the relativity within which all are trapped. It is not that God is found within the human soul, but that the need for him can be awakened only by turning away from *divertissements* to self-knowledge. The call is to recognise within oneself the "feeble instinct of happiness... and... and miseries of blindness". This unresolved contradiction gives birth to a desire for resolution, for a higher rationality which can embrace the unavoidably contradictory nature of human discourse, a desire which opens the heart for the touch of grace.

Referring to L291, Wetsel claims: "The whole of Revelation... ultimately points to *'la folie de la Croix'*."[86] This however sits uneasily with his claims for the efficacy in Pascal's mind of proofs addressed to the unbeliever. It is either one or the other. Pascal points the unbeliever not to proofs which convince, but to the folly and wisdom of the cross: to both the need for and provision of salvation as the key to the puzzle. When that need is existentially grasped, and the provision recognised, then the way is open to that higher rationality, the explanation which embraces the contradictory nature of human experience, namely the reality of the God who hides himself from those who test him, but reveals himself to those who search for him.

The "convincing proofs" serve to confirm the faith of believers, not to argue unbelievers towards faith. If the entry point to faith is an awareness of the need for salvation, rather than proofs, then Pascal's argument is not as dependent as Wetsel thinks on, for example, the exact historical inerrancy of the Bible. Arguments from prophecy and miracle stand alongside nature itself, which, when viewed from the right perspective, shines forth with proofs of God. To be sure, Pascal does think the proofs are compelling, but only for those who have the inclination to believe, who regard them from the perspective of the foolishness of the cross. Scriptural proofs simply confirm the validity of a perspective already taken up on moral grounds. They therefore play less of a role in Pascal's approach to bringing an unbeliever to faith than is often thought.

PASCAL BETWEEN DESCARTES AND MONTAIGNE

Our conclusions obviously sit much closer to those of Sara Melzer, in her insistence on Pascal's belief in the fallen nature of all human discourse, "trapped in the prison-house of language", The centre of Pascal's appeal for Melzer is his rejection of Classical/Cartesian certainties. Truth is unavailable within a fallen world where God remains hidden. It is possible to go beyond Melzer to point out two consequences of an understanding of the place of the wisdom and folly of the cross for Pascal.

First, Pascal refuses to commend Christianity on the basis that it can be shown to be true, yet he does so not out of necessity, nor out of a fideistic abandonment of rationality (as Melzer implies) or a lack of confidence in its ultimate truth. Rather, his method is dictated by strictly theological factors. Given the nature of Pascal's God, as the Augustinian God known by the heart and not reason, and given the fallen state of human understanding, clouded by the passions, such an attempt would be self-defeating. The only God susceptible to proof by reason is the God of the philosophers, who is none other than an idol.

Secondly, Pascal's apologetic is aimed not just at the pretensions of classical discourse, represented in his own day by Descartes, but also at the sceptical tradition represented by Montaigne. Melzer stresses Pascal's rejection of the former of these, but as the *Entretien avec M. Saci* shows, Pascal denies just as much the despairing scepticism of Pyrrhonism. Both are equally at fault, because they are only partial readings of the way things are, and can convince only by silencing the legitimate voice of the other. Both Epictetus and Montaigne offer totalizing readings of the world. Neither is adequate because each ignores the opposing perspective. Both claim too much for themselves, and ignore either the uncertainty and ambivalence of the fallen world, or the instinct for happiness and truth which lies buried within the human condition.

To borrow the language of Derrida, as Melzer does, Pascal too believes in *différance*, plurality as the nature of things in a fallen world. He believes in opposite perspectives which must always be held together within that world, and which for him can be reconciled only outside this world in the unfallen realm of eternity. While "truth lies beyond our scope, and is an unattainable quarry… it is no earthly denizen", yet still " it is at home in heaven, resting with God, to be known only in so far as it pleases him to reveal it".[87] Truth is a stranger in this fallen world, but the touch of grace, the realisation of the need for salvation gives the believer a light which begins to make out shapes in the darkness. Truth is fundamentally eschatological for Pascal, obtainable here and now only by living within the tension of this world and the next, living within a fallen creation, yet called to belong to the life of God.

It is because he believes that this world is provisional, fallen, and therefore not the ultimate reality that Pascal can still point to the possibility of knowledge and truth, but only from the standpoint of a knowledge of one's own inability to arrive at it unaided. Knowledge is possible, but only by a careful balance of opposites, a simultaneous grasp of human *grandeur* and *misère*, taught only by grace and personal experiential revelation. True, this 'discourse of the Fall' equally lacks the status of proof. It cannot be established from the perspective of unbelief, yet it can be adopted by the non-rational experiential and moral realignment which the Wager represents. For Pascal, the Wager is not blind choice; rather, it opens the eyes. Human folly and fallenness are not the last word, nor the inevitable end. Hence, Lucien Goldmann's understanding of the hidden God as a "tragic vision" does not quite capture Pascal's mind, because it implies an inevitability about human separation from God. Pascal might rather have called it a comic (or perhaps tragi-comic) vision, implying a serious condition but one which is not inevitable, and from which there is the possibility of a joyful outcome, the certainty of faith.[88]

The major question posed by Descartes in seventeenth century intellectual life was the question of epistemology. Pascal refuses to be swayed by this: his diagnosis of the human condition insists that the essential problem is not primarily epistemological, but soteriological.[89] It is not a failure to understand God, it is a failure to love him. This insight flows directly out of his understanding of the nature of the Augustinian God approached in love. The cross, revealing[90] both the God whose will is to save and the gravity of sin which has corrupted nature, lies at the heart of his answer to this condition. Pascal can fairly be described as working with a *theologia crucis:* Christianity for him is essentially "the religion of a humiliated God" (*la religion d'un Dieu humilié*).[91] And the only ones who can find the *Dieu humilié* are those with a *coeur humilié*.[92]

Historically, Pascal represents a strident voice raised in protest against the totalizing claims of both rationalism and scepticism at the beginning of the modern Cartesian era. The claim to total knowledge must be abandoned, as must the claim of the total impossibility of knowledge. Instead there must be the admission of both the possibility and the limitations of knowledge, the weakness and frailty of human reason. A restored rationality can begin only at the point of a radical renunciation of mastery, the admission of confusion, sin and the need for salvation, of *anéantissement de soi.* It is no accident that his protest arises out of his insistence on the precise nature of God as the Augustinian, Jansenist God, known only by those who love him, hidden from those who examine him, revealed paradoxically in Christ crucified. It is in the name of a *theologia crucis* that Pascal is able to unmask the pretension of these claims to encompass everything within a unified total knowledge. Pascal aims to bring unbelievers to the cross, to an awareness of the frailty of their reason, the overpowering influence of their passions, and consequently to their need of redemption. Only then can the touch of grace enable light to dawn.

Notes:

[1]This is true for a wide variety of commentators on Pascal, both older writers such as J-E d'Angers, *Pascal et ses Précurseurs*; J. Russier, *La Foi Selon Pascal*;

Broome, *Pascal*, and also more recent writers such as N. Hammond, *Playing with Truth: Language and the Human Condition in Pascal's Pensées* (Oxford: Clarendon, 1994); Melzer, *Discourses of the Fall*. For an opposing view, arguing that the *Pari* is an earlier piece, written for a particular type of person, and was not intended to play a significant part in the Apology, see M-R. and M. Le Guern, *Les Pensées de Pascal* (Paris: Larousse, 1972), 34-55.

[2]S. Melzer, "Sin and Signs in Pascal's Pensées", *Meaning Structure & History*, ed. Wetsel, 94.

[3]D. Wetsel, *L'Ecriture et le Reste*, 218.

[4]L291.

[5]"*Cela fait bien condamner ceux qui n'en sont pas, mais non pas croire ceux qui en sont. Ce qui les fait croire est la croix* - ne evacuata sit crux." L842.

[6]Another is L110.

[7]"*ils ont une disposition intérieure toute sainte et [que] ce qu'ils entendent dire de notre religion y est conforme*".

[8]"*Il n'en faut pas davantage pour persuader des hommes qui ont cette disposition dans le coeur et qui ont cette connaissance de leur devoir et de leur incapacité*."

[9]L380.

[10]"*les choses sont vraies ou fausses selon la face par où on les regarde*". L539.

[11]"*qu'il vaincrait la mort par sa mort*" (L253) "*Source des contrariétés. Un Dieu humilié et jusqu'à la mort de la croix.... Un Messie triomphant de la mort par sa mort.*" (L241).

[12]L256: "*ils l'ont méconnu de même dans son abaissement et dans sa mort.*" Also L593.

[13]L503. See also L689 for the same principle in reading Montaigne: "*Ce n'est pas dans Montaigne mais dans moi que je trouve tout ce que j'y vois.*"

[14]Cf. L6, 148.

[15]"*qui sont de faibles arguments, la raison étant flexible à tout*".

[16]"*prouver la divinité par les ouvrages de la nature*".

[17]L14.

[18]L228, 427 (paragraph 1).

[19]L131.

[20]L439.

[21]L404.

[22]L93.

[23]L93.

[24]L130: "*S'il se vante je l'abaisse. S'il s'abaisse je le vante. Et le contredis toujours. Jusqu'à ce qu'il comprenne qu'il est un monstre incompréhensible.*"

[25]L44.

[26]L48.

[27]L110. The point is explained at greater length in Pascal's *De l'Esprit géométrique et de l'art de persuader*.

[28]e.g. L60, 61, 66.

[29]L701: *"Quand on veut reprendre avec utilité et montrer à un autre qu'il se trompe il faut observer par quel côté il envisage la chose, car elle est vraie ordinairement de ce côté-là et lui avouer cette vérité, mais lui découvrir le côté par où elle est fausse."*

[30]L619: *"Tous leurs principes sont vrais, des pyrrhoniens, des stoïques, des athées, etc... mais leurs conclusions sont fausses, parce que les principes opposés sont vrais aussi."*

[31]*"... de telle sorte qu'on demeure convaincu que nous ne pensons pas mieux à présent que dans quelque songe dont nous ne nous éveillons qu'à la mort."* Entretien, *Œuvres*, 294.

[32]*Entretien, Œuvres*, 296.

[33]*"ils ruinent la vérité aussi bien que les faussetés l'un de l'autre.. ils se brisent et s'anéantissent pour faire place à la vérité de l'Évangile".Entretien, Œuvres,* 296.

[34]L545.

[35]L697.

[36]For the search for permanence, rest and stability in the Pensées, see P. Sellier, "Sur les fleuves de Babylone", and Broome, *Pascal*, 141-2.

[37]For example, statements such as the famous *"le silence éternel de ces espaces infinis m'effraie"* (L201) is most likely spoken from the perspective of unbelief, whereas *"tout y éclate des preuves de ces deux vérités"* (L449) comes from the mouth of one who already believes. See R. Parish, "Mais qui Parle? Voice and Persona in the 'Pensées'", *SCFS* 8 (1986), 23-40.

[38]L56.

[39]*"Notre nature est dans le mouvement, le repos entier est la mort."* L641. See also L682: *"Mouvement infini".*

[40]*"notre raison est toujours déçue par linconstance des apparences".* L199.

[41]The fact that the simple word *deux* occurs 184 times in the *Pensées* illustrates this point vividly.

[42]L199.

[43]Hammond, *Playing with Truth*, part II, ch. 3. The book takes up this theme to argue how Pascal's shifting use of language contributes to a sense of unease and to the necessity of wagering to find sure ground.

[44]*"La raison naturelle est le dernier effort de notre puissance... soit en la grâce ou en la nature, Dieu n'assemble pas ordinairement les choses extrêmes sans les faire venir aux approches dans un milieu qui en apaise la contrariété. Or la raison est moyenne entre la première verité divine et l'ignorance du monde matériel".* Théologie naturelle (1633). Taken from J. Eymard, *Yves de Paris* (Paris: Bloud & Gay, 1964), 77.

[45]e.g. Calvet, *La Littérature Religieuse*, ch. 6.

[46]Pintard, "Pascal et les libertins", *Pascal Présent*, 105-30.

[47]Mesnard, *Les Pensées,* 123ff.

[48]Wetsel, *Pascal and Disbelief,* ch. 1.

[49]L119: "*...sachant combien sa connaissance s'est obscurcie par les passions*".

[50]The principle is well expressed in a letter from Pascal to his sister in 1648: "*toutes choses parlent de Dieu à ceux qui le connaissent, et qu'elles le découvrent à tout ceux qui l'aiment, ces mêmes choses le cachent à tous ceux qui ne le connaissent pas.*" *Œuvres,* 273.

[51]L308: "*O qu'il est venu en grande pompe et en une prodigieuse magnificence aux yeux du coeur et qui voyent la sagesse.*"

[52]L739.

[53]L380, 382, 821.

[54]J. Morgan, "Pascal's Three Orders", *MLR* 72 (1978), 755-66, warns against the habit of reading too much into the theme of the 'three orders' as a central doctrine for Pascal.

[55]See Davidson, *The Origins of Certainty,* chs. 1 and 5 for an extended examination of this fragment and its implications for Pascal's view of how certainty is achieved.

[56]B. Howells, "The Interpretation of Pascal's 'Pari'", *MLR* 79 (1984), 45-63.

[57]Cf. "*vous êtes embarqués*".

[58]This again seems a direct reference to 1 Corinthians 1:18-31.

[59]"*apprenez au moins que votre impuissance à croire vient de vos passions. Puisque la raison vous y porte et que néanmoins, vous ne le pouver, travaillez donc non pas à vous convaincre par l'argumentation des preuves de Dieu, mais par la diminution de vos passions*".

[60]Howells, "Interpretation", 57 (his italics).

[61]Ibid., 61 (his italics).

[62]E. Gilson, "Le sens du terme 'abêtir' chez Blaise Pascal", *Les Idées et les Lettres* (2nd ed.; Paris: J. Vrin, 1955), 263-74; Sellier, *Pascal et St Augustin,* 552. I take it that *abêtir* is the verb Pascal intended here, despite various other suggestions. See the discussion in *French Studies* 17 (1963), 1-13; 18 (1964), 29-32, 244-6; 19 (1965), 379-84.

[63]Towards the end of L418, the Port-Royal edition follows the original manuscript up to "*suivre la manière par où ils ont commencé*", but then, instead of continuing as Pascal does with "*C'est en faisant tout comme s'ils croyaient*", leading up to the use of *abêtir,* it paraphrases rather lamely with "*imitiez leurs actions extérieurs, si vous pouvez entrer dans leurs disposition intérieurs*". Cf. the facsimile of the 1670 Port Royal edition in *Images et Témoins de l'age classique 2,* eds. G. Couton and J. Jehasse (Université de la Region de la Rhone-Alpes, 1972). See also D.A. Askew, "Pascal's Pari in the Port-Royal Edition", *AJFS* 5 (1968), 155-82, where the two versions are laid out side by side. Askew concludes that Pascal's editors present him as more of a rationalist, confident in the capacity of 'proofs' to convince, than he really was.

[64]See Howells, "Interpretation", 59, n.39.

[65]R. Parish, "Automate et sacrement: figures de l'incarnation chez Pascal," in proceedings of conference held at the University of Saint-Etienne, October 1995, entitled "Les avatars de l'augustinisme" (*Acts* forthcoming).

[66]Alban Krailsheimer's translation: *Pensées*, 152.

[67]L695, 809.

[68]The Wager is a particularly clear and dramatic expression of Pascal's method, but precisely because it summarises so much of his argument elsewhere, it is difficult to see that it introduces anything particularly new to his argument. The acknowledgement of the foolishness of Christianity from the perspective of unbelief, the insistence upon the irrational basis of all perspectives, and the consequent appeal to moral rather than intellectual change are all paralleled elsewhere in the *Pensées*.

[69]"*ceux à qui il plaît à Dieu de donner cette grâce, se portent d'eux-mêmes par leur libre arbitre à préférer infailliblement Dieu à la créature*". *Ecrits sur la Grâce, Œuvres*, 318. "*Toutes nos bonnes actions ont deux sources: l'une notre volonté, l'autre, la volonté de Dieu.*" 323. Pascal sees the process of falling away from Christian faith as a *double délaissement,* whereby God lets the backslider go, which is then confirmed by his continuation to reject God, in response to which God finally abandons him.

[70]Wanting to believe is a sign for Pascal that God's grace is already operating upon a person. See *Le Mystère de Jésus: "Tu ne me chercherais pas si tu ne m'avais trouvé.*" Also in the *Ecrits sur la Grâce: "celui qui disait:* cherchez votre serviteur, *avait sans doute déjà été cherché et trouvé.*" *Œuvres*, 322. See also L482.

[71]L271.

[72]H. Gouhier, *Blaise Pascal: Conversion et Apologétique* (Paris: J. Vrin, 1986), 128: "*un amour de Dieu tel qu'il exclut tous les autres et qu'il se manifeste dans la haine de soi-même*".

[73]This point is made at length in Pascal's "Sur la conversion du pécheur".

[74]Gouhier, *Conversion* ch. 2 shows how *haine de soi* for Pascal means not the annihilation of one's own will, as it did for François de Sales, but a hatred of one's own tendency to self-love.

[75]L378.

[76]L373, 378, 978, 1006.

[77]L123, 220, 373, 380, 381, 564, 597, 618.

[78]L418.

[79]L131, 167, 170, 373.

[80]L271.

[81]"*Renonciation totale et douce... Soumission totale à Jésus-Christ et à mon directeur.*" (from the *Mémorial*) Note also the references to his own experience in the *Pari*, e.g.: "*sachez qu'il est fait par un homme qui s'est mis à genoux*

auparavant et après, pour prier cet être infini et sans parties, auquel il soumet tout le sien..."
[82]Wetsel, *l'Écriture*, 217.
[83]Ibid., 218.
[84]If there is an exception, it comes only within the perspective of faith. See the repeated use of *'hors la foi'* in L131: outside faith, nothing sure can be known.
[85]Wetsel does not discuss this fragment.
[86]Ibid., 220.
[87]L131.
[88] Goldmann, *The Hidden God.*
[89]Cf. S. Williams, *Revelation and Reconciliation* (Cambridge: CUP, 1995), 20-3.
[90]L253 makes it clear that the cross is a revelation (*ouverture*) of God for Pascal.
[91]L220.
[92]L394.

Fifteen: Polemics, Piety and Politics

PASCAL'S POLEMICS

The coincidence of Pascal's spiritual development alongside a
time of advances in scientific understanding, the political and social
unrest in mid-seventeenth century France known as the *fronde*, and
the controversy over the Five Propositions attributed to Jansenius
alerts the student of his thought to place it carefully within this
theological, spiritual, intellectual and political context. In short,
Pascal's thinking was shaped both by a spiritual tradition and by
polemical necessity, his somewhat complex relationship with
Jansenism and Port-Royal, and the polemic against *dogmatistes,
pyrrhoniens*[1] and Jesuits. We have seen how Pascal's theology and
the apologetics which grew from it was shaped by the theme of the
cross, as a sign of the foolishness of Christianity, as the central point
from which to make sense of the world, and as the means of
conversion. This chapter will proceed to show how this perspective
gave Pascal a vantage point from which he could conduct an

effective polemical campaign on three separate fronts, against the confident rationalism of Cartesian *dogmatistes*, the sceptical doubt of the *pyrrhoniens*, and the moral laxism of the Jesuits.

THE LIMITS OF RATIONALISM

Pascal makes conscious use of both sceptical and rationalist arguments, frequently playing them off against each other.[2] Pascal was clearly indebted to Montaigne in his more sceptical arguments, and had quite obviously read and used the ideas of other writers working with such ideas[3] such as Charron[4] and Grotius.[5] Pascal is unusual in seventeenth century apologetics precisely for this reason, that he used the arguments of such writers, rather than setting himself to oppose them, as most others did.[6] On the other hand, he recognises the strong point of *dogmatisme*, namely that nature does give intimations of fundamental principles which cannot be doubted. The human inability to prove anything of any great significance confounds dogmatism, the instinct for truth confounds scepticism.[7]

Dogmatistes fail to take into account the Fall, human sinfulness, and the resulting spiritual, moral and intellectual blindness. Pascal often uses sceptical arguments to make this point, but his argument is fundamentally theological. It is because of the Fall that all perspectives are relative, we are condemned to endless movement, and no firm ground can be found. Those confident of rational powers fail to come to terms with the foolishness of Christianity, which bars the way to an objective, direct rational knowledge of God. God is hidden from the *dogmatistes*, and until they recognise their sin and their need for the sacrifice of the cross, they remain in a false light, thinking they see while they are blind. Reason is always blinded by passion, and until the moral issue of desire is addressed, it is useless as a tool for discovering truth.

THE FAILURE OF SCEPTICISM

Sceptical *Pyrrhoniens*, on the other hand, propose universal doubt, where nothing can be known at all. For Pascal, however, the revelation of God in Christ who was crucified is the vital clue which makes sense of everything else, once the inner disposition to believe has been given. Knowledge is possible, to those who have grasped the fundamental principle which the cross proclaims: the tragedy and yet the potential of human life. Truth is the sole possession of God, yet the cross is the sign (*chiffre*) which St Paul gives,[8] which reveals as well as conceals. Its message alone is able to change a person and make him capable of knowing (*connaître*).[9] The Pyrrhonists have failed to account for the way in which God does make knowledge possible, so that their reductionism, although true from the perspective of indifference, is not total, and is overcome from the perspective of faith. Pascal's qualification, "There is no certainty, *apart from faith*"[10] in L131 is highly significant. The phrase *hors la foi* is repeated rhythmically through the first paragraph of this fragment, to indicate the crucial exception he makes to their universal scepticism. The phrase is given content by Pascal's insistence that outside Jesus Christ there can be no self-knowledge or knowledge of God, life or death.[11] Conversely, *in* Jesus Christ there is true knowledge, which not even the acids of scepticism can destroy.

The ability of the cross both to reveal and conceal God, to offer both "infinite wisdom and folly"[12] confounds both dogmatist and sceptic, and provides Pascal with a polemical weapon to confound both at once.

JESUIT COMPROMISE

The cross also gives Pascal the perspective from which to combat the Jesuits of his time. In the 5th *Lettre Provinciale,* Pascal alludes to the *Querelle des Rites,* a contemporary dispute over Jesuit missionary practice in Indo-China. Pascal accuses the Jesuits in India and China of playing down the cross where it is controversial, adjusting the content of the gospel to please their hearers: "When they are in countries where a crucified God is regarded as folly, they suppress the scandal of the cross, and preach only Christ in glory, and not Christ in agony."[13]

This thought recurs to Pascal during the writing of the *Pensées*, where the similarity of language (an explicit reference to 1 Corinthians 1:22) implies a reference to the same dispute:

> *For the Jews require a sign, and the Greeks seek after wisdom, but we preach Christ crucified*
> *But full of signs and full of wisdom.*
> *But you preach Christ not crucified and a religion without miracles and without wisdom.*[14]

The *Querelle des Rites* was principally a dispute between Dominican and Jesuit missionaries which spilled over into their European headquarters to become a major issue in French Catholicism from the mid sixteenth until the late eighteenth century. It concerned various syncretistic practices endorsed by Jesuit missionaries, yet the role of this 'hiding of the cross' was by no means the only question involved. In 1639, Jean-Baptiste de Moralez, a Dominican priest, wrote to *Père* Manuel Dias, who was responsible for oversight of Jesuit missionaries to complain of similar syncretistic practices. His list included allowing Christian converts to sacrifice to idols, worship ancestors and Confucius at local temples, too liberal an attitude to absolution, and equivocation when asked whether Confucius was damned. It did not include the accusation of veiling crucifixes.[15] This practice was clearly one of the points at issue, the Jesuits having removed the crucifix from the altars of mission churches because the Chinese regarded it with distaste,[16] but it was only one of many disputed practices. When Pascal picks up the dispute then, he makes a deliberate choice to focus on the issue of hiding the cross, accusing the Jesuits of this practice, and implying that behind it lies a more fundamental principle of Jesuit ideology.

Pascal's accusation is that not just in Indo-China, but also in France, they preach 'Christ not crucified'. The context of the 5th Provincial Letter is a discussion of the Jesuits' "obliging and accommodating conduct... how they open their arms to the whole world". In other words, it concerns the Jesuits' understanding of conversion. For Pascal, their moral laxism suggests that it is possible to become a true Christian without the need for deep moral change. Jesuit moral theology allows a person to receive absolution, attend mass, and live with a clear conscience without any change of behaviour. When he accuses them of preaching 'Christ not crucified', of suppressing the scandal of the cross, Pascal's charge is that they have neglected the third aspect of the cross which we noted in the *Pensées*, the cross as signifying the profound moral realignment that needs to take place if a person is to come to know and love God. When they "hide the mystery of the cross", they deny Pascal's fundamental insight that conversion, the change of perspective takes place only through moral, not intellectual reorientation. It is therefore typical of the Jesuits to begin to omit the conventional sign of the cross when writing the monogram IHS.[17] Here, the polemic of both the *Lettres Provinciales* and the *Pensées* coincide.[18]

These satirical letters accuse the Jesuits of justifying moral laxity by rationalising inappropriate behaviour in order not to offend anyone. They bend the rules because they want to make it easy for people to be Christian without too much sacrifice. Pascal's objection is not however to the process of rationalisation. His remedy is not to urge them to give up wrong motives and replace them with pure ones, or to argue with purer reason. The Jesuit problem is the universal problem, in that *everyone* rationalises on the basis of unacknowledged and hidden desires. Jesuit casuistry may be a particularly blatant example of it, but in principle it is trapped in the same dilemma as all human thinking. Human passions and desires lie deeper than human reason, and reason is always controlled by hidden desires, not the other way round. Pascal's objection to Jesuit moral theology is not the Cartesian one that they have abused reason by using it to justify conclusions adopted on other grounds. It is instead the Jansenist objection that they are not aware that they have done so. They have failed to appreciate that the real driving force behind their moral theology is unworthy passions, the desire to make life easy for their converts by turning a blind eye to unchristian practice. They have failed to confront the root of the problem, and therefore offer a spurious salvation. Sidelining the cross in their missionary strategy is therefore symbolic of a more fundamental theological trend. They ignore the cross both in the sense that it stands for human corruption, the frailty of reason and the need for salvation, and also in that it stands for the need for the crucifixion of the passions, and the encouragement of a desire for God, if rationality is to be based on a surer foundation. Jesuit missionary activity ignores the need for deep-rooted spiritual change, for a profound awareness of sin and the moral re-orientation urged in the Wager. It is a superficial analysis of the human condition, and proposes a superficial solution to that condition.

Pascal's polemics as well as his apologetics are therefore conducted from the perspective of the cross. The three aspects we noticed in the *Pensées* correspond to the three objects of his polemic: Christian faith as foolishness confounds the *dogmatistes,* as wisdom it confounds the *pyrrhoniens*, and as the way of the cross, the path of moral realignment, it confounds the *Jésuites*. On all three fronts, Pascal opposes forms of belief which lack a sense of moral or religious seriousness. While dogmatism and scepticism are too superficial in that both fail to encompass the valid insights of the other, the Jesuit way is too superficial in that it leaves the sinner untouched and unchanged.

PASCAL, JANSENISM AND JESUIT POWER

We have seen the importance of Pascal's Augustinian understanding of God for the fundamental structure of his Apology. He had at some point read carefully the works of Augustine, presumably in the Louvain edition of 1576-77.[19] Yet his Augustinianism is clearly mediated through, and coloured by, Jansenist influence. We need therefore to look beyond this direct encounter with Augustine for the sources of Pascal's *theologia crucis*. It is also important to be precise in identifying which aspects of Jansenism mediated this belief to Pascal. This is a vital question in exploring the origins of his *theologia crucis*, especially when it is placed alongside Luther's as an example of the reappropriation of Pauline themes and ideas in 1 Corinthians.

The problem of defining Jansenism has frequently perplexed its students.[20] Some have spoken of the difficulty of defining it intellectually,[21] others of its sheer variety of expressions.[22] Four separate strands of interpretation stand out in the study of the rise and function of Jansenism in seventeenth century France, each of which stresses a different aspect of the movement.

SOCIOLOGICAL FACTORS

Sainte-Beuve read the movement as the religious enterprise of the *bourgeois* aristocracy in France,[23] while Paul Bénichou's masterly study of the seventeenth century placed the social level of the Jansenists a little lower, among the mainstream *bourgeoisie* reacting with a hostile and repressed dignity towards the aristocracy at whose hands their fortunes had suffered.[24] Lucien Goldmann saw Jansenism as a spiritual expression of the declining fortunes of the *noblesse de robe*, reflecting their vulnerability at the hands of a fluctuating economy and their loss of status and power to the rising *commissaire* class.[25]

This attempt to place or perhaps even explain Jansenism sociologically has come in for increased criticism in more recent studies. René Taveneaux has called the whole approach '*fragile*',[26] pointing out how on its own terms, the crisis was not between different classes, but within one class, between new and old bourgeoisie, while also drawing attention to the difficulties involved in explaining religious and spiritual movements purely on sociological grounds. Françoise Hildesheimer similarly points out the weaknesses of Goldmann's thesis, that in fact the *noblesse de robe* was one of the main supports of the monarchy at start of the century. Antipathy towards it emerged after the *fronde*, not before it, and did not really show itself properly until the eighteenth century.[27]

POLITICAL FACTORS

A number of recent studies have linked Jansenism to the *fronde*, and have either alleged real political involvement in the rebellion on the part of individual Jansenists, or seen the movement as the spiritual expression of the same social and political factors which prompted the *fronde*. Alexander Sedgwick points out the links between Port-Royal and the Parisian *curés* responsible for the religious *fronde*, and highlights evidence that père Antoine Arnauld's eldest son, Arnauld D'Andilly wrote anonymous pamphlets against Cardinal Mazarin.[28] René Taveneaux sees the movement as the spiritual equivalent of the political unrest of the *fronde*.[29] These interpretations tend to stress the gulf between the atmosphere and values of Port-Royal and the Court circles surrounding Louis XIV, as well as Jansenist opposition to French foreign policy during this period. Saint-Cyran, the Jansenist spiritual leader, was clearly imprisoned by Cardinal Richelieu at Vincennes in 1638 for reasons as much political as theological, the Cardinal taking exception to his resistance to authority as much as to his views on the necessity of contrition, not just attrition for absolution.[30] There was a widespread feeling in Jansenist and *dévot* circles that the war against Spain, another Catholic country, was morally and spiritually wrong, particularly when it involved alliances with Protestant countries.

Alongside these readings of the movement lies a recurrent theme of recent study of Jansenism which stresses the movement's resistance to authority, and loyalty to the principle of the intellectual and spiritual autonomy of the individual. This began with Paul Bénichou, who argued that Jansenism failed because of its resistance to authority and independence of conscience, the only expressions of bourgeois sensibility unacceptable in Louis XIV's France.[31] Jansenism was thus a movement of protest against the absolutism of both the French Church and the French Royal Court. Both Sedgwick and Taveneaux similarly argue that the Jansenists' self-sufficiency, their emphasis upon the individual and this freedom of his conscience ironically contributed towards rather than stemmed the tide of the Enlightenment in France.[32] Despite being a conservative movement socially, paternalistic in its attitude to the poverty brought about by the wars of religion,[33] it therefore made a significant contribution to social change in France, but one contrary to that which it probably would have wished.

THEOLOGICAL FACTORS

A third aspect of Jansenism, and historically perhaps its most notorious, is its theological standpoint. The problems of definition mentioned above are far from new. Even in its own day, the controversy over the *question de droit* and the *question de fait* bore witness to the difficulty of ascribing a precise and agreed meaning to Jansenist theology. Whether defined by Jansenius's *Augustinus,* the 'Five Propositions' of Nicholas Cornet, allegedly summarising Jansenius's teaching, or by Port-Royal Logic, the movement has always been hard to tie down theologically. Jansenius's own theology was clearly of an extreme Augustinian form, yet it is debatable how much of the loyalty of the nuns of Port-Royal's to that theology was in fact displaced loyalty to their favourite Saint-Cyran rather than to Jansenius, a Belgian academic who had died before the book was even published. Many of the Port-Royal nuns, for example, who agonised at length over signing the *formulaire* condemning the book had not read this 1300-page work of complicated theology.[34] Jean Orcibal's work has shown how Saint-Cyran, who was after all the guiding spirit of Jansenism until his death, gained much of his Augustinianism from Bérulle rather than from Jansenius.[35] Even after Saint-Cyran's death in 1643, when the effective leadership of the party passed to Antoine Arnauld, much of the controversy surrounding Jansenism concerned its spiritual teaching, such as Arnauld's views expressed in *De la fréquente communion* and *La Théologie morale des Jésuites*. In time, the focus of debate became the "Five Propositions", and the question of whether or not they were an accurate description of Jansenius's teaching. As a result, the finer details of Jansenius's own theology, although an important symbol of resistance to the Molinist tendencies of Jesuit theology and humanist confidence, became actually tangential to the main lines of the movement.

SPIRITUAL FACTORS

As a form of spirituality, Jansenism has received a good deal of attention. Jean Orcibal's extensive work has uncovered the spiritual predecessors of Saint-Cyran, tracing a line through Bérulle, François de Sales, to Saint-Cyran himself, Mère Angélique and the beginnings of Port-Royal and on to Antoine Arnauld and Nicole. The spiritual authority of Saint-Cyran in Port-Royal was exercised principally through his influence on its Abbess, Mère Marie-Angélique de Sainte-Madeleine, whom he had met in 1621, after she had conceived a desire to reform the Cistercian convent at Port-Royal, originally founded in 1608. His entry into prison if anything increased that spiritual power, through his extensive correspondence in which he disseminated a wide range of spiritual advice,[36] and through his enhanced status as a martyr for what Jansenists saw as true Christian theology and spirituality. This spiritual authority enabled him to gather a significant following, all of whom still owed a certain loyalty and debt to him for many years to come.[37] The true centre of Port-Royal lay not so much in Jansenius, but in Saint-Cyran and his spiritual legacy.

PASCAL AND JANSENIST SPIRITUALITY

Pascal's relationship to Jansenism is complicated, due to several factors. He did not take the common Jansenist route into isolation after his 'second' conversion, and deliberately refused to become one of the *Solitaires* at Port-Royal aux Granges. Although he clearly took up the cudgels on behalf of the Jansenists in the *Provinciales*, Pascal's references to Jansenism in the *Pensées* are cryptic to say the least, at once stage favouring the Jesuits' position over that of the Jansenists,[38] and even denying that he was a Jansenist.[39] The value of the evidence of Père Beurrier, who administered the last rites at Pascal's deathbed, and who suggested that he died reconciled to the

Pope, and renouncing Jansenism, is disputed.[40] Roman Catholic
writers, anxious to rescue Pascal for orthodoxy, have often used this
evidence to distance him from Jansenism, emphasising the extent of
his disagreement with de Sacy.[41] Baudin's conclusion was that
Pascal's critique of Jansenism was in its nascent stage at the time of
his death.[42] So, how much of a Jansenist was he?

We have already argued that the Jansenist understanding of God
profoundly influenced Pascal's theology and apologetics. Although
Mme Périer mentions that he had read Jansenius's works, Pascal
does not show a clear debt to Jansenius's teaching, as opposed to
what he received directly from Augustine. In fact the *Pensées* show
a decided ambivalence towards the movement at times. Similarly
Pascal shows little overt interest in the political side of the
movement. He hardly mentions the *fronde*, pausing only to reject its
injustice,[43] and if the account of his sister Mme Périer is to be
believed, resisting all attempts to persuade him to join in the
rebellion against the king.[44] Pascal's Christ-centred theology and
apologetics derives not so much from the purely theological or
sociological or political aspects of the Jansenist movement, as from
its spirituality.

Both Saint-Cyran's Augustinianism[45] and his Christocentrism
derive from Pierre de Bérulle, whom he had first met in 1620.
Bérulle's incarnation-centred spirituality, impregnated with
Augustine, clearly made a deep impression on the young Saint-
Cyran, at that time know as Jean Duvergier de Hauranne. This
Christocentricity stands out in Saint-Cyran's later spiritual writings,
and as Jean Orcibal has noted: "The Bérullian imitation of Jesus, in
which Condren saw a participation in his annihilation thus becomes
in the hands of the Director of Port-Royal, an association with his
cross... This is Saint-Cyran's most original idea."[46]

For Saint-Cyran, identification with Jesus on the cross, imitation
of him in his humility and suffering[47] was the centre of Christian
spirituality. For Saint-Cyran, "The whole of religion consists only
in humility."[48] "Jesus Christ and St. John show clearly by their
example, that the whole gospel consists in humility."[49] Self-
abasement and conformity to the cross are constant themes within

his teaching.[50] He even foreshadows Pascal's own use of the term *le Dieu humilié*.[51]

Pascal takes many of his own characteristic themes from this spiritual tradition. The *Dieu caché* has often been recognised as a common theme within Jansenism[52] and Saint-Cyran shows a similar interest to that of Pascal in the identity of God as the God of the Patriarchs.[53]   Pascal takes these motifs and develops them in his own characteristic way. We have touched on the way Pascal deepened and extended Nicole and Arnauld's ideas of God's tendency to hide the truth about himself. Similarly, Saint-Cyran's God of the Patriarchs as opposed to the idols of the nations around Israel becomes for Pascal the God of the Patriarchs, "not of the philosophers and scholars". The *Dieu humilié* becomes the *Dieu crucifié*. In each of these, Pascal has radicalised and *theologised* the spiritual tradition before him. He has taken a characteristic Jansenist theme and turned it into a characteristic of the God to whom he wishes to bring unbelievers. Saint-Cyran's spiritual idea of *renouvellement*, a psychological process whereby the penitent is deprived of the Eucharist and absolution for several weeks to intensify desire for God, and shock him into separation from the world, becomes for Pascal the process of moral change needed to begin to believe the Christian faith. The same dynamic is at work, namely that the deepest choices we make are not intellectual ones, but made with the heart, the instinct.

Although Pascal never met him, given the continuing strength of the cult of Saint-Cyran at Port-Royal,[54] and given Pascal's close connection with the convent through his sister and the *Solitaires*, it is not surprising that Pascal's theology shows the distinctive imprint of the spiritual tradition which flowed from Bérulle through Saint-Cyran into the community there. This was a spiritual tradition which stressed the incarnation, the cross and human sin. At the centre of its spirituality was the the Fall, the incarnation and passion of Christ as the means by which it is overcome, and the need for profound inner spiritual renewal, to be found through humility, prayer, and introspection, rather than intellectual endeavour.[55]   Pascal's Christocentricity, and within that, his focus upon the cross of Christ as the sign of the foolishness of Christianity, the key to true understanding of revelation, and the means of conversion, derived not from the rigid Augustinianism of Jansenius nor deferral of temporal or political power, nor the modified Cartesianism of Arnauld and Nicole, but from the rich vein of Counter-Reformation spirituality represented by Port-Royal. As such, it represents a spiritual tradition within seventeenth century Catholicism which, like that to which Luther was heir, reacted against the Aristotelian tradition of natural theology, the tradition of Aquinas, and now for Pascal, of the Council of Trent.[56]

PASCAL AND JANSENIST POLITICS

Pascal's relationship with Jansenism towards the end of his life was enigmatic. It is quite probable that had he lived, Pascal would have found himself more distanced from the Cartesian philosophy of Arnauld and Nicole, and thus from 'official' Jansenism. Henri Gouhier reminds us, as Sainte-Beuve had done before him, of the important distinction between Port-Royal and Jansenism: that though they are inseparably linked, they refer to subtly different tendencies within the same movement.[57] Pascal may more properly be said to be a friend of Port-Royal than of Jansenism proper, as the former represents the spiritual as opposed to the theological or political aspects of the latter.

Although Pascal did not show a great deal of interest in the *fronde*, and while his immediate successors tried to distance him from any political motive in his actions[58], it is clear that the matter is not as simple as it may seem. Pascal, following Saint-Cyran, may have retreated from explicit involvement in political life, but his life and thought carry inevitable political implications. The *Lettres Provinciales* have a clear polemical and political edge, directed against the Jesuit campaign to crush Jansenist opposition. Even the *Pensées* have political significance which, though less explicit, is nonetheless incontrovertible. If they were founded upon the insight that Christian apologetic can work only when based upon the Jansenist Augustinian God, and that other forms of contemporary apologetic were totally missing the point, they must be read as an implicit critique of the Jesuits, the theology of the Sorbonne, and, in Pascal's stress on the need for moral reorientation, even as a critique of the royal Court of Louis XIV.

Louis Cognet has pointed out how the way of life adopted by the *Solitaires* at Port-Royal-des-Champs, and their conscious rejection of social status was " a kind of permanent defiance, of negation and also derision towards the fundamental values upon which society was based".[59] The *Solitaires* may not have seen their actions as political, but Richelieu certainly did, imprisoning his former friend Saint-Cyran because he and the movement he represented constituted a threat to the Cardinal's own position, founded on a delicate interplay of political and spiritual power. As Cognet puts it: "The Institution of the *Solitaires* is a quiet, perhaps inconsequential, yet eloquent protest against the politics of the Cardinal-Minister."[60]

Although Pascal never joined the *Solitaires* at Port-Royal-des-Champs, it is clear that he led a version of the same kind of lifestyle near to the end of his days.[61] His sister tells how he refused to employ a servant, insisted on making his own bed, sold as many possessions as he could to give the proceeds to the poor. He kept only those possessions which were necessary, ate only plain food, hung no tapestry in his bedroom, and took especial interest not in the rich and influential whom he had courted during his 'worldly period', but in the poor of Paris.[62] Such a lifestyle, particularly the adoption of manual labour, scandalous for a man of Pascal's rank, could not but be a statement of protest, an opting-out of the way of life sanctioned by the Jesuit-inspired theology of the academy of his time. Pascal's asceticism should be read at least partly in this light. It was not merely world-renouncing negativity, but an eloquent form of dissent from the economically comfortable, morally lax and socially divisive values of his contemporaries, which took little notice of the poor, and which was validated by a theology which suggested that conversion to Christ made few demands for moral and economic change. This course of action is entirely in continuity with the content of the *Pensées,* shaped as it was by the theme of the cross theologically, apologetically and experientially. Pascal's austerity was a practical expression of his theological dissent from the values of the controlling theology of his time.[63]

"In the French seventeenth century a theological opinion was a political event."[64] Viscount St Cyres' reminder is undoubtedly true. Pascal's opposition to the Jesuits in the *Lettres Provinciales* could not fail to be political. The *Pensées*, as we have seen, also have their political edge. The combination of Pascal's literary attack on the Jesuits, and his dissociation from the affluent style of the royal court are linked. As royal absolutism progressed under Richelieu and Mazarin, it was increasingly allied to a cult of the King as an object of distant admiration and even worship, expressed in the love for detailed ostentation, for elaborate displays of wealth and power. Those who lost out were clearly those in the lower reaches of the *bourgeoisie* and below, whose opposition gradually petered out after the collapse of the *fronde* in 1653.[65] The Jesuits were firmly tied in to this royal cult and court, and from the perspective of a critic such as Pascal, served to legitimate this way of life. Louis XIV himself placed a great deal of confidence in the Jesuits, who often provided spiritual direction to the great and the good, and education to their children. The Jesuit Père Annat, Louis XIV's confessor from 1654-70 was strongly anti-Jansenist, and Jesuits "undeniably exercised an excessive degree of influence upon the king."[66] Pascal's protest against Jesuit casuistry and sleight of hand, ignoring the place of the cross in Christian life and theology was an attack on an attempt to justify affluence, the abuse of power, and rivalry, values he saw alive and well in the royal court. It was a protest against a form of theology which could be used to legitimise an oppressive and ostentatious régime, far removed from the spirit of the crucified Christ.

Like Paul's and Luther's, Pascal's theology of the cross stood as a protest against claims to totalizing power and dominance, whether ideological (as in *dogmatisme* or *pyrrhonisme*) or ecclesiastical and political (as in the Society of Jesus). Like Luther's it utilised the themes and language of 1 Corinthians 1-2, and developed out of anti-scholastic traditions of spirituality, traditions which stand in line as a critique of the dominant Thomist rationalism, of the God accessible either by human works or by human observation. There are of course differences in emphasis, and the notable differences in their theologies of grace. Yet still their theologies play a similar role in opposing human self-assertion, issuing in claims to power and control. The protest is made in the name of the God who reveals himself at the cross of Christ.

Notes:

[1] See the opposition Pascal makes between these two in L4, 109, 208 and at length in 131.

[2] E.g. L131.

[3] See Pintard, "Pascal et les libertins".

[4] Pascal had read, but was unimpressed by Charron: "*les divisions de Charron, qui attristent et ennuient*", L780.

[5] L498.

[6] M. de Saci's opinion, as expressed in the *Entretien*, shows the degree of suspicion in *dévot* circles to the use of such literature.

[7] L406.

[8] L268.

[9] L291.

[10] "*n'ayant point de certitude* hors la foi".

[11] L416, 417, 449.

[12] L458, see also 291, 842.

[13] "...*quand ils se trouvent en des pays où un Dieu crucifié passe pour folie, ils suppriment le scandale de la croix, et ne prêchent que Jésus-Christ glorieux, et non pas Jésus-Christ souffrant*". *Œuvres*, 388. English Translation in ed. A. J. Krailsheimer, *Blaise Pascal: The Provincial Letters* (Harmondsworth: Penguin, 1967), 76.

[14] L834.

[15] Text in Etiemble, *Les Jésuites en Chine: La Querelle des Rites 1552-1773* (Paris: René Julliard, 1966), 89-90.

[16] See *New Cambridge Modern History Vol.V: The Ascendancy of France 1648-88*, ed. F.L. Carsten (Cambridge: C.U.P., 1961), 408f.

[17] 11th *Lettre Provinciale. Œuvres*, 423. ET, 174.

[18] R. Parish, *Pascal's Lettres Provinciales: A Study in Polemic* (Oxford: Clarendon, 1989) argues that the two works share a fundamental unity of purpose and perspective. On this particular point, see 82-3: "the burden of the refutation

in the *Lettres Provinciales* is identical to that in the *Pensées*: the Society of Jesus, by its suppression of the 'scandale de la Croix' and all that follows from it... does not just offend the sacred truth; it also, it is asserted - in paradoxically, the very act of proselytizing - makes the claims of Christianity inefficacious and so, ultimately, unbelievable."

[19]For Pascal's knowledge of the Fathers (and particularly Augustine) from an early age, see both the evidence of extensive quotation in the *Écrits sur la Grâce*, and Sellier, *Pascal et Saint Augustin*, 11-18. Sellier concludes that the report in the *Entretien* that de Sacy was surprised to see Pascal had discovered Augustinian ideas without reading Augustine, is due to Fontaine's inadequate knowledge of the breadth of Pascal's reading, not to Pascal's ignorance of Augustine. Père Beurrier mentions in passing that Pascal had kept his copies of Augustine's works when he sold all his other books; *Pascal: Pensées sur la Religion et sur autres sujets III: Documents*, 3 vols. (Paris: Editions du Luxembourg, 1951), 54.

[20]Taveneaux, "Jansénisme et vie sociale". A. Sedgwick, *Jansenism*, 93.

[21]Cognet, *Le Jansénisme* (Paris: Presses Universitaires de France, 1961), 123, speaks of *"la quasi-impossibilité de donner au mot jansénisme un contenu intellectual précis"*.

[22]F. Hildesheimer, *Le Jansénisme en France aux XVIIe et XVIIIe siècles* (Paris: Publisud, 1991), 100-4.

[23]Sainte-Beuve, *Port-Royal I*, 2 vols.; presented and annotated by M. Leroy (Paris: Gallimard, 1953 - originally published 1840-59).

[24]P. Bénichou, *Morales du Grand Siècle* (Paris: Gallimard, 1948), 184-6.

[25]L. Goldmann, *The Hidden God*, cf. chs. 6 and 7.

[26]Taveneaux, "Jansénisme et vie sociale", 25.

[27]Hildesheimer, *Le Jansénisme*, 93f.

[28]Sedgwick, *Jansenism*, 59-63.

[29]Taveneaux, "Jansénisme et vie sociale", 23.

[30]Goldmann, *Hidden God*, 114-5; N. Abercrombie, *The Origins of Jansenism* (Oxford: Clarendon, 1936), 188.

[31]Bénichou, *Morales*, 181-213.

[32]Sedgwick, *Jansenism*, 198; Taveneaux, "Jansénisme et vie sociale", 32-3.

[33]R. Taveneaux, "Port-Royal, les pauvres et la pauvreté", *Jansénisme et Réforme Catholique*, 45-62.

[34]Cognet, *Le Jansénisme*, 77-8.

[35]J. Orcibal, *Jean Duvergier de Hauranne, abbé de Saint-Cyran, et son temps*, 2 vols. (Paris: J. Vrin, 1947-48). Also *Saint-Cyran et le Jansénisme* (Paris: Éditions du Seuil, 1961), 10-22, 55-85.

[36]*Lettres Inédites de Jean Duvergier de Hauranne*, A. Barnes, ed. *Les Origines du Jansénisme* vol. IV (Paris: J. Vrin, 1962).

[37]Abercrombie, *Origins*, 187-94.

[38]L786.

[39]L955: "*Vous dites que je suis janséniste, que le P.R. soutient les 5 p[ropositions]. et qu'ainsi je les soutiens. 3 mensonges.*"

[40]Beurrier does not mention Jansenism by name, but is keen to show that Pascal died in "*soumission à l'Eglise et au Souverain Pontife*". *Documents*, 56. Gilberte Pascal's *Vie*, however, denies that Pascal made any "*rétractation*" on his death-bed, (*Œuvres*, 33).

[41]e.g. J. Chaix-Ruy, *Pascal et Port-Royal* (Paris: Félix Alcan, 1930), 106, 161.

[42]E. Baudin, *Études Historiques et Critiques sur la Philosophie de Pascal, II. Sa Philosophie Morale: Pascal, les libertins et les jansénistes* (Neuchâtel: Éditions de la Baconnière, 1946), 93-8.

[43]L85.

[44]*Vie de Monsieur Pascal*, *Œuvres*, 30.

[45]Cognet, *Le Jansénisme*, 21-2

[46]"*L'imitation bérullienne de Jésus, dans laquelle Condren voyait une participation à son anéantissement, devient ainsi chez le directeur de Port-Royal une association à sa croix.... Telle est l'idée la plus originale de Saint-Cyran.*" J. Orcibal, *Jean Duvergier de Hauranne*, 678.

[47]"*Jésus-Christ a répondu si humblement à ses juges.... il faut faire de même.*" J. Orcibal, "La Spiritualité de Saint-Cyran avec ses Écrits de Piété Inédits" *Les Origines du Jansénisme* vol. V (Paris: J. Vrin, 1962), 196.

[48]"*Toute la religion n'est qu'humilité.*" ibid., 393. See the whole section from 391-420.

[49]"*Jésus-Christ et saint Jean montrent bien par leurs exemples que tout l'Evangile consiste en l'humilité.*" ibid., 190, no. 23.

[50]"*La vocation de Dieu, ce qui nous obligera à nous tenir sans cesse dans l'humilité et dans l'abaissement de nous-mêmes.*" ibid., 394.

[51]"*...un Dieu humilié dans tous ses mystères, dans sa vie, dans la suite de ses actions et de sa mort*". ibid., 395. "*Un Dieu s'étant autant abaissé qu'un homme s'était voulu élever*" (quoted in Orcibal, *Saint-Cyran et le Jansénisme*,133).

[52]Calvet, *La Littérature Religieuse*, 240-2, Goldmann, *Hidden God*, 161.

[53]"*...le Dieu d'Abraham seul, était le vrai Dieu*": J. Orcibal, *Lettres Inédites de Jean Duvergier de Hauranne*, 315.

[54]Sedgwick, *Jansenism*, 31.

[55]In fact Port-Royal always showed a distinct distrust in intellectualism. See Sedgwick, *Jansenism*, 87.

[56]Kearns, *Ideas*, 6-11.

[57]Gouhier, "Pascal et les humanismes de son temps," 81. Louis Cognet expresses the relationship well: "*Port-Royal est un milieu spiritual riche complexe, issu de la Contre-Réforme, et où le jansénisme, mouvement théologique lui-même fort polymorphe a trouvé un terrain favorable.*" "Le Mépris du monde à Port-Royal et dans le Jansénisme," *RAM* 41 (1965), 387-402, (here, 387-8).

[58]Mme Périer asserts Pascal's loyalty to the King in her *Vie de Monsieur Pascal*,

Œuvres, 30

[59]"*un sorte de défi permanent, de négation et presque de dérision à l'égard des valeurs fondamentales sur lesquelles reposait le cadre social*", Cognet, "Mépris du monde", 396. See also Briggs, *Communities of Belief*, 347-8.

[60]"*L'institution des Solitaires est une muette et peut-être inconséquente, mais éloquante, protestation contre la politique du cardinal-ministre.*" Cognet, "Mépris du monde", 397.

[61]As did a number of others, e.g., M. De Fossé: cf R. Taveneaux, "Port-Royal ou l'héroisme de la sainteté", *Jansénisme et Réforme Catholique*, 35-44 (first published 1974). Taveneaux confirms that apart from the extreme Barcosian wing, the ideal for Port-Royal was not negative renunciation, but a heroic ideal of detachment from and rejection of the secular world's values.

[62]Taveneaux, "Port-Royal, les pauvres et la pauvreté", shows how poverty and care for the poor were a primary vocation for the devotees of Port-Royal.

[63]The later Pascal is often seen as more extreme in his rejection of the world than the earlier. So, for example, in the three attitudes which Jansenism adopted towards the world, total rejection (e.g., Barcos), worldly extremism (e.g., Jacqueline Pascal), and theological justification/argumentation (e.g., Arnauld, Nicole), Taveneaux suggests that the later Pascal fits into the first, whereas at the time of the *Lettres Provinciales* he would fit under the second. My understanding of the significance of Pascal's asceticism places it in greater continuity with the protest of the *Lettres*, and therefore would suggest that even the later Pascal fits better under the second category. See Taveneaux, "Jansénisme et vie sociale", 25-6.

[64]Viscount St. Cyres, "The Gallican Church", *Cambridge Modern* History Vol. V (Cambridge: C.U.P., 1934), 83.

[65]Cf. J. Lough, *An Introduction to Seventeenth Century France* (London: Longmans 1954), 127-32.

[66]F. Bluche, *Louis XIV* (Oxford: Blackwell, 1990; original French edition 1984), 390-1.

Conclusion

Sixteen: The Theology of the Cross: Power, Truth and Love

The theology of the cross is a strand of Christian theology, often sidelined from the mainstream academic tradition, yet sustained by engagement with important biblical themes, in the context of prayer and devotion. Reflection on the themes and language of Paul's teaching in 1 Cor.1-2 in the context of traditions of popular piety and prayer nourished this theology, and kept it from being entirely forgotten, when it only occasionally became explicit in the theology of the academy. In this area at least, theology follows in the footsteps of prayer and spiritual life, and devotion is one step ahead of theology.

In fact, a *theologia crucis* opposes the notion of purely *academic* theology, in the sense of theology conducted purely within the 'academy', without the personal involvement of the theologian. If Christian theology has to take account of the precise historical nature of God's self-revelation in Christ as crucified, then it can be undertaken only by those who experience a kind of crucifixion or powerlessness within their own existence. For Paul the form of crucifixion was social, his voluntary adoption of the socially weak position of the artisan labourer, rather than the other more socially prominent options open to him as a travelling 'sophist'. For Luther, the form was experiential: the experience of temptation, despair and judgement which is the only preparation for grace.[1] For Pascal, the form was intellectual and moral, the fundamental moral reorientation, the willingness to become stupid (*abêtir*) in order to arrive at the perspective from which truth can be seen. For all three, true theology is foolishness in the sense that from the outside it must appear as foolishness. To be a theologian one needs to become foolish, whether socially, experientially or morally: theology cannot be done from the safety of objective distance. As Luther expressed it in his Preface to 1 Corinthians, written in 1530, yet published in the 1546 edition of his German Bible:

> The desire to be wise and the pretence of cleverness in the gospel are the very things that really give offence and hinder the knowledge of God. Yet such people can never know our Lord Christ, unless they first become fools again, and humbly let themselves be taught and led by the simple Word of God.[2]

Yet despite its ambivalent relationship with 'academic theology', the theology of the cross still seeks to address it. In particular, it has always been firmly contextual theology, addressing issues of power within the church and society, and the ways in which this is so often underpinned by ideology. The last stage in this journey must therefore be an investigation into the continuing relevance of this theology today.

THE POWER OF THE CROSS

The fundamental insight lying at the heart of the theology of the cross is the notion that God acts in the present in continuity with the way he has acted in the past. In asserting the paradigmatic nature of the cross, or in other words, that the cross represents the characteristic pattern of God's action in the world, these theologians claim that the cross can never be just a soteriological event, which remains locked in the past, but is a paradigm of the way in which God *always* works. For this reason, atonement theologies which regard the cross as purely a past action, the benefits of which one simply enjoys in the present, are inadequate if they fail to make the connection between God's action in Christ and God's action in the ongoing life of the church or the Christian. All three of these theologians oppose forms of theology which would divide the two, and fail to see the cross as determinative for *present* Christian experience as well as past divine action. None of them opposes the traditional affirmation of the soteriological efficacy of Christ's death on the cross; in fact this soteriological basis provides the grounds on which they argue for the *theological* significance of the cross.[3] The cross can be seen as a paradigm for God's action in the world now, precisely because it was the way in which God worked salvation in Christ. It continues to represent the essential sign of the action of God. God deals with the church and the Christian now in the same way as he dealt with Christ. The cross acts as God's signature, the mark of his action in the present. Just as God revealed himself, and worked salvation through a crucified Messiah, God still works in and through what is to conventional human understanding, weak, powerless and apparently irrational rather than through what is strong, powerful and reasonable.

This basic insight gives rise to a "discourse of the cross", which in turns contains a particular understanding of the nature of power. This can best be described in terms of two connected ideas, or to be more exact, two realisations.

The first is that in the light of the cross, human power counts for nothing before God. At the heart of the disputes in the church in first century Corinth, involving a complex interrelation of power and ideology, lay the assumption that social status and philosophical knowledge counted for something within the church, acting as a criterion of worth. Paul's response to this was not to take sides with his supporters in re-asserting his authority over the church, but to recast the debate by reminding them of the cross. If the cross of Christ is understood as God's wisdom and power, then God works out his comprehensive purposes through a death reserved for slaves, criminals and rebellious outsiders.[4] To despise slaves or artisans within the Christian congregation is therefore to despise those who in fact are closer to the place where God himself was found in Christ. Similarly, the message that the cross is God's wisdom offends against all standards of rhetorical and philosophical sense. Although new, socially fluid Corinthian society placed great store by social status and philosophical sophistication and rhetorical ability, in the light of the cross, both are rendered irrelevant.

For Luther, the issue initially concerned human works and their place in the scheme of salvation. Luther's developing understanding of the cross as the paradigm of God's action demanded that God must humble sinners, bringing them to a realisation of their own emptiness, before he can raise them to new life and salvation. This means that the claim to offer works to contribute to salvation is not only unnecessary, it is the very thing which prevents salvation from taking place. In turn this critique led to a wide-ranging attack not just on late medieval scholasticism or the university syllabus, but on the papacy and its use of power.

For Pascal, again there was a complex relationship between the powers of human reason, moral capacity and political power. The cross, representing the drama of fall and redemption, the priority of the moral rather than the intellectual in the knowledge of God, indicates that without the predisposition to believe, effected by grace, human reason was powerless to make sense of the ambiguous revelation of the hidden God. Pascal's theology of the cross contained also an implicit critique not only of the royal court of Louis XIV, but also the casuistic Jesuit moral theology which seemed to justify it.

For all three, a theology of the cross involved a struggle against ideologies which were foreign to true Christian theology. In turn these ideologies led to critiques of configurations of power in the church. True power begins with a realisation of one's own powerlessness before God, when the point is reached where a person grasps the ineffectiveness of their own power, whether rational, moral or social, before God. This brings us to the second of the two fundamental ideas which stand at the heart of this theology.

The result of this realisation of powerlessness before God is the power to surrender power, the ability to relinquish rights or privileges, for the sake of another, and out of identification with Christ. Paul's repeated claim to have chosen not to make use of his "rights" (the word ἐξουσία is repeated throughout 1 Cor.9) is typical of his understanding of how power is to operate within the Christian community. In specific terms, such privileges might be the right to dine at pagan temples which wealthy Corinthian Christians claimed, and which Paul asks them to forego. To be truly wise, these richer Christians needed to forego such rights, and eat alongside the poorer fellow-Christians at the Lord's table, in the same way as Paul had, in imitation of the cross, given up his right to financial assistance and social respectability. This was of course, not because pagan gods have any power in themselves, but purely as an act of love and consideration for those poorer Christians who would never be invited to such meals, and who think it scandalous that their Christian brothers and sisters should stroll out after the Christian Eucharist to move on to a meal at a pagan temple. In other words, power is to be expressed and exercised through love.

These 'rights' to be surrendered might equally be the late medieval papacy's 'right' to lavish ostentation and a politically significant role within the empire. Again, they might be the privileged position of the Jesuits in seventeenth century France as confessors to the wealthy and powerful, or the right to a socially prominent and comfortable life such as Pascal himself renounced towards the end of his life.

Yet questions remain. Is this outlook simply the diseased and anaesthetising denial of life which Nietzsche feared? Is it simply another power-game under another name, whereby religious authority is used to impose a constricting ethic upon others? How does this understanding of power, the power to surrender rights for the sake of the other, relate to contemporary notions of power? One way to explore these questions will be to examine this 'discourse of the cross' in the light of one of the most prominent recent theorists on the nature of power, Michel Foucault.

MICHEL FOUCAULT ON POWER AND TRUTH

Whereas his previous work contained implicit discussion of the operation of power, it was only after 1968, the Paris student uprisings which took place in that year, and Foucault's own move to the Collège de France, that power and its relation to knowledge and discourse took up an explicit and prominent place in his work.[5] Writing against the background of the Parisian Marxist Left, Foucault developed an understanding of power which began to distance itself from notions common in those circles. In *Folie et Déraison* and *Naissance de la Clinique*[6] he had already called into question the assumption that our understanding and treatment of a phenomenon such as mental illness had actually improved or progressed. This 'archaeological' approach to knowledge aimed to show how, under different historical 'epistemes', madness had been conceptualised and then treated in different ways, and yet the underlying rationale had by no means been an inexorable advance in knowledge and an increasingly humane manner of treatment. Instead, these different ways of treating madness, all conditioned by discourses which reflect their own contemporary historical possibilities, were simply different from and discontinuous with one another. They may share the impulse to silence and confine the mad, but simply do it in different, and by no means improving ways. What we see when we look at this concept 'madness' is determined not by 'what it is', but by the discourse which surrounds the act of looking. As a result, these shifts from one historical episteme to another are to be understood not in continuity from one another, as was traditionally thought under the notion of the 'history of ideas', but as simply a series of breaks or discontinuities, ruptures in history. Foucault's aim is to describe these discontinuities, and to demonstrate the lack of coherence in the history of the study of madness and its treatment.

After 1968, although it is more of a development within his understanding than a replacement of one idea for another, Foucault's method shifts from what he calls 'archaeology' to 'genealogy'. This shift includes two notable features. First, Foucault shows a much greater awareness of the role of power and its relationship to discourse. A genealogical approach, (influenced of course by Nietzsche's 1887 work, "On the Genealogy of Morals"), refuses to search for the origins of ideas, or for the historical essence of phenomena, but rather sees them as developing arbitrarily, with no guiding intention; it is merely the "search for descent".[7] Whereas his earlier studies had tended to work with an underlying concept of madness which remained constant, while its interpretation changed,[8] the genealogical method is less confident that there can be such an unchanging essence as 'madness' or 'sexuality' or even 'human nature'.

Secondly, the archaeological approach could describe these historical shifts in understanding in terms of distinct historical events. Such events might include, in the case of the birth of the Asylum, the establishment of the Hôpital Général in Paris in 1656, the freeing of the inmates of Bicêtre by Pinel in 1794, or the establishment of the asylum by Samuel Tuke in York around the same time.[9] The genealogical method, with its greater interest in questions of power and how it operates, tends not to see such deliberate acts as particularly significant. Instead, it sees power as operating through networks of relations, in unseen, dispersed mechanisms located very often in institutions, not controlled by anyone in particular, but developing arbitrarily and unintentionally through discourse. Genealogy listens carefully to hidden voices from the past, perspectives which have been lost or forgotten in the grander schemes of discourse into which they did not fit. Foucault, in fact, defines genealogy at one point as "the union of erudite knowledge and local memories which allows us to establish a historical knowledge of struggles and to make use of this knowledge tactically today".[10] It is this concern with struggle, with analysis of how the struggles of power operate in quiet, unnoticed and minute ways which distinguishes Foucault's genealogical approach. He wants to elucidate just how discourse which we normally take to be true and scientifically established actually manages to impose its view of things upon us.[11]

Foucault's understanding of power therefore moves away from a more classical Marxist view. For the Marxist, power was concentrated in the hands of the ruling classes, and needed to be wrested from their grasp, and placed into the hands of the proletariat. Foucault however, denies that power is concentrated in any one place. It is so dispersed in relations within society that it is impossible to talk of claiming power, or overthrowing it in a Marxist revolutionary sense. What can never be tied down can never be seized. *Surveiller et Punir*[12], published in 1975 presents society not as controlled by any one political party, social class, or coercive institution such as the army or police, but by a whole series of small mechanisms operative in human relationships and institutions. The prison for example is studied not according to a hidden plan devised by a nameless (or named) bureaucrat, but as a 'disciplinary régime' which orders the minute details of the lives of inmates, which enables constant visibility and therefore constant control. The history of the prison is then, for Foucault, a story of the way in which a class of people is created which is analysed, observed, documented and thus controlled. It is not that this procedure is deliberately planned or orchestrated by those in power, it is merely an illustration of the way in which discourse (the concept of the criminal, the means of collecting information about them etc.) is related to power, or the ability to control.

The other major illustration of this approach to power was Foucault's study of sexuality, published in his unfinished project, "The History of Sexuality", three volumes of which were published between 1976 and 1984.[13] Here, Foucault's question is not the Freudian one: "Why are we sexually repressed?" but rather, "Why do we feel the need to keep on saying we are sexually repressed?"[14] Opposing what he calls "the Repressive Hypothesis", Foucault sees the eighteenth and nineteenth centuries, for example, not as a time when sexuality was hushed up, but on the contrary, as a time when it was talked about and worried over more than ever. Whether in the post-Tridentine intensification of the practice of religious confession, or the analysis of the psychiatrist, the doctor or the pimp, Foucault unearths what he sees as a typically Victorian need to talk about, to codify, to describe and administer sex. As he concludes:

> What is peculiar to modern societies, in fact, is not that they consigned sex to a shadow existence, but that they dedicated themselves to speaking of it *ad infinitum*, while exploiting it as *the* secret.[15]

The attempt to master or control sex thus generates a discourse about it, a discourse which in turn creates mechanisms of power. For example, as Foucault points out, while thinking of themselves as sexually liberated in their freedom to talk about sex, modern societies tend to have very restrictive and harsh expectations about how a body should look, the kinds of bodies which are acceptable, and the kind which are not.[16] In this case, discourse produces a very powerful image which demands that bodies look a certain way, and which then generates whole industries and cadres of experts to facilitate conformity to that image.

Running throughout his argument is a rejection of the typically Freudian idea (which he also thinks is Stoic and Christian), that sexuality is a deeply hidden constant within human nature, an underlying 'truth' or innate impulse which, in the Stoic/Christian version, has to be carefully controlled, or in the Freudian version, has only recently been liberated from centuries of repression. For Foucault, power does not repress sexuality because there is nothing to repress. Sex has in fact been turned into sexuality, in other words, talk about sex. It is not so much that powerful people have repressed sexuality, as that the notion of sexuality itself enables supervision, surveillance, control over people's bodies, and thus over society. 'Sexuality' is therefore not a basic human property, but an historical construct. Again it is not that this process is controlled by some hidden body of people manipulating its whole operation: no one person or body is in control. It may develop into coherent strategies, but it is impossible to identify who or what designed or intended such strategies. It is more that power, where it is exercised, cannot help but produce discourse,[17] and this discourse about sex in turn produces power.

Foucault insists therefore that it is a mistake to see power as something essentially negative or repressive:

> If power were never anything but repressive, if it never did anything but to say no, do you really think one would be brought to obey it? What makes power hold good, what makes it accepted, is simply the fact that it doesn't only weigh on us as a force that says no, but that it traverses and produces things, it induces pleasure, forms knowledge, produces discourse.[18]

Power is essentially creative and productive, and in particular, it produces discourse, which in turn produces power. It does not repress hidden realities, as Foucault does not believe there are such hidden realities to repress - to this extent he embraces an extreme nominalism. Instead, it produces new forms, new discourses, habits and expectations which shape the way we view the world. Likewise, to see power as operating only through the machinery of the State apparatus is also to misunderstand it.[19] Power operates through social structures, conventions, through small-scale techniques and tactics whereby at one point one individual or group exercises power, and at another point they are at the receiving end of its operation. Power circulates freely in societies,[20] so that each person is at different times both the subject and object of its workings. Power exists in the spaces between people; in relationships. It is to be found everywhere, is inevitably present, so that it is impossible to think of a society devoid of power relations. Foucault abandons the Enlightenment dream that knowledge is a means to escaping or controlling the workings of power: instead, in ironic fashion, knowledge actually produces power.

Through this analysis of power, Foucault aims to show the basically contingent nature of all discourse, of concepts which we so often take for granted, such as sexuality, discipline or human nature. 'Man' is for him a recent invention. Previously, God was the unchanging essence which guaranteed the truth of what we perceive, the fixed point upon which knowledge could be built. The modern age, argues Foucault, having dispensed with the notion of God, replaces it with 'Human Nature' as the fixed essence which guarantees knowledge and becomes the object of research within the social and psychological sciences. In the modern period these sciences have designated 'Man' or 'human nature' as the basic concept to be studied and explained. Foucault argues that they have not so much suddenly discovered Man, as invented him.[21]

The point is often made, and rightly so, that Foucault is not trying to found a new system, a better programme for social change, but is intent instead on destabilising those systems which are available. He aims to establish a kind of hermeneutic of suspicion, and is perhaps best described, in the words of John Rajchman, as "the great sceptic of our times",[22] or as Alan Sheridan puts it: "a slayer of dragons, a breaker of systems".[23] For Foucault, the social sciences, modern rationalism, psychoanalysis, in fact all Knowledge, Reason and Truth are contingent and accidental in their origins. None of them can claim to represent the unchanging nature of things. Truth or discourse can never be purely neutral: it is always implicated within social relations, serving to create power at some points within social networks, and to remove it at others. Neither truth nor knowledge can never exist apart from power, neither can power exist apart from truth or knowledge. Foucault's own observation is that his studies do not offer 'Truth' nor even a new theory to replace others, but a "box of tools" to dismantle old theories, and perhaps to begin building new, particularly local and small-scale, ones.[24] Foucault himself insists that he is not merely a cynic, but is better described as a sceptic: "my point is not that everything is bad, but that everything is dangerous."[25] He does not try to offer 'alternatives' to current ways of thinking, but to encourage alertness for the dangers inherent in any particular discourse, and a technique for mounting a critique of disciplinary power. He offers "a critical analysis of the prevailing regime of truth and its effects of power",[26] a critique of the ways in which the distinction between what is true and false, legitimate and illegitimate, has been used to govern societies in the past and by implication, in the present. This might involve the rediscovery of what Foucault calls 'local knowledges', or *le savoir de gens*, perspectives on a more popular level which have been disqualified from a hearing by victorious modes of discourse in operation in the past.[27] Yet it is not that these subjugated voices are any more true than the dominant ones, they merely remind us of the precarious and provisional nature of what we tend to take as self-evident. Foucault asks what are the effects of a body of 'Truth'. How does power work within it? Truth is a social and human construct, and power is created and used by it. Power usually works in present day societies by a process of normalisation, of a series of expectations that individuals conform to certain norms of what is expected or assumed to be appropriate and true, in whole range of different areas, including the sexual, the psychological and the political. The effect is that for Foucault, "all knowledge rests upon injustice (that there is no right, not even in the act of knowing, to truth, or a foundation for truth)".[28]

We can perhaps summarise this by isolating four distinctive marks of Foucault's analysis of power and its relation to truth.

1.   He indicates the inevitability of power-relations, and insists that power is endemic in human society. It cannot be abandoned and must not be ignored.

2.   For Foucault, truth is intimately connected with power. Power is not so much repressive of an underlying reality, as productive of versions of reality. Truth produces power, and power produces truth.

3.   He resists the idea of a gradual process of 'enlightenment', whereby societies progress towards greater degrees of understanding and freedom. He denies the possibility of any Hegelian kind of historicism, or even of the value of revolution or liberation. 'Liberation' can mean only the replacement of one set of arbitrary and contingent values by another.

4.   Foucault offers not a new theory of power, but rather a new way of understanding how it operates within societies, namely that it is not exercised in a centralised, deliberate fashion, but in a dispersed network of relations. It is not to be studied from the centre outwards, but from the periphery inwards. This analysis leads to a critique of disciplinary power, or the attempts of any powerful group to impose a view of reality on others, and thus to control or dominate.

FOUCAULT'S CRITICS

This analytic of power has of course not gone unchallenged. Foucault's critics have focused on a number of areas in which they feel he has failed to offer a satisfactory account of the power-truth relationship. These criticisms can be boiled down to a few distinct angles of attack.

A FAILURE TO CONSTRUCT

Foucault has been accused of failing to offer alternatives, solutions, or actual social or political forms which might replace what he himself criticizes. Similarly, he is taken to task because his view of power as ubiquitous suggests that resistance is futile. Jürgen Habermas calls Foucault a neo-conservative because he rejected the idea that revolution could achieve anything, and because he appeared to deny the usefulness of politics or the effectiveness of political activity to change the State.[29] Michael Walzer, in an important essay, thinks that Foucault's ideas lead merely to anarchism or even nihilism, and that the great weakness of his political theory is his refusal "however tentatively and critically... to construct(s) a new setting and propose(s) new codes and categories".[30] Foucault abandons politics, and for Habermas and Walzer, politics matter. According to them, Foucault tries to adopt a position outside history, in mid-air, critiquing all epistemes impartially, yet not being part of any himself. Yet no-one can stand outside history.[31] Even if he does advocate small-scale localised action based on his 'tools' for critique of power, he does not and cannot give any hope of finding anything better, nor helping anyone recognise anything better when they see it. If at the end of the day, there is just power and little else, and if power is endemic within societies, how might we distinguish between different configurations of power in order to reject one and accept another?

HIDDEN ASSUMPTIONS?

This is closely connected to another line of argument. Foucault has been criticised for smuggling in assumptions which are necessary for his analytics to work, yet which he rejects in principle. This is the essence of Derrida's critique of Foucault, when he denies the possibility of what Foucault is trying to do in writing a history of madness without recourse to an external rationality which makes sense of the data he surveys.[32] If we are to prefer one configuration of power to another (which Foucault must think possible, given that he does advocate resistance to power, a "hyper- and pessimistic activism",[33] the only way he can make such judgements is by introducing criteria to which in theory he denies any foundation. So, a valid question remains: what are we to make of Foucault's own standpoint if there are no independent standpoints?[34] Foucault's answer, that his is a kind of analytic waiting for the political realities which will validate it, fails to convince, because of the absence of criteria by which we might decide whether these future political realities can ever validate the critique.[35] On his own terms, even Foucault's limited and tentative suggestion of struggle and resistance cannot really mean a great deal, or promise anything better than what we already have.

THE MEANING OF POWER

Charles Taylor identifies Foucault's view of power as anonymous, dispersed among social networks, and yet not actually exercised by anyone in particular. He considers the idea that power can act with the effect of domination, yet without a subjective purpose behind it, to be basically unintelligible. To speak, as Foucault does, of power as domination (at least in some contexts), must involve notions of truth and liberation from that domination.[36] Foucault wants to hold onto the idea that discourse or truth effectively dominates by operations of power, yet to deny that any specific subject acts to effect this. For Taylor, Foucault appears to be trying to have his cake and eat it. In a similar way, Steven Lukes, who develops the relativistic thesis that the social sciences use a number of conflicting and models of power, tends to think of power as essentially 'power over' others. His view of power involves its deliberate exercise by agents. As a result, he considers that Foucault fails to account for or explain how individuals use power, when in a conscious position to do so, and with a sense of responsibility for its use.[37]

A LIMITED PERSPECTIVE?

Another critique accuses Foucault of insufficient attention to varieties of political environment, and of underestimating the extent to which living in a western liberal democracy has affected his outlook. France in the late 60s and early 70s may not have been the most stable and content of societies, but at least it offered the possibility of protest and resistance within a fundamentally liberal framework. Walzer suggests that the nature of the political context matters a great deal, in that only within a more liberal, and less totalitarian context is the kind of 'local resistance' of which Foucault speaks, possible.[38] The success of such resistance depends to some degree on support or at least recognition from the State itself, which in a totalitarian setting will hardly be forthcoming. Edward Said points out how Foucault's disillusionment with ideas of liberation and progress towards a more just society is not shared by Third World intellectuals and peoples, and those whose daily experience reinforces a strong sense of political or social oppression. Power may "circulate freely" in western European democracies such as the France of the 1970s, but arguably less so in Stalin's Russia or Pol Pot's Cambodia. Cornel West makes much the same point although not directly addressed to Foucault, when he suggests that postmodern discourse from the likes of Lyotard and Habermas have little to say to the experience of despair and the absurd common to many in black urban America. In contrast, in such a setting, West finds the Christian narratives of the Bible "empowering and enabling".[39]

Foucault speaks as a western post-imperialist intellectual, less aware than he might be of the real existence of differentials of 'justice' within the world, and thus his approach fails to satisfy or offer much help to those minority groups who are at the receiving end of significant economic or political repression. Despite his protests, Foucault can come over as a rather jaded, cynical westerner, not able to offer much where the need to build community, re-configure power and establish a sense of equality is more urgent than to offer a critique of present forms.

EITHER-OR?

Several critics think Foucault too simplistic, stark and oppositional, seeing no alternatives, for example, between dispersed and centralised power, or between rejection of the entire project of modernity and nostalgic clinging to it. While Foucault suggests that the only alternative to State- or Sovereign-centred power is this kind of dispersed power, owned and exercised anonymously, Taylor argues that there is in between these two options, other political and social forms such as "civic humanism", or the freedom of the individual to give or withhold a contribution to society.[40] Again, Habermas suggest that between naïve acceptance and outright rejection of modernity there is a space for what he calls "communicative rationality".[41] Likewise, Walzer points out that just because it is possible to detect in modern societies a growth in surveillance and social control, this does not mean that modern society has become a prison. In noticing some similarities between them, this oppositional character of Foucault's thought fails to notice the large difference there is between living in society and living in prison, and elides the important space between them.

These criticisms, although effective to varying degrees, still stand as areas of debate over Michel Foucault's work. Rather than enter into a detailed evaluation of each one, our purpose is to relate the theology of the cross to Foucault's understanding of power, to examine both the similarities and important differences between them.

FOUCAULT AND THE THEOLOGY OF THE CROSS

When this 'discourse of the cross' is placed alongside Foucault's, the first notable surprise is a high degree of similarity between them. Many of their suspicions are shared, and they call attention to similar difficulties in the approach to knowledge and truth. To take the four marks of Foucault's analysis outlined above, we can see ways in which Paul, Luther and Pascal can be seen to adopt analogous positions.

1.   Foucault highlights the importance of issues of power within human communities, and maintains that power is an inevitable part of the relations which make up those communities. In a similar way, the theology of the cross sees power as a vital issue, and one which Christian communities must address. The power relations which exist within those communities to some extent define them, and the way those power relations are configured goes a long way towards determining whether they are acting in a genuinely Christian or sub-Christian fashion. If the Son of God died as a powerless victim of political and religious necessities, then a theology built from this point raises the issue of power and how it operates within the church, in a quite specific way. Foucault reminds us of the hidden but determinative nature of power relations, and the theology of the cross does the same.

2.   Foucault again points to the inescapable relationship between power and truth, discourse and domination. Likewise, the theology of the cross is keenly aware of this relationship, and how power produces a discourse to legitimate it, and that discourse in turn produces power. Each of our three theologians turned to a theology of the cross to mount a critique of the use of theology to legitimate the abuse of power within his own historical setting, doing so by exposing the uncertain foundations of the discourse which produces the power relations they criticise. Paul's critique of Apollos' supporters in Corinth acts by pointing out the inconsistency of holding faith in the crucified and risen Christ alongside an ideology which values social status and denies Resurrection. Luther's critique

of the late medieval church was effective precisely because it did not just expose structural faults or moral decline, simply recommending different action, but because it tackled questions of discourse; in other words, it centred on the Word and its connection with works, not just the deed.[42] His gradual realisation that God worked through weakness and suffering, through human passivity, not activity, led in turn to his effective and historically significant critique of the ostentatious elaboration of both the papal church and scholastic theology, the symbiosis of the *philosophi et principati*. Pascal's later life and work constituted a developing critique of the power of the Jesuits, as well as a protest against the ostentation of cultured Parisian society and its indifference to the poor. These power relations are intimately related to ideology, the Jesuits with their Molinist theology, and the *libertins* with their laissez-faire scepticism. So Pascal's critique is again focused on the interplay between what is accepted as 'true' and the power relations which emerge from that discourse. In each case, the relationship between power and discourse is marked: each claim to power is rooted in an ideology which legitimates it, and each of these three theologians turns to a theology centred upon the cross to counter it. Like Foucault's critique, the theology of the cross understands well the relationship between truth and power, and the ability of versions of 'truth' to deliver power.

3.   Foucault rejects the possibility of Enlightenment, of gradual progress towards truth through knowledge. The theology of the cross in a comparable manner rejects the power of human reason to provide foundations for knowledge. These three theologians all contain a deep suspicion of human understanding, of "the wisdom of the world" (Paul), "Mistress Reason" (Luther), and "*la superbe raison*" (Pascal). They too despair of any slow inexorable advance towards peace and truth and security within human society. The similarities and differences between their views of reason can be illustrated by a striking parallelism of phraseology between Michel Foucault and Blaise Pascal.

Foucault reckons that "truth is a thing of this world";[43] Pascal thinks "*la vérité.. ne demeure pas en terre*".[44] There appears at first sight to be a direct contradiction between these two statements, yet when we realise they are talking of different things when they speak of truth, their similarity becomes apparent. By 'truth' Foucault means human discourse which might claim to be 'true', but which is merely contingent and accidental, unable to claim any foundation in reality. Pascal means God's truth, which for him, as we have seen above, is unavailable to human rationality, yet is fundamentally eschatological, to be known in its fullness only when God reveals it, or in the direct encounter with God. Of course Foucault implicitly denies the existence of Pascal's eschatological truth, yet in one important sense, they agree on one thing, that ultimate Truth is not to be found within this world. Any scientific or rationally constructed 'truth' which we may think we possess is in fact illusory. They differ over the existence of a truth beyond this world, "lying in the lap of God, to be known only in so far as it please him to reveal it", as Pascal puts it, but they are at one in their scepticism about human claims to possess ultimate 'true' Truth. Both Foucault and the theology of the cross share this air of suspicion, a sceptical perspective on truth within this world.

This theology constantly calls into question the outward appearance of things, and acts as a reminder that things may not be as they seem. It insists that what is normally thought of as self-evidently strong, reasonable and effective, may not necessarily be so. Corinthian rhetoric, Aristotelian philosophy and Cartesian rationality may have seemed to be the bases upon which the church could build unassailable positions in first century Corinth, sixteenth century Europe and seventeenth century France, but the theology of the cross raised searching questions about each. If God is revealed in such a shameful and unexpected place as a cross, then human reason and values, which cannot begin to understand why this should be, are forced to admit defeat. Pascal in particular develops a sophisticated deconstruction of human rationality as a foundation for knowledge, yet Paul and Luther also share this sense that thinking about God, human experience and society cannot begin from any conventional foundation, but must begin at the cross.

4.   Foucault tries to enable a critique of the operation of disciplinary power, by an analysis of the way power relations work at the micro- rather than the macro-level of society. The 'discourse of the cross' is also sensitive to such concerns. Behind small differences in eating times, menu and seating arrangements in the Corinthian eucharist, Paul sees issues of power at work, establishing relations which serve the interests of the wealthy 'Apollos group' over against the socially inferior. Behind the apparently minor practice of Indulgences, Luther sees issues both of theology and power. Indulgences fleece the poor by resting on a soteriology of human works and their significant role in salvation. Behind the *"Querelle des Rites"* and the easy-going attitude to confession and absolution in Jesuit circles, Pascal also sees issues of power. These are instances of the Jesuit practice of admitting to Christian fellowship those whom they are keen to cultivate, yet who fail to grasp the distinctive nature of Christian living. In each case, there is an awareness of how power works through hidden mechanisms and practices, which are in turn built upon and produce the versions of reality which confirm them. The theology of the cross therefore does not just raise a critique of centralised power, the power of leaders, popes and kings. It also asks about the way power operates within Christian communities, whether they are places where mutual submission is to be found, where each member looks to the good of the other, whether in the small-scale, micro-level relations in church life, the life of the crucified Christ is expressed in acts of simple love for one another.

This is not of course to claim that the theology of the cross has anticipated Foucault precisely. It is more that he makes explicit several factors which lie implicit within the theology of the cross. It is also to suggest that this type of theology can act as an alternative critical process to Foucault's analysis, particularly in a Christian setting. The theology of the cross raises the issue of power; it asks about the forms of discourse which actually give rise to a church's power relations, and how influenced they are by non- or sub-Christian paradigms; it questions the expectations of conventional rationality, reminding the Christian community that "God's ways are not our ways", and it alerts that community to the way in which small-scale mechanisms express the inner dynamic at work within its own society.

Yet, for all their similarity, there are of course significant differences between the two kinds of critique. Can the theology of the cross answer some of the questions which Foucault's critique raises, and behind him, those of Nietzsche himself?

THE THEOLOGY OF THE CROSS IN A POSTMODERN WORLD

POWER OR TRUTH?

Foucault questions Reason because he thinks there is no Truth waiting to be found by it. Pascal questions it because although he thinks such Truth is to be found, fallen human reason is not capable of grasping it. The theology of the cross itself comes under the scrutiny of Foucault's critique as yet another claim to tell a Truth which Foucault would himself want to deconstruct. Furthermore, might it not be just another claim to power, undergirded by its own discourse? After all, as Elizabeth Castelli points out, Paul can be accused of adopting a position of dominance in his relations with the Corinthians,[45] threatening them with punishment (4:21) and judging and expelling an offender (5:3,13). Luther's interventions into the Peasants' War also seem to reinforce conventional notions of disciplinary power, and Pascal is not averse to using his rhetorical skill in a deliberately provocative way in the Provincial Letters, arguably another use of a type of power, in his struggle with the Jesuits.

The theology of the cross does claim to offer a Truth. It does claim to point to a way of discovering Truth which is ultimately 'True', not just the socially constructed version which Foucault proposes. Yet the kind of Truth asserted by the theology of the cross differs significantly from the kind of truths which Foucault undermines, both in its content and in the means by which it is accessed.

The kind of Truth exhibited in the cross cannot be grasped from a position of power, but only from the perspective of weakness, of a profound awareness of powerlessness. This is particularly clear in Luther's approach, where his hermeneutic of the cross maintains that the God revealed on the cross can be understood only *from* the cross of the believer. For Luther, suffering and weakness are the true teachers of wisdom, as they lead to a sense of despair about one's own capacities, and a readiness to hear the promise of God. Thus Luther stresses the role of experience in knowledge. Knowledge of this kind of truth can never be a purely abstract, speculative, analytic process, but requires the existential embracing of powerlessness before God and people. Luther's criticisms of scholastic theology flow directly from this: that it does not know what the experience of weakness and powerlessness is like. Whereas human power produces 'truth' in Foucault's sense (i.e. human discourse), powerlessness produces 'Truth' in an ultimate sense, a dimension which Foucault misses altogether.

Although this alternative understanding of Truth is perhaps clearest in Luther, it is still present in Paul and Pascal. When Paul claims that "none of the rulers of this age understood this" (1 Cor.2:8) or that self-giving ἀγάπη, not γνῶσις is the authentic content of wisdom, he too suggests a line of thinking in which powerlessness is the criterion for Truth. The path he recommends is not the path of power, but of self-giving love which does not seek to exert power over others, but surrenders rights for the sake of others in the congregation. Pascal's contention that moral reorientation, *anéantissement de soi*, needs to take place before true understanding can begin, also lies along the same lines.

This version of Truth is different from the kinds of discourse which Foucault has in mind, because it is not merely a matter of discourse. The theology of the cross is suspicious of any theology which claims to offer a kind of objective detached knowledge of God which can be comprehensively codified, defined propositionally, or which has verifiable foundations, universally accessible and certain. This approach leads in Pascal's words, not to the God of Abraham, Isaac and Jacob, but to the god of the philosophers. The path to Truth is not so much epistemological as soteriological: only within the experience of a truly humbling encounter with God can the Truth about him begin to be grasped.

If this is another power-game, it is of a very different kind from that which Foucault identifies. The theology of the cross speaks of a kind of power which emerges from a position of powerlessness. Moreover, the power which this discourse produces, is power not to dominate or to control, but to love, to enable and to release. It is not so much power *over* others, but a power to give oneself *for* others. The Truth which it proclaims is not so much a will to power as a will to love. It holds out the vision of a community built not upon relations determined by domination, but relations where power and privilege are at the service of others, rather than serving to divide and oppress.

CONFORMITY OR FREEDOM?

This is of course a contentious claim, since one of the criticisms levelled at power by Foucault among others is that it works by a process of normalisation, insisting on conformity to predetermined patterns. Castelli explicitly accuses Paul of doing just this in Corinth in his call for the Christians there to imitate him. The claim that theology which begins at the cross leads to a greater sense of freedom needs a good deal of explanation and clarification, not to say defence.

Luther's attitude to the Peasants' Uprising of 1524-6, where notoriously, Luther eventually advised the rulers of Germany to suppress the peasant rebellion with as much violence as it took can serve as a test case. It is important in this context, because Luther explicitly appeals to the theology of the cross in a way which seems to recommend political quietism from the peasants.[46] Although it is hard to justify Luther's extreme position, more recent scholarship has tended to point up how common his reaction was amongst his contemporaries. Although more eirenic souls like Melancthon disapproved of his language, many other reformers such as Urbanus Rhegius and Nikolaus von Amsdorf took up a similar position to

Luther.[47] No doubt Luther's deep medieval fear of anarchy and his fear for the fortunes of the Evangelical movement coloured his approach strongly, and perhaps accounts for some of his more lurid language in the notorious "Against the Robbing and Murdering Hordes of Peasants". Without being able to go into the question in great detail here, it is quite clear from the texts that Luther's opposition to the peasants does not stem from disagreement with the justice of their cause, or a desire that they should not triumph in it, but rather from his conviction that the theology of the cross can sanction only a non-violent response to injustice. Luther accuses the nobles themselves of oppressing the peasants and goes so far as to declare to them that "it is not the peasants who are resisting you, it is God himself".[48] The Twelve Articles which contain the peasants' grievances, in so far as they protest against economic oppression, are in Luther's eyes "right and just".[49] Luther in fact takes their side in the dispute, yet where he differs sharply, is on the tactics they use. For him, to resort to violence in pursuit of their aims is to trust to worldly methods, not Christian ones, to trust to human activity rather than to the Word of God. It is not that their cause is unjust, or that rulers have a perfect right to use their power to treat the peasants as they please, it is just that the peasants are going about it the wrong way. Their avowedly godly aims can never be achieved by human actions, but only by the action of the Word. They are called to "triumph by suffering, not by fists". Luther's negative response to the peasants was determined by a dispute over methods, not substance. In other words, the theology of the cross here does not encourage silent submissiveness. Luther does encourage resistance to power wielded by the rulers in an abusive way, but insists that to be true to the cross, it has to be of a non-violent kind, which is for him not only more consistently Christian, but ultimately more effective. Luther might be accused of political naivety, but not social injustice.

Whatever judgement we arrive at concerning Luther's contributions to the Peasants' War, what is perhaps of more interest in connection with the question of whether or not the theology of the cross encourages a stifling conformity, is Luther's doctrine of

Christian Freedom. Luther's 1520 treatise, "The Freedom of a Christian", contrasts a notion of Christian liberty based on the dialectic of law and gospel, to the totalitarian regime of the papal curia, which by means of "forces and bans", brooks no contradiction, and burns the books of those who oppose it.[50] It is a vision of Christian liberty which flows directly from his theology of the cross, and begins, as we have seen before, with powerlessness. It begins with a person "being truly humbled and reduced to nothing in his own eyes... so that he may be justified and saved".[51] Justifying faith then frees the believer from anxiety over his own salvation, identity or value, and gives him the dignity of being the free lord of all things. Yet Luther defines this lordship or power quite carefully, not as producing disciplinary power, or even social control over others; it is power to rule over and thus be free from the demands of religious authority, life, death, sin and so on.[52] The Christian is then freely (not under compulsion, Luther is careful to insist), able and willing to give himself for his neighbour:

> Although the Christian is thus free from all works, he ought in this liberty, to empty himself, take upon himself the form of a servant, be made in the likeness of men, be found in human form, and to serve, help, and in every way deal with his neighbour as he sees that God through Christ has dealt and still deals with him.[53]

This freedom or power is therefore modelled on God's freedom and power, as expressed in Christ, hence the borrowing of language from the Christological hymn in Philippians 2. Divine freedom and power is used not for domination but for service, and its characteristic mark is the cross, its willingness to give itself for the other. In Luther's context, this freedom expressed itself on the one hand as freedom from the demands of religious observance or acts of mercy, understood as the techniques by which some strands of late medieval theological piety demanded submission and conformity. Yet, on the other hand, it is a freedom and power to be able freely to choose to give oneself for the interests of other people.

A complementary perspective can be found in Paul's encouragement of Christian diversity in Corinth. As we have seen above, Castelli misses the mark when she accuses Paul of imposing "sameness" on the congregation in Corinth. In chapter 12 in particular, Paul is keen to encourage and safeguard the ethnic, social and charismatic diversity within the church in Corinth. If he does impose a norm upon the church, it is to insist that this diversity must be preserved. In fact, the chapter protests against those who would impose an expectation that all charismatic gifting should be hierarchically valued. Paul's argument in the whole letter is designed to make significant space within the community for Christians at the lower end of the Corinthian social spectrum, in opposition to those who would wish to give significance only to those at the higher end. This is of course, perfectly consistent with Paul's passionate concern that both Gentiles and Jews find a place alongside one another within the new Christian communities, a concern which, while not prominent in 1 Corinthians, comes to the fore in Galatians and Romans. The same dynamic is at work in Romans 14, where in discussing the strong and the weak, he agrees with the strong, yet expects them to act in ways which do not exclude and disenfranchise the weak.[54]

On the other hand, it would be false to contend that there is no sense of boundary or limit within this type of theology, or that the theology of the cross does not lay down any expectations of norms of behaviour within the Christian community. Paul does impose moral constraints upon the church in Corinth, and Pascal in particular seems to be drawing much stricter lines between what is and is not acceptable than the Jesuits did with their easy-going moral laxity. Yet this difficulty arises only when freedom is understood as licence. It is important to grasp that what Luther means by freedom does not correspond to a more general notion of freedom found outside and independent of Christian discourse. There can never be an accessible, independent and neutral notion of liberty which commands universal assent and to which Christian theology must conform. As we have seen above, for Luther, human freedom finds its meaning in God's freedom. Divine freedom is not an abstract ideal which more resembles licence to do whatever God pleases, but it is freedom or power to go to a cross, freedom to surrender privilege and liberty for the sake of his creation, freedom to protect the weak and vulnerable. As an example, Paul's image of himself as the Corinthians' "father", to which Castelli objects, only leads him to urge rather than compel imitation. It is not a demand for obedience, which is what would be expected, as Castelli shows, from a father in the ancient world, but an offer of example. If he does threaten to "come with a rod" (1 Cor.4:21), whatever action he proposes is directed at those who would disparage the 'weak': it is power exercised to protect those who would otherwise be mistreated and ignored.

Freedom for these theologians is defined in specifically Christian terms. The Truth about God does have its own discipline. Yet the point is that this discipline demands that those who exercise it do so for the well-being and freedom of the other. It is not an absolute liberty which frees the subject from all obligation, but a freedom and power which demands and enables the freedom of the other.

A DENIAL OF LIFE?

For the alert reader, the figure of Nietzsche lurks behind this discussion. Nietzsche's attack on Christianity was direct and informed. Nietzsche accuses Christianity of being the great denial of Life, with its tale of guilt and sin inducing shame, self-hatred and opposition to all vigour, strength and life. For him, the whole edifice of Christianity is destructive of life and passion, reducing existence to a dull, compliant mediocrity. Christian theologians have sometimes tried to evade this critique by suggesting that he did not understand the real Christian God, but only the pale Enlightenment shadow. Yet that is to underestimate Nietzsche's grasp of Christianity: perhaps he above all its critics, understood it best. The God whom Nietzsche attacked was not just the God of the philosophers, the God of Descartes.[55] Nietzsche knew Pascal and Luther, and for all his respect for them as thinkers, it is Pascal's and Luther's God whom he rejects. Nietzsche aims right at the heart of the God of the cross, the theology of the cross. It is precisely the "crucified God" whom he finds "seductive, intoxicating, anaesthetising and corrupting".[56]

Again, there is neither time nor space at this stage for an exhaustive analysis of Nietzsche here. Yet his attack on the theology of the cross in a backhanded way, confirms Luther's and particularly Pascal's suspicion that the moral precedes the epistemological when it comes to the rejection of God. As Stephen Williams argues, Nietzsche's objection to this God is not so much to do with reason as with taste.[57] Nietzsche objects finally, not to the irrationality of Christianity, but to what he sees as its depravity.

Yet is the theology of the cross really a denial of life? Does it really stamp out all active energy, vigour, intensity and strength? This chapter has argued that the theology of the cross can best be understood in two steps, in the recognition of powerlessness before God, and subsequently, a power to surrender privilege or rights for the good of the other. In these, Nietzsche can see only passivity and negativity. Yet to understand the giving up of oneself as a *power* suggests that this part of the equation is a lot more active than might seem apparent. To actively seek the good of a neighbour, a friend or an enemy, even at the cost of one's own rights is hardly a call for limp-wristed inactivity. Paul can hardly be accused of an ascetic passivity in his missionary activity, or even his leather-working. Luther makes a clear distinction between the kind of passivity required for salvation and the subsequent vigorous activity expected in the Christian life, the passionate concern for a greater degree of justice, health, equality not for oneself, but for the neighbour. Even Pascal's asceticism has an unmistakable political meaning, as eloquent protest against Parisian disregard for the poor, and ostentatious opulence. This is not asceticism for asceticism's sake. It is not, as Nietzsche feared,[58] a denial of life, a willing embrace of suffering for its own sake, but rather, the freely chosen surrender of what would normally be considered a 'right' *for the sake of the other*. In contrast to Nietzsche's elitist and aristocratic vision, these privileges are to be given up, as is especially clear in the case of the Corinthian church, in order that others within the Christian community might benefit. In response to Nietzsche's criticism that Christianity is a "No to Life", we might be tempted to ask "whose Life?" This theology is not so much a No to Life, as a Yes to the life of the other.

The theology of the cross by no means demands a quietist abandonment of all intensity of feeling or enterprise of action, it simply directs it differently. Such privileges, rights, strengths that one has, are not to be abandoned as something evil (Foucault's reminder of the inevitability of power in society and our inability to abandon it entirely is useful here), but are to be put to the use of the neighbour in the essentially communal setting which the theology of the cross demands. This goal is one which can engage every passion and desire which Nietzsche fears is destroyed in Christianity.

Karl Barth's criticism of Nietzsche was in part that he was a "solitary",[59] unappreciative of society or belonging, a factor he derided as belonging to the herd instinct. One does not have to endorse Barth's personal suspicions about Nietzsche to concede his basic point, that Nietzsche's model leant more towards the solitary than the social, lone heroism rather than communal neighbourliness. It is perhaps this point which expresses one of the essential differences between Nietzsche and the theology of the cross. The latter is very much a social vision, one which is intended to build communities and enable them to function in new and more satisfying ways. It also highlights a nagging concern about Foucault, that for all his suspicious mind, his social critique, he is much better at destroying than building. Yet is it not crucial to build as well as destroy? Is it not vital, alongside unmasking fraudulent power-relations, to be able to build functioning societies where power is shared and relatively equally dispersed, and where the less regarded members are not forgotten? This kind of theology is not to be seen as fostering an individual spirituality which encourages submissiveness and passivity as ends in themselves. If it has sometimes been understood in that way, then it fails to realise its potential, and falls subject to Nietzsche's critique. Instead, it is a theology which is designed to operate in the setting of the Christian community, to enable new kinds of relationships, and to reconceptualize power relations. Understood in a narrowly individualistic way, it can easily become a kind of aimless asceticism. Understood as the dynamic for Christian community, it comes into its own as the kind of discourse which will build rather than destroy community.

Furthermore, it is a theology which avoids many of the criticisms levelled at Foucault's understanding of power. Like Foucault, the theology of the cross has a suspicious mind about the workings of power, yet at the same time it also offers a model of power which promises to build community, not just to analyse it. It aims to facilitate the building of a community where, "each of you looks not only to your own interests, but also to the interests of others, having this mind among yourselves, which is yours in Christ Jesus, who, though he was in the form of God, emptied himself, taking the form of a servant, humbling himself unto death, even death on a cross". The discourse of the cross gives criteria whereby social forms can be evaluated. Alongside the poverty and weakness of the cross, the snobbery of Apollos' fan club, the authoritarian manner of the late medieval papacy and the opulence of the Royal Court of Louis XIV all jarred. Leadership which consciously or unconsciously draws power to itself, rather than sharing power with others always comes under the judgement of the cross, in a church which, living under the cross must be *semper reformandum*.

Perhaps most importantly, while Foucault offers little help to those experiencing the harshness of inequality in the third world, or those who look in hungrily on the affluence of the West, the theology of the cross has something to say. As many liberation theologians have seen,[60] it calls those who exercise power over them in these instances to a realisation of a more fundamental powerlessness, and a subsequent praxis which restores power to those who lack it. It insists that power is employed to restrain injustice and inequality, and to value those whose experience of life resembles the cross. It speaks directly to the 'poor', not by dulling their sense of injustice by an opiate of the abstract spiritual value of suffering, but by privileging them as the ones who, being in most ways powerless, can teach those who exercise a greater degree of power the beginning of wisdom.

This type of theology is in effect a call for Christian communities to enact, rather than just to analyse or to understand, theology. It calls for a sense of mutuality, a will not to power or to knowledge, but to love and belonging. For the theology of the cross can be realised only in community, within the power relations of the social networks operative between members of churches, their leaders, their preachers, and their people.

Notes:

[1]Cf. the importance of *tentatio* as a hermeneutical principle alongside *oratio* and *meditatio* in Luther's Preface to the 1539 Wittenberg edition of his German writings, (LW 34, 283-88).

[2]WA DB 7.83-7, (LW 35.380-3).

[3]Cf. Luther's words: "Therefore this text – 'he bore our sins' - must be understood particularly thoroughly, as the foundation upon which stands the whole of the New Testament or the Gospel, as that which alone distinguishes us and our religion from all other religions." (quoted by Brunner, *Mediator*, 435-6). See the whole of WA 25.328.19-330.14.

[4]Hengel, *Crucifixion*, 46-63.

[5]See A. Sheridan, *Michel Foucault: The Will to Truth* (London: Routledge, 1980), 113.

[6]M. Foucault, *Folie et Déraison: Histoire de la Folie à l'âge classique* (Paris: Plon, 1961); *Naissance de la Clinique* (Paris: PUF, 1963).

[7]"Nietzsche, Genealogy, History", ed. P. Rabinow, *A Foucault Reader* (London: Penguin, 1984), 76-100, here 82.

[8]See the piece entitled "Truth and Power" in *Power/Knowledge*, 109-33. "When I wrote Madness and Civilisation... I think indeed that I was positing the existence of a sort of living, voluble and anxious madness, which the mechanism of power and psychiatry were supposed to repress and reduce to silence. But it seems to me now that the notion of repression is quite inadequate for capturing what is precisely the productive aspect of power." (118-9).

[9]M. Foucault, *Histoire de la folie à l'age classique* (Paris: Gallimard, 1972), esp. Part 1 ch. II, and Part 3, ch.IV.

[10]*Power/Knowledge*, 83.

[11]"…it is really against the effects of the power of a discourse that is considered to be scientific that genealogy must wage its struggle." *Power/Knowledge*, 84.

[12]*Surveiller et Punir* (Paris: Gallimard, 1975).

[13]*La Volonté de Savoir* (Paris: Gallimard, 1971); *L'Usage des Plaisirs* (Paris: Gallimard, 1984); *Le Souci de Soi* (Paris: Gallimard, 1984). Foucault planned six volumes, but died in 1984 before the fourth was written.

[14]Cf. *The Foucault Reader*, 297.

[15]From *A History of Sexuality* Vol. 1, in *Foucault Reader*, 316.

[16]See "Body/Power", *Power/Knowledge*, 55-62. Here, 57.

[17]"We are subjected to the production of truth through power, and we cannot exercise power except through the production of truth." *Power/Knowledge*, 93.

[18]"Truth and Power", *Power/Knowledge* 119.

[19]"I don't want to say that the State isn't important; what I want to say is that relations of power, and hence the analysis that must be made of them, necessarily extend beyond the limits of the State. In two senses: first of all because the State, for all the omnipotence of its apparatuses, is far from being able to occupy the whole field of actual power relations, and further, because the State can only operate on the basis of other, already existing power relations." *Power/Knowledge*, 122.

[20]*Power/Knowledge*, 98-9.

[21]See M. Foucault, *Les Mots et les choses: une archéologie des sciences humaines* (Paris: Gallimard, 1966); ET: *The Order of Things: An Archaeology of the Human Sciences* (New York: Pantheon, 1970), 312-20.

[22]J. Rajchman, *Michel Foucault: The Freedom of Philosophy* (New York: Columbia University Press, 1985), 2.

[23]Sheridan, *The Will to Truth*, 225.

[24]*Power/Knowledge*, 145, See also M. Foucault and G. Deleuze, "Intellectuals and Power," ed. D.F. Bouchard, *Language, Counter-Memory, Practice: Selected Essays and Interviews* (Ithaca, Cornell University Press, 1977), 208. See also D. Shumway, *Michel Foucault* (Charlottesville: University Press of Virginia, 1989), 156-62 for a valuable discussion of uses to which these "tools" might be put.

[25]"On the Genealogy of Ethics: An Overview of Work in Progress", *A Foucault Reader*, 340-72, here, 343. Where possible, reference will be made to this selection of Foucault's works, simply for ease of access.

[26]B. Smart, "The Politics of Truth and the Problem of Hegemony", ed. D.C. Hoy, *Foucault: A Critical Reader* (Oxford: Blackwell, 1986), 157-73, here, 169.

[27]See *Power/Knowledge*, 81-4.

[28]"Nietzsche, Genealogy, History", *Foucault Reader* 95.

[29]See J. Habermas, "Modernity - An Incomplete Project", reprinted in ed. P. Brooker, *Modernism/Postmodernism* (London: Longman, 1992), 125-38.

[30]M. Walzer, "The Politics of Michel Foucault", ed. Hoy, *A Critical Reader*, 51-68, here, 67.

[31]See Charles Taylor's remarks in ed. Hoy, *A Critical Reader*, 98.

[32]J. Derrida, "Cogito and the History of Madness", *Writing and Difference*, 31-63.

[33]Foucault, "Genealogy of Ethics", 343.

[34]Nancy Fraser asks similar questions: "Why is struggle preferable to submission? Why ought domination to be resisted?" in "Foucault on modern power: empirical insights and normative confusions". *Praxis International* Vol. 1 (1981), 238.

[35]J. Baudrillard's critique in *Forget Foucault* (New York: Semiotexte, 1987) is along similar lines.

[36]ed. Hoy, *A Critical Reader*, 90-3.

[37]S. Lukes, *Power: A Radical View* (London: Macmillan, 1974). For a study of the differences between Lukes' and Foucault's understandings of power, see "D. C. Hoy, "Power, Repression, Progress: Foucault, Lukes and the Frankfurt School", ed. Hoy, *A Critical Reader*, 123-147.

[38]ed. Hoy, *A Critical Reader*, 66.

[39]C. West, "Black Culture and Postmodernism", in ed. Brooker, *Modernism/Postmodernism*, 213-24.

[40]See ed. Hoy, *A Critical Reader*, 82-3.

[41]Habermas, "Modernity", 131.

[42]Gerhard Ebeling makes this point: "The Reformation did not remain a matter of words, but went on to action, because the necessity of the whole Reformation and what happened in it was so profoundly understood that it became clear that the Reformation could only be comprehended not as a matter of specific actions, but wholly as a matter of the word, and the word alone." *Luther: An Introduction to his Thought* (London: Collins, 1972), 60-1.

[43]*Power/Knowledge*, 131.

[44]L131

[45]Castelli, *Imitating Paul*.

[46]"*Leyden, Leyden, Creuz, Creuz ist der Christen recht, des und keyn anders.*" *Admonition to Peace*, WA 18.310.28-9. (LW.46.29)

[47]R. Kolb, "The Theologians and the Peasants: Conservative Evangelical Reactions to the German Peasants' Revolt", *ARG* 79 (1978), 103-31.

[48]*Admonition to Peace*, WA 18.295.4-6 (LW 46.20).

[49]Ibid., 22.

[50]See particularly, Luther's *On the Babylonian Captivity of the Church*, WA 6.497-573, and *Why the Books of the Pope and his Disciples were burned by Doctor Martin Luther*, WA 7.161-82, both from the same year, 1520.

[51]WA 7.53.1-3.

[52]"First, with respect to the kingship, every Christian is by faith so exalted above all things that, by virtue of a spiritual power, he is lord of all things without exception, so that nothing can do him any harm.... This not to say that every Christian is placed over all things to have and to control them by physical power

- a madness with which some churchmen are afflicted - for such power belongs to kings, princes, and other men on earth... As a matter of fact, the more Christian a man is, the more evils, sufferings, and deaths he must endure, as we see in Christ the first-born prince himself, and in all his brethren the saints. The power of which we speak is spiritual..." WA.7.57.2-14. (LW 31.354-5).

[53]WA.7.65.32-6 (LW 31.366).

[54]See in connection with this point, R. Jewett, *Christian Tolerance: Paul's Message to the Modern Church* (Philadelphia: Westminster, 1982).

[55]"Nietzsche rejected the genuine article, not a caricature of Christianity." Williams, *Revelation*, 108. For the wider argument, see the whole of chapter 4.

[56]F. Nietzsche *On the Genealogy of Morals* (ed. & trans. D. Smith; Oxford: O.U.P., 1996), 21.

[57]Williams quotes Nietzsche's claim in *The Gay Science* III.132, that "What is now decisive against Christianity is our taste, no longer our reasons". *Revelation*, 95.

[58]e.g. Nietzsche's essay, "What is the Meaning of Ascetic Ideals?" in *Genealogy of Morals*, 77-136.

[59]K. Barth, *Protestant Theology in the Nineteenth Century* (London: S.C.M. 1972), 342.

[60]For example, L. Boff, *Way of the Cross: Way of Justice* (Maryknoll: Orbis, 1988); J. Sobrino, *Christology at the Crossroads: A Latin American View* (London: S.C.M., 1978) 217-35; *The Principle of Mercy: Taking the Crucified People from the Cross* (Maryknoll: Orbis, 1994).

Postscript: The Theology of the Cross in the Church

How might the type of theology explored in this book be expressed in the church and in Christian experience? Foucault reminds us that power, and perhaps even its legitimised form, authority, is an inevitable aspect of any community. The task is therefore not to eliminate power, or to pretend that the set of relationships that exist within a community such as a church can somehow operate without some kind of power being wielded, whether recognised or not. It is more a question of how to think about power, about how power can be conceived, or about 'how things get done' within the church.

Of course, to raise these issues may at first be a bit embarrassing for the church, as it has for a long time been associated with authoritarian power and domination. Since the day when Constantine emerged from an internal power-struggle within the Roman empire, and adopted the God of the Christians as his patron god at the start of the fourth century, Christianity in the western world has tried to influence society from a position of authority. For most of the time since then, the church's image has continued to be that of domination. The complex administrative system of the medieval papal church legislated for the details of spiritual and social life across Europe, and even tried to extend this control eastwards through the crusades. Even after the Reformation, the rise of Lutheran, Reformed, and Roman Catholic orthodoxies encouraged a kind of intellectual and doctrinal conformity, parts of which rested on a rug which both the Enlightenment and Romanticism pulled energetically from under the church's feet. Even in more recent times, the church's willingness to bless the guns being sent off to fight the First World War, and its continued position as part of an increasingly questioned establishment, do not tend to make it the first place one might look to find lessons on the use of power.

Now that the notion of authority is questioned, the church finds itself struggling to come to terms with a new situation. It has sought to dominate and occasionally repress with its claim to possess the truth about God, the world, humankind and everything else. It will need to rethink its notion of power and how it operates, if it is to play a significant part in this post-authoritarian world.

To be effective and responsible, the theology of the cross first of all suggests that authority is best exercised by those who have directly experienced their own limitations and powerlessness. In pastoral ministry, it is often remarkable that the experience of sickness, or grief, or even of humiliation can be the beginning of true wisdom. These experiences can for the first time deflate exalted opinions of one's own self-importance. They can for the first time open the eyes of the blind and proud to the needs and suffering of others. This is by no means to romanticise such painful experiences, nor to say that they should be sought out in some kind of spiritual masochism. It is to say, however, that power, as Christians understand it, is best exercised by those who have been humbled before God and before others.

Secondly, we have seen that true power is the ability to give up privilege for the sake of another. It is a rare and prized ability to surrender what we might expect to be entitled to, for the sake of others. In 1905, Albert Schweitzer, already author of a ground-breaking work in New Testament studies, shocked the academic world of his time by announcing that he was to give up his promising academic career to train as a doctor, with the intention of working in equatorial Africa. Later, he recalled the unexpected opposition he faced in carrying out his plan:

> My relatives and friends all joined in expostulating with me on the folly of my enterprise. I was a man, they said, who was burying the talent entrusted to him and wanted to work with false currency. Work among savages I ought to leave to those who would not thereby be compelled to leave gifts and acquirements in science and art unused.

He found himself accused of conceit, of romantic disappointment, of professional frustration at the slowness of his career progression, even though his was a career which had already brought him more recognition at the age of twenty-nine than most academics ever achieve. His action went so much against the grain that his contemporaries found it almost impossible to understand. To give up privilege for the sake of another is not to be taken for granted. It is indeed a power, a remarkable ability.

Power can be described as the capability to influence people or situations and to transform them. For the theology of the cross, what transforms people and situations in the last analysis is not so much imposed authority, but love: not the power to dominate, but the power, the ability to love. In fact both of these perspectives on power expressed through powerlessness focus on this ability to love. The painful experience of powerlessness can often lead to a new appreciation of the struggles of others, and the will to do something about them. The surrender of rights for the sake of another, is of the essence of love itself. The theology of the cross insists that whatever power or authority is exercised over others, whether recognised or not, is power for others, rather than power over others.

It is within the Christian community that such a vision will need to be taken with the utmost seriousness. Before it proclaims its message, perhaps the first task for churches in a post-Christian and post-authoritarian world will be to demonstrate new relationships, new communities based not upon clerical authority, nor reproducing traditional social divisions between richer and poorer, educated and uneducated, but on the freedom found when "each one looks out not only for his own interests, but also for the interests of others." (Philp.2:4) These churches will be places where the narrative of the cross provides the dynamic to enable the "will to love" not the "will to power" to drive its relationships and life.

The significance of this understanding of power does not stop with the church, however. One of the few universal values in a pluralist society is the toleration of difference. Yet how can toleration cope with Evil? Toleration of another culture, and renunciation of the desire to change it is a very fine thing, yet when that 'culture' is oppressive of what most would see as human rights, when people suffer innocently, then toleration is not enough, there is need for transformation. The theology of the cross proposes that God transforms the human condition not through the exercise of imposed power, but through apparently powerless love. The deepest forms of transformation take place not through force, but through love, the surrender of power and privilege; not in a negation of Life, as Nietzsche feared, but in a radical affirmation of the life of another.

Especially in pluralist western society, the notion of love, which goes beyond toleration, actively to seek the benefit and welfare of others is a vital quality. That culture will also need not just the recognition of the value of such love, but discover the dynamic to enable it to grow. This "word of the cross", the picture of a God who gives himself in love for his damaged creation, suffering at the hands of, yet also for the sake of those he had created, had the dynamic to do just that for Paul, for Luther, for Pascal, and for Albert Schweitzer. If the church can first reclaim it again for itself, that word of the cross, the story of power expressed through the willing acceptance of powerlessness, may yet be able to provide that dynamic for the emerging culture of the West as it makes its way in a new millennium.

Abbreviations

A&G	Arndt and Gingrich: Greek-English Lexicon
ABR	American Benedictine Review
AJFS	Australian Journal of French Studies
ANCL	*Ante-Nicene Christian Library*
ARG	Archiv für Reformationsgeschichte
AWA2	Archiv zur Weimarer Ausgabe Band 2
BHT	Beiträge zur Historischen Theologie
Bib	Biblica
CBQ	Catholic Biblical Quarterly
CistStud	Cistercian Studies
CP	Classical Philology
CTQ	Concordia Theological Quarterly
DL	*Lives of Eminent Philosophers (Diogenes Laertius)*
DRN	*De Rerum Natura (Lucretius)*
EvTh	Evangelische Theologie
FKDG	Forschungen zur Kirchen- und Dogmengeschichte
Greg	Gregorianum
ICC	International Critical Commentary
Int	Interpretation
JAAR	Journal of the American Academy of Religion
JBL	Journal of Biblical Literature
JHI	Journal of the History of Ideas
JRel	Journal of Religion

JRH	Journal of Religious History
JSNT	Journal for the Study of the New Testament
JTS	Journal of Theological Studies
LJB	Luther-Jahrbuch
LuthW	Lutheran World
MLR	Modern Languages Review
MonS	Monastic Studies
NovT	Novum Testamentum
NTS	New Testament Studies
RAM	Revue d'Ascétique et de Mystique
RHE	Revue d'Histoire Ecclésiastique
SBL	Society for Biblical Literature
SCFS	Seventeenth Century French Studies
SGR	Studien in den Grundlagen der Reformation
SJT	Scottish Journal of Theology
SMRT	Studies in Medieval and Reformation Thought
SNTSMS	Society for New Testament Studies Monograph Series
SVEC	Studies on Voltaire and the Eighteenth Century
TDNT	Theological Dictionary of the New Testament *(Kittel)*
ThSt	Theological Studies
THStKr	Theologische Studien und Kritiken
TynBul	Tyndale Bulletin
Them	Themelios
Th	Theology
ThZ	Theologische Zeitschrift
TNS	The New Scholasticism
WA	Weimarer Ausgabe (Luther's Works)
WADB	Weimarer Ausgabe (Deutsche Bibel)
WATr	Weimarer Ausgabe (Tischreden)
WBC	Word Biblical Commentary
WSCF	World Student Christian Federation
ZKG	Zeitschrift für Kirchengeschichte
ZNW	Zeitschrift für die neutestamentliche Wissenschaft
ZTK	Zeitschrift für Theologie und Kirche

Bibliography

PRIMARY TEXTS

Aelred of Rievaulx, *Treatises, The Pastoral Prayer* (ed. D. Knowles; Kalamazoo: Cistercian Publications, 1982)

Arndt, W.F. and Gingrich, F.W., *A Greek-English Lexicon of the New Testament and Other Early Christian Literature* (2nd ed.; Chicago: University of Chicago Press, 1979)

Anselm, *S. Anselmi Cantuarensis Archiepiscopi: Omnia Opera* (4 vols.; ed. F.S. Shmitt; Rome/Edinburgh: Nelson, 1938-68)

Aquinas, *Summa Theologiae Vol. 54* (ed. & trans. R.T.A. Murphy OP; London: Blackfriars/Eyre & Spottiswoode, 1965)

Bernard of Clairvaux, *On the Song of Songs* (Cistercian Fathers Series 7; trans. K. Walsh OCSO; Kalamazoo: Cistercian Publications, 1976)

Cicero, *Tusculan Disputations* (Loeb; London: Heinemann, 1960)

Epicurus, *Epicurus: The Extant Remains* (ed. C. Bailey; Oxford: Clarendon, 1926)

Philodemus, *On Methods of Inference* (ed. P.H. and E.A. De Lacy; Naples: Bibliopolis, 1978)

Diogenes Laertius, *Lives of Eminent Philosophers II* (Loeb; Cambridge, Mass.: Harvard University Press, 1925)

Gray, D., *A Selection of Religious Lyrics* (Oxford: Clarendon, 1975)

Kempis, Thomas à, *De Imitatione Christi* (ed. T. Lupo; Vatican: Libreria Editrice Vaticana, 1982)

Lucian, *Alexander the False Prophet* (Loeb; Cambridge, Mass.: Harvard University Press, 1925)

Lucretius, *De Rerum Natura* (Loeb; Cambridge, Mass.: Harvard University Press, 1924)

Luther, *D. M. Luthers Werke. Kritische Gesamtausgabe* (Weimar: Böhlau, 1883-)

D.M. Luthers Werke: Tischreden (Weimar: Böhlau, 1883-)

Luther's Works (55 vols.; St Louis: Concordia, 1955-75)

Complete commentary on the first twenty-two psalms. Now first translated by Henry Cole (London, 1826)

Pascal, *Œuvres Complètes* (Paris: Editions du Seuil, 1963)

Pensées sur la Religion et sur autres sujets III: Documents (3 vols.; Paris: Editions du Luxembourg, 1951)

Le manuscrit des Pensées de Pascal 1662 (ed. L. Lafuma; Paris: Les Libraires Associés, 1962)

Plutarch, *Moralia* (Loeb; 16 vols.; London: Heinemann, 1969)

Quintilian, *Institutio Oratoria* (Loeb; 4 vols.; London: Heinemann, 1968-70)

Seneca, *Moral Essays* (Loeb; 3 vols.; London: Heinemann, 1964-70)

Ad Lucilium Epistulae Morales (Loeb; 3 vols.; Cambridge, Mass.: Harvard University Press, 1967-70)

Tertullian, *Adversus Marcionem* (ed. & trans. E. Evans; Oxford: OUP, 1972)

De Carne Christi (ed. & trans. E. Evans; London: SPCK, 1956)

Adversus Praxean (ANCL XV) ET: E. Evans, *Tertullian's Treatise against Praxeas* (London: SPCK 1948)

SECONDARY TEXTS

PAUL:

Allo, E-B., *Saint-Paul Première Epitre aux Corinthiens* (Paris: Gabalda, 1934)

Bachmann, P., *Der erste Brief des Paulus an die Korinther* (Leipzig: A Deichert, 1905)

Bailey, K.E., "Recovering the Poetic Structure of 1Cor. 1:17-2:2", *NovT* 17 (1975), 265-96

Baird, W., "The Idea of Wisdom in 1Cor.2:6," *Int* 13 (1959), 425-32

Barbour, R.S., "Wisdom and the Cross in 1Cor.2:6", eds. C. Andresen and G. Klein, *Theologia Crucis - Signum Crucis: Festschrift für Erich Dinkler* (Tübingen: Mohr/Siebeck, 1979), 57-71

Barclay, J.M.G., "Mirror-Reading a Polemical Letter: Galatians as a Test Case", *JSNT* 31 (1987), 73-93

Barrett, C.K., *Essays on Paul* (London: SPCK, 1982)
A Commentary on the First Epistle to the Corinthians (2nd ed.n; London: A. & C. Black, 1971)
The Epistle to the Romans (London: A. & C. Black, 1957)

Barton, S.C., "Paul and the Cross: A Sociological Approach", *Th* 85 (1982), 13-19
"Paul's Sense of Place: an Anthropological Approach to Community Formation in Corinth", *NTS* 32 (1986), 225-46

Bernard, J.H., "The Connexion between the Fifth and Sixth Chapters of 1 Corinthians", *The Expositor* (1907), 433-43

Betz, O., "Der gekreuzigte Christus, unsere Weisheit und Gerechtigkeit (Der alttestimentliche Hintergrund von 1 Korinther 1-2)", *Tradition and Interpretation in the New Testament: Essays in Honor of E.E. Ellis for his 60th Birthday*, eds. G.F. Hawthorne and O. Betz (Grand Rapids: Eerdmans, 1987), 195-215

Black, D.A., *Paul, Apostle of Weakness: Astheneia and its Cognates in the Pauline Literature* (New York: Peter Lang, 1984)

Borgen, P., "Catalogues of Vices, the Apostolic Decree, and the Jerusalem Meeting", *The Social World of Formative Christianity and Judaism: Essays in tribute to H.C. Kee* (Philadelphia: Fortress, 1988), 121-33

Bousset, W., "Der Erste Brief an die Korinther", *Die Schriften des Neuen Testaments Vol 2*, ed. J. Weiss (Göttingen: Vandenhoeck & Ruprecht, 1917-18), 72-161

Branick, V.P., "Source and Redaction Analysis of 1Cor. 1-3", *JBL* 101 (1982), 251-69

Brown, A.R., *The Cross and Human Transformation* (Minneapolis: Fortress, 1995)

Brown, R.D., *Lucretius on Love and Sex* (Leiden: Brill, 1987)

Bruce, F.F., *1 and 2 Corinthians* (New Century Bible; London: Oliphants, 1971)
The Acts of the Apostles (Grand Rapids: Eerdmans, 1990)

Castelli, E., *Imitating Paul: A Discourse of Power* (Louisville: Westminster/John Knox Press, 1991)

Cerfaux, L., "Vestiges d'un florilège dans 1Cor. 1:18-3:24?", *RHE* 27 (1931), 521-34

Clarke, A.D., *Secular and Christian Leadership in Corinth: A Socio-Historical and Exegetical Study of 1 Corinthians 1-6* (Leiden: Brill, 1993)

Conzelmann, H., *1 Corinthians* (Hermeneia; Philadelphia: Fortress, 1975)
"Paulus und die Weisheit", *NTS* 12 (1965), 231-44

Cousar, C.B., *A Theology of the Cross: The Death of Jesus in the Pauline Letters* (Minneapolis: Fortress, 1990)

Cranfield, C.E.B., *The Epistle to the Romans* (ICC; 2 vols; Edinburgh: T. & T. Clark, 1979)

Dahl, N.A., "Paul and the Church at Corinth according to 1 Corinthians 1:10-4:21", *Christian History and Interpretation: Studies presented to John Knox*, eds. W.R.Farmer, C.F.D Moule and R.R. Niebuhr (Cambridge: CUP, 1967)

Davis, J.A., *Wisdom and Spirit: An Investigation of 1 Corinthians 1:18-3:20 against the background of Jewish Sapiental Traditions in the Greco-Roman Period* (Lanham: University Press of America, 1984)

Deissmann, A.,*Light from the Ancient East: The New Testament illustrated by recently discovered texts of the Greco-Roman world* (London: Hodder, 1927)

De Wette, W.M.L., *Kurze Erklärung der Briefe an die Korinther* (Leipzig: Weidmann, 1845)

De Witt, N.W., *St Paul and Epicurus* (Minneapolis: University of Minneapolis Press, 1954)
"Organisation and Procedure in Epicurean Groups", *CP* 31 (1936), 205-11

Dunn, J.D.G., *Romans 9-16* (WBC 38b; Dallas: Word, 1988)

Ellis, E.E., "'Wisdom' and "Knowledge" in 1 Corinthians", *TynBul* 25 (1974), 82-98
"Traditions in 1 Corinthians", *NTS* 32 (1986), 481-502
"Christ Crucified", *Reconciliation and Hope. New Testament Essays in Atonement and Eschatology Presented to L.L. Morris*, ed. R. Banks (Exeter: Paternoster, 1974), 69-75

Engberg-Pederson, T., "The Gospel and Social Practice according to 1 Corinthians," *NTS* 33 (1987) 557-84

Engels, D., *Roman Corinth: An Alternative Model for the Classical City* (Chicago: University of Chicago, 1990)

Fee, G., *The First Epistle to the Corinthians* (NICNT; Grand Rapids: Eerdmans, 1987)

Festugière, A.J., *Epicurus and his Gods* (New York: Russell & Russell, 1955)

Fitch, W.O., "Paul, Apollos, Cephas, Christ", *Th* 74 (1971), 18-24

Fitzgerald, J.T., *Cracks in an Earthen Vessel: An Examination of the Catalogues of Hardships in the Corinthian Correspondence* (Atlanta: Scholars Press, 1988)

Furnish, V.P., "Belonging to Christ: A Paradigm for Ethics in 1st Corinthians", *Int* 44 (1990), 145-57

Gaskin, J., (ed.), *The Epicurean Philosophers* (Everyman; London: J.M. Dent, 1995)

Gill, D.W.J., "Head-covering in 1 Corinthians 11.2-16", *TynBul* 41 (1990), 245-60

Glucker, J., *Antiochus and the Late Academy* (Göttingen: Vandenhoeck & Ruprecht, 1978)

Gosling, J.C.B. and Taylor, C.C.W., *The Greeks on Pleasure* (Oxford: Clarendon, 1982)

Goulder, M.D., *A Tale of Two Missions* (London: SCM, 1994)
"Σοφία in 1 Corinthians", *NTS* 37 (1991), 516-34

Grant, R.M., *Gnosticism and Early Christianity* (2nd ed.; New York: Columbia University Press, 1966)

Gundry, R.H., *Mark - A Commentary on His Apology for the Cross* (Grand Rapids: Eerdmans, 1993)

Haenchen, E., *The Acts of the Apostles* (Oxford: Blackwell, 1971)

Hanson, A.T., *The Paradox of the Cross in the Thought of St. Paul* (Sheffield: JSOT Press, 1987)

Hengel, M., *Crucifixion* (London: SCM, 1977)

Héring, J., *The First Epistle of Saint Paul to the Corinthians* (London: Epworth, 1962)

Hitchcock, F.R.M., "Who are the 'People of Chloe' in 1Cor.1:11?" *JTS* 25 (1923), 163-7

Hock, R.F., "Paul's Tentmaking and the Problem of his Social Class," *JBL* 97 (1978), 555-64
The Social Context of Paul's Ministry: Tentmaking and Apostleship (Philadelphia: Fortress, 1980)

Horrell, D., *The Social Ethos of the Corinthian Correspondence: Interests and Ideology from 1 Corinthians to 1 Clement* (Studies of the New Testament and Its World; Edinburgh, T. & T. Clark, 1996)

Horsley, R.A., "Wisdom of Word and Words of Wisdom in Corinth", *CBQ* 39 (1977), 224-39

"'How can some of you say there is no Resurrection of the Dead?' Spiritual Elitism in Corinth", *NovT* 20 (1978), 203-31

"Gnosis in Corinth: 1 Corinthians 8:1-6", *NTS* 27 (1980), 32-51

(ed.) *Paul and Empire: Religion and Power in Roman Imperial Society* (Harrisburg: Trinity Press International, 1997)

Hurd, J.C.,   *The Origin of 1 Corinthians* (London: SPCK, 1965)

Jewett, R.,   *Dating Paul's Life* (London: SCM, 1979)

Christian Tolerance: Paul's Message to the Modern Church (Philadelphia: Westminster, 1982)

Jones, H., *The Epicurean Tradition* (London: Routledge, 1989)

Judge, E.A., "The Early Christians as a Scholastic Community", *JRH* 1.i (1960-61), 4-15; 1.ii, 125-37

The Social Pattern of Christian Groups in the First Century (London: Tyndale, 1960)

Kähler, M. "Das Kreuz: Grund und Mass für die Christologie", (Gütersloh, C. Bertelsmann, 1911)

Käsemann, E., "The Disciples of John the Baptist in Ephesus", *Essays on New Testament Themes* (London: SCM, 1964), 136-48

"The Saving Significance of the Death of Jesus in Paul", *Perspectives on Paul* (London: SCM, 1971), 32-59

New Testament Questions for Today (London: SCM, 1969)

Koester, H., *History, Culture, Religion of the Hellenistic Age* (New York: Walter de Gruyter, 1982)

Lake, K., *The Earlier Epistles of Paul: Their Motive and Origin* (London: Rivingtons, 1914)

Lampe, P., "Theological Wisdom and the 'Word of the Cross': The Rhetorical Scheme in 1Cor. 1-4", *Int* 44 (1990), 117-31

Litfin, D., *St. Paul's Theology of Proclamation: 1 Corinthians 1-4 and Greco-Roman Rhetoric* (Cambridge: CUP, 1994)

Lüdemann, G.,   *Paul: Apostle to the Gentiles: Studies in Chronology* (London: SCM, 1984)

Opposition to Paul in Jewish Christianity (Minneapolis: Fortress, 1989)

Lütgert, W., *Freiheitspredigt und Schwärmgeister in Korinth. Ein Beitrag zur Charakteristik der Christuspartei* (Gütersloh: C. Bertelsmann, 1908)

Luz, U., "Theologia Crucis als Mitte der Theologie im Neuen Testament", *EvTh* 34 (1974), 116-41

Macrae, G., "Gnosis in Corinth", *Int* 26 (1972), 489-91

Malherbe, A.J., "Self-Definition among Epicureans and Cynics", *Jewish and Christian Self-Definition Vol 3* (eds. B.F. Meyer and E.P. Sanders; London: SCM, 1982), 46-59.
Social Aspects of Early Christianity (Baton Rouge: Louisiana State University Press, 1977)
"The Beasts at Ephesus", *JBL* 87 (1968), 71-80

Malina, B.J., *The New Testament World: Insights from Cultural Anthropology* (London: SCM, 1981)

Marshall, P., *Enmity in Corinth: Social Conventions in Paul's Relations with the Corinthians* (Tübingen: Mohr/Siebeck, 1987)

Martin, D.B., *Slavery as Salvation: The Metaphor of Slavery in Pauline Christianity* (New Haven: Yale University Press, 1990)
"Tongues of Angels and Other Status Indicators", *JAAR* 59 (1991), 547-89
The Corinthian Body (New Haven: Yale University Press, 1995)

Martyn, J.L., "Apocalyptic Antinomies in Paul's letter to the Galatians", *NTS* 31 (1985), 410-24

Meeks, W.A., *The First Urban Christians: The Social World of the Apostle Paul* (New Haven: Yale University Press, 1983)
The Moral World of the First Christians (London: SPCK, 1987)

Merritt, B.D., (ed.) *Corinth: Vol VIII.i: Greek Inscriptions* (Cambridge, Mass.: Harvard University Press, 1931)

Miller, G.W., "'ΑΡΧΟΝΤΩΝ ΤΟΥ ΑΙΩΝΟΣ ΤΟΥΤΟΥ' - A New Look at 1Cor.2:6-8", *JBL* (1972), 522-8

Mitchell, M., *Paul and the Rhetoric of Reconciliation: An Exegetical Investigation of the Language and Composition of 1 Corinthians* (Tübingen: Mohr/Siebeck, 1991)

Munck, J., *The Church without Factions: Studies in 1 Corinthians 1-4* (London: SCM, 1959)

Murphy-O'Connor, J., *St Paul's Corinth: Texts and Archaeology* (Wilmington: Michael Glazier, 1983)

Neyrey, J.H., "The Form and Background of the Polemic in 2 Peter", JBL 99 (1980), 407-31

Nielsen, H.K., "Paulus' Verwendung des Begriffes Δυναμις: Eine Replik zur Kreuzestheologie", *Die Paulinische Literatur und Theologie* (ed. S. Petersen; Aarhus: Vandenhoeck & Ruprecht, 1980), 137-58

Painter, J., "Paul and the Πνευματικοι at Corinth", *Paul and Paulinism: Essays in honour of C.K. Barrett*, eds. M.D. Hooker and S.G. Wilson (London: SPCK, 1982), 237-50

Pearson, B.A., "Philo, Gnosis and the New Testament", *The New Testament and Gnosis: Essays in honour of Robert McLachlan Wilson*, eds. A.H.B. Logan and A.J.M. Wedderburn (Edinburgh: T. & T. Clark, 1983), 73-89

The Pneumatikos-Psychikos Terminology in 1 Corinthians: A Study in the Theology of the Corinthian Opponents of Paul and Its Relation to Gnosticism (Atlanta: Scholars Press, 1973)

Peterson, E., "1 Korinther 1:18 und die Thematik des jüdischen Busstages", *Bib* 32 (1951), 97-103

Plank, K.A., *Paul and the Irony of Affliction* (Atlanta: Scholars Press, 1987)

Pogoloff, S.M., *Logos and Sophia: The Rhetorical Situation of 1 Corinthians* (Atlanta: Scholars Press, 1992)

Richardson, N., *Paul's Language about God* (JSNT 99; Sheffield: Sheffield Academic Press, 1994)

Richardson, P., "The Thunderbolt in Q and the Wise Man in Corinth", *From Jesus to Paul, Studies in Honour of Francis Wright Beare*, eds. P. Richardson and J.C. Hurd (Waterloo: Wilfred Laurier University Press, 1984), 91-111

Rist, J.M., *Epicurus: An Introduction* (Cambridge: CUP, 1972)

Sanders, E.P., *Paul & Palestinian Judaism* (London: SCM, 1977)

Paul, the Law & the Jewish People (London: SCM, 1983)

Schlatter, A., "Das Kreuz Jesu unsere Versöhnung mit Gott", *Gesunde Lehre - Reden und Aufsätze* (Velbert im Rheinland: Freizeiten, 1929)

Schmithals, W., *Gnosis in Corinth: An Investigation of the Letters to the Corinthians* (Nashville: Abingdon, 1971)

"The *Corpus Paulinum* and Gnosis", *The New Testament and Gnosis: Essays in honour of Robert McLachlan Wilson*, ed. A.H.B. Logan and A.J.M. Wedderburn; Edinburgh: T. & T. Clark, 1983), 107-24

Schüssler Fiorenza, E., *In Memory of Her: A Feminist Theological Reconstruction of Christian Origins* (London: SCM, 1983)

Schütz, J., *Paul and the Anatomy of Apostolic Authority* (SNTSMS 26; Cambridge: CUP, 1975)

Scroggs, R. "Paul: Σοφός and Πνευματικὸς," *NTS* 14 (1967-8), 33-55

"The Sociological Interpretation of the New Testament: The Present State of Research", *NTS* 26 (1980)

Sellin, G., "Das Geheimnis der Weisheit und das Rätsel der 'Christuspartei' (zu 1 Kor. 1-4)", *ZNW* 73 (1982), 69-96

Stendahl, K., *Paul Among Jews and Gentiles* (Philadelphia: Fortress, 1976)

Stowers, S.K., "Social Status, Public Speaking and Private Teaching: The Circumstances of Paul's Preaching Activity", *NovT* 26 (1984), 59-82

Stuhlmacher, P., "Eighteen Theses on Paul's Theology of the Cross", *Reconciliation, Law and Righteousness: Essays in Biblical Theology* (Philadelphia: Fortress, 1986), 155-68

"The Hermeneutical Significance of 1Cor. 2:6-16", *Tradition and Interpretation in the New Testament: Essays in Honor of E.E. Ellis for his 60th Birthday*, eds. G.F. Hawthorne and O. Betz; (Grand Rapids: Eerdmans, 1987), 328-47

Theissen, G., *The Social Setting of Pauline Christianity* (Edinburgh: T. & T. Clark, 1982)

Psychological Aspects of Pauline Theology (Edinburgh: T. & T. Clark, 1987)

Thiselton, A.C., "Realised Eschatology at Corinth", *NTS* 24 (1978), 510-26

Tomlin, G.S., "Christians and Epicureans in 1 Corinthians", *JSNT* 68 (1997), 51-72

Viering, F., *Das Kreuzetod Jesu: Interpretation eines theologischen Gutachtens* (Gütersloh: Gerd Mohn, 1967)

Wedderburn, A. J. M., "The Denial of the Resurrection in Corinth", *Baptism and Resurrection* (Tübingen: Mohr-Siebeck, 1987), 1-37

Weder, H., *Das Kreuz Jesu bei Paulus* (Göttingen: Vandenhoeck & Ruprecht, 1981)

Weiss, J., *Der erste Korintherbrief* (Göttingen: Vandenhoeck & Ruprecht, 1910)

Welborn, L.L., "On the Discord in Corinth: 1 Corinthians 4 and Ancient Politics", *JBL* 106 (1987), 85-111

Wenham, D., *Paul: Follower of Jesus or Founder of Christianity?* (Grand Rapids: Eerdmans, 1995)

Wilckens, U., *Weisheit und Torheit* (Tübingen: Mohr/Siebeck, 1959)

"Zu I Kor. 2:1-16", *Theologia Crucis - Signum Crucis: Festschrift für Erich Dinkler*, eds. C. Andresen and G. Klein; (Tübingen: Mohr/Siebeck, 1979), 501-39

Willis, W., "The 'Mind of Christ' in 1 Corinthians 2:16", *Bib* 70 (1989), 110-22

Wilson, R. McL., "Gnosis at Corinth", *Paul and Paulinism: Essays in honour of C.K.Barrett*, eds. M.D. Hooker and S.G. Wilson; (London: SPCK, 1982)

"How Gnostic were the Corinthians?", *NTS* 19 (1972), 65-74

Winter, M., *Pneumatiker und Psychiker in Korinth: Zum religionsgeschichtliche Hintergrund von 1 Kor.2:6-3:4* (Marburg: N.G. Elwert, 1975)

Winter, B.W., "Civil Litigation in Corinth: the Forensic Background to 1Cor.6:1-8", *NTS* 37 (1991), 559-72

Wire, A.C., *The Corinthian Women Prophets: A Reconstruction through Paul's Rhetoric* (Minneapolis: Fortress, 1990)

Witherington, B., *Jesus the Sage: The Pilgrimage of Wisdom* (Edinburgh: T. & T. Clark, 1994)

Conflict and Community in Corinth (Grand Rapids: Eerdmans, 1995)

Wright, N.T., "A New Tübingen School? Ernst Käsemann and his commentary on Romans", *Them* 7 (1982), 6-16

Wuellner, W., "Haggadic Homily Genre in 1Cor.1-3", *JBL* 89 (1970), 199-204

"The Sociological Implications of 1Cor.1:26-28 Reconsidered," *Studia Evangelica. VI*, ed. E.A. Livingstone (Berlin: Akademie, 1973), 666-72

"Tradition and Interpretation of the 'Wise- Powerful- Noble-' Triad in 1Cor.1:26", *Studia Evangelica VII*, ed. E.A. Livingstone; (Berlin: Akademie, 1982), 557-62

Yamauchi, E., *Pre-Christian Gnosticism* (London: Tyndale, 1973)

Yarbrough, O.L., *Not like the Gentiles: Marriage Rules in the Letters of Paul* (SBL 80; Atlanta: Scholars Press, 1985)

LUTHER:

Althaus, P., *The Theology of Martin Luther* (Philadelphia: Fortress, 1966)

Appel, H., *Anfechtung und Trost im Spätmittelalter und bei Luther* (Leipzig: M. Heinsius, 1938)

Bagchi, D., *Luther's Earliest Opponents: Catholic Controversialists, 1518-1525* (Minneapolis: Fortress, 1991)

Bandt, H.,*Luthers Lehre vom verborgenen Gott* (Berlin: Evangelische Verlagsanstalt, 1958)

Barnes, T.D., *Tertullian: A Historical and Literary Study* (Oxford: Clarendon, 1985)

Bauer, K.,*Die Wittenberger Universitätstheologie und die Anfänge der Deutschen Reformation* (Tübingen: Mohr/Siebeck, 1928)

"Die Heidelberg Disputation Luthers", *ZKG* 21 (1900), 231-68, 299-329

Baus, K., *Handbook of Church History Vol I: From the Apostolic Community to Constantine* (London: Burns & Oates, 1965)

Beintker, H.,*Die Überwindung der Anfechtung bei Luther: Eine Studie zu seiner Theologie nach den Operationes in Psalmos 1519-21* (Berlin: Evangelische Verlagsanstalt, 1954)

Bell, T., "Pater Bernardus. Bernard de Clairvaux par Martin Luther", *Citeaux* 41 (1991), 233-55
Divus Bernardus: Bernhard von Clairvaux in Martin Luthers Schriften (von Zabern: Mainz, 1993)

Benrath, G.A. "Luther und die Mystik - ein Kurzbericht", *Zur Lage der Lutherforschung Heute*, ed. P. Manns (Wiesbaden: Franz Steiner, 1982), 44-58

Bizer, E., *Fides ex Auditu* (Neukirchen: Kreis Moers, 1958)

Blaumeiser, H., *Martin Luthers Kreuzestheologie: Schlüssel zu seiner Deutung von Mensch und Wirklichkeit; eine Untersuchung anhand der Operationes in Psalmos 1519-1521* (Paderborn: Bonifatius, 1995)

Boehmer, H., *Luthers erste Vorlesung* (BVSAW 75.1; Leipzig: S. Hirzel, 1923)
Road to Reformation (Cleveland: Meridian, 1957)

Bornkamm, H.,"Iustitia Dei beim jungen Luther", ed. B. Lohse, *Der Durchbruch der Reformatorischen Erkenntnis bei Luther* (Darmstadt: Wissenschaftliche Buchgesellschaft, 1968), 115-62

Brecht, M., *Martin Luther: His Road to Reformation 1483-1521* (Philadelphia: Fortress, 1985)
"Randbemerkungen in Luthers Ausgaben der 'Deutsch Theologia'", (*LJB* 47; Göttingen: Vandenhoeck & Ruprecht, 1980), 11-32

Bredero, A.H., *Bernard of Clairvaux: between Cult and History* (Edinburgh, T. & T. Clark, 1996)

Cargill Thompson, W.D.J., "The Problem of Luther's 'Tower Experience' and its Place in his Intellectual Development", *Studies in the Reformation: Luther to Hooker*, ed. C.W. Dugmore (London: Athlone Press, 1980), 60-80

Cessario, R. OP, *The Godly Image: Christ and Salvation in Catholic Thought from Anselm to Aquinas* (Petersham, Mass.: St. Bede's, 1990)

Courtenay, W.J., "Nominalism and Late Medieval Thought: A Bibliographical Essay", *ThSt* 33 (1972), 716-34
"Nominalism and Late Medieval Religion", *The Pursuit of Holiness in Late Medieval and Renaissance Religion*, ed. C. Trinkaus and H. Oberman (Leiden: Brill, 1974), 26-59
"Late Medieval Nominalism Revisited: 1972-1982", *JHI* 44 (1983), 159-64

Damerau, R., *Die Demut in der Theologie Luthers,* (SGR 5; Giessen: Wilhelm Schmitz, 1967)

Davies, B., *The Thought of Thomas Aquinas* (Oxford: Clarendon Press, 1992)

Dickens, A.G. *The German Nation and Martin Luther* (London: Fontana: 1976)

Ebeling, G., "Die Anfänge von Luthers Hermeneutik", *Lutherstudien* 1 (Tübingen: Mohr/Siebeck, 1971), 1-68
Luther: An Introduction to his Thought (London: Collins, 1972)

Eckermann, K.W., "Luther's Kreuzestheologie. Zur Frage nach ihrem Ursprung", *Catholica* 37 (1983), 306-17

Ellwein, E., "Die Entfaltung der theologia crucis in Luthers Hebräerbriefvorlesung", *Theologische Aufsätze: Karl Barth zum 50. Geburtstag,* ed. E. Wolf (Münich: Kaiser, 1936), 382-404

Elze, M., "Züge spätmittelalterlicher Frömmigkeit in Luthers Theologie", *ZTK* 62 (1965), 382-402
"Das Verständnis der Passion Jesu im Ausgehenden Mittelalter und bei Luther", *Geist und Geschichte der Reformation: Festgabe H. Rückert,* ed. H. Liebling and K. Scholder (Berlin: Walter de Gruyter, 1966), 127-51

Ficker, J., "Zu den Bemerkungen Luthers in Taulers Sermones (Augsburg 1508)", *THStKr* 107 (1936), 46-64

Forde, G.O., *On Being a Theologian of the Cross: Reflections on Luther's Heidelberg Disputation 1518* (Grand Rapids: Eerdmans, 1997)

Gerrish, B.A., *Grace and Reason; A Study in the Theology of Luther* (Oxford: Clarendon, 1962)
"To the Unknown God: Luther and Calvin on the Hiddenness of God", *JRel* 53 (1973), 263-92
"By Faith Alone: Medium and Message in Luther's Gospel", The *Old Protestantism and the New: Essays on the Reformation Heritage* (Edinburgh: T. & T. Clark, 1982), 69-89

Grane, L.,*Contra Gabrielum: Luthers Auseinandersetzung mit Gabriel Biel in der Disputatio contra scholasticam theologiam 1517* (Copenhagen: Gyldendal, 1962)
Modus Loquendi Theologicus: Luthers Kampf um die Erneuerung der Theologie 1515-1518 (Leiden: Brill, 1975)
"Luther and Scholasticism", *Luther and Learning: the Wittenberg University Luther Symposium,* ed. M.J. Harran (Selinsgrove: Associated University Presses, 1985), 52-68

Greschat, M. and Lottes, G. (eds.), *Luther in seiner Zeit: Persönlichkeit und Wirken des Reformators* (Stuttgart: Kohlhammer, 1997)

Hagen, K., "Changes in the Understanding of Luther: the Development of the Young Luther", *ThSt* 29 (1968), 472-96

Hägglund, B., *The Background of Luther's Doctrine of Justification in Late Medieval Theology* (Philadelphia: Fortress, 1971)

Hall, B., "*Hoc est Corpus Meum*: The Centrality of the Real Presence for Luther", *Luther: Theologian for Catholics and Protestants*, ed. G. Yule; (Edinburgh: T. & T. Clark, 1985), 112-44

Hamm, B., *Frömmigkeit am Anfang des 16. Jahrhunderts: Studien zu Johannes von Paltz und seinem Umkreis* (BHT 65; Tübingen: Mohr/Siebeck, 1982)

Harran, M.J., *Luther on Conversion: The Early Years* (Ithaca: Cornell University Press, 1983)

Hendrix, S.H., *Luther and the Papacy: Stages in a Reformation Conflict* (Philadelphia: Fortress, 1981)

Hirsch, E., "Initium Theologiae Lutheri", *Lutherstudien II* (Gütersloh: C. Bertelsmann, 1954)

Holl, K., *Gesammelte Aufsätze zur Kirchengeschichte Vol 1: Luther* (Tübingen: Mohr/Siebeck, 1921)

Hopkins, J., *A Companion to the Study of St. Anselm* (Minneapolis: University of Minnesota Press, 1972)

Janz, D.R., *Luther and Late Medieval Thomism: A Study in Theological Anthropology* (Waterloo: Wilfred Laurier University Press, 1983) *Luther on Thomas Aquinas: The Angelic Doctor in the Thought of the Reformer* (Wiesbaden: Franz Steiner, 1989)

Kleineidam, E., "Ursprung und Gegenstand der Theologie bei Bernhard von Clairvaux und Martin Luther", *Dienst der Vermittlung: Festschrift zum 25-jahrigen Bestehen des philosophisch-theologischen Studiums in Priesterseminar Erfurt*, eds. W Ernst, K. Feiereis and F. Hoffmann (Leipzig: St. Benno, 1977), 221-47

Kolb, R., "The Theologians and the Peasants: Conservative Evangelical Reactions to the German Peasants' Revolt", *ARG* 79 (1978), 103-31

Loewenich, W. von, *Luther's Theology of the Cross* (Belfast: Christian Journals, 1976)

Lohse, B., *Mönchtum und Reformation: Luthers Auseinander-setzung mit dem Mönchsideal des Mittelalters* (FKDG 12; Göttingen: Vandenhoeck & Ruprecht, 1963) *Martin Luther: An Introduction to his Life and Work* (Edinburgh: T. & T. Clark, 1986)

"Luther und Bernhard von Clairvaux", *Bernhard von Clairvaux: Rezeption und Wirkung im Mittelalter und in der Neuzeit*, ed. K. Elm (Wiesbaden: Harrassowitz, 1994), 271-301

Lortz., J., *Die Reformation in Deutschland* (4th ed..; Freiburg: Herder, 1982)

Matsuura, J., "Restbestände aus der Bibliotek des Erfurter Augustinerklosters zu Luthers Zeit und bisher unbekannte eigenhändige Notizen Luthers", *Lutheriana: Zum 500. Geburtstag Martin Luthers von den Mitarbeitern der Weimarer Ausgabe* (AWA 5; Köln: Böhlau, 1984)

McGrath, A.E.,"'Mira et Nova diffinitio iustitiae': Luther and Scholastic Doctrines of Justification",*ARG* 74 (1983), 37-60

Luther's Theology of the Cross (Oxford, Blackwell, 1984)

The Intellectual Origins of the European Reformation (Blackwell: Oxford, 1987)

"The Christology of Hugolino of Orvieto", *Schwerpunkte und Wirkungen des Sentenzkommentars Hugolins von Orvieto O.E.S.A.*, ed. W. Eckermann O.S.A (Würzburg: Augustinus, 1990), 253-62

McSorley, H.J., *Luther Right or Wrong? An Ecumenical-Theological Study of Luther's Major Work, the Bondage of the Will* (Minneapolis/New York: Newman, 1969)

Modalsli, O., "Die Heidelberger Disputation im Lichte der evangelischen Neuentdeckung Luthers", (*LJB 47;* Göttingen: Vandenhoeck & Ruprecht, 1980), 33-9

Mozley, J.K., *The Impassibility of God* (Cambridge: CUP, 1926)

Mühlen,K-H zur.,*Nos extra Nos: Luthers Theologie zwischen Mystik und Scholastik* (Tübingen: Mohr/Siebeck, 1972)

Nicol, M., *Meditation bei Luther* (FKDG 34; Göttingen: Vandenhoeck & Ruprecht, 1984)

Oberman, H.A., *The Harvest of Medieval Theology: Gabriel Biel and Late Medieval Nominalism* (Cambridge, Mass.: Harvard, 1963)

Forerunners of the Reformation: The Shape of Late Medieval Thought (London: Lutterworth, 1967)

The Dawn of the Reformation: Essays in Late Medieval and Early Reformation Thought (Edinburgh: T. &. T. Clark, 1986)

The Reformation, Roots and Ramifications (Edinburgh: T. & T. Clark, 1994)

Ozment, S.E., *Homo Spiritualis: A Comparative Study of the Anthropology of Johannes Tauler, Jean Gerson and Martin Luther (1509-1516) in the Context of their Theological Thought* (Leiden: Brill, 1969)

"Homo Viator: Luther and Late Medieval Theology", *The Reformation in Medieval Perspective*, ed. S. E. Ozment (Chicago: Quadrangle, 1971), 142-54

"Mysticism, Nominalism and Dissent," *The Pursuit of Holiness in Late Medieval and Renaissance Religion*, ed. C. Trinkaus and H. Oberman; Leiden: Brill, 1974), 67-92

"Luther and the Late Middle Ages: The Formation of Reformation Thought", *Transition and Revolution: Problems and Issues of European Renaissance and Reformation History*, ed. R.M. Kingdon (Minneapolis: Burgess, 1974), 112-28

The Age of Reform 1250-1550; An Intellectual and Religious History of Late Medieval and Reformation Europe (New Haven: Yale University Press, 1980)

Pinomaa, L., *Der Existentielle Charakter der Theologie Luthers* (Helsinki: Suomalainen Tiedeakatemia, 1940)

Posset, F., "Bible Reading 'With Closed Eyes' in the Monastic Tradition: An Overlooked Aspect of Martin Luther's Hermeneutic", *ABR* 38 (1987), 293-306

"Monastic Influence on Martin Luther", *MonS* 18 (1988), 136-63

"Recommendations by Martin Luther of St. Bernard's 'On Consideration'", *CistStud* 25 (1990), 25-36

"Divus Bernardus: Saint Bernard as Spiritual and Theological Mentor of the Reformer Martin Luther", *Bernardus Magister: Papers presented at the Nonacentenary Celebration of the Birth of Saint Bernard of Clairvaux*, ed. J.R. Sommerfeldt (Spencer MA: Cistercian Publications, 1992), 517-32

Post, R.R., *The Modern Devotion: Confrontation with Reformation and Humanism* (SMRT 3; Leiden, Brill, 1968)

Prenter, R., *Der Barmherzige Richter: Iustitia dei passiva in Luthers Dictata super Psalterium 1513-1515* (Copenhagen: Universitetsforlaget I Aarhus, 1961)

Rohr, J. von,"Medieval Consolation and the Young Luther's Despair", *Reformation Studies: Essays in Honour of R.H. Bainton*, ed. F.H. Littell (Richmond: John Knox, 1962), 61-74

Ross, E.M., *The Grief of God: Images of the Suffering Jesus in Late Medieval England* (Oxford, OUP, 1997)

Ruh, K., "Zur Theologie des mittelalterlichen Passionstraktats", *ThZ* 6 (1950), 17-39

Rupp, G., *The Righteousness of God: Luther Studies* (London: Hodder, 1953)

"Luther's 95 Theses and the Theology of the Cross", ed. C.S. Meyer, *Luther for an Ecumenical Age: Essays in Commemoration of the 450th Anniversary of the Reformation* (St. Louis: Concordia, 1967), 67-81

Saarnivaara, U., *Luther Discovers the Gospel: New Light upon Luther's Way from Medieval Catholicism to Evangelical Faith* (St Louis: Concordia, 1951)

Schwarz, R.,"Luther's Inalienable Inheritance of Monastic Theology", *ABR* 39 (1988), 430-50

Steinmetz, D.C., *Misericordia Dei: The Theology of Johannes von Staupitz in Its Late Medieval Setting* (Leiden: Brill, 1968)
Luther and Staupitz: An Essay in the Intellectual Origins of the Protestant Reformation (Durham, N. Carolina: Duke University Press, 1980)
Luther in Context (Bloomington: Indiana, 1986)

Swanson, R.N., *Religion and Devotion in Europe, c.1215-c.1515* (Cambridge Medieval textbooks; Cambridge: CUP, 1995)

Tomlin, G.S., "The Medieval Origins of Luther's Theology of the Cross", *ARG* 89 (1998), 22-40.

Vercruysse, J.E., "Luther's Theology of the Cross at the time of the Heidelberg Disputation", *Greg* 57 (1976), 523-48

Vogelsang, E., *Die Anfänge von Luthers Christologie nach der ersten Psalmenvorlesung* (Berlin: Walter de Gruyter, 1929)
Der Angefochtene Christus bei Luther (Berlin: Walter de Gruyter, 1932)

Wendorf, H., "Der Durchbruch der neuen Erkenntnis Luthers im Lichte der handschriftlichen Überlieferungen", *Historische Vierteljahrschrift* (1932)

Wicks, J., *Man's Yearning for Grace: Luther's Early Spiritual Teaching* (Washington: Corpus, 1968)

Zeller, W., "Luther und die Mystik", *Theologie und Frömmigkeit. Gesammelte Aufsätze 2*, ed. B. Jaspert (Marburg: N.G. Elwert, 1978)

PASCAL

Abercrombie, N., *The Origins of Jansenism* (Oxford: Clarendon, 1936)

Angers, J.E. d'., *L'Apologétique en France de 1580 à 1670: Pascal et ses Précurseurs* (Paris: Nouvelles Editions Latines, 1954)

Askew, D.A., "Pascal's Pari in the Port-Royal Edition", *AJFS* 5 (1968), 155-82

Aston, T.H., *Crisis in Europe 1560-1660: Essays from Past and Present* (London: Routledge & Kegan Paul, 1965)

Barnes, A., *Lettres Inédites de Jean Duvergier de Hauranne: Les Origines du Jansénisme Vol. IV* (Paris: J. Vrin, 1962)

Baudin, E., *Études Historiques et Critiques sur la Philosophie de Pascal, II: Sa Philosophie Morale: Pascal, les libertins et les jansénistes* (Neuchâtel: Editions de la Baconnière, 1946)

Bénichou, P., *Morales du Grand Siècle* (Paris: Gallimard, 1948)

Bluche, F., *Louis XIV* (Oxford: Blackwell, 1990)

Brémond, H., *Nicole: Œuvres Choisies* (Paris: Bloud, 1909)

Briggs, R., *Communities of Belief: Cultural and Social Tensions in Early Modern France* (Oxford: Clarendon, 1989)

Broome, J.H., *Pascal* (London: Edward Arnold, 1965)

Calvet, J., *La Littérature Religieuse de François de Sales à Fénelon* (Paris: J. de Gigord, 1938)

Carsten, F.L., (ed.), *New Cambridge Modern History Vol.V: The Ascendancy of France 1648-88* (Cambridge: CUP, 1961)

Chaix-Ruy, J., *Pascal et Port-Royal* (Paris: Félix Alcan, 1930)

Cognet, L., *Le Jansénisme* (Paris: Presses Universitaires de France, 1961) "Le Mépris du monde à Port-Royal et dans le Jansénisme", *RAM* 41 (1965), 387-402

Couton, G., and Jehasse, J. (eds.), *Images et Témoins de l'age classique 2* (Université de la Region de la Rhone-Alpes, 1972)

Davidson, H.M. and Dubé, P.H. (eds.), *Concordance to the Pensées* (Ithaca: Cornell University Press, 1975)

Davidson, H.M. *The Origins of Certainty* (Chicago: University of Chicago Press, 1979) *Pascal and the Arts of the Mind* (Cambridge: CUP, 1993)

Ehrard, J.,"Pascal au siècle des lumières", *Pascal Présent*, ed. Faculté des lettres de Clermont (Clermont-Ferrand: G. de Bussac, 1962), 231-55

Etiemble, *Les Jésuites en Chine: La Querelle des Rites 1552-1773* (Paris: René Julliard, 1966)

Eymard, J., *Yves de Paris* (Paris: Bloud & Gay, 1964)

Fletcher, F.T.H., *Pascal and the Mystical Tradition* (Oxford: Blackwell, 1954)

Gilson, E., "Le sens du terme 'abêtir' chez Blaise Pascal", *Les Idées et les Lettres* (2nd ed.; Paris: J. Vrin, 1955), 263-74

Goldmann, L., *The Hidden God: A Study of Tragic Vision in the Pensées of Pascal and the Tragedies of Racine* (London: Routledge & Kegan Paul, 1964)

Gouhier, H., "Pascal et les humanismes de son temps", *Pascal Présent*, ed. Faculté des lettres de Clermont (Clermont-Ferrand: G. de Bussac, 1962) *Blaise Pascal: Conversion et Apologétique* (Paris: J. Vrin, 1986)

Hammond, N., *Playing with Truth: Language and the Human Condition in Pascal's Pensées* (Oxford: Clarendon Press, 1994)

Hildesheimer, F., *Le Jansénisme en France aux XVIIe et XVIIIe siècles* (Paris: Publisud, 1991)

Howells, B., "The Interpretation of Pascal's 'Pari'", *MLR* 79 (1984), 45-63

Jordan, J. (ed.),*Gambling on God: Essays on Pascal's Wager* (Lanham: Rowman & Littlefield, 1994)

Kearns, E.J., *Ideas in Seventeenth-Century France* (Manchester: Manchester University Press, 1979)

Kolakowski, L., *God Owes Us Nothing: A Brief Remark on Pascal's Religion and the Spirit of Jansenism* (Chicago: University of Chicago Press, 1995)

Krailsheimer, A.J., *Studies in Self-Interest from Descartes to Bruyère* (Oxford: Clarendon, 1962)

Le Guern, M-R. & M., *Les Pensées de Pascal* (Paris: Larousse, 1972)

Lough, J., *An Introduction to Seventeenth Century France* (London: Longmans, 1954)

McBride, R., *Aspects of Seventeenth Century French Drama and Thought* (London: Macmillan, 1979)

Melzer, S., *Discourses of the Fall: A Study of Pascal's Pensées* (Berkeley: University of California Press, 1986)
"Sin and Signs in Pascal's Pensées", *Meaning, Structure and History in the Pensées of Pascal* Biblio 17, ed. D. Wetsel (Paris: Papers on French Seventeenth Century Literature, 1990)

Mesnard, J., *Pascal* (5th ed.), Connaissance des Lettres (Paris: Hatier, 1967)
Les Pensées de Pascal (Paris: SEDES, 1976)

Miel, J., *Pascal and Theology* (Baltimore: John Hopkins, 1969)

Morgan, J., "Pascal's Three Orders", *MLR* 72 (1978), 755-66

Natoli, C.M., *Nietzsche and Pascal on Christianity* (New York: Lang, 1985)

Nelson, R.J.,*Pascal, Adversary and Advocate* (Cambridge Mass.: Harvard University Press, 1981)

Norman, B., *Portraits of Thought: Knowledge, Methods and Style in Pascal* (Columbus: Ohio State University Press, 1988)

Orcibal, J., *Jean Duvergier de Hauranne, abbé de Saint-Cyran, et son temps* (2 vols.; Paris: J. Vrin, 1947-48)

Saint-Cyran et le Jansénisme (Paris: Éditions du Seuil, 1961)

La Spiritualité de Saint-Cyran avec ses Écrits de Piété Inédits: Les Origines du Jansénisme Vol. V (Paris: J. Vrin, 1962)

Parish, R., "Mais qui Parle? Voice and Persona in the 'Pensées'", *SCFS* 8 (1986), 23-40

Pascal's Lettres Provinciales: A Study in Polemic (Oxford: Clarendon, 1989)

"Automate et sacrement: figures de l'incarnation chez Pascal", in proceedings of conference held at the University of Saint-Etienne, October 1995, entitled *"Les avatars de l'augustinisme"* (*Acts* forthcoming)

Pintard, R., "Pascal et les libertins", *Pascal Présent*, ed. Faculté des lettres de Clermont (Clermont-Ferrand: G. de Bussac, 1962), 105-30

Russier, J., *La Foi Selon Pascal* (2 vols.; Paris: Presses Universitaires de France, 1949)

Ryan, J.K., "The Argument of the Wager in Pascal and Others", *TNS* 19 (1945), 233-50

Sainte Beuve, *Port-Royal* (2 vols; texte présenté et annotaté par M. Leroy; Paris: Gallimard, 1953)

Sedgwick, A., *Jansenism in Seventeenth Century France: Voices from the Wilderness* (Charlottesville: University Press of Virginia, 1977)

Sellier, P., *Pascal et Saint Augustin* (Paris: Armand Colin, 1970)

"'Sur les fleuves de Babylone': The Fluidity of the World and the Search for Permanence in the Pensées", *Meaning, Structure & History in the Pensées of Pascal* Biblio 17, ed. D. Wetsel (Paris: Papers on French Seventeenth Century Literature, 1990)

Taveneaux, R., *Jansénisme et Réforme Catholique* (Nancy: Presses Universitaires de Nancy, 1992)

Topliss, P., *The Rhetoric of Pascal: A Study of His Art of Persuasion in the 'Provinciales' and the 'Pensées'* (Leicester: Leicester University Press, 1966)

Vamos, M., *Pascal's Pensées and the Enlightenment: the Roots of a Misunderstanding* (SVEC XCVII; Oxford: OUP, 1972) 17-145

Ward, A.W., Prothero, G.W., Leathes, S., (eds.) *The Cambridge Modern History Vol. V: The Age of Louis XIV* (Cambridge: CUP, 1934)

Wetsel, D., *Pascal and Disbelief: Catechesis and Conversion in the Pensées* (Washington D.C.: Catholic University of America, 1994)

L'Ecriture et le Reste: The Pensées of Pascal in the Exegetical Tradition of Port-Royal (Columbus: Ohio State University Press, 1981)

Williams, S.N., *Revelation and Reconciliation* (Cambridge: CUP, 1995)

GENERAL:

Bauckham, R.J., *Moltmann: Messianic Theology in the Making* (Basingstoke: Marshall Pickering, 1987)

Barth, K., *Protestant Theology in the Nineteenth Century* (London: SCM 1972)

Baudrillard, J., *Forget Foucault* (New York: Semiotexte, 1987)

Boff, L., *Way of the Cross: Way of Justice* (Maryknoll: Orbis, 1988)

Bonhoeffer, D., *Letters and Papers from Prison* (London: SCM, 1953)

Brooker, P. (ed.), *Modernism/Postmodernism* (London: Longman, 1992)

Brunner, E., *The Mediator* (London: Lutterworth, 1934)

Caputo, J.D., "Mysticism and Transgression: Derrida and Meister Eckhart", ed. H.J. Silverman, *Derrida and Deconstruction* (New York: Routledge, 1989), 24-39

Derrida, J., *Writing and Difference* (London: Routledge, 1978)

Flynn, B., "Derrida and Foucault: Madness and Writing," *Derrida and Deconstruction* (ed. H.J. Silverman; New York: Routledge, 1989), 201-18

Foucault, M.,
Power/Knowledge: Selected Interviews and Other Writings 1972-77, edited by Colin Gordon (New York: Harvester Wheatsheaf, 1980)
Folie et Déraison: Histoire de la Folie à l'âge classique (Paris: Plon, 1961)
Naissance de la Clinique (Paris: PUF, 1963)
"Nietzsche, Genealogy, History", ed. P. Rabinow, *A Foucault Reader* (London: Penguin, 1984)
Surveiller et Punir (Paris: Gallimard, 1975)
La Volonté de Savoir (Paris: Gallimard, 1971)
L'Usage des Plaisirs (Paris: Gallimard, 1984)
Le Souci de Soi (Paris: Gallimard, 1984)
The History of Sexuality (3 vols.; London: Allen Lane, 1979-88)
ed. P. Rabinow, *A Foucault Reader* (London: Penguin, 1984)
Les Mots et les choses: une archéologie des sciences humaines (Paris: Gallimard, 1966); ET: *The Order of Things: An Archaeology of the Human Sciences* (New York: Pantheon, 1970)

Foucault, M. and Deleuze, G., "Intellectuals and Power", ed. D.F. Bouchard, *Language, Counter-Memory, Practice: Selected Essays and Interviews* (Ithaca, Cornell University Press, 1977)

Fraser, N., "Foucault on modern power: empirical insights and normative confusions", *Praxis International* Vol. 1 (1981)

Hall, D.J.,*Hope Against Hope: Towards an Indigenous Theology of the Cross* (WSCF Books 1.3.3; WSCF: Geneva, 1971)
  God and Human Suffering: An Exercise in the Theology of the Cross (Minneapolis: Augsburg, 1986)

Hoy, D.C. (ed.), *Foucault: A Critical Reader* (Oxford: Blackwell, 1986)

Jüngel, E.,   *God as the Mystery of the World* (Edinburgh: T. & T. Clark, 1983)

Kitamori, K.,   *A Theology of the Pain of God*, (London: SCM, 1966)

Lukes, S., *Power: A Radical View* (London: Macmillan, 1974).

Lyotard, J-F., *La Condition Postmoderne: Rapport sur le Savoir* (Paris: Editions de Minuit, 1979)
  "Answering the Question: What is Postmodernism", *Modernism/ Postmodernism*, ed. P. Brooker (London: Longman, 1992), 139-50

McHoul, A., and Grace, W., *A Foucault Primer: Discourse, Power and the Subject* (London: UCL, 1995)

Moltmann, J., *The Crucified God* (London: SCM, 1974)
  Theology Today (London: SCM, 1988)

Nietzsche, F., *On the Genealogy of Morals* (ed. and trans. D. Smith; Oxford: OUP, 1996. First published 1887)

Rajchman, J., *Michel Foucault: The Freedom of Philosophy* (New York: Columbia University Press, 1985)

Sheridan, A., *Michel Foucault: The Will to Truth* (London: Routledge, 1980)

Shumway, D., *Michel Foucault* (Charlottesville: University Press of Virginia, 1989)

Sobrino, J., *Christology at the Crossroads: A Latin American View* (London: SCM, 1978)
  The Principle of Mercy: Taking the Crucified People from the Cross (Maryknoll: Orbis, 1994).

Thiselton, A.C.,   *Interpreting God and the Postmodern Self: On Meaning, Manipulation and Promise* (Edinburgh: T. & T. Clark, 1995)

Tomlin, G.S., "The Theology of the Cross: Subversive Theology for a Postmodern World?", *Themelios* 23.1 (1997), 59-73

Index

Abercrombie, N., 272

Aelred of Rievaulx, 134, 136, 139, 150

Angers, J. d', 207-8, 223, 226, 232, 250

Anselm, 122-4, 127, 136, 144

Apollos, 22, 23, 25, 26, 29-35, 41-56, 78, 79, 82, 83, 85-91, 93, 94, 96, 293, 296, 306

Aquinas, Thomas, 124-6, 127, 144, 187, 194, 268

Aristotle, 112, 185, 186, 190, 268

Arnauld, Antoine, 212, 263-8, 274

Atonement, 103, 123, 231, 279

Augustine of Hippo, 123-4, 132, 141, 151, 154, 155, 157, 195, 261, 266, 272

Augustinian Order, 114, 129, 131, 133, 134, 137, 142, 149, 191, 207-8

Augustinian theology, 209, 211-3, 220, 222, 232, 248, 250, 261, 264, 266, 268-9, 272

Augustiniana, Schola Moderna, 126, 151

Authority, 311-4

Bandt, H., 153, 193, 194

Barnes, A., 273

Barth, K., 6, 305, 310

Baudrillard., J., 309

Bell, T., 111-2, 116, 148, 195

Bénichou, P., 262-3, 272

Bernard of Clairvaux, 130-33, 140, 144, 145, 146, 160, 167, 178, 188, 193, 195

Bérulle, 264-7

Beurrier, 266, 272, 273

Biel, Gabriel, 130, 131, 135-6, 139, 146, 150, 153, 161, 193

Bizer, E., 155, 165

Boehmer, H., 14, 170, 179

Bonhoeffer, D., 6, 227

Bornkamm, H., 155, 165

Branick, V.P., 16-7, 21, 54

Brecht, M., 147, 153

Broome, J.H., 224, 251, 252

Brown, A., 99-100, 106, 107, 117

Brown, R.D., 67, 77

Calvet, J., 224, 227, 253, 273

Cargill Thompson, W.D.J., 166

Castelli, E., 98-9, 106, 297, 299,

Paternoster Biblical and Theological Monographs

An established series of doctoral theses of high academic standard
(All titles paperback, 229 x 152mm)

Joseph Abraham
Eve: Accused or Acquitted?
A Reconsideration of Feminist Readings of the Creation Narrative Texts in Genesis 1–3

Two contrary views dominate contemporary feminist biblical scholarship. One finds in the Bible an unequivocal equality between the sexes from the very creation of humanity, whilst the other sees the biblical text as irredeemably patriarchal and androcentric. Dr. Abraham enters into dialogue with both camps as well as introducing his own method of approach. An invaluable tool for any one who is interested in this contemporary debate.

2003/ 0-85364-971-5 / xxiv + 272pp

Emil Bartos
Deification in Eastern Orthodox Theology
An Evaluation and Critique of the Theology of Dumitru Staniloae

Bartos studies a fundamental yet neglected aspect of Orthodox theology: deification. By examining the doctrines of anthropology, christology, soteriology and ecclesiology as they relate to deification, he provides an important contribution to contemporary dialogue between Eastern and Western theologians.

1999 / 0-85364-956-1 / xi + 370pp

Jonathan F. Bayes
The Weakness of the Law
God's Law and the Christian in New Testament Perspective

A study of the four New Testament books which refer to the law as weak (Acts, Romans, Galatians, Hebrews) leads to a defence of the third use in the Reformed debate about the law in the life of the believer.

2000 / 0-85364-957-X / xi + 244pp

Mark Bonnington
The Antioch Episode of Galatians 2:11-14 in Historical and Cultural Context

The Galatians 2 'incident' in Antioch over table-fellowship suggests significant disagreement between the leading apostles. This book analyses the background to the disagreement by locating the incident within the dynamics of social interaction between Jews and Gentiles. It proposes a new way of understanding the relationship between the individuals and issues involved.

2004 / 1-84227-050-8 /

Mark Bredin
Jesus, Revolutionary of Peace
A Non-violent Christology in the Book of Revelation

This book aims to demonstrate that the figure of Jesus in the Book of Revelation can best be understood as an active non-violent revolutionary.

2003 / 1-84227-153-9 / xviii + 262pp

Colin J. Bulley
The Priesthood of Some Believers
Developments in the Christian Literature of the First Three Centuries

The first in-depth treatment of early Christian texts on the priesthood of all believers shows that the developing priesthood of the ordained related closely to the division between laity and clergy and had deleterious effects on the practice of the general priesthood.

2000 / 1-84227-034-6 / xii + 336pp

Daniel J-S Chae
Paul as Apostle to the Gentiles
His Apostolic Self-awareness and its Influence on the Soteriological Argument in Romans

Opposing 'the post-Holocaust interpretation of Romans', Daniel Chae competently demonstrates that Paul argues for the equality of Jew and Gentile in Romans. Chae's fresh exegetical interpretation is academically outstanding and spiritually encouraging.

1997 / 0-85364-829-8 / xiv + 378pp

Luke L. Cheung
The Genre, Composition and Hermeneutics of the Epistle of James
The present work examines the employment of the wisdom genre with a certain compositional structure and the interpretation of the law through the Jesus' tradition of the double love command by the author of the Epistle of James to serve his purpose in promoting perfection and warning against doubleness among the eschatologically renewed people of God in the Diaspora.

2003 / 1-84227-062-1 / xvi + 372pp

Andrew C. Clark
Parallel Lives
The Relation of Paul to the Apostles in the Lucan Perspective
This study of the Peter-Paul parallels in Acts argues that their purpose was to emphasize the themes of continuity in salvation history and the unity of the Jewish and Gentile missions. New light is shed on Luke's literary techniques, partly through a comparison with Plutarch.

2001 / 1-84227-035-4 / xviii + 384pp

Sylvia I Collinson
Making Disciples
The Significance of Jesus' Educational Strategy for Today's Church
This study examines the biblical practice of discipling, formulates a definition, and makes comparisons with modern models of education. A recommendation is made for greater attention to its practice today.

2004 / 1-84227-116-4 /

Stephen M. Dunning
The Crisis and the Quest
A Kierkegaardian Reading of Charles Williams
Employing Kierkegaardian categories and analysis, this study investigates both the central crisis in Charles Williams's authorship between hermetism and Christianity (Kierkegaard's Religions A and B), and the quest to resolve this crisis, a quest that ultimately presses the bounds of orthodoxy.

2000 / 0-85364-985-5 / xxiv + 254pp

Keith Ferdinando
The Triumph of Christ in African Perspective
A Study of Demonology and Redemption in the African Context
The book explores the implications of the gospel for traditional African fears of occult aggression. It analyses such traditional approaches to suffering and biblical responses to fears of demonic evil, concluding with an evaluation of African beliefs from the perspective of the gospel.

1999 / 0-85364-830-1 / xvii + 450pp

Andrew Goddard
Living the Word, Resisting the World
The Life and Thought of Jacques Ellul
This work offers a definitive study of both the life and thought of the French Reformed thinker Jacques Ellul (1912-1994). It will prove an indispensable resource for those interested in this influential theologian and sociologist and for Christian ethics and political thought generally.

2002 / 1-84227-053-2 / xxiv + 378pp

Scott J. Hafemann
Suffering and Ministry in the Spirit
Paul's Defence of His Ministry in 2 Corinthians 2:14–3:3
Shedding new light on the way Paul defended his apostleship, the author offers a careful, detailed study of 2 Corinthians 2:14–3:3 linked with other key passages throughout 1 and 2 Corinthians. Demonstrating the unity and coherence of Paul's argument in this passage, the author shows that Paul's suffering served as the vehicle for revealing God's power and glory through the Spirit.

2000 / 0-85364-967-7 / xiv + 262pp

John G. Kelly
One God, One People
The Differentiated Unity of the People of God in the Theology of Jürgen Moltmann
The author expounds and critiques Moltmann's doctrine of God and highlights the systematic connections between it and Moltmann's influential discussion of Israel. He then proposes a fresh approach to Jewish-Christian relations building on Moltmann's work using insights from Habermas and Rawls.

2004 / 0-85346-969-3 /

Mark Lovatt
Confronting the Will-to-Power
A Reconsideration of the Theology of Reinhold Neibuhr
Confronting the Will-to-Power is an analysis of the theology of Reinhold Niebuhr, arguing that his work is an attempt to identify, and provide a practical theological answer to, the existence and nature of human evil.

2001 / 1-84227-054-0 / xvii + 218pp

Neil B. MacDonald
Karl Barth and the Strange New World within the Bible
Barth, Wittgenstein, and the Metadilemmas of the Enlightenment
Barth's discovery of the strange new world within the Bible is examined in the context of Kant, Hume, Overbeck, and, most importantly, Wittgenstein. MacDonald covers some fundamental issues in theology today: epistemology, the final form of the text and biblical truth-claims.

2000 / 0-85364-970-7 / xxvi + 374pp

Gillian McCulloch
The Deconstruction of Dualism in Theology
With Reference to Eco-feminist Theology and New Age Spirituality
This book challenges eco-theological anti-dualism in Christian theology, arguing that dualism has a twofold function in Christian religious discourse. Firstly, it enables us to express the discontinuities and divisions that are part of the process of reality. Secondly, dualistic language allows us to express the mysteries of divine transcendence/immanence and the survival of the soul without collapsing into monism and materialism, both of which are problematic for Christian epistemology.

2002 / 1-84227-044-3 / xii + 282pp

Leslie McCurdy
Attributes and Atonement
The Holy Love of God in the Theology of P.T. Forsyth
Attributes and Atonement is an intriguing full-length study of P.T. Forsyth's doctrine of the cross as it relates particularly to God's holy love. It includes an unparalleled bibliography of both primary and secondary material relating to Forsyth.

1999 / 0-85364-833-6 / xii + 328pp

Nozomu Miyahira
Towards a Theology of the Concord of God
A Japanese Perspective on the Trinity
This book introduces a new Japanese theology and a unique Trinitarian formula based on the Japanese intellectual climate: three betweennesses and one concord. It also presents a new interpretation of the Trinity, a co-subordinationism, which is in line with orthodox Trinitarianism; each single person of the Trinity is eternally and equally subordinate (or serviceable) to the other persons, so that they retain the mutual dynamic equality.
2000 / 0-85364-863-8 / xiv + 256pp

Stephen Motyer
Your Father the Devil?
A New Approach to John and 'The Jews'
Who are 'the Jews' in John's Gospel? Defending John against the charge of antisemitism, Motyer argues that, far from demonising the Jews, the Gospel seeks to present Jesus as 'Good News for Jews' in a late first century setting.
1997 / 0-85364-832-8 / xiii + 260pp

Eddy José Muskus
The Origins and Early Development of Liberation Theology in Latin America
With Particular Reference to Gustavo Gutiérrez
This work challenges the fundamental premise of Liberation Theology, 'opting for the poor', and its claim that Christ is found in them. It also argues that Liberation Theology emerged as a direct result of the failure of the Roman Catholic Church in Latin America.
2002 / 0-85364-974-X / xiv + 296pp

Esther Ng
Reconstructing Christian Origins?
The Feminist Theology of Elizabeth Schüssler Fiorenza: An Evaluation
In a detailed evaluation, the author challenges Elizabeth Schüssler Fiorenza's reconstruction of early Christian origins and her underlying presuppositions. The author also presents her own views on women's roles both then and now.
2002 / 1-84227-055-9 / xxiv + 468pp

Ian Paul
Power to See the World Anew
The Value of Paul Ricoeur's Hermeneutic of Metaphor in Interpreting the Symbolism of Revelation 12 and 13
This book is a study of the hermeneutics of metaphor of Paul Ricoeur, one of the most important writers on hermeneutics and metaphor of the last century. It sets out the key points of his theory, important criticisms of his work, and how his approach, modified in the light of these criticisms, offers a methodological framework for reading apocalyptic texts.

2004 / 1-84227-056-7 /

David Powys
'Hell': A Hard Look at a Hard Question
The Fate of the Unrighteous in New Testament Thought
This comprehensive treatment seeks to unlock the original meaning of terms and phrases long thought to support the traditional doctrine of hell. It concludes that there is an alternative – one which is more biblical, and which can positively revive the rationale for Christian mission.

1999 / 0-85364-831-X / xxii + 478pp

Ed Rybarczyk
Beyond Salvation
Eastern Orthodoxy and Classical Pentecostalism on becoming like Christ
Despite their historical and cultural differences, Eastern Orthodox Christians and Classical Pentecostals share some surprising similarities. This study locates both Traditions within their cultural and philosophical meta-contexts and suggests avenues of mutual understanding.

2003 / 1-84227-144-X / xii + 426pp approx

Signe Sandsmark
Is World View Neutral Education Possible and Desirable?
A Christian Response to Liberal Arguments
(Published jointly with
The Stapleford Centre)
This thesis discusses reasons for belief in world view neutrality, and argues that 'neutral' education will have a hidden, but strong world view influence. It discusses the place for Christian education in the common school.

2000 / 0-85364-973-1 / xiv + 182pp

Andrew Sloane
On being a Christian in the Academy
Nicholas Wolterstorff and the Practice of Christian Scholarship
An exposition and critical appraisal of Nicholas Wolterstorff's epistemology in the light of the philosophy of science, and an application of his thought to the practice of Christian scholarship.
2003 / 1-84227-058-3 / xvi + 274pp

Daniel Strange
The Possibility of Salvation Among the Unevangelised
An Analysis of Inclusivism in Recent Evangelical Theology
For evangelical theologians the 'fate of the unevangelised' impinges upon fundamental tenets of evangelical identity. The position known as 'inclusivism', defined by the belief that the unevangelised can be ontologically saved by Christ whilst being epistemologically unaware of him, has been defended most vigorously by the Canadian evangelical Clark H. Pinnock. Through a detailed analysis and critique of Pinnock's work, this book examines a cluster of issues surrounding the unevangelised and its implication for christology, soteriology and the doctrine of revelation.
2002 / 1-84227-047-8 / xviii + 362pp

G.Michael Thomas
The Extent of the Atonement
A Dilemma for Reformed Theology from Calvin to the Consensus
A study of the way Reformed theology addressed the question, 'Did Christ die for all, or for the elect only?', commencing with John Calvin, and including debates with Lutheranism, the Synod of Dort and the teaching of Moïse Amyraut.
1997 / 0-85364-828-X / ix + 275pp

Mark Thompson
A Sure Ground on which to Stand
The Relation of Authority and Interpretative Method of Luther's Approach to Scripture
This study attempts a fresh examination of the most significant of Luther's comments on the nature and use of Scripture, locating each in its literary and historical context. It explores a series of connections in Luther's thought, analysing his scattered statements in terms of four categories reflected in his own terminology: inspiration, unity, clarity and sufficiency. In particular, it seeks to identify those elements which enable Luther to move with confidence between his statements about the authority of Scripture and his interpretative method.
2003 / 1-84227-145-8 / xvi + 322pp

Graham Tomlin
The Power of the Cross
Theology and the Death of Christ in Paul, Luther and Pascal
This book explores the theology of the cross in St Paul, Luther and Pascal. It offers new perspectives on the theology of each, and some implications for the nature of power, apologetics, theology and church life in a postmodern context.

1999 / 0-85364-984-7 / xiv + 344pp

Kevin Walton
Thou Traveller Unknown
The Presence and Absence of God in the Jacob Narrative
The author offers a fresh reading of the story of Jacob in the book of Genesis through the paradox of divine presence and absence. The work also seeks to make a contribution to Pentateuchal studies by bringing together a close reading of the final text with historical critical insights, doing justice to the text's historical depth, final form and canonical status.

2003 / 1-84227-059-1 / xvi + 238pp

Graham J. Watts
Revelation and the Spirit
A Comparative Study of the Relationship between the Doctrine of Revelation and Pneumatology in the Theology of Eberhard Jüngel and of Wolfhart Pannenberg
The relationship between Revelation and pneumatology is relatively unexplored. This approach offers a fresh angle on two important twentieth century theologians and raises pneumatological questions which are theologically crucial and relevant to mission in a post modern culture.

2003 / 1-84227-104-0 / xxii + 232pp

Alistair Wilson
When Will These Things Happen?
A Study of Jesus as Judge in Matthew 21–25
This study seeks to allow Matthew's carefully constructed presentation of Jesus to be given full weight in the modern evaluation of Jesus' eschatology. Careful analysis of the text of Matthew 21–25 reveals Jesus to be standing firmly in the Jewish prophetic and wisdom traditions as he proclaims and enacts imminent judgement on the Jewish authorities then boldly claims the central role in the final and universal judgement.

2004 / 1-84227-146-6 / approx xvi + 292pp

Nigel G. Wright
Disavowing Constantine
Mission, Church and the Social Order in the Theologies of John Howard
Yoder and Jürgen Moltmann
This book is a timely restatement of a radical theology of church and state in the Anabaptist and Baptist tradition. Dr. Wright constructs his argument in dialogue and debate with Yoder and Moltmann, major contributors to a free church perspective.
2000 / 0-85364-978-2 / xv + 252pp

Stephen Wright
The Voice of Jesus
Studies in the Interpretation of Six Gospel Parables
This literary study considers how the 'voice' of Jesus has been heard in different periods of parable interpretation, and how the categories of figure and trope may help us towards a sensitive reading of the parables today.
2000 / 0-85364-975-8 / xiv + 280pp

PATERNOSTER PRESS

The Paternoster Press,
PO Box 300, Carlisle, Cumbria CA3 0QS, United Kingdom
Web: www.paternoster-publishing.com